T0324543

Back from the Collapse

American Prairie and the Restoration
of Great Plains Wildlife

CURTIS H. FREESE

University of Nebraska Press

LINCOLN

© 2023 by Curtis H. Freese

All rights reserved
Manufactured in the United States of America

The University of Nebraska Press is part of a land-grant institution with campuses and programs on the past, present, and future homelands of the Pawnee, Ponca, Otoe-Missouria, Omaha, Dakota, Lakota, Kaw, Cheyenne, and Arapaho Peoples, as well as those of the relocated Ho-Chunk, Sac and Fox, and Iowa Peoples.

Library of Congress Cataloging-in-Publication Data

Names: Freese, Curtis H., author.
Title: Back from the collapse: American Prairie and the restoration of Great Plains wildlife / Curtis H. Freese.
Description: Lincoln: University of Nebraska Press, 2023 | Includes bibliographical references and index.
Identifiers: LCCN 2022043593
ISBN 9781496231321 (paperback)
ISBN 9781496236630 (epub)
ISBN 9781496236647 (pdf)
Subjects: LCSH: Prairie restoration—Great Plains. | Wildlife reintroduction—Great Plains. | Great Plains—History. | BISAC: NATURE / Environmental Conservation & Protection | NATURE / Ecosystems & Habitats / Plains & Prairies
Classification: LCC QH104.5.G73 F74 2023 |
DDC 333.74/1530978—dc23/eng/20220923
LC record available at https://lccn.loc.gov/2022043593

Set in Minion Pro by Scribe Inc.

CONTENTS

ILLUSTRATIONS

Figures

Tables

Drawings

ACKNOWLEDGMENTS

I've lost count of the generous, knowledgeable, unselfish ways that so many people helped me in researching and writing this book. No one has done more to educate me about the lands and wildlife of northeast Montana than Randy Matchett, longtime biologist for the Charles M. Russell National Wildlife Refuge. Randy also read, patiently corrected, and offered helpful suggestions for several chapters. Steve Forrest, Sean Gerrity, Daniel Kinka, and Mike Stark also stand out for time invested and countless helpful discussions and suggestions as they read the entire manuscript. Damien Austin, Andy Boyce, Patrick Braaten, Robert Bramblett, Alison Fox, Scott Heidebrink, Craig Knowles, Kyran Kunkel, Jeffrey Lockwood, and Hila Shamon helped with many enlightening discussions and constructive critiques of individual chapters.

For a diverse range of help—from stimulating discussions, sharing observations, fact-checking, and explaining concepts, to guiding my search for and accessing of a vast literature on a wide range of topics—thanks go to Ellen Anderson, Katy Beattie, Nicole Davis, Jesse DeVoe, Nicolle Fugere, Patricia Gilbert-Ball, Luke Holmquist, Larry Igl, Mike Kautz, Eliza Krause, David Mech, Dakota Meeks, Alexandra Morphew, Ellie Oakley, Sarah Olimb, Paul Santavy, John Sauer, Scott Somershoe, Mark Sommer, Scott Thompson, Brian Tornabene, Stephanie Tucker, Cliff Wallis, and Jane Wright. Arizona's Pima County Library and the University of Arizona library were invaluable for accessing publications.

A hearty thanks to Eric Cline for patiently handling my ever-changing ideas to skillfully produce such eye-pleasing and readable maps and graphs.

A sincere thanks to Damien Austin, David Driscoll, Greg Lavaty, Dennis Lingohr, Marky Mutchler, Gib Myers, Michael Schilz, and Johnny Stutzman for permitting me to use their photos.

A special thank you to Clark Whitehorn, executive editor of Bison Books, for supporting the idea for this book from the outset and for deftly and patiently guiding me through the manuscript preparation and publishing process. Also at the University of Nebraska Press, a sincere thanks to Ann Baker, Tish Fobben, Taylor Rothgeb, Rosemary Sekora, and Andrea Shahan, all of whom were a delight to work with as they skillfully steered me and the book through manuscript preparation, design, production, and marketing. My earnest thanks to Brianna Blackburn at Scribe for patiently and skillfully managing the storm of my seemingly endless questions about and changes to the manuscript during the book's copyediting and production. As copyeditor of the manuscript, Sam Martin deserves my hearty thank you for so patiently and carefully catching and correcting the innumerable errors in my prose and manuscript preparation and for suggesting edits to better communicate what I wanted to say. To Douglas Easton, thank you for producing such a thorough and usable index.

My wife, Heather Bentz, and daughter, Erica Freese, gave unflagging and loving support and encouragement from beginning to end. They also read the entire manuscript and brought discerning eyes, as only family can, to catching my tired colloquialisms and naked efforts at trying to be too clever. And it was especially a joy to work with Erica as we figured out which species would be the subjects of her thirteen pen-and-ink drawings and then to see the results provide a wonderful artistic touch to the book.

INTRODUCTION

I grew up on a farm in the tallgrass prairie region of eastern Iowa in the 1950s and '60s. As a result, I was afflicted at an early age with the prairie strain of a common, but then unnamed, malady. Because those afflicted are generally unaware of the symptoms, the malady wasn't named or widely recognized until 1995. That's when fisheries biologist Daniel Pauly coined the term *shifting baseline syndrome* (SBS) to describe how, as fish stocks and the size of fish declined due to decades of overfishing, the perceptions of each new generation of fisheries biologists regarding the baseline of what constituted natural fish populations shifted to smaller stocks and fish.[1] This malady, sometimes called "environmental generational amnesia," isn't restricted to biologists or to fisheries. The public is also highly susceptible, and SBS can occur wherever wildlife populations have experienced long-term declines. This is bad for conservation. The persistent downgrading of what biologists and the public consider the natural environment and healthy wildlife populations leads to complacency about current degraded ecological conditions and to ever-weaker conservation goals and outcomes.[2]

The history and current condition of Great Plains grasslands and wildlife offer prime conditions for particularly severe cases of SBS. My journey with the malady offers an example.

Fields of grain and hay surrounded our farmstead, and a creek (pronounced "crick") ran through the 80 acres across the road. Pheasants nested in the hayfields in the spring and fed in the harvested cornfields in the fall, but the creek offered "wild" habitat where I could fish for chubs, set traps on muskrat slides, and hunt pheasants and rabbits hiding in the creek-side tall grass and shrubs. Our farm's wildlife habitat—croplands with a creek or grassy draw or two running through them—was typical of nearly every farm in Iowa. Others may be less susceptible than me, but that image was firmly etched in my adolescent brain as the baseline of what healthy wildlife and wildlife habitat looked like in Iowa.

SBS is, fortunately, at least partially reversible, and my syndrome began to improve when I became a wildlife student at Iowa State University. There I learned that just one-tenth of a percent of the tallgrass prairie that once covered Iowa remained and many wildlife species that were once common, like bison (*Bison bison*) and wolves (*Canis lupus*), had disappeared a century ago. A class field trip to study the prairie often meant searching old cemeteries and railroad rights-of-way for a patch that had escaped the plow. I also remember being wowed by a field trip to a prairie marsh and its waterfowl—but then learning that 99% of the marshes that once blanketed north-central Iowa had been drained for cropland. Those patches of prairie and isolated marshes were like precious gems that, based on my adolescent baseline, were exciting to see. But as I learned what had once been, my slow recovery from SBS left me lamenting what had been lost.

In Iowa and elsewhere across the Great Plains, one has to rely on old photos, historic accounts, and a vivid imagination to envision what the original horizon-to-horizon native prairie and its wildlife looked like. It was, per the title of environmental historian Dan Flores's book on the topic, the American Serengeti, where, by all accounts, one of the world's most extraordinary panoramas of wildlife once existed.[3] But imagining such a scene doesn't cut it any more than seeing the score to a favorite song is equivalent to hearing it. Consequently, I fear society's baseline will continue its two-century, multigenerational shift to ever-lower standards for prairie conservation. As a result, many prairie species whose populations collapsed many years ago or have suffered long-term declines will continue to be ignored or, at best, confined to remnant populations with unduly modest goals for their recovery. Beyond concerns about the status of individual species are the often insidious effects their demise has on the function and health of prairie ecosystems. At the broadest level, the depleted wildlife heritage of the prairie and our ignorance of what's been lost translate into underappreciation of the prairie itself and a diminished will to save it from the killer threat of all threats, the plow. The flip side of this is the appalling dearth and generally small size of national parks, wildlife refuges, and other protected areas across the Great Plains and, with a few exceptions, little being done to rectify the situation. At this point, prairies are being plowed up faster than they are being protected.

Without experiencing firsthand the historic wildlife diversity and abundance of the Great Plains, I doubt a case of sbs can ever fully be reversed. The chance, however, for anyone to ever again enjoy this experience seemed, not too long ago, far-fetched. But then, a little more than 20 years ago, a group of people recognized the potential of a region in northeast Montana for resurrecting this experience. Millions of acres of prairie and associated habitats in the region remained intact. Based on descriptions by Native peoples and early explorers, the lands once harbored a stunning diversity and abundance of wildlife. The region offered our best chance to reassemble the native wildlife community within a vast reserve large enough to preserve the ecosystem to its fullest potential. So was born American Prairie, a nonprofit organization whose mission is to assemble, through land acquisition and the stitching together of associated public lands, a 3.2-million-acre (5,000-square-mile) prairie reserve, an area 1.5 times the size of Yellowstone National Park. The goal is to build a protected area where the visitor will be able to experience an endless sea of grass teeming with wildlife on a scale not seen in more than 200 years. The project area is in the 180-million-acre Northern Great Plains, an ecoregion recognized as a global priority for grassland conservation[4] that lies within the 620-million-acre Great Plains (fig. 1).

In the spirit of full disclosure and as explained more in chapter 1, I was involved in American Prairie's founding and served briefly as

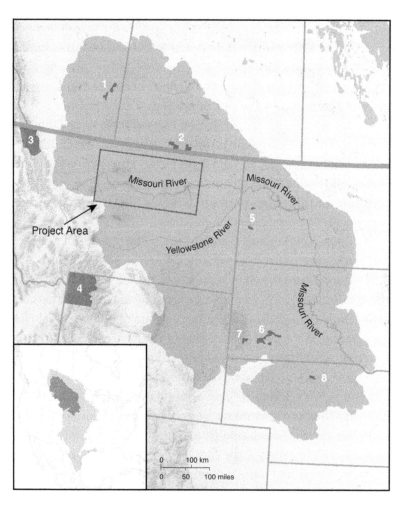

FIG. 1. Location of the Northern Great Plains within the Great Plains (*dark gray and light gray in inset*) and location of America Prairie–Russell Refuge region (project area) and of major protected areas mentioned in the text: (1) Suffield National Wildlife Area, (2) Grasslands National Park, (3) Glacier National Park, (4) Yellowstone National Park, (5) Theodore Roosevelt National Park, (6) Badlands National Park, (7) Wind Cave National Park, (8) Valentine National Wildlife Refuge. Created by Eric Cline.

its first executive director before handing the reins to Sean Gerrity, who skillfully shepherded the growth of the organization for many years. I have continued since to be involved with the organization's work, first as the director of the Northern Great Plains Program of the World Wildlife Fund (WWF), a partner with American Prairie during its early years, and subsequently as an individual assisting on various projects. To be clear, the ideas and opinions I express in this book are mine alone. They do not necessarily represent those of American Prairie or any other institution or individual.

The core of the protected area consists of American Prairie's deeded lands and leased public lands and the 1.1-million-acre Charles M. Russell National Wildlife Refuge (C. M. Russell Refuge). I call the protected area composed of the lands of these two institutions the American Prairie–Russell Refuge. American Prairie is still acquiring lands and thus the final boundaries of the 3.2-million-acre protected area are yet to be determined. Throughout the book, however, the discussion often concerns a larger landscape of northeast Montana—the region of about 15 million acres shown in figure 2 or even somewhat larger. I refer to this larger landscape as the American Prairie–Russell Refuge region.

The vegetation of the Northern Great Plains is variously referred to as short-grass prairie, mixed-grass prairie, steppe, and where sagebrush (*Artemisia* spp.) is abundant, sagebrush steppe. Throughout the book, except where more detail is required, I use interchangeably the terms *prairie* and *grassland* when referring to these various vegetation types. I occasionally refer to these vegetation types as *rangelands* in the context of livestock management, where the term is commonly used.

I have three goals for this book, which, combined, I hope engender strong support for the work and vision of American Prairie and its collaborators and, more broadly, inspire and encourage large-scale restoration of wildlife across the Great Plains through the creation of new and larger protected areas and employment of other mechanisms that enable wildlife to flourish.

The first goal is to raise awareness of the evolutionary history of the American Prairie–Russell Refuge region. Just like getting

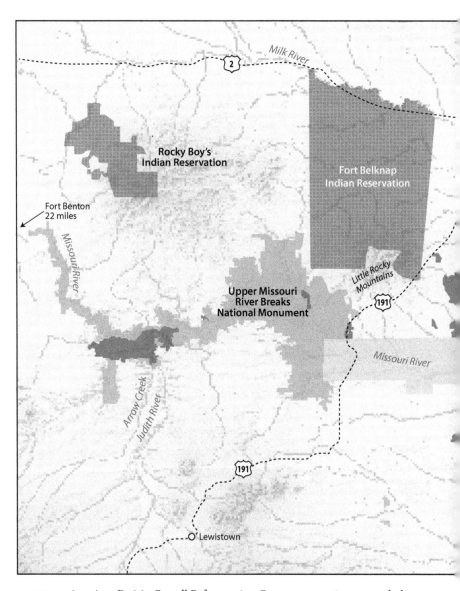

FIG. 2. American Prairie–Russell Refuge region. Because properties are regularly being acquired, go to americanprairie.org for an updated map of American Prairie lands. Created by Eric Cline.

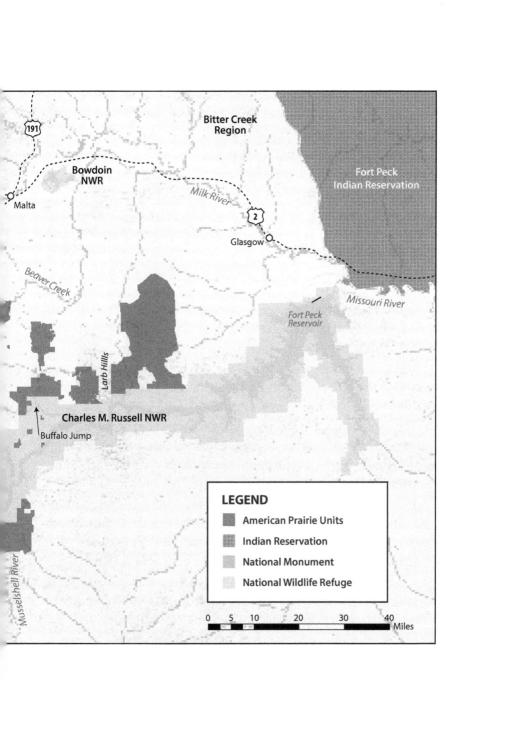

to know a person or an old house, one cannot understand and fully appreciate the American Prairie–Russell Refuge region without knowing how a constellation of often contrasting forces and events—large-scale and small, long-term and short—forged the region's landscape and biodiversity. In a few tens of millions of years it went from subtropical forest and shallow sea to the edge of a continental ice sheet to semiarid grassland. Massive extinctions that snuffed out most life in the region opened the door to the explosive evolution and immigration of other species. Descendants of fish found in the region's rivers when dinosaurs prowled the shores still swim today in its waters while all the dinosaurs—except birds—are only present as fossils in those shores' eroding cliffs. Species whose evolutionary journey began here 100 million years ago mix with species that arrived from Eurasia less than 20,000 years ago. Mountains that rose in the west cast a rain shadow that often leaves the region parched but also delivers the Missouri River to quench that thirst. Two major waves of human immigration, one from the northwest thousands of years ago and the other from the east hundreds of years ago, also profoundly affected the region's wildlife.

The second goal is to create greater awareness of the historic diversity and abundance of the region's wildlife and of the widespread collapse of wildlife populations caused by Euro-American settlement. By "collapse" I mean a species' population declined by 90% or more since Europeans arrived on America's shores. Bison have garnered the vast majority of words written about the collapse of Great Plains wildlife. I understand that—they're big and iconic and were driven to the edge of extinction. But the attention to bison tends to obscure the widespread annihilation of other wildlife. Since we have only anecdotal accounts of pre-Euro-American population levels, my estimates of which species' populations declined by 90% required some speculation. For most species, however, collapses of that magnitude or greater are obvious. Within the American Prairie–Russell Refuge region, according to my tally, population collapses have swept through at a minimum 14 mammal species, 8 bird species, 1 fish species, and 1 insect species—at least 24 species in all. There are surely more, but data on population trends are too sparse to confidently identify them. No place in the Great Plains has been spared from similar devastation of its wildlife. While some populations have begun to recover, others are still collapsing with no certainty regarding if and when it will end. I'll refrain, when reviewing each population collapse, how it may have lowered our baseline for what's normal. But be aware that in each case, SBS may be subconsciously trying to trick us into setting overly modest targets for restoring populations.

My third goal is to fire our imaginations by providing rough estimates of what fully restored wildlife populations could look like with 3.2 million acres of prairie dedicated to biodiversity conservation. My focus is on the science and management involved in restoring these populations. Perhaps by starting in one area—representing just half of a percent of the Great Plains—we can begin to rebuild both wildlife populations and society's understanding of and appreciation for the rich heritage of grassland wildlife that once graced the core of the continent. The fate of the tallgrass prairie tells me that we should not wait, that there is urgency in making that vision a reality.

Since purchasing its first property in 2004, American Prairie, as this book went to press, has acquired 452,428 acres of deeded lands and leased public lands. Combined with the 1.1-million-acre C. M. Russell Refuge, American Prairie is half way toward its 3.2-million-acre goal. The vision of a protected area for the Great Plains large enough to restore all native wildlife, hatched more than 20 years ago, is taking shape. A growing number of visitors are awed—and their baselines shifted for the better—by what they experience. George Horse Capture Jr., director of Aaniiih Nakoda Tours and an advisor to American Prairie, succinctly captured the degree of society's environmental amnesia about prairies and the reserve's curative powers for first-time visitors: it was, he said, "almost like they accidentally found something they didn't know they were looking for."[5]

An inhabitant of sagebrush steppe habitat, the sagebrush checkerspot butterfly (*Chlosyne acastus*) has strikingly patterned white, black, and orange wings. Drawing by Erica Freese.

BACK FROM THE COLLAPSE

PART ONE

History

Powerfully built for digging, the American badger prefers grassland habitats,
where ground squirrels and prairie dogs are among its favorite prey.
Drawing by Erica Freese.

ONE

How It Started

A few miles north of the Missouri River on the Charles M. Russell National Wildlife Refuge in northeast Montana, a steep, 80-foot-high embankment rises above Fourchette Creek. Twelve drivelines consisting of hundreds of rock cairns leading to the edge at the top of the embankment—as well as teepee rings, old bison bones, and projectile points from more than 1,000 years ago near the bottom—mark this as a buffalo jump, where Native people killed bison by driving them over the precipice. A five-gallon-bucket-sized stone on a rise overlooking the jump shows well-worn etchings, perhaps an ancient guide for how to run the bison between the rock cairns and over the edge.[1] The buffalo jump is early evidence that wildlife, in this case bison, had long been abundant in this region.

In the spring of 1805 the Lewis and Clark Expedition was approaching the region of the buffalo jump. After journeying up the Missouri River through present-day North Dakota, where they reported low wildlife numbers, on May 8, 1805, they reached the mouth of the Milk River. Meriwether Lewis wrote that day, "We saw a great number buffaloe, Elk, common and Black taled deer, goats beaver and wolves. Capt C. killed a beaver and a wolf, the party killed 3 beaver and a deer. We can send out at any time and obtain whatever species of meat the country affords in as large quantity as we wish."[2] (Lewis's "goats" were pronghorn [*Antilocapra americana*].) Grizzly bears (*Ursus arctos*) were particularly abundant—and intimidating to expedition members—while they traveled through the region.

Less than 200 years later, in August 2000, about 30 conservationists were gathered for a two-day meeting in Bozeman, Montana,
the beginning of what would become a loose coalition called the
Northern Plains Conservation Network (NPCN). It was an eclectic
group. Notable figures in conservation biology were there, including Michael Soulé, a founder of the discipline of conservation biology, and Eric Dinerstein, then head of conservation science for
World Wildlife Fund (WWF). Other national organizations—The
Nature Conservancy, Sierra Club, and Defenders of Wildlife—were
also represented. Most participants, however, were from local or
regional organizations from across the Northern Great Plains. The
gathering's purpose was to identify conservation priorities in
the Northern Great Plains. Maps were on display and meeting participants were pointing to areas they think should be priorities,
places like the Badlands region of South Dakota, Thunder Basin
in Wyoming, the Sandhills of Nebraska, and Grasslands National
Park in Saskatchewan. Others argued for urgent action on endangered species such as the black-footed ferret and changes in government farm policies to eliminate incentives to plow up native
prairie. As I recall, at one point during the conference someone
said, "It's a no brainer. We don't need more analysis to agree that
one place stands out as a top priority." That place was the Montana
Glaciated Plains, a region of northeast Montana that encompasses
the buffalo jump and the locations of Lewis and Clark's stirring
wildlife reports. The region lies primarily between the Milk and
Missouri Rivers as far west as the western boundary of the Fort
Belknap Indian Reservation. A vote by participants confirmed
that the region would be the number-one priority for action by the
newly formed NPCN. The goal: to create a vast nature reserve to
restore and conserve one of the most outstanding landscapes for
wildlife in the Great Plains—and for that matter, in the world.

Data from conservation science presented at the meeting provided new layers of evidence that beyond its historic populations of
bison, wolves, and grizzly bears, the Montana Glaciated Plains stood
out according to other measures of biodiversity. An assessment of
conservation priorities in the Northern Great Plains completed by

The Nature Conservancy in 1999 ranked the Montana Glaciated Plains as "very high priority," their highest designation based on biodiversity value and urgency of threats.[3] The region was exceptionally intact, the most extensive, never-been-plowed prairie on glaciated soils in North America. A seminal 1996 paper by prairie ecologist Fritz Knopf showed the Montana Glaciated Plains contained the greatest diversity of grassland breeding birds in North America.[4] Research by biologist Jonathan Proctor (who was at the meeting) found that much of the Montana Glaciated Plains had good habitat for black-tailed prairie dogs (*Cynomys ludovicianus*), and prairie dogs were increasingly being recognized as a "keystone species"—a species that, relative to its abundance, greatly influences the structure and species diversity of an ecosystem.[5] The region encompassed reintroduction sites for the black-footed ferret (*Mustela nigripes*), one of North America's most endangered species. Historic reports clearly indicated that the Montana Glaciated Plains had been prime habitat for bison and other wild ungulates. Importantly, the region consisted mostly of public lands held by the C. M. Russell Refuge and Bureau of Land Management (BLM) that might be more readily steered toward wildlife restoration than regions dominated by private land ownership.

Conservation Flyover Country

Prairie scientists and advocates came to that first Bozeman meeting with a collective gripe—a score that needed settling. The grasslands of the Great Plains and, more generally, the temperate grasslands of the world had for too long taken a back seat to forest, wetland, coastal, and other ecosystems. For most of the continent's conservation history the Great Plains had been "flyover country," even before transcontinental air travel popularized the term. A 1993 tally of U.S. organizations devoted to various habitats—nine for forests, four for the Great Lakes, five for coastal areas, six for rivers, two for caves, three for deserts, two for polar regions, and zero for grasslands—showed the region still lacked a large constituency.[6] It was time for grassland conservationists to raise their voices to be heard, and they needed a game plan for doing so. Participants only had to point to the history and current state of conservation in the Great Plains to back their claim. The era of establishing the continent's largest and most iconic parks, from Yellowstone in 1872 and Banff in 1885 to Great Smoky Mountains in 1934 and Everglades in 1947, came and went without the creation of a single large-scale Great Plains national park.

Although the Great Plains had been ignored, two early visionaries had called for creating a large protected area in the region. First was George Catlin, renowned painter and early ethnographer of North America's Native peoples. While exploring the Great Plains of the Dakotas in the 1830s, Catlin became concerned regarding the plight of Native peoples and bison. He wrote of the massive slaughter of bison and how, having "seen this noble animal in all its pride and glory, to contemplate it so rapidly wasting from the world" left him "melancholy."[7] Catlin's interest in preserving prairie wildlife and Native peoples led him to propose in his 1841 book *Letters and Notes on the Manners, Customs, and Condition of the North American Indians* an idea new to the Americas: "What a beautiful and thrilling specimen for America to preserve and hold up to the view of her refined citizens and the world, in future ages! A Nation's Park, containing man and beast, in all the wild and freshness of their nature's beauty!"[8] Although the Great Plains, its wildlife, and its people fired Catlin's imagination for creating "A Nation's Park," the subsequent national park movement focused on the nation's forests, mountains, and other nongrassland habitats.

Montana photographer Laton A. Huffman—whose photos chronicled the rapidly changing land, wildlife, and peoples of the plains of eastern Montana during the late 1800s and early 1900s—called for the nation to create a "great pasture" in the region between the Missouri and Yellowstone Rivers of eastern Montana and "to fence it with a great woven wire to banish forever the skin hunters, maybe enlist them in an army of wardens. How and where the great park gates should be guarded, how tame the wild things would get—bison, antelope and elk—and too how splendid twould be when the yellow-green carpet of spring had come, to see it all teeming with life."[9]

The early 1900s brought the first modest breakthroughs for establishing Great Plains protected areas. In 1901 President William McKinley created the 59,000-acre Wichita Forest Reserve in Oklahoma, now named Wichita Mountains National Wildlife Refuge. In 1903 President Theodore Roosevelt created the 33,847-acre Wind Cave National Park in South Dakota. Not much else happened in the way of new protected areas until the 1930s and 1940s when the C. M. Russell Refuge, Badlands National Park in South Dakota, and Theodore Roosevelt National Park in North Dakota were established. This brief surge quickly tapered off, with only a very modest increase in protected-area coverage of the U.S. Great Plains since then. Canada created its largest Great Plains protected area, Grasslands National Park, in 1981 and its second largest, Suffield National Wildlife Area, in 2003. We'll look at the size of these protected areas later.

Although these protected areas are important, at the time of the Bozeman meeting in 2000, they and a few others covered just 1% of the Great Plains. As one of the least-protected biomes in North America,[10] meeting participants recognized that far more and larger protected areas were needed to restore and conserve the full sweep of Great Plains biodiversity.

One reason for the region's sparse protected area coverage is that compared to forests, wetlands, and mountains, grasslands are instantly colonizable by agricultural settlers. Open the livestock gate and a palatable spread of grasses and forbs is ready for grazing. Turn over the prairie sod with a spade or plow and the rich topsoil is ready for crops. No forest to clear, wetlands to drain, or alpine rock and ice to endure. Railroad salesmen pitched the promise of riches by running cattle and tilling the soil rather than, as they did for Yellowstone, touting the financial rewards of scenic tourism. Fueled by the rising demand for beef in the East and in mining towns of the West and facilitated by the westward expansion of railroads, horrific persecution of Native peoples, and various government programs to transfer public lands to homesteaders in the United States and Canada, livestock numbers and open-range ranching boomed during the last three decades of the 19th century.[11] Any wildlife that might compete with livestock for grass, eat livestock, or bring a quick buck vanished. By the mid-1880s the last herds of wild bison, once numbering in the tens of millions, were gone from the Great Plains. All large mammals—elk (*Cervus canadensis*), mule deer (*Odocoileus hemionus*), white-tailed deer (*Odocoileus virginianus*), pronghorn, bighorn sheep (*Ovis canadensis*), wolves, grizzly bears, and pumas (*Puma concolor*)—met similar fates over the next 30 years. The demise of many smaller species followed. The devastation was swift and broad. From Alberta and Saskatchewan to Texas, no area of the Great Plains was spared. The idea of creating a national park or refuge the size of Yellowstone National Park never had a chance.

This story of agriculture getting the jump on protected areas has been repeated in temperate grasslands around the world. Globally, of the world's 14 terrestrial biomes, the temperate grasslands, savannas, and shrublands biome is the least protected, with 4.6% designated as protected.[12] Participants in the Bozeman meeting pointed to a rash of growing threats to biodiversity in the Northern Great Plains that added urgency to correcting this oversight. Energy development—oil, coal, natural gas, and coalbed methane—was chopping up and degrading grasslands and rivers and streams. Wetlands continued to be drained. Government farm subsidies and new crop-production technologies were causing a resurgence in the plowing of native prairie. Livestock grazing practices continued to homogenize grassland habitats and degrade streams and riparian areas.

Meeting participants proposed a diversity of tools to confront these challenges: reform energy and farm policies, improve how millions of acres of federal grazing lands in the region are managed, create new incentives for private landowners to improve land management practices, and others. But as had already been demonstrated in diverse biomes around the globe, large protected areas had to be the cornerstone for restoring and protecting biodiversity.

The year 2000, the start of a new millennium and time of the Bozeman conference, was perhaps the tipping point for forging and realizing a vision for building large protected areas in the Great

Plains. New research and developments in biological, socioeconomic, and political spheres during the last three decades of the
1900s were providing justification and a heightened awareness of
the need and potential for biodiversity conservation at much larger
scales. More to the point, the mix of these three spheres had arguably
produced the perfect brew for launching a bold project to create a multi-million-acre reserve on the Great Plains of Montana.

Sagebrush Rebellion and New Environmental Policies

Agriculture in the Great Plains experienced rather halcyon times after
the Dust Bowl, especially from the mid-1960s to the mid-1970s as
crop and livestock production benefited from major improvements
in irrigation, pest management, fertilizer, tillage practices, crop
varieties, and financial and market subsidies. Then in the mid-
1970s, boom again turned to bust as several factors converged to
drive down farm and ranch income that led to the farm crisis of
the early 1980s. The most rural, least irrigated regions of the Great
Plains—areas of high biodiversity value in many cases—were among
the hardest hit, as agricultural income in these regions continued
to decline through the 1990s and into the new millennium. The
farm crisis, in turn, further accelerated the population decline
of the rural Great Plains that had begun in the 1920s. More than
ever, young people raised in farm and ranch country in the Great
Plains were moving out in search of new opportunities, and the
remaining population was grayer than ever.[13]

While these trends were well known and there was considerable
handwringing by the region's residents and politicians over what
to do, it took a radical proposal by two East Coast academics to
change the course of debates about the region's future. It's a mystery to me how the 1987 article "The Great Plains: Dust to Dust"
in the relatively obscure academic journal *Planning* by Rutgers
University geographers Debora and Frank Popper leapt across the
gap from academia to the center of political discourse. But leap it
did, and the "Buffalo Commons" they proposed in the article hit
a nerve that deeply penetrated the region's collective psyche. The
Poppers predicted that "much of the Plains will inexorably suffer

near-total desertion over the next generation."[14] Their solution was to deprivatize the region—essentially reverse what the Homestead Acts had done—through a government program to buy the region's private lands and turn them into a commons with abundant bison and other wildlife, much as it had been when Native peoples shared the land and its resources. "The Buffalo Commons," they predicted, "will become the world's largest historic preservation project, the ultimate national park."[15]

Although the Poppers were excoriated across the Great Plains, the region's ongoing agricultural struggles and population loss have slowly eroded some of the denialism about the region's plight. In succeeding years, the Poppers recast the Buffalo Commons as a metaphor for how the Great Plains should change as they recognized that, rather than a government-led effort, individuals, nonprofit organizations, and Native peoples were beginning to lead the region's transformation.[16] Regardless of how the change might unfold, their proposal for setting aside most of the Great Plains provided an anchor point against which any other proposal for creating a large park or reserve would seem modest in comparison. But it also put those resistant to change on guard and "Buffalo Commons" became a four-letter word in ranch country.

Even novelists weighed in regarding the need for big protected areas in the Great Plains. In James A. Michener's 1974 bestseller, *Centennial*, Colorado rancher Paul Garret spends a lot of time reflecting on the harsh conditions of rangeland living and how Native peoples seem to have a better approach to living with the land than white people. Garret eventually concludes, "What the United States ought to do is take the money we're spending on Southeast Asia and space shots and build a barbed wire fence around the whole state of Wyoming. . . . Declare Wyoming a national park and treat it as such."[17] With the not-so-subtle title *Buffalo Commons*, Montana author Richard Wheeler's 1998 novel is about a wealthy man who buys ranches to eventually assemble a huge reserve for bison and other wildlife.[18]

On the political front, new federal policies were being viewed by the ranch community as threats to their way of life, particularly for ranchers who had long enjoyed rather unencumbered and inexpensive grazing privileges on public lands. Many ranchers in the Northern Great Plains depend on grazing allotments on BLM lands and National Grasslands for their livestock operations. No one, it seemed, outside of the grazing allotment holders and respective federal management agencies, paid much attention to management of these federal lands. Then came a string of new federal policies—the 1970 National Environmental Policy Act (NEPA), the 1973 Endangered Species Act (ESA), and in 1976, the National Forest Management Act (NFMA) and the Federal Land Policy and Management Act (FLPMA), among others—that increasingly gave environmental and recreational values greater influence over both public grazing lands and, in the case of the ESA, private lands. FLPMA caught the most attention because it emphasized the importance of multiple use and of giving attention to wildlife and their habitats and to wilderness values in the management of about 175 million acres of BLM lands across the Great Plains and other western states.[19]

Following Newton's Third Law of Motion that for every action there is an equal and opposite reaction, FLPMA was the primary spark that ignited the backlash of the Sagebrush Rebellion. The economic crisis of the early 1980s in farm and ranch country only added oxygen to the conflagration. Rather than FLPMA's emphasis on keeping BLM lands in federal ownership and giving the public more say in how federal lands in the West are managed, the Sagebrush Rebellion sought to have most federal lands, especially BLM rangelands, turned over to the states or to the private sector—ranching and mining interests in particular. The rebellion found political backing at the highest level when Ronald Reagan became president in 1981 and, while calling himself a "rebel," appointed James Watt as Secretary of the Interior. (I recall vividly, when I worked in the Department of the Interior in Washington DC in 1981, attending a gathering of Interior employees to hear Secretary Watt introduce himself and his vision for the agency. The reaction of most of my fellow coworkers to his speech can best be summarized as stunned silence. *Time* later named Watt one of the 10 worst cabinet members in history.[20]) Reagan and Watt, however, never pushed hard for a transfer of federal lands; they just worked to make Interior friendlier to ranching and mining interests.[21]

The Sagebrush Rebellion served to broaden public awareness of the value of public lands, especially of BLM grasslands, whose management had received relatively little attention compared to federal forestlands. The result was a stronger resolve by conservationists to protect these lands for their biodiversity values.

The political tide changed in 1993 when Bill Clinton became president and appointed Bruce Babbitt as Secretary of the Interior. Signaling an interest in the conservation value of BLM lands, in 1996 and 1997 the Clinton administration designated several BLM units as Wilderness Study Areas in the plains and Missouri River breaks of northeast Montana. On January 17, 2001, three days before leaving office, President Clinton created by proclamation the 377,000-acre Upper Missouri River Breaks National Monument (Upper Missouri Monument), consisting of BLM lands on both sides of the Missouri River upriver from the C. M. Russell Refuge. Although designation as a monument had little effect on how the BLM lands in the monument were managed, the proclamation created a firestorm of protests across the plains of eastern Montana about the government locking up land in ranch country.

The Science of Bigger Is Better

Rapidly growing recognition of the biological diversity crisis and the ballooning roster of endangered species in North America and globally gave rise in the 1980s to the new discipline of conservation biology.[22] The term *biological diversity*, soon shortened to *biodiversity*, entered the conservation lexicon as an expression for the entire spectrum of plant and animal species, of their genetic diversity, and of the ecosystems they inhabit. Conservation biology pushed scientific research beyond the utilitarian focus of how to sustainably harvest wildlife and forests to the broader challenge of how to save all species, their long-term evolutionary potential, and the diversity and functioning of the planet's ecosystems.[23]

The justification for creating large protected areas had been mostly based on the aesthetics of their wilderness values, but that started to change around 1980 when research in conservation biology began to offer scientific evidence that large areas were needed to conserve the full sweep of a region's biodiversity.[24] A kick-start to that idea was a book published in 1967, *The Theory of Island Biogeography* by Robert T. MacArthur and Edward O. Wilson.[25] MacArthur and Wilson's theory explains in scientific terms what makes sense intuitively: larger islands tend to be able to hold more species than smaller islands. They also note that, compared to highly isolated islands, islands closer to the mainland (or to other islands) tend to have more species because they can be more easily reached by colonizing species from the mainland. A logical extension of their theory is that isolated patches of forest, grassland, or other habitats surrounded by human development are the equivalent of islands. The theory was readily transmuted for application regarding how big protected areas should be, where they should be located, and how they should be managed.

Building on the theory of island biogeography, several new biological concepts emerged in the 1970s and 1980s that aimed to provide a more scientific, biodiversity-oriented approach to the design and management of protected areas. A central question in this debate was how large do reserves need to be to conserve biodiversity? Not surprisingly, the answer seemed to be "It depends."[26]

"It depends" spawned an explosion of new research questions and graduate theses for the field of conservation biology. The term *habitat fragmentation* was coined to describe what happens when previously intact habitats are chopped up—fragmented—by roads, fences, dams, deforestation, and other developments.[27] *Wildlife corridors* of intact habitat were proposed as remedies to connect protected areas and wildlife populations isolated by fragmentation.[28]

Researchers also looked at reserve configuration, particularly the *perimeter-to-area ratio*—the perimeter, or boundary, of an area relative to the acres within the area.[29] A protected area that is long and narrow or that is irregularly shaped with the boundary occasionally curving in near the center of the area has a high

perimeter-to-area ratio. This means that negative influences outside the boundary, such as poachers or invasive nonnative species, can more readily reach the core of a protected area. It also
means a greater likelihood that wildlife within the protected area
will wander into unprotected terrain outside the boundary.

Two other concepts, *minimum viable population* (MVP) and
population viability analysis (PVA), emerged to estimate the risk of
species going extinct.[30] Of particular interest was the question
of how large a species' population should be in order to have a low
probability (say, 5%) of going extinct over a long period of time
(say, 1,000 years). Intuitively it makes sense that small populations are more vulnerable to extinction than large populations. A
small population, especially if restricted to a small area, is likely
more vulnerable to elimination by a single catastrophic event,
such as a flood or fire or disease, than a large population. Small
populations are also susceptible to two types of genetic problems,
inbreeding and genetic drift, which increase the risk of extinction. *Inbreeding* (relatives mating with each other) leads to the
expression of deleterious genes. *Genetic drift* is the random loss
of genetic diversity that occurs when variations of a gene—the
alleles—fail to get passed on from one generation to the next.
The smaller a population, the more likely alleles will be lost. It's
like starting with a large bowl of hundreds of red, white, and blue
marbles (the alleles of a gene in a population) and then picking
just five marbles from the bowl to represent the animals that survive and breed. There's a good chance that at least one of the colors
will be missing. The loss of alleles can reduce a population's ability to respond genetically through natural selection to changing
conditions—climate change, new diseases, and so on—thereby making it more prone to extinction. Geneticists, for example, posited
that, depending on the species, a population of at least 500 to more
than 1,000 animals would be needed to avoid the loss of genetic
diversity and inbreeding problems. The upshot is that to conserve
species that occur at low population densities (such as wolves,
grizzly bears, and pumas), reserves of millions of acres may be
needed.[31]

The importance of making reserves large enough to support viable populations of big predators was reinforced by research showing their powerful top-down role in shaping ecosystems.[32] The term *trophic cascade* was coined to describe what happens when removal of big carnivores leads to large increases in populations of the herbivores they eat, which, in turn, results in so much plant life being consumed that the ecosystem collapses.[33] Big carnivores are *umbrella species*. According to the concept, reserves that are big enough to support umbrella species should be able to conserve other species that have smaller area requirements.

The mounting theoretical evidence supporting the creation of large reserves was forcefully driven home in 1987 when the biologist William D. Newmark, based on his research of mammalian extinctions in 14 western North American parks, concluded in a seminal paper that "all but the largest western North American parks are too small to retain an intact mammalian fauna."[34] Even Yellowstone National Park, at 2.2 million acres—the second largest one he examined—isn't big enough.

Although conservation biology was making progress toward science-based estimates of how big reserves needed to be, it was still hard for conservation biologists to avoid the not-very-scientific quip "The bigger the better."

Great Plains Protected Areas Fall Short

How do Great Plains protected areas stack up in light of these concepts from conservation biology? Five of the six largest protected areas in the Great Plains have high perimeter-to-area ratios. The largest, the 1.1-million-acre C. M. Russell Refuge, is approximately 140 miles long and 10 miles wide, with the Missouri River and the 245,000-acre Fort Peck Reservoir running through its middle. Prairie habitat is a fringe running the length of both sides of the refuge. The next-largest protected area, the 242,756-acre Badlands National Park in South Dakota, is about 50 miles long by 3–6 miles wide, narrowing down to less than 2 miles wide in places, and a large portion of the park is a detached unit. The third largest, Grasslands National Park in Saskatchewan, around 180,000 acres

in 2020 but slated to grow to 224,000 acres, is divided into east
and west units separated by about 10 miles of provincial livestock
grazing lands. Fourth is the 113,000-acre Suffield National Wildlife Area in Alberta, also fragmented into two separate management units. Valentine National Wildlife Refuge in the Sandhills
of Nebraska, the fifth largest at 73,000 acres, is one contiguous
area that mostly falls within a square shape and thus has a favor-
able perimeter-to-area ratio. Theodore Roosevelt National Park
in North Dakota covers 70,447 acres and is fragmented into two
geographically separate management units. All other public protected areas in the Great Plains are less than 70,000 acres, and the
management of many of these is also compromised by problematic
configurations and fragmentation. Every one of these protected
areas is entirely or nearly entirely surrounded by lands devoted
primarily to livestock ranching and crops. For some species (bison,
wolves, prairie dogs, and others) and for some ecological processes (stream flow, pollination, seed dispersal, fire, and others)
these protected areas are, to varying degrees, islands in a sea of
incompatible land uses.

Given these contorted configurations, the relatively small size
of most of their management units, and the agricultural landscapes
that surround them, it's not surprising that no national park, wildlife refuge, or other public protected area in the Great Plains harbors the full suite of native species. Biologists, including some of
North America's most imminent, had expressed dismay about this
problem for six decades leading up to the 2000 Bozeman conference. In 1940 Victor Cahalane, then chief of National Park Wildlife,
citing work by the plant ecologist Victor Shelford and with support by the Ecological Society of America, proposed the creation
of a Great Plains reserve of at least one million acres. He argued
that a large grassland reserve is important not only for ecological
and research reasons but also to ensure the greatest inspirational
value.[35] At a national parks conference in 1976, Durwood Allen,
one of the founders of wildlife conservation science, lamented that
all Great Plains parks "fall far short on size and fauna they contain" and that a great grassland park "is our most obvious 'hole'

in the nation's program of wildland preservation."[36] Daniel Licht, then an ecologist with the U.S. National Park Service, in his 1997 book *Ecology and Economics of the Great Plains*, expresses the same sentiment: "There are few naturally functioning ecosystems in the lower forty-eight states, and absolutely none in the vast grasslands of the center of North America."[37] Licht marshals a raft of compelling data about the troubled agricultural economy of the Great Plains and threats to the region's biodiversity to argue for creating several large protected areas of more than a million acres each.

Global Conservation Trends and Ecoregion Conservation

Let's step back for a moment to look broadly at U.S. and global trends in the growth of national parks, wildlife refuges, and other types of protected areas, particularly big ones. While the era of creating large protected areas in the lower 48 U.S. states ended in the 1930s (the exception is the 5,270-square-mile Death Valley National Park, created in 1994, where competing land uses were of minor concern), global trends in protected area creation offered a distinctly different story. Globally, in 1970 about 1.16 million square miles, 2% of the Earth's land surface, were protected. This was about to change dramatically as concerns about the rapid loss of wildlife and wildlands from the Arctic to the tropics catalyzed a global surge in protected area creation. Within 30 years, by 2000, the coverage had increased fivefold to 5.8 million square miles, 10% of the world's land area.[38]

This global trend made the lackluster condition of protected areas in the Great Plains all the more untenable, particularly for those of us who had worked internationally. For naysayers who thought the idea of building a multi-million-acre grassland reserve in eastern Montana was a pipe dream, the counterpoint was to ask how other regions of the world with often extreme poverty, high human population densities, rampant development pressures, nascent and impoverished park agencies, and often far more intimidating wildlife (tigers, lions, elephants, rhinoceros) than historically found on the Great Plains, could be building impressive systems of parks and reserves. If they could do it, or were at least willing to try, surely, we thought, we can aim just as high in a region with a human population density of one person per square mile (and declining) where the ecosystem is still relatively intact and faces few development pressures.

Increasing recognition of the need for conservationists to work at larger geographic scales and to ensure that all ecosystems are represented in the world's protected areas fostered the birth of another important concept during the 1990s: ecoregion-based conservation.[39] Ecoregions, such as the Northern Great Plains, are large areas characterized by a particular climate and suite of species and ecological communities. wwf, The Nature Conservancy, and other conservation organizations began using ecoregions as the primary framework for conservation planning in the 1990s in an attempt to incorporate all the dimensions of biodiversity across large landscapes. By the end of the 1990s, wwf had identified the Northern Great Plains as one of its "Global 200" priority ecoregions. Temperate grasslands were now in the same priority league as the tropical forest of the Amazon, Congo, and Southeast Asia that were garnering so much attention by wwf and other international conservation groups.

Of Ferrets, Bison, and Birds

Other less theoretical developments of particular relevance to Great Plains conservation unfolded during the 1980s and 1990s that encouraged participants to think big at the Bozeman conference. In 1981 one of those miracles that too rarely happen in wildlife conservation occurred on the windswept grasslands near Meeteeste, Wyoming, thanks to a rancher's dog bringing home its day's quarry: a dead black-footed ferret. Endemic (found only there) to the Great Plains and thought extinct, the ferret was discovered to be still among the living—but barely (more about this in chapter 9).[40] None, as far as anyone knew, remained anywhere else in the wild and the black-footed ferret was then—and still is—among the most endangered mammals in North America. Ferrets prey almost exclusively on prairie dogs and live only in prairie dog colonies, and thus their recovery would require restoring hundreds of thousands of acres of prairie dog colonies.[41] With prairie dog populations at 2% of their pre-Euro-American abundance in the Great Plains due to habitat loss, rancher intolerance, an introduced disease, and government-funded eradication programs, the ferret offered conservationists a compelling biological justification for restoring big prairie dog populations.

Threats to the biodiversity of the Great Plains were further highlighted in 1996 with the publication of *Prairie Conservation: Preserving North America's Most Endangered Ecosystem*, a book edited by the ecologists Fred Samson and Fritz Knopf.[42] They continued with the book title's message when the following year in another book, *Ecology and Conservation of Great Plains Vertebrates*, they stated, "The grasslands of the Great Plains remain the nation's most threatened ecosystem."[43] Among the many threats to the region's grasslands, the most destructive was then, and still is, sodbusting—the plow-up of native grasslands for crop production. Technological advances in crop production and ecologically perverse federal farm subsidies that encouraged cultivation of grasslands marginally—or not at all—suitable for crop production were contributing to the ongoing conversion of prairie to cropland.[44]

Birds emerged as early indicators of the threats facing Great Plains biodiversity. The plight of grassland birds was captured by Knopf in his 1996 *Prairie Legacies—Birds* when he wrote what has become one of the most widely quoted statements in North American grassland conservation literature: "As a group, grassland birds in general and endemic grassland birds specifically have shown steeper, more consistent, and more geographically widespread declines than any other behavioral or ecological guild of North American species."[45]

The plight of the American bison was also gaining increasing attention among conservationists during the 1980s and 1990s. As later became evident when Steve Forrest compiled historical data for a paper, "Second Chance for the Plains Bison," which Steve and I and several colleagues published in 2006, the total population of plains bison in conservation herds hadn't budged upward in 70 years—it had been stuck at around 20,000 since the 1930s.[46]

Moreover, most of these were in small herds of a few hundred animals with the attendant risks of inbreeding and loss of genetic diversity, and all but a handful of herds were fenced in and managed under highly artificial ecological conditions. This situation starkly contrasted with growing awareness that bison historically played a large ecological role in the prairie ecosystem, when massive herds could freely roam and graze across the landscape.[47] With wild bison occupying a fraction of 1% of their historic range in the Great Plains, bold action was needed to begin to rebuild anything that came close to resembling those historic herds and their effects on the prairie ecosystem.

Another threat to wild bison came to the attention of conservationists in 1995 with the publication of a paper showing that bison in several conservation herds—and by implication in possibly most herds in North America—had some cattle genes in their DNA (*introgressed*, in the language of geneticists), the result of attempts to crossbreed bison and cattle a century earlier.[48] Adding to the concern—and considerable confusion in terms of public awareness—was the fact that bison numbers in private commercial herds in North America had grown dramatically and numbered more than 300,000 by the end of the century.[49] While the public was seeing more bison than ever on farms and ranches in the United States and Canada and wondering, "What's the worry?," conservationists were concerned that artificial selection by bison producers catering to the commodity meat market were breeding for big rumps, small humps, and an easy-to-handle, docile animal. Bison domestication was a threat to the wild bison genome and to public recognition of the bison's plight.

Books about bison, such as David Dary's *The Buffalo Book: The Full Saga of the American Animal* and Valerius Geist's *Buffalo Nation: History and Legend of the North American Bison*, were raising awareness of the bison's iconic position in Great Plains natural and human history and its close call with extinction.[50] Stephen Ambrose's 1996 bestseller, *Undaunted Courage: Meriwether Lewis, Thomas Jefferson, and the Opening of the American West*, provides compelling testimony from the Lewis and Clark journals of the wildlife spectacle the Great Plains once harbored and offered a vision for what might be restored.[51]

Great Plains Native nations were also greatly expanding their efforts during this period to restore the bison's economic and cultural values as several reservations, including some in Montana, began reintroducing bison. In 1992 the InterTribal Bison Cooperative (now the InterTribal Buffalo Council) was established to help Native nations restore bison.[52]

The assaults on biodiversity were adding up: The Great Plains was home to the continent's most-endangered mammal and the largest number of imperiled birds. It was the most-threatened ecosystem and its most iconic species, the Americas' biggest land animal, was at a conservation dead end and maybe going in reverse. Further, there existed no protected area large enough to restore and conserve the full sweep of wildlife that the region once harbored. The silver lining in all this bad news was that it offered hope that the region would finally get the attention it had long deserved. The Bozeman meeting of the NPCN in 2000 set in motion the creation of an organization with a vision: to assemble a protected area on the plains of northeast Montana for restoring that wildlife spectacle.

A 3.2-Million-Acre Prairie Wildlife Reserve

Within a year of the NPCN meeting's decision to launch a project in the Montana Glaciated Plains, Steve Forrest and I had filed articles of incorporation for creating American Prairie as a nonprofit organization with the sole mission of carrying out the project. Because WWF had designated the Northern Great Plains as one of its global priority ecoregions, it provided crucial start-up support for American Prairie. The history of American Prairie and the scores of individuals and institutions involved in its growth and success since the idea was hatched is, in itself, a book-length story to be told elsewhere.

Plans for assembling the American Prairie–Russell Refuge were based on a combination of science and practicality. William Newmark's seminal paper on species extinctions in parks in western North America suggests that a prairie reserve should be several million acres in size to avoid losing species.[53] Independently, bison biologist Dale Lott, in his book *American Bison: A Natural History* published in 2002, states that a reserve of 5,000 square miles (3.2 million acres) would be needed to fully restore a population of wild bison and their ecological role in the grassland ecosystem.[54] Some ecological processes, such as the interaction of fire and grazers (especially bison), can only be captured at large scales.[55] Similarly, conserving hydrological processes is best achieved by including the full reach of streams and their watersheds. Viable populations of wolves, grizzly bears, and puma require millions of acres.[56] A vast area would also be needed to capture the region's richness of grassland birds and potential for restoring populations of the black-tailed prairie dog and endangered black-footed ferret. The protected area needed to include the region's vast array of habitats—the Missouri River and its tributaries, their floodplain forests, the rugged Missouri River breaks and badlands, the glaciated plains to the north of the river and unglaciated plains to the south, and connectivity to the pine-forested slopes of the Little Rocky Mountains. Perhaps as important as any of the above considerations was the potential for permanently protecting a region where 90% of the prairie and associated habitats were in natural or near-natural condition.

From the outset, the basic strategy was for American Prairie to purchase ranches as they came up for sale and to link American Prairie lands with the C. M. Russell Refuge to create one large protected area.[57] The deeded portion of ranches in the region generally come with leased BLM and state trust lands that are transferred with the property when it changes hands. Although nearly all BLM lands in the region are leased for livestock grazing, BLM's mission requires that its lands also be managed for biodiversity conservation and recreation, among other uses.[58] BLM lands cannot be converted to croplands, an obvious cornerstone for conserving grasslands. State trust lands are managed by the state of Montana with the goal of generating revenue for public schools; they are mostly leased for grazing and farming in the American Prairie–Russell Refuge region.[59] Managed by the U.S. Fish

and Wildlife Service, the refuge's primary purpose is wildlife conservation. Up to two-thirds of the refuge is leased for livestock
grazing, but grazing is managed to meet biodiversity conservation objectives.[60] The 377,000-acre Upper Missouri Monument,
administered by BLM, is important for ecological, geological, and
cultural resources, although the monument's 2008 management
plan provides modest additional protection for these resources
beyond that provided for other BLM lands. Nearly all monument
lands are leased for livestock grazing like other BLM lands in the
region. Encompassed within the refuge and monument is the 149-
mile Upper Missouri Wild and Scenic River, extending from Fort
Benton to where Highway 191 crosses the Missouri River near the
western boundary of the C. M. Russell Refuge.

The boundaries for assembling the American Prairie–Russell
Refuge are not rigid but reflect existing land uses and importance
to wildlife. Generally, the west end of the Upper Missouri Monument forms a practical western boundary. The 675,000-acre Fort
Belknap Indian Reservation partially defines a western and northern boundary. The rest of the northern boundary is comprised of
extensive cropland and other developments on private lands along
the Highway 2 and Milk River corridor. The 15,551-acre Bowdoin
National Wildlife Refuge, containing large wetlands and upland
prairie habitat, is along this corridor. The east end of the C. M. Russell Refuge is a logical eastern limit. There are less obvious practical
limits to the south of the refuge and Upper Missouri Monument.

At roughly the halfway mark in acreage, much work remains
for American Prairie and its collaborators and supporters to assemble and mold this mosaic of land ownership into a seamlessly managed 3.2-million-acre American Prairie–Russell Refuge. As noted
in the introduction, my concern in this book is not how that gets
done. Rather, I offer a biodiversity-oriented perspective on the
history of this landscape and explore what it could look like with
populations of all native wildlife restored.

To eat, the plains hog-nosed snake (*Heterodon nasicus*) uses its shovel-shaped snout to dig out toads, and to avoid being eaten it often feigns death by rolling on its back with its mouth open and tongue hanging out. Drawing by Erica Freese.

TWO

From Sea, Ice, and Forest Emerges a Prairie

Like chapter 1, the buffalo jump on the Charles M. Russell National Wildlife Refuge is a good place to start this chapter. But instead of going forward from the time Native peoples used the jump, we'll wind the reel further back in time. Go back 20–15 kya (thousand years ago) and, rather than the steep embankment rising over Fourchette Creek in the semiarid prairie, the site is at the southern edge of a continental ice sheet. Some years it is buried under the grinding ice, and other years, when the ice sheet has retreated, it is a soggy wetland bathed by the melting ice. Crank the reel back to 75–65 mya (million years ago) and the site of the buffalo jump is on the western edge of the Western Interior Seaway, first covered by the seaway's warm waters and then, as the sea's edge retreats to the east, slowly surfacing to become a vast coastal swamp and, later, a lush subtropical forest that is then scorched by a massive bolide striking Earth. Reel back the shifting continental plates to 500 mya and the region of the buffalo jump sits astride the equator.[1]

As this rewind suggests and as will become apparent in this chapter and the next, the American Prairie–Russell Refuge region's landscape and biodiversity were forged by extreme geologic and climatic changes that, literally, kept life on the edge. If, like people, adversity and diverse experiences forge interesting characters and life stories, the American Prairie–Russell Refuge region must offer a storied history.

The American Prairie–Russell Refuge region today, like every other place on Earth, is a snapshot of two intertwined histories, one physical and one biological, that have played out over time imme-morial. The region's landscape and biodiversity are the legacy of mil-lions of years of not only sweeping climatic and geologic changes but also massive extinctions, explosive plant and animal evolution, globetrotting plant and animal migrations, and prehistoric and his-toric human influence. The imprints of this legacy are sometimes obvious, such as fossil-laden sedimentary rocks exposed on a cliff face along the Missouri River. Others are subtle or invisible, like a species' genetic code shaped by millions of years of natural selec-tion. Each species has its own evolutionary story, some that can be traced back tens of millions of years, others only thousands.

Warm seas, frigid ice sheets, boreal forests, subtropical forests, woodlands and savannas, and grasslands—few species could evolve fast enough to keep up with the changing conditions. As the habi-tat changed, most species either moved out or went extinct while others moved in. Consequently, the American Prairie–Russell Refuge region's plants and animals are a melting pot of species, some evolutionarily homegrown in North America but most arriv-ing as immigrants from far-off places.

The Paleozoic: A Warm, Shallow Sea under a Tropical Sun

A good time to begin our evolutionary journey is about a half bil-lion years ago, near the beginning of the Paleozoic Era (see table 1). The Paleozoic left some of the earliest imprints visible today on the American Prairie–Russell Refuge landscape. Finding the North-ern Great Plains, much less the American Prairie–Russell Refuge region, on a map from a half billion years ago, however, isn't easy. North America was tipped on its side—north was east, east was south, and so on—and was part of Laurentia, a Paleozoic conti-nent hovering over the equator and mostly covered by a shallow tropical sea.[2] By the end of the Paleozoic, Laurentia had fused with the supercontinent Gondwana to form the larger supercontinent Pangaea, which incorporated nearly all the land masses on Earth.[3]

The warm shallow seas that covered western North America during most of the Paleozoic nurtured the evolution of new life-forms at a dizzying pace. Plants and arthropods emerged from the

Table 1. Geologic time scales, mya = million years ago, kya = thousand years ago

Era	Period	Epoch
Paleozoic (542.0–251.0 mya)		
Mesozoic (251.0–66.0 mya)	Triassic (251.0–199.6 mya)	
	Jurassic (199.6–145.5 mya)	
	Cretaceous (145.5–66.0 mya)	
Cenozoic (66.0 mya–present)		Paleocene (66.0–55.8 mya)
		Eocene (55.8–33.9 mya)
		Oligocene (33.9–23.03 mya)
		Miocene (23.03–5.332 mya)
		Pliocene (5.332–2.588 mya)
		Pleistocene (2.588 mya–11,700 kya)
		Holocene (11,700 kya–present)

Source: University of California Museum of Paleontology, "Online Exhibits"

seas to occupy land early in the Paleozoic. By the end of the era, a shallow sea was retreating to the west from eastern Montana, and cycads, ferns, and primitive conifers were spreading across the land. The first reptiles had also evolved, and a lineage that would eventually give rise to the mammals, the synapsids, had split off from the reptiles.[4]

The legacy of Paleozoic life is etched in the economy and associated environmental concerns of the Northern Great Plains today. The productive shallow seas that repeatedly covered central North America during the Paleozoic deposited massive amounts of algae and plankton on the sea floor. With heat, high pressure, and time, these transformed into the oil and gas deposits of the Williston Basin, centered over western North Dakota and extending into the American Prairie–Russell Refuge region.[5] The basin's Bakken Formation, deposited about 300 mya, is currently under heavy oil and gas exploitation in western North Dakota.

One does not need to drill for oil to find sedimentary layers from the Paleozoic in the American Prairie–Russell Refuge region. After crossing north over the Missouri River on Highway 191 and emerging onto the prairie, a driver sees these layers surrounding much of the Little Rocky Mountains. The Madison Formation, deposited on the sea bottom about 340 mya, laid buried until about 50 mya when hot plasma pushed its way up through 1.7-billion-year-old Precambrian rock and then through layers of Madison Limestone to create the 15-mile-wide igneous dome forming the core of the Little Rocky Mountains. The light-colored Madison Limestone was thrust on edge to girdle much of the Little Rockies with a fortress-like appearance.[6] Today the limestone cliffs offer nesting places for prairie falcons (*Falco mexicanus*) and golden eagles (*Aguila chrysaetos*).

The Paleozoic ended 251 mya with the greatest extinction of life in Earth's history. The end-Permian extinction (named after the last period of the Paleozoic) saw more than an estimated 90% of species vanish.[7] Although the cause is unknown and widely debated, we do know that by nearly snuffing out life on Earth, the end-Permian extinction opened up vast ecological niches for the next evolutionary explosion of biodiversity during a new era, the Mesozoic.

The Mesozoic: Dinosaurs Take Charge

Known as the Age of Reptiles, geological and evolutionary events of the Mesozoic Era are firmly etched in the landscape of the American Prairie–Russell Refuge region. Pangaea began to break apart in the early Mesozoic as North America migrated north from the equator and rotated counterclockwise toward today's cardinal directions. During the first period of the Mesozoic, the Triassic (251–200 mya), ecological niches left by the end-Permian extinction were quickly filled. Dinosaurs, pterosaurs (the first flying vertebrates), and the earliest shrew-like mammals all appeared during the Triassic. A major extinction of terrestrial vertebrates marked the end of the Triassic, but the dinosaurs survived and quickly rose to ever-larger sizes and dominance during the next period, the Jurassic (200–145 mya).[8]

The Western Interior Seaway covered nearly the entire Northern Great Plains, including the American Prairie–Russell Refuge region, during the middle Jurassic. By the end of the Jurassic the seaway had retreated from eastern Montana to expose a vast coastal plain of subtropical forest where dinosaurs reigned.[9] Mammals generally remained rat sized and smaller and were mostly insectivorous.[10] The late Jurassic, 165–145 mya, also marked the first appearance of a distinct dinosaur lineage—birds.[11]

Although ferns and gymnosperms (nonflowering plants with naked seeds, unprotected by a fruit, such as conifers and cycads) dominated plant life of the Northern Great Plains at the start of the Cretaceous Period (145–66 mya), by the middle Cretaceous, angiosperms—flowering plants—were undergoing explosive speciation.[12] By producing flowers and encapsulating their seeds in fruit, angiosperms brought a new strategy to plant reproduction. Flower pollination, fruits, broad leaves, higher plant productivity, and other features presented a cornucopia of novel niches for animals to exploit. The first angiosperms were animal pollinated, which quickly led to the appearance of the common ancestor of one of the most diverse and important lineages of pollinating insects—bees.[13] By the end of the Cretaceous, flowering plants had unequivocally displaced gymnosperms as the most diverse form of plant life on Earth, including in the Northern Great Plains.[14]

During the middle and late Cretaceous, 110–70 mya, Pangaea continued to break up and North America became a stand-alone continent. About this same time the Western Interior Seaway returned to cover nearly the entire Great Plains, extending from the Gulf of Mexico to the Arctic Ocean and splitting North America into two land masses. The American Prairie–Russell Refuge region was on the western edge of the seaway and thus was subject to its ebb and flow and the resulting ecological extremes ranging from a warm, shallow sea, to a coastal environment of river deltas and marshes, to *terra firme* covered by subtropical forest. Sand settling to the bottom of this shallow sea created the sandstone of the distinctive white cliffs of the Upper Missouri River Breaks National Monument.

About 70 mya and 100 miles west of the American Prairie–Russell Refuge, the Rocky Mountains were on the rise as the North American Plate rumpled like a gigantic rug as it slid west over the subducting Farallon Plate. Called the Laramide Orogeny, those first years of mountain growth also marked the birth of the future Missouri River as newly formed mountain-fed streams carved new channels to the east and across the plains.[15]

Although mammals showed some diversification in form and in the ecological niches they filled near the end of the Cretaceous, nearly all were still small and insectivorous. Dinosaurs continued to rule the terrestrial realm. Similarly, birds were minor players compared to flying predatory pterosaurs with 30-foot wingspans. No place in North America has a richer fossil trove, especially of dinosaurs, from the last years of the Cretaceous than the Hell Creek Formation, named for Hell Creek in the southeast section of the C. M. Russell Refuge. With its sedimentary layers exposed throughout much of the American Prairie–Russell Refuge region and nearby areas of the Northern Great Plains, Hell Creek is particularly famous for fossils of *Tyrannosaurus rex* and *Triceratops*.[16] While *T. rex* prowled the river deltas on the western edge of the Western Interior Seaway, ancestors of two fish found in the Missouri River today, the pallid sturgeon (*Scaphirhynchus albus*) and American paddlefish (*Polydon spathula*), were cruising the bottoms of the region's rivers.[17]

What a lush, exuberant place the American Prairie–Russell Refuge region must have been in the late Cretaceous: warm and humid with a subtropical forest and slow-flowing rivers merging into massive deltas on the edge of a shallow, warm interior seaway, its western shoreline slowly retreating from eastern Montana into the Dakotas. Dinosaurs, pterosaurs, crocodiles, marine reptiles, and fish, some massive in size, abounded. Insects thrived on the abundant plant growth. Bees were undergoing rapid speciation to begin a long-term, coevolutionary pollination dance with the radiation of flowering plants. Mammals and birds were there in more subtle forms and numbers. Life was evolving and changing, as it always had, but ecologists studying the Northern Great

Plains then would have had little reason to think that dinosaurs wouldn't be dominating the terrestrial realm for tens of millions of years into the future—through to today.

Then all hell broke loose.

Six to ten miles in diameter and traveling an estimated 12 miles per second, an asteroid slammed into Mexico's Yucatan Peninsula about 66 mya. It gouged a hole, the Chicxulub Crater, roughly 110 miles in diameter and 12 miles deep. The Earth's crust vaporized at the impact site. The pressure pulse, 600-mile-per-hour winds, 10,000°F plasma gases, trillions of tons of molten material ejected into the atmosphere, magnitude-10 earthquakes, and a mile-high tsunami that emanated from the impact shredded, cooked, drowned, and generally annihilated life, especially terrestrial life, for thousands of miles around the impact site. Though located 1,500–2,000 miles away, the molten, ejected material began raining down on the Northern Great Plains a few minutes to hours after impact, heating the atmosphere several hundred degrees Fahrenheit and torching vegetation and animal life.[18] Among the ejected material was melted glass that hardened when it fell to Earth. These glass spherules, about one millimeter in diameter, are prevalent in not only Northern Great Plains sediments from that time but also in the gill rakers of the region's fossil paddlefish and pallid sturgeon, the fish apparently having inhaled the spherules within a few hours after the asteroid struck.[19] Nearly all the Americas' forests burned. The global repercussions on life, lasting a few years to possibly centuries after the impact, likely occurred when the massive amounts of gases and soot released into the atmosphere squelched photosynthesis and plunged the Earth's land surface into a deep freeze—the "impact winter."[20]

It's hard to imagine the scene—and the silence—of the apocalyptic landscape of charred and decaying plants and dying and decomposing animals in the Northern Great Plains and elsewhere around the globe. The K-Pg extinction event (*K* is for *Kriede*, German for "Cretaceous"; *Pg* stands for *Paleogene*, the first period of the Cenozoic) marks the end of the Cretaceous and beginning of the Cenozoic Era. Globally, only 12% of all terrestrial species survived. All dinosaurs, except birds, vanished from the Earth. Based on Hell Creek data, the Northern Great Plains was not spared. An estimated 78% of the region's plant species and 75% of mammal species went extinct.[21] Arboreal birds were especially hard hit, presumably because forests were obliterated, while ground-dwelling birds fared much better.[22] Some groups such as bony fish, amphibians, and turtles came through the event relatively unscathed.[23] Life at the bottom of a river is a good place to be when mayhem reigns above the surface.

The Cenozoic: The Rise of Mammals and Grasslands

The Great Plains—and North America—entered the Cenozoic Era, the period from 66 mya to today, with a devastated landscape and depauperate flora and fauna caused by the K-Pg extinction. After the impact winter, the climate quickly turned warm and humid. Tropical-to-subtropical forests soon covered the land. The Western Interior Seaway was retreating due to regional uplift and mountain building in western North America and was nearly gone from the Northern Great Plains by 60 mya.[24] The Cenozoic is commonly known as the Age of Mammals because it was a time when mammalian evolution and radiation boomed, but the era could also justifiably be called the "Age of Birds" or the "Age of Flowering Plants" or, of particular relevance here, the "Age of Grasses."

Climate and Geology

Climatic and geologic changes during the Cenozoic would dramatically alter the Northern Great Plains ecosystem. The warming trend continued in the early Cenozoic, with the average global temperature peaking at hothouse levels about 50 mya. A global cooling and drying trend then began and has generally continued ever since (viewed at the scale of millions of years).[25] The continued rise of the Rocky Mountains, nearing completion 40 mya, cast a rain shadow over the Northern Great Plains.[26] The westerly, moisture-laden winds from the Pacific coast dropped most of their water content over the mountains, leaving warming and desiccating winds to descend onto the plains to the east. The Rocky Mountain uplift extended to eastern Montana, elevating the American Prairie–Russell Refuge region from below sea level to its present elevation of 2,000–3,500 feet. The sediments carried by the rivers flowing out of the emerging Rocky Mountains and deposited in the interior seaway and rivers' deltas in eastern Montana during the late Cretaceous were now subject to the growing flow and erosive force of the Missouri River, a process that continues today. The Missouri River now runs 500–1,000 feet below the surrounding prairie and the river's 2-to-10-mile-wide valley is lined with water- and wind-sculpted badlands, cliffs of Cretaceous sedimentary rocks, and a highly dissected, rugged terrain known as the Missouri River breaks. As noted earlier, another prominent geologic feature of the American Prairie–Russell Refuge region that emerged early in the Cenozoic, about 50 mya, is the conifer-forested Little Rocky Mountains, rising 2,000–3,000 feet above the surrounding land.[27]

One of the most significant geologic events that would overwhelmingly influence the biodiversity of North America and, eventually, South America for millions of years up to the present was unfolding far to the northwest at the start of the Cenozoic. A land bridge linking Eurasia to North America probably emerged around the time of the K-Pg extinction. This first Bering Land Bridge of the Cenozoic lasted maybe a million years before it disappeared, but a few million years later it returned—a pattern of emergence and submergence of the land bridge that would continue throughout the Cenozoic.[28] The newly exposed land was more than what one envisions as a "bridge." While the gap between the two continents is about 50 miles, the terrestrial connection bridging the gap was sometimes 500–1,000 miles wide, essentially forming a supercontinent of Eurasia and North America. Along with the land bridge itself, the adjoining regions of far eastern Siberia and of northern Alaska and northern Yukon are called Beringia. The bridge has been North America's link to the diverse plant and animal species of Eurasia since the K-Pg extinction. Movement has occurred in both directions, but the flow has been disproportionately west to east, Eurasia to North America.[29]

Of minor consequence for the Northern Great Plains, but of immense importance to South America, one other land bridge merits mention. The Isthmus of Panama opened the gates for what paleontologists call the Great American Biotic Interchange (GABI), the two-way dispersal of terrestrial mammals between North and South America. GABI probably started with island-hopping between the two continents about 10 mya before the isthmus emerged and accelerated with the full emergence of the isthmus a few million years later. GABI was also a lopsided exchange. Lineages of immigrant mammals from North America represent about half of South America's mammal species while only 10% of North American mammals are of South American ancestry—and even fewer made it north of Mexico.[30] That's reflected in the fact that only one South American representative of GABI, the porcupine (*Erethizon dorsatum*), occurs in the American Prairie–Russell Refuge region. Another, the Virginia opossum (*Didelphis virginiana*)—the only marsupial in North American north of Mexico—has recently expanded its range northwest into southern areas of the Northern Great Plains.[31]

After about 50 million years of a slow cooling trend, the global climate turned turbulent during the second-to-last epoch of the Cenozoic, the Pleistocene (2.6 mya–11,700 kya). As the temperature bottomed out—the average global temperature at the start of the Pleistocene was 30–35°F cooler than 50 million years earlier—North America and Eurasia entered an ice age. The first ice sheet to cover extensive areas of North America may have occurred 850 kya, with alternating cycles of warm interglacial periods and ice-sheet-forming cold glacial periods occurring roughly every 100,000 years since. Once again, plants and animals across much of the Northern Great Plains, including the American Prairie–Russell Refuge region, were living on the edge. This time, rather than the edge of an interior seaway, it was the southern edge of the Laurentide Ice Sheet that advanced and retreated 10 or more times across the region throughout the last million years.[32] With ice sheets covering half of the continent during glacial periods and average global temperature varying by 15–20°F between glacial and interglacial periods, plants and animals had to shift their ranges hundreds to thousands of miles, mostly north and south, across the Great Plains in response to the advancing and retreating ice sheet and associated swings in climate.

Determining the geographic extent of each glacial period is difficult because each succeeding glacial period's scouring ice and deposits obliterated evidence of the preceding one. The last glacial period, the Wisconsin around 75–10 kya, left the greatest visible mark on the Northern Great Plains landscape, when two ice sheets dominated climatic, geological, and biological events. The Laurentide Ice Sheet covered nearly all of Canada and the northern United States from the Atlantic coast to the base of the Rocky Mountains, and the Cordilleran Ice Sheet covered the northern Rocky Mountains to the Pacific coast.[33] During what's called the "Last Glacial Maximum," about 26–19 mya, these two ice sheets fused along the eastern base of the Rocky Mountains to form one vast sheet that spanned from coast to coast.

The Laurentide Ice Sheet during the Last Glacial Maximum was a half-mile thick near its southern edge along the Missouri River and two-to-three-miles thick in northern Canada.[34] Like pressing the palm of your hand on a ball of pizza dough, the ice sheet's weight pushed its edges out to act like a giant bulldozer, leveling the land (except for island mountains like the Little Rockies and Bear's Paw) to its current gently rolling condition and leaving thousands of oversized divots known as "prairie potholes." The base of the advancing ice sheet ground, mixed, picked up, and carried soils and rocks to be later deposited, sometimes hundreds of miles away, as glacial till in layers from a few feet to hundreds of feet thick. The biggest of these deposits, called erratics, are granite and gneiss boulders—some as big as a house and many the size of a car—carried from as far away as northern Manitoba and the Canadian Shield.[35] Unglaciated lands to the south of the river are also often gently rolling but, lacking the leveling effects of the ice sheet, are punctuated by buttes and badlands. Their soils are derived from shale and sandstone, less productive for plant growth than the glacial till to the north.

The Laurentide Ice Sheet also altered the region's rivers. A time-lapse aerial video of the Missouri River covering the last million years would show the big river being whiplashed and choked by advancing and retreating ice. The first whiplash occurred during one or more of the Pleistocene's early glacial periods, when the ice sheets pushed and rerouted the river from a trajectory to the northeast, where it emptied into Hudson Bay, to its current course to the southeast, where it merges with the Mississippi River.[36]

The second whiplash occurred during the Wisconsin glacial period, when the southern edge of the Laurentide Ice Sheet grew for a few thousand years before reaching its maximum southern extent about 20 kya. Before the Wisconsin glacial period, the Missouri flowed north of the Bear's Paw and Little Rocky Mountains through the valley of the present-day Milk River. Current thinking is that the Laurentide Ice Sheet pushed the Missouri River south about 50 miles to its current course as the melt waters along the ice sheet's edge carved out a new channel. Today, the Missouri rejoins its old pre-ice-sheet channel at the mouth of the Milk River a few miles downstream from the Fort Peck Dam.[37]

The time-lapse video would also show how the thick ice sheet during the Wisconsin glacial period blocked the Missouri River in at least five places through the plains of eastern Montana, creating a series of large glacial lakes. One of them—Glacial Lake Musselshell, which covered more than one million acres, four times the size of the Fort Peck Reservoir—played a central role in establishing the course of the Missouri River through the C. M. Russell Refuge. At some point the ice sheet lobe blocked both the Missouri and Musselshell Rivers sufficiently to raise the glacial lake's level until it breached the Larb Hills south of the ice sheet's edge. The disgorging lake waters proceeded to gouge out the current southern deviation—the L in UL Bend—in the Missouri River's channel near the center of the C. M. Russell Refuge.[38]

The periodic formation of ice sheets around the Northern Hemisphere and in Antarctica during the Pleistocene had far-reaching consequences for biodiversity in the Northern Great Plains and across the Americas. At their glacial maximum the ice sheets held

enough water to lower sea levels several hundred feet to repeatedly expose the Bering Land Bridge. Ocean currents kept Beringia
ice free and relatively verdant, thereby creating an avenue for animal and plant movement between the two continents.[39] However,
when the Laurentide and Cordilleran Ice Sheets fused during the
Last Glacial Maximum, they closed off what had been a thousand-
mile ice-free corridor through which animals and, potentially,
humans could travel between Beringia and Montana and the rest
of the continent south of the ice sheets. As the ice sheets melted
the ice-free corridor slowly opened about 15–13.4 kya.[40] As we
will see below, the timing of the closing and opening of this ice-
free corridor occupies center stage in debates about the peopling
of the Americas.

By about 11.5 kya, the Laurentide Ice Sheet had receded beyond
the northeast corner of Montana into southern Saskatchewan and
north of the Missouri River through North Dakota. Glacial meltwater created wet conditions over extensive areas south of the
ice sheet's receding edge. Soon, however, the ongoing retreat of
the ice sheet led to warmer and drier conditions that favored the
spread of grasslands.[41]

Evolutionary Adaptations to the Spread of Grasslands

The K-Pg extinctions created a veritable petri dish for evolutionary innovation and speciation during the Cenozoic. Globally, the
evolution of flowering plants into new forms and species continued at a blistering pace. Grasses, making their first appearance in
North America around 55 mya, quickly radiated into scores of open-
habitat species in North America 40–30 mya, although forests still
dominated the Great Plains at that time. By 25–15 mya, forests of
the Great Plains increasingly gave way to open woodlands and
savannas and then, 5–2 mya, to grassland habitats.[42] Adapting to
their windswept, open habitat, grasses abandoned animal pollination and showy flowers in favor of wind pollination and inconspicuous flowers.[43] Although the Cenozoic's drying and cooling trend
may have helped drive the spread of grasslands, intense browsing
of trees and shrubs by megaherbivores (herbivores weighing more

than 2,000 pounds) such as mastodons and gomphotheres and changes in feeding behavior by other herbivores may have created the ecological space for grassland expansion.[44]

Grazing and aridity were major forces shaping the evolution of grasses.[45] Although grasses employ various strategies to avoid being eaten, natural selection seems to have decided that, rather than expending lots of resources on building defense mechanisms against the cellulose-digesting firepower of grazers, a better strategy was to develop the capacity to survive and reproduce while being eaten. In contrast to most flowering plants, grasses keep their nutrient reserves underground and their main growing points at the plant's base just above the ground. As a result, when a grazer—or fire or extreme aridity—has lopped off or desiccated their leaves and stems, even down to the ground, grasses can grow back.[46]

Storing nutrient reserves underground and growing deep roots to secure water is also a strategy for surviving arid conditions. Few and narrow leaves aboveground reduce water loss through leaves when plants breathe. Leaves with high cellulose content may be adaptive to dry conditions and confer resistance to grazers by being tougher to chew and digest. Grasses grow quickly in the spring when there is moisture and then desiccate their leaves quickly to avoid losing moisture during the heat of summer. A brief period of growth when the plant is most nutritious may also be a way to avoid being found and eaten by grazers.[47]

An important development in the evolution of grasses and other plants was a two-pronged approach to dealing with temperature extremes. Most plant species in the world use what is called the C3 photosynthetic pathway (indicating the number of carbon atoms involved). This is a highly efficient mode of photosynthesis under moderate temperatures and moderate to high atmospheric levels of carbon dioxide. Plants with a C4 pathway, in contrast, do better under conditions of warm temperatures and low carbon dioxide.[48] These two types of grass are known colloquially as "cool season grasses" and "warm season grasses" because C3 grasses grow best in cooler regions (about 65–75°F), such as Northern Great Plains, and C4 grasses grow best in the warmer Southern Great Plains (about

90–95°F). Consequently, in the Northern Great Plains, including the American Prairie–Russell Refuge region, cool-season grasses, such as western wheatgrass (*Pascopyrum smithii*) and green needle grass (*Nassella viridula*), dominate both in terms of species diversity and abundance. These species grow mostly in the spring and fall when temperatures are cooler. However, a few warm-season grass species, such as blue grama (*Bouteloua gracilis*) and buffalo grass (*Bouteloua dactyloides*), that are common in the region grow better during the heat of summer.[49]

While bees, butterflies, beetles, and most other insect groups got their start in the Cretaceous, a new group of insects that would eventually play a central role in the grasslands of North American and the world, grasshoppers, appeared around 60 mya. Perhaps first evolving in South America and then migrating to Africa, Europe, and North America, grasshoppers radiated into 6,700 species and generally represent more than 50% of the biomass of all insects in grasslands.[50]

Bird speciation also surged after the K-Pg extinction event. By 50 mya nearly all modern orders of birds had emerged.[51] By 6–4 mya, ancestors of some of today's Great Plains grassland specialists, such as Sprague's pipit (*Anthus spragueii*), thick-billed longspur (*Rhynchophanes mccownii*), chestnut-collared longspur (*Calcarius ornatus*), and meadowlarks (*Sturnella* spp.), had appeared.[52]

No taxonomic group, however, responded as dramatically, and with as rich a fossil record from which to reconstruct its history, as mammals. Mammals experimented by evolving into various lineages and species of diverse shapes and sizes for living in the tropical and subtropical forests of the early Cenozoic.

Evidence is mounting that one such experiment that unfolded in the Northern Great Plains was especially significant for life on Earth: the region may be the birthplace of primates. *Purgatorius*—named for Purgatory Hill, near the eastern edge of the American Prairie–Russell Refuge region, where its fossils were first found—is generally considered the oldest known fossil of a primate and likely the ancestor of all living primates, including humans.[53] The oldest *Purgatorius* fossils (all teeth) found thus far, from the southeastern portion of the American Prairie–Russell Refuge region, are from animals that probably lived only 105,000–139,000 years after the K-Pg extinction.[54] Ankle bones discovered in the same area show the first step toward the evolution of grasping hands and feet that characterize modern primates. Shrew-like *Purgatorius* was adapted to arboreal living and likely ate insects and the fruits of the angiosperm trees that recolonized the devastated landscape.[55] *Purgatorius* fossils have been found in several areas of the American Prairie–Russell Refuge region and elsewhere in the Northern Great Plains but nowhere else.[56] Like *Purgatorius*, other early primate species subsequently appeared and disappeared from North America's fossil record during the first half of the Cenozoic. The last one, an inhabitant of the Northern Great Plains and other western regions, vanished from the fossil record 26 mya.[57] That was the end of the continent's primates until the arrival of an evolutionary bookend to *Purgatorius*: *Homo sapiens* (more about their arrival later).

Vast numbers of mammal species came and went in North America during the early Cenozoic.[58] Among the lineages that survived, rodents, lagomorphs (hares and rabbits), ungulates (hoofed mammals), and carnivores stand out for both their evolutionary adaptations to survival and their ecological importance in today's grassland ecosystems.

Lagomorphs first emerged in North America and rodents probably originated in Eurasia. Regardless of their origins, the two lineages repeatedly crossed the Bering Land Bridge throughout much of the Cenozoic.[59] Rodents radiated into numerous and diverse forms. Today roughly 38 species of rodents inhabit the Northern Great Plains, far outnumbering species in any other mammalian order.[60] Out of that scramble of rodents emerged two keystone species, the black-tailed prairie dog and American beaver (*Castor canadensis*). Lagomorph radiation was not nearly as prolific, with five species—two jackrabbits and three hares—inhabiting the Northern Great Plains.[61] They are often significant herbivores as well as prey for snakes, raptors, and carnivores in western grasslands.

Grassland living led to unique evolutionary adaptations by rodents and lagomorphs. Fifty million years ago all North American rodents and lagomorphs had brachydont—low-crowned—teeth, the crown type of dogs, cats, and humans. But as open habitats and grasslands spread, North American rodents and lagomorphs evolved hypsodont—high-crowned—teeth. About the same time, a new tooth strategy appeared—nonstop growth, called hypselodonty. By 2 mya, 60% of rodents and lagomorphs had either hypsodont or hypselodont crowns. The cause? The need to counter the constant tooth wear caused by grit and soil ingested when living and foraging on or under the ground.[62]

And indeed, rodents increasingly went underground. Fossoriality (burrowing) became a prominent evolutionary strategy for temperate grassland rodents as a way to avoid predators and as thermal refuge from aboveground temperature extremes.[63] Two groups of rodents of the Great Plains grasslands, prairie dogs and ground squirrels, also became highly social by forming large colonies, an evolutionary adaptation by fossorial and semifossorial herbivorous mammals to grassland habitats around the world.[64] The resulting digging and churning of soil added complexity to the grassland ecosystem; the burrows became habitat for other mammals, arthropods, amphibians, reptiles, and even a bird (the burrowing owl [*Athene cunicularia*]); and burrow occupants became prey for a diversity of grassland predators.

Natural selection in lagomorphs honed a different strategy for avoiding predators in open grasslands: speed. Cursoriality—running—was achieved by evolving long limbs, epitomized by jackrabbits. Saltation—hopping—is a similar strategy employed by hares and kangaroo rats.[65]

Ungulates participated in what was arguably the most striking evolutionary change among mammals after the K-Pg extinction—a rapid and massive increase in body size in response to the plethora of empty big-dinosaur niches. Within the first 20 million years of the Cenozoic the largest mammals in North America increased three orders of magnitude—one thousand times—from a few pounds to thousands of pounds.[66]

Today's two lineages of ungulates, the taxonomic orders Perissodactyla and Artiodactyla, first appeared in the early Cenozoic about

55 mya.[67] Perissodactyls are odd-toed ungulates, so named because they walk on either one (horses) or three (tapirs and rhinos) toes. Artiodactyls, even-toed ungulates who walk on two toes, include bison, sheep, deer, pronghorn, camelids, and peccaries, among others. Perissodactyls flourished, with some, such as the rhino-sized brontotheres ("thunder beasts"), achieving massive sizes. Artiodactyls also evolved into large and bizarre (to our eyes) forms, such as the bull-bison-sized, warthog-like entelodonts, also known as "hell pigs." As forest inhabitants, early ungulates were browsers, feeding on the leaves, shoots, and buds of flowering plants.[68]

Perissodactyl diversity boomed throughout the middle Cenozoic. By 20–15 mya as many as eight species of equids (horses) coexisted in the Great Plains, with two or three species of rhinos often in the mix.[69] Artiodactyls diversified as well. Antilocaprids (pronghorns), which first appeared in North America's fossil record at least 20 mya, thrived with perhaps a half dozen species inhabiting the Great Plains at the same time.[70] Ancestors of today's peccaries (*Pecari* spp.), camels, and muskox (*Ovibus moschatus*) were also Great Plains inhabitants. In sum, at the peak of ungulate diversity 20–10 mya, 20–29 species coexisted in the Great Plains, rivaling the diversity of today's Serengeti-Mara ecosystem in Africa. Ungulate diversity slowly declined after 12 mya, mostly due to browsing species disappearing as grasslands continued to crowd out woodland habitats.[71]

The transition from forest to grassland living during the Cenozoic favored several evolutionary trends in ungulates. Grasses have a higher cellulose content than flowering plants, and ungulates can digest cellulose only through fermentation by gut-inhabiting microbes. Because fermentation is more efficient as body size increases (up to a point), ungulates evolved larger body sizes in order to better utilize the growing abundance of grass during the mid- to late Cenozoic.[72]

Ungulates have evolved two basic approaches to extracting nutrients from plant cellulose via microbial fermentation.[73] Hindgut fermentation, which occurs after the food passes through the stomach and small intestine, was employed by the first ungulates and today occurs in all perissodactyls, such as the horse and rhino. Herbivores ranging from rabbits to elephants—and to some extent omnivorous humans—also use this system. The basic digestive strategy is to extract nutrients by eating a lot and passing the food quickly through the digestive system.

A distinctly different digestive strategy, foregut fermentation, evolved in some artiodactyls in the late Oligocene, about 39–32 mya.[74] Ruminants are species with foregut fermentation and a four-chambered stomach. When ruminants ingest a mouthful of plant material, it's first fermented in vats of bacteria in the first two chambers of the stomach, then regurgitated back to the mouth for rumination—chewing cud—to further break it down, and then swallowed again for further fermentation before passing on to the third and fourth stomachs for more digestion and nutrient absorption. Food moves much more slowly through the ruminant's digestive system in this process of breaking down the cellulose.[75] All extant native ungulates of the Great Plains—pronghorn, bighorn sheep, deer, elk, moose (*Alces alces*), and bison—are ruminants.

Ungulates, like rodents and lagomorphs, also went from low-crowned to high-crowned teeth during their transition from browsing in forests to grazing in open grassland environments. Higher-crowned teeth were probably an adaptation to the increased amount of grit and soil that comes with eating close to the ground in dusty, semiarid grasslands, as well as to the high content of abrasive phytoliths (composed of silica) in grasses. Moreover, the high cellulose levels and possibly lower nutritive value of grasses require more eating and chewing, which causes more tooth wear.[76] The high crown may also help the root anchor the tooth during chewing.[77]

The transition from forest to grassland living triggered interrelated evolutionary changes in behavior and mobility. Behaviorally, ungulates adapted to open habitats by becoming more gregarious and forming herds, by developing larger home ranges, and by becoming more migratory as they tracked the highly variable and dispersed productivity of grassland ecosystems.[78] The formation of herds in open habitats, in turn, favored the evolution of polygyny (one male mating with multiple females), as males could more readily watch and control several females and repel intruding males. Intensified male–male competition likely selected for larger body size in males, resulting in sexual dimorphism whereby males are much larger than females. Antipredator behavior also changed as hiding to avoid predators, effective in closed forest habitats, gave way to escape as a better strategy. Herd formation could also be an effective antipredator strategy: there are more animals for defense and more ears, eyes, and noses for predator detection.[79]

Hand in hand with these behavioral changes, ungulates took the cursorial approach to grassland living by evolving three anatomical adaptations: longer legs, fewer digits, and hooves.[80] Terrestrial mammals have three basic foot postures. The original, primitive posture is flat-footed—called plantigrady—as in humans, bears, and raccoons. The next evolutionary step is walking on digits only—digitigrady—as in cats and dogs. The final step is walking on hooves located on the tips of the digits—ungulugrady—as in ungulates. In most perissodactyls the primitive condition of five or more digits was reduced to only the third toe, which became hooved and touched the ground, as is evident in horses. In artiodactyls the third and fourth toes were retained as hooves, as in bison and deer. These changes probably reduced stress on leg and foot bones caused by the increase in ungulate body size and enabled more efficient walking to cover the larger home ranges that ungulates have in grasslands compared to forests.

Ungulates of the Great Plains were joined by an imposing caste of megaherbivores during the late Cenozoic. Arriving from the north via the Bering Land Bridge were three proboscidean lineages—gomphotheres (several genera), mastodons (*Mammut* spp.), and mammoths (*Mammuthus* spp.). From the south, crossing the Isthmus of Panama, came giant ground sloths (several genera) from South America.[81] These massive plant eaters surely had large and diverse effects on Great Plains biodiversity, from altering the structure and composition of plant communities to influencing the assembly and evolution of the predators that hunted them, including Paleoindians.[82] As the only grazer among these four lineages of megaherbivores, mammoths in particular flourished on the Great Plains grasslands, including the American Prairie–Russell Refuge region, during the Pleistocene.[83]

Interestingly, as the end of the Miocene approached about 5 mya, pronghorns were the only lineage represented of the seven native ungulate lineages living in today's American Prairie–Russell Refuge region. The rest of the ungulate caste was about to arrive. After their ancestral forms migrated across the Bering Land Bridge about 5 mya, the mule deer and white-tailed deer evolved into their present form during the Pleistocene.[84] Bighorn sheep immigrated to North America across the Bering Land Bridge a few hundred thousand years ago but probably didn't arrive in the Northern Great Plains until about 100 kya.[85] The steppe bison (*Bison priscus*) arrived from Eurasia 195–135 kya. Despite confronting a diverse community of large grazers, the steppe bison and its descendants quickly spread south across the continent. According to bison paleontologist Duane Froese and colleagues, "The entry of bison stands with human arrival as one of the most successful mammalian dispersals into North America during the last million years."[86] The steppe bison soon evolved into various forms, including the giant long-horned bison (*Bison latifrons*), with horns spanning nearly seven feet and males almost twice the size of today's plains bison—perhaps an evolutionary response to fend off the big carnivores of that period. Elk and moose were the last ungulate immigrants from Eurasia to arrive in North America, apparently crossing the Bering Land Bridge 15–11 kya before it was again inundated.[87]

Like other mammals, early carnivore evolution was shaped by forest living. In the closed forests of the first half of the Cenozoic, carnivores were primarily ambush predators, some weighing more than 1,000 pounds, that could take on the era's large herbivores. This produced a fascinating menagerie of large predators that came and went throughout the Cenozoic. Among the lineages that survived are six families of carnivores native to the Northern Great Plains today: Mustelidae (weasel family), Ursidae (bears), Canidae (dogs), Felidae (cats), Procyonidae (raccoons), and Mephitidae (skunks), all first appearing during the middle

Cenozoic about 45–20 mya. Some lineages originated in North America and others in Eurasia, but repeated migrations east and west across the Bering Land Bridge were the norm.[88] I focus on the first four—mustelids, ursids, canids, and felids—because of their evolutionary history and conservation significance in the Northern Great Plains.

Mustelid evolution mostly honed in on exploiting the abundance of grassland rodents as prey. Among the largest mustelids to emerge was the American badger, which evolved an unparalleled digging ability to prey on fossorial rodents. The smaller mustelids—the long-tailed weasel (*Mustela frenata*), least weasel (*Mustela nivalis*), and black-footed ferret—evolved small, slender bodies and short legs to get at burrow inhabitants. The mink (*Neovison vison*) and river otter (*Lontra canadensis*) took distinctly different evolutionary routes by becoming semiaquatic predators.[89]

Three ursid lineages inhabited the Northern Great Plains during the Pleistocene. The ancestor of the American black bear (*Ursus americanus*) may have been the first to arrive, having crossed the Bering Land Bridge to North America perhaps 3.5 mya.[90] Appearing about 1.5 mya, the 2,000-pound giant short-faced bear (*Arctodus simus*) was the largest carnivore to ever inhabit the Northern Great Plains.[91] The species may have relied on its intimidating size to be the ultimate kleptoparasite by robbing wolves, big cats, and perhaps humans of their kills. Last to cross the land bridge was the grizzly bear, arriving in the Northern Great Plains during an ice-free interglacial period 130–71 kya.[92]

Canids responded to grassland living by transitioning from plantigrade to digitigrade feet as well as undergoing other anatomical adaptations to cursoriality. The change enabled them to cover large distances more efficiently as grasslands spread and their prey became more migratory, as well as improving their ability to pursue prey over long distances.[93] Ancestors of today's gray wolf and coyote (*Canis latrans*) diverged 4.5–1.8 mya; the continental origin—Eurasia or North America—of the ancestor is uncertain.[94]

Three types of wolves probably inhabited North America during the late Pleistocene. The burly dire wolf (*Canis dirus*), about one-quarter larger than today's gray wolf, dominated the canid niche in the southern half of North America during the late Pleistocene.[95] During that time the gray wolf appears to have evolved into two morphological types, the modern gray wolf and the Beringian wolf, that occupied the northern half of the continent. The Beringian wolf was somewhere between the dire wolf and modern gray wolf in burliness and was likely the most common wolf of the Northern Great Plains near the end of the Pleistocene. The dire and Beringian wolves were clearly made for taking on North America's big herbivores. Fossil and genomic evidence suggests that wherever the dire wolf or Beringian wolf was common, the gray wolf was scarce or absent.[96]

The Great Plains acquired an impressive lineup of big felids—the saber-tooth cat (*Smilodon* spp.), scimitar-tooth cat (*Homotherium latidens*), American cheetah (*Miracinonyx trumani*), and American lion (*Panthera atrox*)—to prey on the region's ungulates and megaherbivores during the Pliocene and Pleistocene.[97] The common ancestor of the puma, bobcat (*Lynx rufus*), and lynx (*Lynx canadensis*) may have diverged in Eurasia around 7 mya.[98] Around 6 mya a puma-like cat invaded North American from Eurasia. This ancestor subsequently diverged about 3.2 mya into the American cheetah and the lineage of today's puma. The American cheetah, like the similar-looking but not closely related African cheetah (*Acinonyx jubatus*), was clearly a cat made for high-speed chases of ungulates across Great Plains grasslands.[99] The earliest puma fossil dates to about 1 mya in Argentina and the earliest fossil from North America is about 200,000 years old, suggesting that the ancestor of all living pumas evolved in South America.[100]

Humans were among the last mammalian immigrants to disperse across the land bridge from Eurasia to North America and to spread across the continent. When, where, and how they did so remain contentious questions for archeologists and paleontologists. A remarkable recent discovery of human footprints in White Sands National Park, New Mexico, provides robust evidence that humans populated much of at least the western half of North America by 22 kya, about 5,000 years sooner than previously solid evidence indicated. This suggests that humans could have migrated south from Beringia before the ice-free corridor between the Laurentide and Cordilleran Ice Sheets coalesced, or possibly via an ice-free route along the Pacific coast.[101]

People of the early Paleoindian cultures of North America—pre-Clovis, Clovis, Folsom, and others—were big game hunters. The projectiles and other tools characterizing each culture and the bones of the mammals they butchered are found at archeological sites across the Northern Great Plains and elsewhere in North America. Not only were ungulates like bison, horses, and camels hunted, but these early hunters were superpredators, adept at killing even adults of the proboscideans—mammoths, mastodons, and gomphotheres—that the big carnivores could not.[102] Paleoindians enjoyed this diversity of big game for several thousand years in North America.

As the end of the Pleistocene drew near, a nature walk through the American Prairie–Russell Refuge region—or nearly anywhere in the Northern Great Plains—would have overwhelmed the senses. The spring chorus of grassland birds and perhaps the yips of prairie dogs would have been notable, but the eyes would quickly register that this was an ecosystem dominated by ungulates, carnivores, and megaherbivores. A few, epitomized by the 22-pound dwarf pronghorn (*Capromeryx minor*), were small. But most were large and some were gigantic, topping out at the 20,000-pound Columbian mammoth (*Mammuthus columbi*). Whether walking through the grasslands, riparian forests, or wetlands and shrublands on the continental ice sheet's edge, one may have encountered big cats, big bears, wolves, proboscideans, Jefferson's ground sloths (*Megalonyx jeffersonii*), steppe bison, helmeted muskox (*Bootherium bombifrons*), and various species of horses, pronghorns, and camels, among other ungulates. It was not a place to let your guard down while bird watching or photographing prairie flowers. One can only imagine—and admire—the survival skills of Paleoindians living in this bestiary.

Then disaster struck. Another extinction spasm turned the biological world on its head.

The End-Pleistocene Extinction

Similar to the K-Pg extinction event, the end-Pleistocene extinction happened with speed, with geographic breadth, and with a bias against big sizes. In North America, between roughly 14–11 kya, all mammalian species weighing more than 2,200 pounds went extinct, along with more than 50% of those weighing between 70 and 2,200 pounds and 20% of those weighing between 32 and 70 pounds. Two mammalian orders, Proboscidea and Perissodactyla, disappeared from the continent.[103] Gone were the mammoth, mastodon, horse, camel, ground sloth, shrub ox, four big cat species, two wolf species/subspecies, giant short-faced bear, giant beaver, and dozens of other mammalian species. Most were inhabitants of the American Prairie–Russell Refuge region.[104] Notably, among ungulates the only survivors—bison, bighorn sheep, pronghorn, mule deer, white-tailed deer, elk, and moose—were ruminants (the four-stomach foregut fermenters). Gone were all the single-stomach, hindgut-fermenting herbivores, but it's unclear why.[105] With somewhat different timing, Australia and South America experienced similarly big extinctions of large animals, while extinction levels in Eurasia and Africa were much lower.[106]

What happened? The two leading explanations are climatic fluctuations and the aboriginal overkill hypothesis. Major changes in climate—such as the Younger Dryas cold interval, when temperatures dropped around the world 12.9–11.7 kya—are hypothesized to have caused ecological changes that wiped out the large mammals. The aboriginal overkill hypothesis argues that when humans colonized North America, they found an abundance of large herbivores that evolved in the absence of hunting and thus had little fear of humans; they were therefore quickly hunted to extinction as the Paleoindian population spread across the continent.[107] The disappearance of large herbivores, such as proboscideans, whether due to climate change or human hunting, could have resulted in a cascade of massive ecosystem changes ranging from altered vegetation to the extinction of the big carnivores that ate them.[108] Aboriginal overkill and climatic changes may have worked in tandem to cause the extinctions.[109]

Extinction of the mammoth and other commonly hunted mega-herbivores forced a major shift in Paleoindian hunting strategies and diet. Several bison kill sites in the Northern Great Plains date to immediately after the mammoth's extinction and the last of the mammoth kill sites. One of the oldest, dated to around 15.5–12.2 kya, is the Mill Iron site in southeast Montana, where bones of ancient bison occur with Paleoindian projectile points.[110]

Whether or not North America's Paleoindians caused or contributed to the end-Pleistocene extinction, they were certainly witnesses to it from beginning to end. One wonders what changes they saw during this period. Could people who lived in the American Prairie–Russell Refuge region explain why dozens of large mammals that had shaped and dominated their lives for millennia, both those they preyed on and those they feared and competed with for food, were growing scarce and vanishing? The end-Pleistocene extinction must have caused sweeping adaptations to the new environment among the survivors—Paleoindians and wildlife alike. It also ushered in a new epoch, the Holocene, which would eventually produce its own sweeping changes that, again, would challenge the survival skills of wildlife, especially large mammals, and lead to more extinctions. In this case, however, there would be no debate about humans being the cause.

After nesting in western grasslands, Swainson's hawks migrate 6,000 miles to wintering grounds in southern South America, the longest migration of any North American raptor. Drawing by Erica Freese.

THREE

Holocene Wildlife Settle In

After a two-hour walk from their camp on the north side of the Missouri River, they spot what they were looking for—a herd of ancient bison, several miles to the west, grazing on a wide ridge on the edge of a large prairie dog town. Pronghorn graze nearby, and below the ridge, elk are browsing willows along a stream. Seven to eight feet tall at their hump, the bison look huge next to the pronghorn. Not far from the herd, the next ridge over, a wolf pack lounges in the late afternoon sun. It's a spring day in the first years of the Holocene, about 11,500 years ago, and the two Paleoindian men, scouting for tomorrow's hunt, have ascended to a high point of the Larb Hills, five miles north of their riverside camp. If the bison stay on the ridge for the night, the two men agree that in the morning they may be able to drive the herd over a steep embankment at the end of the ridge where hunters with atlatls and spears can, in the chaos, get close enough for efficient kills.

After mentally marking the location of the bison, they look back south toward their clan's riverside camp and visualize a route that they and their fellow hunters will take before sunrise to stalk the herd. The clan's camp sits along the river where, a few hundred years earlier, Glacial Lake Musselshell breached a low point in the Larb Hills and emptied as it cut a new channel to the east. Fifty miles to the west the Little Rocky Mountains rise 2,500 feet above the surrounding lands. To the north, far beyond the hunters' view, is the melting edge of the Laurentide Ice Sheet, now finally, after advancing and retreating three or four times over the last 10,000 years, in retreat for good from the region. The rolling landscape before them is a parkland of spruce, aspen, and willows surrounding ponds filled by the ice sheet's meltwater and large patches of sagebrush and grass on higher ground.

Back at camp that evening the children's chatter about practicing their hunting skills on prairie dogs soon subsides as the elders begin to tell stories around the campfire. Their voices are accompanied by the "shush, shush, shush" of women scraping hides and "chip, chip, chip" of hunters knapping their fluted points for the morning's hunt. Some elders recall when the spruce parkland extended far to the south of the river, but the grasslands have been spreading north, aided by tree-killing grassland fires. Bison, pronghorn, and prairie dogs have kept pace with the grassland's northward advance. They discuss how bison prefer grazing north of the river on the lush vegetation that grows on the deep soil left by the retreating ice sheet. Bison, they note, are especially attracted to grasses growing on recently burned areas and on the edges of prairie dog towns. The best hunters know these relationships.

As happens most nights, the elders eventually turn to telling stories, some passed down through generations, about strange-looking, big, and dangerous animals. The stories usually start with the biggest animal, one that was two and a half men high at the shoulder with long tusks and a big snake-like nose, that ran in herds. With bulls tipping the scales at 20,000 pounds, hunting mammoths was difficult and dangerous. Killing the adults was especially difficult, so hunters often tried to isolate younger animals instead. One or two could feed a clan for weeks. The elders recall that their fathers talked of occasionally encountering and killing these beasts, but they have become increasingly rare and none had been seen for years. Smaller animals that earlier generations had hunted—horses, camels, muskox, and others—have also disappeared. No one knows where they went. Fortunately, bison herds have grown much larger and so the clan's ancestors quickly adapted to hunting them.

Tales about stalking a mammoth with spears usually lead to stories about the dangerous big predators that roamed the region until recently—the saber-tooth cat, scimitar-tooth cat, American lion, American cheetah, and giant short-faced bear. Bear stories are a *favorite because the giant short-faced bear was the biggest and most feared of all the predators, a daunting nemesis to hunters. Standing on four legs the bear's shoulders were the height of a man; upright on its hind legs, it was two men tall. If a bear detected the scent of a slayed animal, within minutes it would be charging in to take over the carcass. While several men with spears could usually scare off the other big predators, confronting a short-faced bear often resulted in one or two men being killed or badly injured.*

The elders can recount personal stories of encounters with the bear when they were young hunters. But none have been seen for many years. Like the mammoth and hooved animals, they and almost all the other big predators have vanished in recent generations. Even the smaller cat, the puma, is gone. The only big predators remaining are wolves and a smaller—though still dangerous—brown bear that moved in when the giant short-faced bear disappeared.

Soon everyone retires for the night. The hunters must rise early for a successful bison hunt. If their hunt fails, they may be eating prairie dogs.

As my take on this imaginary Paleoindian clan suggests, the early Holocene in the Northern Great Plains was a new and rapidly changing world for them. New climate, new lands and waters, new plants and animals. The terrain, plants, and animals that greeted the first Paleoindians to arrive in the American Prairie–Russell Refuge region would soon be unrecognizable to their descendants. One of the animals new to the clan may have been the domestic dog, but I left out a line about dogs chewing bones around the campfire because the earliest evidence for dogs accompanying Paleoindians in the Americas is 10 kya (from dog burial sites in Illinois). Dogs diverged from wolves probably in Eurasia around 16 kya. They may have arrived earlier with the first Paleoindian migration south of the ice sheet, but unequivocal fossil evidence is lacking and hard to come by because, among other reasons, distinguishing dog fossils from wolf and coyote fossils is difficult.[1]

The first 2,000–3,000 years of the Holocene, around 11.7–9 kya, must have been a period of massive adjustments for all life, including Paleoindians, in the Northern Great Plains.[2] Dozens of species of mammals, including all the biggest ones, had vanished. New arrivals—elk and moose—joined bison as the biggest ungulates to hunt. The Laurentide Ice Sheet's retreat exposed a waterlogged land of glacial till over the plains north of the Missouri River that hadn't seen the sun in thousands of years—a blank slate for rapid colonization by plants and animals. Land south of the Missouri River, beyond the farthest reach of the ice sheet, was warming up and drying out. Some lands close to the southern margin of the ice appear to have been grassland and sagebrush, while others were woodland or forest but rapidly converting to grassland.[3] The entire food web, from plants to herbivores to predators, was being transformed. Among large mammals, who eats what, who is eaten by whom, and who competes with whom had been altered and greatly simplified. The surviving large herbivores and predators found a plethora of empty large-mammal ecological niches to fill and adjust to.

Herbivores had to adjust to a changing plant world. Boreal and moisture-loving trees and shrubs first rushed in to colonize a landscape of glacial till soaked and laid bare by the melting and retreating ice sheet. The disappearance of landscape-scale ecosystem engineers, especially the mammoth, may have initially favored the spread of woody plants. (Megafauna in Africa, especially elephants, reduce woody species cover by 15–95%.[4]) Arid grasslands, however, soon dominated nearly the entire Northern Great Plains as the climate quickly became warmer and dryer.[5] Bison and pronghorn, with more grass and forbs to eat and less competition, must have flourished. In fact, fossil evidence shows the population of ancient bison on the Great Plains boomed during the end-Pleistocene extinction and into the early Holocene.[6] Meanwhile, bison grew smaller, with the steepest drop in size, about 26%, occurring 12.5–9.25 kya and a further reduction in size around the middle Holocene, 8–2 kya. Several factors may have favored genes for a smaller size. A smaller body may have been adaptive to reduced plant productivity and increased competition for forage caused by the period's warming and drying trend. A smaller body more efficiently dissipates heat. And the extinction of the Pleistocene's large carnivores may have relaxed selection pressure for a defensively large size.[7]

Big carnivores also underwent a big shuffle. The gray wolf probably moved into the Northern Great Plains to replace the larger, now extinct Beringian wolf that had presumably dominated the big canine niche in the northern half of the continent.[8] When gray wolf numbers increased, coyotes vacated the gray wolf niche by shrinking. Perhaps as long as the gray wolf was absent or scarce while the bigger dire and Beringian wolves dominated the continent, the coyote occupied part of the gray wolf niche. Evolution of a more gracile coyote with smaller jaws that had less bone crushing power may also have been driven by the extinction of so many large mammalian herbivores and an increase in smaller mammals in the coyote diet.[9] A similar story unfolded among bears. Fossil evidence suggests the extinction of the giant short-faced bear opened the door to increased numbers of grizzly bears in the Northern Great Plains and elsewhere.[10]

Fossils and genes tell a different story for the puma. As noted in chapter 2, North American pumas probably descended from a population that dispersed north from South America 200 kya.[11] It's possible that pumas, like most other large mammals, vanished from North America near the end of the Pleistocene and that by 10 kya another puma dispersal from South America repopulated North America. More likely, the North American puma population never entirely disappeared but did severely shrink about 20 kya, when suitable habitat became scarce during the Last Glacial Maximum.

The big carnivores that remained after the end-Pleistocene extinction faced a much less competitive and dangerous world. The gray wolf, not the dire or Beringian wolf, was now top dog. The grizzly bear, not the giant short-faced, was top bear. The puma, not the saber-tooth cat, scimitar-tooth cat, or American lion, was top cat.

The other remaining large predator, humans, was also adapting to a less intimidating array of large carnivores to compete with and to avoid being killed by and was further honing its skill in hunting bison, rather than mammoths, as its largest and most challenging prey species. The large surge in bison numbers in the early Holocene must have greatly facilitated this transition, as evidenced by several bison kill sites in the Great Plains.[12]

One can imagine plant and animal species that inhabited the warmer climes of the southern and central Great Plains during the Last Glacial Maximum slowly expanding their ranges to the north as a warmer and drier climate prevailed. Grassland animals, regardless of size or dispersal ability, probably kept pace with the expansion of the grassland ecosystem across the region. Fossils indicate that prairie dogs and ferrets were able to quickly occupy new grassland habitat as it spread north in the wake of the ice sheet's retreat.[13] Today's grassland birds were probably expanding their ranges north with the grassland's advance as well, while undertaking longer annual migrations between Northern Great Plains nesting grounds and wintering grounds in the Southern Great Plains and Chihuahuan Desert grasslands. Small mammals, reptiles, and amphibians, being less mobile, may have colonized the new grasslands more slowly.

The spadefoot toad (*Spea bombifrons*) offers a striking example of range contraction and expansion in response to continental glaciation. About 20 kya, when the Laurentide Ice Sheet covered northern Montana, the spadefoot's range had been reduced to mostly the southwest corner of Arizona. As the ice sheet melted the spadefoot expanded its range north as much as 1,000 miles to again occupy grasslands as far north as the plains of Alberta and Saskatchewan.[14] A quick calculation indicates that, at a minimum—if it started hopping north 20 kya and arrived recently—the spadefoot moved north a minimum of 250 feet per year, a rather impressive march for such a small creature that spends most of the year underground.

All in all, today's guidebook to the plants and wildlife of the Northern Great Plains would have worked quite well in the early Holocene. The biological pieces of today's mixed-grass prairie were falling into place. It was now up to the Holocene climate and other physical forces—and interactions among the species themselves—to hone those pieces into the modern mixed-grass prairie ecosystem.

The Mixed-Grass Prairie and Its Biodiversity

Ecologists cite the interaction of three factors—drought, fire, and grazing—as primarily responsible for shaping the evolution of Great Plains grasslands and their biodiversity.[15] Drought might be more usefully understood in its role as the "bust" in the boom-and-bust climate of the region. Temperature and precipitation are highly variable through time and across the landscape. Average annual precipitation in the American Prairie–Russell Refuge region is 12 inches, but this average masks high year-to-year differences. Periods of wet or dry or of unusually cool or warm weather may last decades. Temperature and precipitation can also be highly variable over short time periods and small distances. Many times I've driven dirt roads in the region that were nearly impassable because of a localized thunderstorm's deluge, only to spin and slide a quarter mile farther onto a dry, dusty road. The average daily high in July is 85°F in the American Prairie–Russell Refuge region while the average daily low in January is 4°F, but summer temperatures above 100°F and winter temperatures below −20°F commonly occur every year. Subzero temperatures combined with high winds and heavy snow challenge the hardiest of animals. The U.S. record for a 24-hour change in temperature of 103°F was recorded in 1972 on the plains of north-central Montana, where it rose from −54°F at 9:00 a.m. on January 14 to 49°F by 8:00 a.m. the next morning.[16]

One of the best methods for tracking changes in vegetation and climate during the Holocene is the record of pollen deposition in lakes. Pollen can be identified to the species or genus of plant, which in turn reveals the climate at the time the pollen was deposited. Pollen cores from lakes in the Northern Great Plains as well as other lines of evidence show a clear warming and drying trend starting around 10 kya, leading to further expansion of xeric grasslands. This trend ended about 5 kya with the onset of a slightly cooler and less arid climate.[17]

While warmer and drier conditions may have favored the spread of grasslands, two other major forces—fire and grazing—were shaping grassland ecosystems. Charcoal in the pollen layers in northwestern North Dakota's Kettle Lake indicate that for at least the last 4,500 years, and probably as far back as 8,500 years, the region's grasslands experienced a roughly 160-year climate-fuel-fire cycle. A wet climatic period produced lush plant growth, creating large fuel loads for both human- and lightning-lit grassland fires. These fires would have limited or prevented encroachment by woody plants, which wetter periods may have favored.[18] Grasses and forbs grow back quickly—within months—after a fire, and the new plant growth is more nutritious than that in unburned areas. Such areas are magnets to bison and other grazers, the third major ecological driver of the mixed-grass prairie. As I'll describe in more detail in later chapters, the interaction of fire and grazers is important for grassland biodiversity.[19]

The adaptations of grasses to aridity discussed in chapter 2 and the diversity of grass species that colonized the Great Plains provide ecological resilience to the region's boom-and-bust climate. An analysis of 426 species of grass from around the world found physiological drought tolerance varied 10-fold among the species.[20] More remarkably, nearly this same range of drought tolerance was found among 52 grass species from a single location in the Great Plains—the Konza Prairie in Kansas. Such a wide range of tolerance among species means the grassland ecosystem can adapt quickly to extreme year-to-year and decade-to-decade swings in precipitation. During relatively wet years, grasses that thrive on moist conditions increase in abundance; during droughts, grasses that do well with little moisture thrive. The upshot is that the roughly 80 species of grass in the American Prairie–Russell Refuge region present diverse survival strategies that maintain the grassland ecosystem through both dry and wet periods.

The sagebrush steppe habitat of the American Prairie–Russell Refuge region offers another lesson in evolutionary ingenuity for living in often arid conditions. Big sagebrush (*Artemisia tridentata*), one of several species of sagebrush in the region, grows both a deep taproot and an extensive network of shallow roots. The shallow root system enables the plant to quickly grab water from a rainstorm. During the day, in a process called "hydraulic lift," the taproot draws up deep-soil moisture and then, at night, releases it into the upper soil where it is available to the shallow root system as well as to other plants.[21] Sagebrush also increases water retention by trapping windblown snow. Moreover, sagebrush is an evergreen with hairy leaves that offer insulation from desiccating hot winds in summer and from cold during winter, enabling the plant to photosynthesize near freezing temperatures. Year-round leaves make it a valuable food source for herbivores during winter, when most everything else is brown and dead. Unlike grasses, however, sagebrush is often killed by fires.

Animals also display adaptations to the localized boom-and-bust climate of the Great Plains. Migration, whether latitudinally north and south, up and down a mountain, or other ways, is obviously the primary adaptation of hundreds of species of insects, birds, mammals, and other organisms to seasonal change in nearly all biomes. Some that breed in the Northern Great Plains are very long distance migrants, such as Swainson's hawk (*Buteo swainsoni*), which migrates to southern South America every winter. A vast majority of grassland birds, however, from sparrows to shorebirds to raptors, escape the inhospitable northern winters by heading to the Gulf of Mexico coastal region and grasslands of the southwest United States and northern Mexico. Some species, however, track resources on a more regional and shorter time scale. Lark buntings (*Calamospiza melanocorys*) shift nesting locations in the Great Plains from year to year to areas receiving recent high levels of precipitation.[22] After breeding, ferruginous hawks (*Buteo regalis*) migrate hundreds of miles within the Great Plains and beyond, to the Columbia Basin of the northwest United States, to track prey resources during the remainder of the summer.[23] Greater sage-grouse (*Centrocercus urophasianus*) move locally in response to snow cover and, in the American Prairie–Russell Refuge region, undertake longer seasonal north-south migrations.[24] Bison, elk, mule deer, and pronghorn regularly migrate

30–40 miles, and sometimes more than 100 miles, between winter and summer ranges.[25]

Like plants, animals have also evolved physiological adaptations
to the aridity of the Northern Great Plains. Dozens of miles separate natural water sources across much of the region, especially
during summer and fall. Diverse species—prairie dogs and smaller
rodents, black-footed ferrets and swift foxes (*Vulpes velox*), snakes
and lizards, and nesting grassland birds—often have no access to
standing water within their territories. All water needs are met by
foods eaten and by being physiologically stingy with water loss.

The plains spadefoot toad epitomizes the oscillating dry-and-
wet, boom-and-bust lifestyle by taking advantage of a brief boom
to breed and mature fast. Spadefoots use their spade-like hind
feet to dig backward to bury themselves until they hit moist soil,
sometimes up to three feet deep, where they estivate for months
during winter and dry periods. They emerge en masse after the
first big rain of spring to explosively breed in muddy, ephemeral
pools of water on the prairie.[26]

Biodiversity at the Time of Euro-American Colonization

Although the distribution and relative abundance of plant species
within each native habitat of the American Prairie–Russell Refuge
region have shifted over the last few hundred years—some due to
Euro-American settlement—the general character of each habitat
probably has not (figs. 3–6). The region's uplands are dominated
by mixed-grass prairie and sagebrush steppe. The two habitats,
however, may blend into each other and are often not as distinct
as the photos suggest. Although grasses and shrubs, especially big
sagebrush, tend to dominate these habitats in terms of ground
cover, forbs generally account for most of the plant species. For
example, a plant survey within a 20-acre area of the sagebrush
steppe shown in figure 4 recorded 96 species of forbs, 23 species
of grasses, and 13 species of shrubs.[27] Uplands also include badlands that range from barren rock outcrops to those with sparse
vegetation composed of short grasses, big sagebrush, and juniper
(*Juniperus* spp.). Ponderosa pine (*Pinus ponderosa*) and Douglas fir

FIG. 3. Major habitats of the American Prairie–Russell Refuge region: a grass-dominated prairie with the Little Rocky Mountains in the distance.
Author's collection.

FIG. 4. Major habitats of the American Prairie–Russell Refuge region: sagebrush steppe being grazed by two bison bulls with the Larb Hills in the distance.
Author's collection.

FIG. 5. Major habitats of the American Prairie–Russell Refuge region: Missouri River breaks and badlands, with Fort Peck Reservoir visible. Courtesy Gib Myers.

FIG. 6. Major habitats of the American Prairie–Russell Refuge region: Missouri River and associated floodplain habitats. Courtesy Gib Myers.

Table 2. Approximate number of native species recorded for
American Prairie–Russell Refuge region and nearby national parks

	American Prairie–Russell Refuge region	Badlands National Park	Yellowstone National Park
Plants	800	444	1,150
Fish	37	17	11
Amphibians	6	5	3
Reptiles	11	9	6
Birds	240	209	289
Mammals	60	49	68

Sources: Charboneau, "Floristic Inventory," 853, 864–75; Charles M. Russell
National Wildlife Refuge, "Wildlife and Habitat"; National Park Service,
"NPspecies"

(*Pseudotsuga menziesii*) dominate the rugged terrain of the Missouri River breaks. The Little Rocky Mountains have a mix of ponderosa pine, lodgepole pine (*Pinus contorta*), and Douglas fir. The riparian habitat of the Missouri River and its major tributaries, such as the Judith and Musselshell Rivers, is dominated by stands of eastern cottonwood (*Populus deltoides*), willows (*Salix* spp.), green ash (*Fraxinus pennsylvanica*), and silver buffaloberry (*Shepherdia argentea*).[28] Most of the streams in the region are intermittent, flowing after rains or snow melt but dry for most of the year.

Table 2 provides a summary of the number of native species of plants and vertebrates recorded in the American Prairie–Russell Refuge region compared to two nearby national parks, Badlands National Park and Yellowstone National Park. Inventories have identified around 786 species of native plants in the two counties, Phillips and Valley, that roughly span the region between the C. M. Russell Refuge and the Canadian border. The C. M. Russell Refuge alone lists about 490 plant species. The most diverse plant families are the Asteraceae (the daisy/sunflower family) with about 120 native species, and the Poacaea (the grasses) with around 80 species.[29]

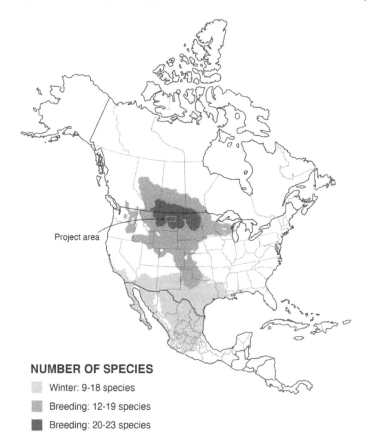

NUMBER OF SPECIES

Winter: 9-18 species

Breeding: 12-19 species

Breeding: 20-23 species

FIG. 7. Regions with the greatest number of species of breeding and wintering grassland birds in North America. Project area indicates the American Prairie–Russell Refuge region. Created by author and Eric Cline (modified from Berlanga et al., *Saving Our Shared Birds*, 20).

The vertebrate numbers are from the C. M. Russell Refuge. Including species found in the coniferous forest of the Little Rocky Mountains would increase some of these numbers. Not evident from the total number of birds documented is that the American Prairie–Russell Refuge region stands out for bird diversity because it lies in an area of the Northern Great Plains that harbors 20–23 species of breeding grassland birds, more than any other area in North America (fig. 7). Ten of these species breed almost exclusively in the Northern Great Plains and thus are considered breeding endemics.[30]

Grasshoppers, because of their economic and ecological importance, and butterflies, because of their showiness (and as pollinators), have been relatively well inventoried. Based on distribution maps on the Montana Natural Heritage website, around 75 species of grasshoppers and 140 species of butterflies occur in the American Prairie–Russell Refuge region.[31] Research is currently underway to assess the region's bee diversity, but a preliminary estimate is 100–200 species based on bee diversity elsewhere in the Great Plains.[32]

Much more complicated than determining the species diversity of a region are efforts to estimate the former abundance of each species. The historic population size of a species can be important for answering several questions and is often a topic of considerable analysis and debate.[33] How much—if at all—did a population decline and, if so, what caused the decline? How did the historic population level of, for example, pumas and wolves alter populations of their ungulate prey, and how, in turn, did ungulate population levels affect populations of the plants they eat? These interactions can have far-reaching effects on the ecosystem and may provide guidance for setting restoration goals.[34] Beyond the innumerable ecological consequences, perceptions of an unbroken prairie extending beyond the horizon occupied by thousands of songbirds, prairie dogs, and large mammals can stir the imagination of people and fuel public support for restoring grassland ecosystems and their biodiversity. Abundance matters both ecologically and emotionally.

Although northern leopard frogs (*Lithobates pipiens*) breed in streams and ponds, they often use nearby grasslands to feed on insects and other invertebrates. Drawing by Erica Freese.

FOUR

From Euro-American Arrival to Today

I've divided Euro-American influence on wildlife in the American Prairie–Russell Refuge region into five time periods. First is the three centuries before the Lewis and Clark expedition, roughly 1500–1805, when the first Euro-American influences—diseases, horses, and guns—arrived in the region. Second is the period from the Lewis and Clark Expedition to the beginning of open-range cattle ranching in the region, from 1806 to around 1880, dominated by the suppression of Native peoples, the fur and hide trade, and unchecked slaughter of wildlife. Third, from the 1880s to the 1920s, is the period of rapid agricultural expansion in both livestock and cropland, resulting in the region's first major plow-up of native prairie and additional collapses of wildlife populations. Fourth is the period between the 1920s and World War II that brought large increases in the extent and types of federal land ownership and management, extensive dam building on the region's streams and rivers, and another wave of wildlife decline. The last period, from the 1940s to today, is characterized by livestock's continued domination of land use, the ongoing government-subsidized conversion of grassland to cropland, a boom in agricultural pesticides, the growth of environmental legislation, and the recognition of the plight of grassland ecosystems and their wildlife. Diverse programs by governments, the private sector, and Native peoples during this period escalated to conserve habitat and restore wildlife populations in the American Prairie–Russell Refuge region.

From 1500 to Lewis and Clark

Our knowledge of wildlife before the arrival of Euro-Americans in the American Prairie–Russell Refuge region comes primarily from Native peoples' oral history, archeological evidence, and animal remains.[1] The first written accounts of wildlife in the region are from the Lewis and Clark expedition's journey up the Missouri River in 1805 and down it in 1806. Unlike the exaggerated descriptions of wildlife encounters by many early explorers and mountain men, the journals of Lewis and Clark are considered highly reliable. No section of their two-year journey, either to the west in the mountains or to the east in the Dakotas, came close to displaying such an abundance of wildlife as the Missouri River corridor through eastern Montana. Observations of bison, elk, mule deer, white-tailed deer, pronghorn, bighorn sheep, wolves, grizzly bears, and beavers, among many other species, were reported nearly every day in some stretches.

Scholars have sliced and diced the expedition's wildlife observations in multiple ways to better understand such differences in wildlife numbers along the expedition's route. Clark himself hinted at the explanation for the abundance of wildlife in eastern Montana when, on August 29, 1806, he wrote, "I have observed that in the country between the nations which are at war with each other the greatest numbers of wild animals are to be found."[2] The "nations" he refers to are Native nations. Other early explorers of western North America also noted that wildlife tended to be numerous in areas where Native peoples were not, suggesting that hunting by Native peoples often significantly affected wildlife numbers.[3]

At the time of the Lewis and Clark Expedition a vast buffer zone between warring Native nations extended from well north of the Missouri River in Montana to well south of the Yellowstone River, from the rivers' confluence in the east to the Rocky Mountain front in the west. Thus, the region appears to have been a de facto refuge from intensive hunting by the various Native nations surrounding the region. As a consequence, Lewis and Clark found a wildlife-rich region as they left present-day North Dakota, where they regularly encountered Native people, and entered the plains of present-day eastern Montana, where few Native people were seen.[4]

The size and location of the Native nations, conflicts among Native nations, and their hunting of wildlife, however, had already been influenced by three Euro-American agents of change before Lewis and Clark ever set foot in the region: horses, exotic diseases, and guns.

Horses of Spanish descent came from the south to the northern plains via InterTribal trade and raids during the first half of the 1700s.[5] Although the availability and rate of adoption of horses varied widely among Native nations of the northern plains, for many Native nations the change from a pedestrian to an equestrian lifestyle profoundly altered their social, demographic, and economic conditions.[6] Mobility was surely an order of magnitude greater with horses rather than dogs serving as the largest beast of burden. Hunting of bison and other game could be conducted much more effectively. The horse also fundamentally changed warring among Native nations. Greater mobility meant more chance for contact and conflict among neighboring Native peoples, horse-mounted warriors were more effective than pedestrian ones, and the horse itself became a valuable resource to fight for. This resulted in large shifts in tribal territories and the buffer zones between them. Social status among tribal members was also affected by horse ownership, and in some areas, horses probably began to compete with bison and pronghorn for forage.[7]

While the horse was arriving to eastern Montana from the south, smallpox, measles, influenza, and other European diseases for which Native people had no or little immunity were spreading into the region from both the south and the east. Between 1730 and 1877 an estimated 50 epidemics struck Native nations of the Northern Great Plains.[8] Smallpox was the deadliest, often killing one-half to all members of a Native community.[9] In fact, Native populations may have been significantly affected by Old World diseases as early as the late 1500s.[10] Epidemics often caused reshuffling of Native territories, as unaffected Native nations quickly occupied territories of those annihilated by disease. James Daschuk notes while examining this question in his book *Clearing the Plains: Disease, Politics of Starvation, and the Loss of Aboriginal Life* that in western Canada, just across the border from Montana, "by 1740, disease was the primary factor in the wholesale redistribution of aboriginal populations."[11] Another smallpox epidemic devastated tribal populations of the northern plains of the United States and Canada during the early 1780s. The decimation of tribal populations by disease and consequent reshuffling of their territories undoubtedly affected hunting of bison and other game decades before Euro-Americans arrived in the region.

Guns, ammunition, and knives from fur traders based around the Great Lakes and Hudson Bay reached the hands of Niitsitapi (Blackfeet), Nakoda (also Nakona or Assiniboine), and other Native nations of the northern plains by the late 1700s. There is little evidence that guns were extensively used for hunting by the region's Native nations until the 1800s, but they were used to wage war on Native nations that lacked them. The Niitsitapi and their allies, for example, appear to have used this advantage in weapons to drive out other Native nations from much of eastern Montana.[12]

It may be that the combination of a massive decline of the Native population due to disease and the existence of a buffer zone between Native nations at the time resulted in the large number and tameness of wildlife encountered by Lewis and Clark in the American Prairie–Russell Refuge region. Consequently, the first Euro-American influence on wildlife numbers in the region may have been to inflate them. Regardless, 1800 appears to have fallen in a boom period for wildlife in a region notorious for boom-and-bust conditions. Hunting intensity and wildlife populations surely had fluctuated widely for millennia. There is little value in trying to establish a "baseline" of wildlife population levels based on historical observations that represent only snapshots in time of a highly dynamic ecosystem.

While the Northern Great Plains and, especially, the American Prairie–Russell Refuge region were teeming with wildlife when Euro-Americans first started arriving, the situation would not last. When Lewis and Clark returned to St. Louis with glowing descriptions of the extensive grasslands and rich wildlife resources of Montana, the Rubicon had been crossed. Another wave of human immigrants, more than 20,000 years after the first, was about to begin. Another faunal collapse would soon follow.

From Lewis and Clark to Open-Range Ranching

The first Euro-American immigrant wave to the plains of eastern Montana was quick to start after the return of the Lewis and Clark Expedition to St. Louis in 1806 with news of abundant beavers in the Upper Missouri River and its tributaries. Before the end of 1807, St. Louis–based merchant and fur trader Manuel Lisa and his crew had navigated 2,000 miles up the Missouri and then Yellowstone Rivers to build a trading post near the mouth of the Bighorn River. The first fur-trading post—the first Euro-American settlement in Montana—was quickly followed by waves of other fur-trading companies and trappers seeking riches from the hides of beavers and other wildlife of the Northern Great Plains and Rocky Mountains. Native peoples also began to participate in the fur trapping and trade business. The Missouri River, cutting through the heart of the American Prairie–Russell Refuge region, was the main corridor of activity for both Euro-Americans and Native peoples involved in the fur trade.[13]

The collapse of the beaver market and beaver population during the 1830s was followed by a growing market for bison robes and the hides of other wild ungulates. In general, any wild animal with fur or a hide—muskrats and otters, raccoons (*Procyon lotor*) and mink, wolves and bears, elk and deer, and so on—had a market and was fair game.[14] No game laws were in place to curtail the ensuing slaughter. The discovery of gold in western Montana in 1862 magnified the demand for a safe and efficient transportation link with eastern markets. The Missouri River was the obvious conduit, but navigating the river was challenging. Improvements in river boat technology—culminating in Missouri River–ready steamboats that could conquer, most of the time, the profusion of the river's snags, sandbars, shallows, and swift currents in Montana—eventually enabled the first steamboat to reach Fort Benton in 1860. Fort

Benton, 2,300 river miles from St Louis, emerged as the upper-most shipping point for furs, gold, and other commodities. In 1867, the peak year, 70 steamboats with 2,200 passengers made it to Fort Benton. Shooting wildlife, especially the bison that were often encountered in massive herds crossing the river, was a favorite pastime of passengers.[15]

Attempting to tap into this river commerce, in 1868 frontier entrepreneurs created a settlement, Fort Musselshell, at the mouth of the Musselshell River in the center of what is now the Charles M. Russell National Wildlife Refuge.[16] With each steamboat requiring 25–30 cords of wood per day to fuel their boilers, "wood-hawks" met the demand by cutting the cottonwood forests lining the river. When not busy cutting wood, many became "wolfers," lacing bison carcasses with strychnine and returning a day or two later to skin dozens of dead wolves for the fur trade. Merchant C. M. Lee's diary documents the rough and dangerous conditions when he lived at the Musselshell trading post from 1868 to 1872.[17] Meat was not in short supply, as bison, elk, and pronghorn were abundant. But attacks by Native people, disturbed by both the growing slaughter of wildlife and now the loss of their forests, were frequent. The completion of the transcontinental railroad through the central plains in 1869 shifted commerce away from risky and seasonal river transport, resulting in declining steamboat traffic and the abandonment of Fort Musselshell and other trading posts along the river. Thus the arrival of the railroad in eastern Montana in 1887 signaled the end of the steamboat era on the Upper Missouri River.[18]

Although Native nations still controlled most of eastern Montana through the early and mid-1800s, the ravages they suffered escalated during this period. Another smallpox epidemic swept through Native populations from 1837 to 1840, killing an estimated 17,200 Native people in the Northern Great Plains and 100,000–300,000 across the continent.[19] Conflict between Native nations and Euro-Americans continued to grow as the gold rush in western Montana brought ever more Euro-Americans to traverse the eastern plains on the Bozeman Trail and Missouri River and again later when the cattle industry and railroads pressed for more lands free of Native people. As of the early 1880s half of the best grazing lands in eastern Montana's plains were on treaty-designated Indian reservations that then covered most of the region.[20] That wouldn't last. From the 1850s to the 1880s the U.S. government reneged on treaties with Native nations, took possession of treaty lands, forced Native peoples' relocation, supported the slaughter of bison as a way to control Native nations, and waged outright war on them.[21] The Battle of the Little Bighorn in southeast Montana in 1876 and the flight of the Nez Perce through eastern Montana in 1877, culminating in the Battle of Bear Paw on the western edge of the American Prairie–Russell Refuge region, are grim milestones in this sordid history of persecution of the region's Native peoples.[22] Eventually Native nations were forced onto much smaller reservations. The Fort Belknap Indian Reservation, home to the Aaniniin (Aaniiih or Gros Ventre) and Nakoda, and the Fort Peck Indian Reservation, home to the Dakota (Sioux) and Nakona, were established in 1888. The Rocky Boy's Reservation, established in 1916, is home to the Ne Hiyawak (Chippewa Cree).[23] All are close neighbors to American Prairie and the C. M. Russell Refuge and, as we'll see later, are conducting valuable wildlife restoration work.

From Livestock Barons to Homesteader Collapse

Despite the gold-fueled growth of Euro-American settlements in western Montana and the river commerce of trappers and hunters in the plains, eastern Montana remained devoid of any significant Euro-American settlement in the 1860s and 1870s. The Homestead Act of 1862, which aimed to spur settlement by offering 160 acres to anyone (except Native people) willing to farm the land, did not catalyze a land rush to eastern Montana.[24] Compared to the well-watered grasslands of the central and eastern Dakotas, the aridity of Montana's plains would challenge even the smartest farmer to make a living on 160 acres. Native nations and the absence of a rail line also deterred Euro-American settlement of eastern Montana and western North Dakota. In 1880 the Montana cattleman and civic leader Granville Stuart reported that he found eastern Montana mostly empty.[25]

That was about to change as demand from eastern markets, eradication of bison, the arrival of the railroads to eastern Montana, and the seizure of former Indian reservation lands opened millions of acres of grassland to livestock grazing. With funding from investors from the East Coast and Europe, cattle numbers in the Montana plains boomed during the 1880s as cattle barons moved herds of shorthorns from the mining region of southwest Montana and cattle drives brought longhorns from Texas.[26] While a total of only four cattle companies incorporated in Montana in 1881 and 1882, 59 companies incorporated from 1884 to 1886.[27] By 1886, the peak of open-range ranching, roughly 664,000 cattle grazed the still-unfenced public lands of Montana's eastern plains.[28] By then the last wild bison of Montana's plains had been killed. The total swap of the region's dominant ungulate grazer from bison to cattle had been completed. The severe winter of 1886–87 killed most of the cattle population of eastern Montana and marked the beginning of the end for the brief era of open-range grazing. Cattle barons and investors lost their shirts and bailed out of the cattle industry. Small-scale cattlemen and homesteaders moved in to create smaller herds and build fences of barbed wire to divide up the range and better control cattle and grazing. Cattle numbers quickly recovered, but the number of sheep was rising even faster. In 1870 the Montana territory had roughly 2,000 sheep, most of them in the intermountain valleys of the western region.[29] By 1895 nearly 1.9 million sheep were in the plains of eastern Montana, along with about 455,500 cattle and 82,500 horses.[30] By 1910 the state's sheep population peaked at around 6 million, most of them in the eastern plains.[31]

The surge in domestic livestock numbers coincided with the collapse not only of the bison population but, as described in chapter 6, of all native ungulates on the plains of Montana. In chapter 7 we'll see how conflict between large carnivores and livestock producers led the Montana territorial government to initiate a bounty system during the open-range era for killing wolves and pumas and, when that was deemed inadequate, the U.S. government in 1915 funded a program to eradicate large carnivores. One important step for wildlife protection, however, occurred when Congress passed the Lacy Act of 1900, the oldest wildlife protection law in the United States. The main purpose of the act at the time was to protect game animals by making it a federal crime to hunt wildlife with the intent of selling it in another state.[32]

The swift transition from wild ungulates to livestock ushered in massive changes in grassland management. Native people managed ungulates by hunting them and using fire to influence where they grazed. Euro-Americans overstocked the range, resulting in extensive overgrazing; built fences to control livestock; impounded and diverted water for livestock and crop irrigation; plowed and seeded land with nonnative plants; and slaughtered not only wild ungulates but also prairie dogs and large carnivores. Grassland fires were largely eliminated by the displacement of Native peoples, reduction of fuel loads by overgrazing, fragmentation of grasslands by croplands and infrastructure, and active fire suppression.[33] This may have been the start of population declines of several species of grassland birds (described in chapter 11).

The first towns of the American Prairie–Russell Refuge region—Lewistown, Malta, and Glasgow—appeared in the 1870s and 1880s. However, not even the arrival of railroad connections to eastern Montana generated a land rush, and the population of the region remained low through the turn of the century. According to Montana historian Mike Malone and his coauthors in their book about the state, "As the twentieth century dawned, the eastern two-thirds of Montana lay wide open, with a settlement or Indian village here and there, occasional herds of cattle and flocks of sheep, and nearly everywhere vast expanses of vacant public land."[34]

Finally, several factors converged to spur a land rush to eastern Montana. The enlarged Homestead Act of 1909 doubled the amount of free land one could receive from 160 acres to 320 acres. Good rains, easy farm credit, and strong grain markets driven by World War I and government price supports, combined with zealous sales pitches by railroad barons and land speculators, created

boom times on eastern Montana's plains. From 1909 to 1923, settlers filed 114,620 homestead claims on nearly 25 million acres of
land in Montana.[35] This period heralded the first big plow-up
of eastern Montana's prairies. Montana's 635,807 acres of cereal
crops in 1909 more than tripled to 2,017,253 acres in 1919, the vast
share in eastern Montana, representing, by far, the largest plow-up
in the United States during that decade.[36]

The boom period in eastern Montana soon turned to bust. In 1917
a new drought began and in 1918 World War I ended. From 1919 to
1925, half of Montana's farmers lost their land. The human population of the American Prairie–Russell Refuge region peaked around
1920 and then began a decline that has continued for 100 years.
Half as many people live in the region today as did in 1920. Rains
returned in the late 1920s, but then the Great Depression struck in
1929 and another multiyear drought, resulting in the Dust Bowl of
the Great Plains, began in 1930.[37] By the 1920s, the population
of every large mammal—adult weight of more than 40 pounds—in
the plains of eastern Montana and, for that matter, across the entire
Great Plains, had collapsed.

From Homesteader Exodus to World War II

With drought and economic depression squeezing ranchers and
farmers and with wolves, pumas, and grizzly bears eradicated in
the Great Plains, the U.S. Biological Survey found a new cause to
justify their pest control budget and jobs. Another so-called var-
mint, the prairie dog, was targeted for eradication. During the
1920s and 1930s the U.S. government's campaign to eradicate prairie
dogs reached the American Prairie–Russell Refuge region in full
force with a massive poisoning program, although ranchers had
already been actively poisoning prairie dogs for years.[38] As we'll
see in chapter 9, the destruction of prairie dog populations also
had devastating effects on the black-footed ferret and other species.

Federal policies and actions in the 1930s brought more changes
in the disposition and management of lands and waters in the
American Prairie–Russell Refuge region than in any decade since.
As part of President Roosevelt's New Deal and setting the stage for

the management and mismanagement of the region's lands for years to come, the first farm bill, the Agriculture Adjustment Act of 1933, allowed farmers to be paid for not growing crops as a means of raising crop prices by limiting production. The act perhaps seemed like a modest measure to help farmers during the Depression, but it meant the farm subsidy genie was out of the bottle, never to return. Subsidies to farmers would diversify and grow after World War II.[39]

Rules governing grazing of public grasslands also changed during the 1930s. Until then, use of the extensive public rangelands in the Northern Great Plains hadn't changed much since the first cattle arrived in the 1800s. Basically, there were no rules. Use of the land was free and ranchers decided for themselves or worked out with neighbors, through both agreeable and disagreeable means, how many livestock to graze and where. It was a perfect tragedy of the commons that resulted in widespread rangeland degradation. This led to passage of the 1934 Taylor Grazing Act and subsequent amendments, which began to impose some order on rancher use of public grazing lands and instituted a modest grazing fee.[40] The act also marked the end of the homesteading of federal lands. The combination of severe rangeland degradation and failed crops during this period led the U.S. government, under the Agricultural Adjustment Act of 1933 and the Bankhead-Jones Farm Tenant Act of 1937, to rescue destitute farmers by approving one of the biggest land buybacks in the country, slightly more than one million acres in four core counties—Blaine, Phillips, Valley, and Fergus—of the American Prairie–Russell Refuge region.[41] These acres are nearly all Bureau of Land Management (BLM) lands today. This government restoration program is responsible for planting much of the crested wheatgrass (*Agropyron cristatum*), a native grass of Eurasia, that plagues millions of acres in eastern Montana. Crested wheat grass often outcompetes native grasses to create monocultural stands, negatively affects ecological processes in grassland soils, and greatly diminishes grassland plant and animal diversity.[42] Many invasive, noxious weeds, some brought into the region intentionally and others not, probably got their start around this time as overgrazing, abandoned croplands, roads, and other disturbances that removed native plant cover opened the door for colonization by nonnative species.[43]

Massive federal investments in managing the region's rivers also emerged in the 1930s. A few small dams had been built in the headwaters of the Missouri River around the turn of the century, but the 1930s marked the beginning of a 30-year era of dam building. With the Great Depression in full swing, President Roosevelt was looking for ways to put people to work and diverse interests were lobbying for building dams on the Missouri River. Massive storage dams were wanted to maintain flows for river navigation, to avert flooding, for irrigation, and for hydropower. The wild, meandering, and unpredictable Missouri River had to be tamed. In 1933 Roosevelt approved funding for construction of the Fort Peck Dam. Construction spanned the period of 1933–40 and at its peak employed 10,500 people.[44] The dam's construction represents one of the largest and most difficult-to-reverse ecological assaults on the American Prairie–Russell Refuge region. As reviewed in chapter 10, no species suffered the consequences more than the pallid sturgeon.

During construction of the Fort Peck Dam, interest grew in establishing a wildlife refuge around and upstream of the future dam's reservoir. In 1935 Olaus J. Murie, one of the century's preeminent wildlife biologists, then employed by the U.S. Bureau of Biological Survey, visited the region and recommended that it be set aside as a game range. In what stands out as one of President Roosevelt's most important actions for wildlife conservation, in 1936 he issued an executive order establishing the Fort Peck Game Range (later renamed the Charles M. Russell National Wildlife Refuge).[45] Spanning 1.1 million acres, it is the second-largest national wildlife refuge in the lower 48 United States and the largest federal protected area in the Great Plains. That same year, Roosevelt established the 15,551-acre Bowdoin Migratory Waterfowl Refuge, later to become the Bowdoin National Wildlife Refuge, 40 miles north of the C. M. Russell Refuge.[46]

Much more land and many miles of streams were affected during the 1930s and 1940s with the construction of thousands of small dams to create stock ponds in the upper reaches of watersheds and to irrigate hay fields in the flood plains of stream systems.[47] Stock ponds were constructed across the uplands to enable cattle, which seldom venture more than a mile or two from water, to graze the entire landscape. The density of stock ponds and small reservoirs in the American Prairie–Russell Refuge region is 0.7–2.6 per square mile, among the highest densities of such impoundments in the Great Plains.[48]

Wildlife management, particularly of game animals, in Montana and elsewhere in the United States got a major boost when Congress passed the 1937 Pittman-Robertson Act, which created an excise tax on firearms, archery equipment, and ammunition to generate funding for state wildlife conservation programs.[49] This new source of funding catalyzed the transition of many state wildlife agencies, including Montana's, to more professional, better equipped, science-based wildlife management—albeit often highly influenced by the states' political winds.

From the 1940s to the Present

After the completion of the Fort Peck Dam in 1940, dam building took a pause during World War II. But the demand for controlling and harvesting the water and power of the Missouri River quickly generated more federal plans and funds for dam construction. Far upriver from the Fort Peck Dam and the American Prairie–Russell Refuge, but with significant downriver effects, two storage dams—Canyon Ferry Dam on the Missouri River and the Tiber Dam on a tributary, the Marias River—were completed in the mid-1950s. Downriver from the Fort Peck Dam, from 1946 to 1966, five more massive main-stem dams were built on the Missouri River in North Dakota and South Dakota with dire consequences for river and riparian habitats and wildlife.

Meanwhile, innovations in pesticides, crop breeding, and farm mechanization, combined with expanding farm subsidies, resulted in more prairie being converted to cropland and the poisoning of wildlife. With the development of DDT, dieldrin, and other synthetic organic pesticides in the 1940s, the use of pesticides exploded after World War II. Agricultural pesticide application in the United States tripled from 200 million pounds in 1960 to more than 600 million pounds by 1980.[50] The toxicological impacts of DDT and dieldrin on wildlife, especially raptors,[51] resulted in organochlorines being replaced by new generations of pesticides, such as organophosphates and neonicotinoids. Though more targeted and less persistent in the environment, recent research shows these chemicals also have serious consequences for wildlife, as we'll see in chapter 11.

This period also brought growing layers of farm subsidies that have been disastrous for grassland ecosystems and biodiversity.[52] The U.S. Congress has seldom met proposed legislation it didn't like when it comes to paying farmers more than their crops are worth, paying them for not planting crops, and covering the risk of planting crops. From 1995 through June 2020 the U.S. government paid landowners in the eight-county region of the American Prairie–Russell Refuge region $2.57 billion in farm subsidies (excluding 2020 crop insurance subsidies). The vast share of these payments were for commodity subsidies, disaster subsidies, and crop insurance subsidies, all of which create incentives for converting grasslands to croplands.[53]

The remainder of the payments, $729 million, were for conservation subsidies—primarily the Conservation Reserve Program. This program, launched under the U.S. Food Security Act of 1985, pays farmers to take land out of production under contracts lasting 10–15 years. The program's goal is to reduce soil erosion and improve water quality and wildlife habitat. Initially, nearly all those lands were planted with nonnative grasses, but recently the program has emphasized native species plantings to serve various biodiversity conservation objectives.[54] Conservation Reserve Program acreages peaked in 2007 and have declined ever since. In 2020, 316,060 acres were enrolled in the eight-county American Prairie–Russell Refuge region.[55] The program's conservation requirements and compliance fall short of what we should expect from the money invested. For example, nationally, from 2007 to 2014, farmers took 15.8 million acres out of the Conservation Reserve

Program, effectively resulting in no lasting conservation benefit for the $8.9 billion they received in payments.[56]

Adding to the plow-up caused by crop subsidies, production of ethanol to meet the U.S. Renewable Fuel Standard imposed in 2005 cranked up market prices for corn and soybeans, fueling more conversion of grasslands to cropland.[57]

Croplands are wastelands for nearly all native plants and animals. The conversion of grasslands to croplands in the U.S. portion of the Northern Great Plains began on the region's western margins in the Dakotas in the late 1800s. The cropland total peaked by 1940, when more than 50% of the eastern Dakotas was cropland, though less than 10% had been converted at that time in most counties in the western portion of the Northern Great Plains.[58] Plow-up to plant the vast wheatfields of southern Alberta and Saskatchewan occurred at this time as well.[59]

Conversion of grasslands to croplands has continued since the 1950s, with a recent surge in the mid-2000s that continued through the 2010s.[60] Determining how many acres of grassland have been converted to cropland since the start of farming in the Great Plains is difficult and has been done on a limited basis.[61] Written records are incomplete, and satellite imagery cannot always readily distinguish tame grasslands (cultivated lands planted with grass) from native grasslands, especially grasslands planted decades ago.[62] Since 2009, however, World Wildlife Fund's Plowprint analyses have tracked conversion of grassland (tame and native) to cropland. Extrapolating from these analyses, a rough estimate for the Great Plains is that 120 million acres of grassland—both native and tame—were converted to cropland from 2000 to 2020.[63] From 2009 to 2020, the period for which annual plow-up data are available, 962,436 acres were converted to cropland in the eight-county region of the American Prairie–Russell Refuge, the equivalent of eight football fields per hour.[64]

Today, about 25% of the Northern Great Plains and 40% of the entire Great Plains of the United States and Canada are in cropland.[65] As suggested above, however, these percentages exclude large acreages of former cropland replanted to grass and other herbaceous cover. The full restoration of biodiversity and eco-system services such as carbon sequestration on these former croplands is slow and seldom complete.

Rangeland management also experienced changes affecting wild-life. As it has since the late 1800s, livestock grazing dominates land use. The eight-county American Prairie–Russell Refuge region had about 320,000 cattle and 236,000 sheep in 1950;[66] by 2017 those numbers were 503,000 cattle and 31,000 sheep.[67] The 1950s saw a surge in rangeland managers advocating for rotational grazing by cattle on private and public rangelands across the West. Rotational grazing comes in many forms, but in short, it involves rotating cat-tle between two, three, four, or more fenced grazing units. A pri-mary objective of rotational grazing is uniform grazing across the landscape—don't let livestock clip the grass too short or leave it too tall anywhere. The objective was reduced to a readily remembered rule of thumb: "Take half, leave half."[68]

The alternative to rotational grazing, the one used by preset-tlement wild bison and that livestock ranchers infrequently use, is continuous grazing, whereby livestock are free to graze across a large area. Research has repeatedly demonstrated that, under moderate stocking rates, continuous grazing is as productive and profitable as, or more than, rotational grazing with equal or greater benefits for grassland health and biodiversity.[69] Neverthe-less, BLM and the U.S. Forest Service have implemented rotational grazing—also called prescribed grazing—on tens of millions of acres that they lease to ranchers for livestock grazing. The Natural Resource Conservation Service (NRCS), which is responsible for assisting private landowners in implementing the U.S. Department of Agriculture's conservation programs, has invested vast resources in rotational grazing on private lands. For example, from 2004 to 2007 on private lands in 17 western states, including Montana, NRCS supported prescribed grazing on nearly 48 million acres of rangelands, along with the installation of 127,000 watering facil-ities and the construction of 5,756 miles of fence.[70] That's enough fence, constructed in just four years, to go from San Francisco to New York City and back again. Fence density in the core of the

American Prairie–Russell Refuge region is commonly 1–3 miles of fence per square mile, while the region to the north up to the Canadian border—Montana's so-called Hi-Line region—has an estimated average fence density of 3.8 miles per square mile.[71] As later chapters describe, fences pose multiple hazards for wildlife.

The surge in oil and gas development in the Great Plains that began in the 1970s and is ongoing has created another source of habitat fragmentation via well pads and access roads, as well as contributing to water, air, and noise pollution. Since 2000 an average of 50,000 new wells have been drilled annually in central North America.[72] Infrastructure for wind energy has recently become another source of habitat fragmentation, and collision with wind turbines is a direct cause of bird and bat mortality. A recent tally shows more than 42,300 wind turbines in the Great Plains.[73]

Climate change in the American Prairie–Russell Refuge region will have potentially far-reaching effects on agriculture and biodiversity. From 1950 to 2015 the average temperature in the region rose about 3.5°F. Projections are that, under various greenhouse gas scenarios, it will increase another 4–6°F by midcentury and 6–10°F by the end of the century. Spring precipitation may increase in the plains of eastern Montana, but higher temperatures will increase rates of drying during the summer, when less rain is expected. The effects of rising temperatures on heat stress on livestock and crops, plant and animal diseases, invasive species, pollinators, forage plants, and other factors are hard to predict but will surely be disruptive.[74]

As noted in chapter 3, native grasslands and wildlife of the American Prairie–Russell Refuge region have evolved with, and are well adapted to, the region's climatic extremes. A warmer and drier climate will undoubtedly cause shifts in the range and number of some species, especially grassland birds (see chapter 11). Some species will adapt, at least partially, to the changed conditions. Some species, whose populations have already been highly compromised by habitat loss and other causes, may be pushed toward extirpation in the region. Overall, however, the native species and ecosystems will be much more resilient to the challenges of a changing climate than will the crop and livestock systems that dominate the region today.

While assaults on biodiversity in the American Prairie–Russell Refuge region have continued, other efforts have advanced since the 1950s to restore and protect the region's natural landscape and biological values. As noted in chapter 1, new federal legislation has addressed growing environmental problems. Because of the 1973 U.S. Endangered Species Act, substantial resources are directed to the American Prairie–Russell Refuge region to conserve two endangered species, the black-footed ferret and the pallid sturgeon, and to avert the listing of a third species whose population has collapsed, the greater sage-grouse, among other species recovery efforts. The 1976 Federal Land and Policy Management Act was particularly significant for the American Prairie–Russell Refuge region because of its mandate for multiple use, including biodiversity conservation, on BLM lands.

The C. M. Russell Refuge for the entirety of this period has been the cornerstone for conserving the region's biodiversity by restoring and protecting habitats and wildlife populations and by being an outdoor laboratory for research aimed at conserving grassland birds, bighorn sheep, the endangered black-footed ferret, and other imperiled species. In 1976 National Wild and Scenic River designation gave recognition and modest additional protection to 149 miles of the Missouri River through the region. In 1993 six areas within the region, totaling 89,030 acres of BLM lands, were designated as Wilderness Study Areas, though Congress has yet to afford additional protection by declaring any of them as a Wilderness Area. The January 2001 declaration by President Clinton that created the Upper Missouri River Breaks National Monument was the most significant federal land decision in the region since the creation of the C. M. Russell Refuge.

The establishment of Grasslands National Park in 1981 in southern Saskatchewan represents another significant governmental contribution to grassland conservation in the region. The Bitter Creek region, consisting of mostly intact grasslands, provides a north-south wildlife corridor between Grasslands National Park and the American Prairie–Russell Refuge. As a result, Grasslands National Park is a northern anchor for grassland birds, pronghorn, and potentially other wildlife that migrate across this transboundary region.[75]

Native peoples of the three Indian reservations in the region—Fort Belknap, Fort Peck, and Rocky Boy's—have also initiated important wildlife restoration programs in recent decades. All three have reintroduced bison, Fort Belknap and Fort Peck have reintroduced the swift fox, and Fort Belknap has reintroduced the endangered black-footed ferret.

Conservation easements by the U.S. Fish and Wildlife Service; the U.S. Department of Agriculture; Montana Fish, Wildlife & Parks; the Montana Land Reliance; and The Nature Conservancy have mushroomed since 1990 to help protect wetlands, grasslands, and forest habitats. As of 2021, at least 224 conservation easements cover 475,492 acres in the eight-county region of the American Prairie–Russell Refuge.[76] As noted above, despite its shortcomings, in 2020 the Conservation Reserve Program provided wildlife habitat by keeping more than 300,000 acres out of cropland in the region. In 2000 The Nature Conservancy purchased the 60,000-acre Matador Ranch in southern Phillips County, which is now a neighbor to American Prairie lands. The Nature Conservancy's grass banking program generally has 10 or more participating ranches that graze cattle for a reduced fee on the Matador in exchange for implementing conservation measures on 200,000–250,000 acres of land each year.[77] Conservation easements and grass-banking programs are important for restoring and conserving habitat and many imperiled grassland species, but none has the goal of restoring the larger or more controversial native species such as bison and wolves.

American Prairie, established in 2002 and with 460,800 acres of deeded and leased public lands as of early 2023, constitutes the region's largest change in land ownership and in the transition from livestock-driven management to biodiversity-driven management since the establishment of the C. M. Russell Refuge. In addition, American Prairie's Wild Sky program, which pays ranchers for wildlife-friendly practices and for having wildlife on their properties (documented by trail cameras), had 16 ranches totaling 72,000 deeded acres enrolled as of early 2023.

Also notable during this period—especially in the last 30 years—is the growth in biodiversity research in the region by scientists from academia, government institutions, and private organizations. The inviting field conditions offered by the C. M. Russell Refuge, the Matador Ranch, the Fort Belknap Indian Reservation, American Prairie, and many ranchers have provided exceptional opportunities for research addressing the conservation of grassland species.

Resilience and Restoration

Despite the diverse assaults on ecological integrity, the American Prairie–Russell Refuge region's biodiversity displays remarkable resilience. A solid ecological foundation exists for restoring what's been lost. Native or seminative vegetation still covers a vast portion of the region and, though it can take decades to restore native plant diversity, cropland can be converted back to prairie. Stretches of undammed streams and rivers remain, and many small dams and water diversions can be removed or will breach on their own to restore more natural conditions.

Already the American Prairie–Russell Refuge offers 1.5 million acres of land devoted primarily to biodiversity conservation, with more land to come. Land conservation work by others in the region is protecting native habitats and wildlife on hundreds of thousands of additional acres. Outreach to and cooperation with ranchers, Native communities, and other natural resource managers are softening the ecological boundaries to make more room for wildlife. Nevertheless, strong opposition by many in the ranching community to large-scale biodiversity conservation and to building a 3.2-million-acre protected area in the region often results in politically mounted obstacles to progress. American Prairie and its many collaborators and supporters, however, are tenacious. While today's opposition can delay prairie and wildlife restoration and the resulting public benefits, the long-term trajectory is toward a more diversified and balanced use of the land and to reclaiming the region's extraordinary wildlife heritage. I use "balanced" loosely. A 3.2-million-acre reserve would represent just 5% of the plains of eastern Montana—a rather modest area compared to the scale of its benefits.

The relative ecological integrity of the region's habitats offers the advantage that, rather than the heavy lifting of habitat restoration that wildlife recovery often requires, few or modest interventions should be needed to bring back populations of most wildlife in the American Prairie–Russell Refuge region. There are exceptions to this generalization, however, and a few species, especially those whose populations have been extirpated or have severely declined, will require extraordinary skill and effort. The next seven chapters tell the stories of 24 species whose populations have collapsed, pathways to restoring their populations, and what their recovery will mean for the ecosystem.

PART TWO

Collapses and Recoveries

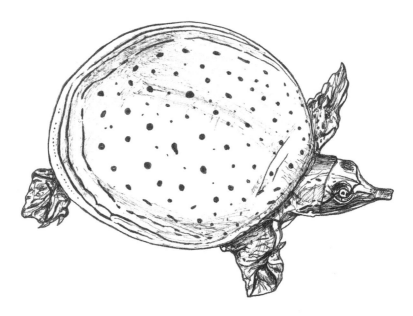

The spiny softshell turtle (*Apalone spinifera*), inhabitant of the Missouri River, has a shell covered with a rough, leathery skin and studded with spines on the front edge. Drawing by Erica Freese.

FIVE

American Beaver and River Otter

In 1805, while Lewis and Clark and their crew ascended the Missouri River into present-day Montana and the American Prairie–Russell Refuge region, American beavers were by far the most important fur-bearing animal in North America. The continental population was estimated at 60–400 million before Euro-American settlement. Beavers were abundant in the Great Plains, perhaps in part because they were generally not hunted by plains Native people for food or fur. Rather, Native people recognized the diverse ecological benefits that beaver engineering offered in their semiarid ecosystem: water, firewood, riparian forests for shelter, and game animals attracted to the water and forests.[1]

But by 1800 North America was the only source of beavers to satisfy the European demand for felt hats and for castoreum (the secretion that beavers mark their territories with, which was widely used for medicinal purposes). Intensive trapping had decimated populations of the European beaver during the 1600s. The resulting beaver shortage was soon relieved by the rapid exploitation of eastern North America's vast beaver populations, which ranged from Newfoundland to Florida, but that relief was short-lived, as intensive trapping during the 1700s also annihilated beavers in the eastern half of the continent.[2] So it was not surprising that Thomas Jefferson's goals for the Lewis and Clark Expedition included an assessment of the potential fur resources, including beavers, of the West.

By the time Lewis and Clark reached the confluence of the Yellowstone and Missouri Rivers near the Montana–North Dakota border in 1805, their journal entries show they were well beyond the zone where eastern beaver populations had been devastated. A couple of Lewis's entries testify to their numbers and ecological effect: on April 27, "Beaver are very abundant, the party kill several of them every day," and the next day, "The beaver have cut great quantities of timber."[3]

The expedition continued to encounter and kill numerous beavers as they proceeded up the Missouri River to the stretch now covered by the Fort Peck Reservoir. Finally, on May 24, as the party began to enter the section of the Missouri River south of the Little Rockies, where the canyon and floodplain narrow, Lewis observed, "Game is becoming more scarce, particularly beaver, of which we have seen but a few for several days the beaver appears to keep pace with the timber as it declines in quantity they also become more scarce."[4]

As noted in the previous chapter, St. Louis entrepreneur Manuel Lisa and his crew were the first to arrive in 1807 to seek a fortune in fur, and soon others followed.[5] By the time the fur trade became well established in Montana in the 1810s, roughly 75,000–100,000 beaver pelts were traded annually in the North American market.[6] Beaver trapping was probably most intense in the American Prairie–Russell Refuge region from 1810 to 1835, when thousands of pelts were traded annually from the Upper Missouri River region of Montana, the Dakotas, Wyoming, and Nebraska.[7] Although records of beavers trapped and traded in the region are lacking, we can assume it didn't take long to trap nearly every beaver along the Missouri River and its tributaries. Beaver dams, beaver lodges, the large food caches of beavers, and beaver-felled timber are like billboards advertising their presence, and beavers create canals that identify regular travel routes.

The demand for beaver pelts sharply declined during the 1830s as hats made from silk rather than from beaver fur became more fashionable. But the drop in demand did not come soon enough. By the 1830s beaver trappers and traders were noting the absence or scarcity of beavers on the Upper Missouri River, and soon both beavers and beaver trappers had mostly disappeared from the region (fig. 8).[8]

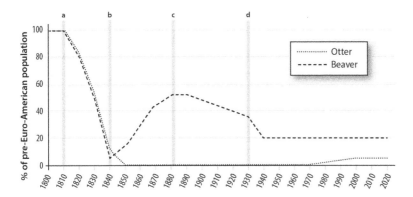

FIG. 8. Postulated population trends of the American beaver and river otter in the American Prairie–Russell Refuge region from 1800 to 2020 as a percentage of population levels before Euro-American colonization. Vertical lines indicate the start of events with likely major effects on the populations: (a) arrival of fur trappers, (b) decline in demand for beaver pelts combined with collapsed beaver and otter populations, (c) livestock degradation of prairie streams, (d) surge in dewatering of prairie streams for stock ponds and irrigation followed by construction of Fort Peck Dam. Created by author and Eric Cline.

North American sales data show another surge in beaver trapping around the 1870s and 1880s.[9] Beaver numbers had at least partially recovered in the Missouri and Yellowstone Rivers of Montana by then (described below), but I've found no accounts detailing the extent of beaver trapping in the region at that time. I suspect beavers reached their low point in the Upper Missouri River during the first era of intensive trapping in the early 1800s. Continentally, however, the beaver population is reported to have reached its nadir around 1900. Regardless of the timing, the continent's beaver population of 60–400 million had crashed to levels that some considered near extinction.[10]

River otters originally inhabited most rivers of the Great Plains, including the plains of eastern Montana.[11] Their populations occurred at low densities, however, as would be expected of a top predator.[12] Lewis and Clark commonly saw river otters while ascending the Missouri River in 1805, though not through the American Prairie–Russell Refuge region, possibly because they were in the region during high spring runoff, when the river's waters are especially turbid. Lewis noted the otter's abundance a few miles above Great Falls on July 12 while offering a possible explanation for why otters were scarce lower on the river: "The otter are now plenty since the water has become sufficiently clear for them to take fish."[13]

The river otter's fur has always attracted top dollar in the market, but because of their low density, otter pelts were never common in the Upper Missouri River fur trade. Like beavers, river otters are easy to trap because they follow well-traveled pathways when inhabiting riparian corridors and they are readily captured incidentally in beaver traps.[14] Even if trappers in the Upper Missouri River were primarily targeting beavers, they would have surely relished finding otters in their traps.

The otter had one more strike against it. River otters are commensals of beavers—they use beaver dens and lodges for resting and raising young, and beaver ponds support fish, frogs, and other otter food.[15] South Dakota's river otter management plan concludes that in the Northern Great Plains, with low gradient streams and harsh winters, self-sustaining populations of river otters are probably limited to streams with significant beaver populations.[16]

High mortality due to trapping in the early 1800s and the degradation of otter habitat caused by the beaver's population collapse must have been the main causes of the river otter's disappearance from the Upper Missouri River region by the end of the fur trapping era. Although the beaver population soon partially recovered, the river otter did not and remained extirpated or extremely rare throughout the Great Plains, including eastern Montana, through the late 1900s.[17] Extensive draining of wetlands, hydrological engineering of streams, livestock damage to streams, and ongoing trapping likely contributed to keeping the otter population from recovering.

Two other semiaquatic mammals found in the Upper Missouri River region—muskrats (*Ondatra zibethicus*) and mink—were also trapped for the fur market during the 1800s. Less conspicuous, less valued, and with a higher reproductive rate than beavers, muskrats and mink probably made it through the era of unregulated trapping without much trouble, although the loss of beaver ponds on smaller streams would have diminished their numbers.[18]

The Keystone Role of Beavers

What were the ecological consequences of the beaver's population collapse? Like a keystone in a masonry arch, which has a central role in preventing the arch's collapse, the beaver is a keystone species because of its central role in forging the structure and species diversity of Great Plains streams and riparian areas that influence the wildlife of surrounding grasslands.[19] Beavers are the ultimate ecosystem engineers, surpassed only by humans in their ability to alter the landscape and what grows on it. Especially in dryland ecosystems, beavers exhibit two distinct lifestyles. Beavers inhabiting streams and sometimes small rivers construct dams to retain water and build lodges for shelter. In large rivers, such as the Missouri River, beavers do not build dams—it's neither possible nor necessary for water retention. Instead, they excavate bank dens for shelter. The vast majority of research on beavers and their ecological effects has been conducted in ecosystems where water is not in short supply—the boreal forests of Canada, the Rocky Mountains, and eastern North America. Beavers are much less studied in semiarid systems such as the western Great Plains, where, because water is generally scarce, their hydrological engineering effects are magnified. The beaver's two main engineering feats with big ecological consequences in semiarid grasslands are the construction of dams on small streams and the clipping and felling of shrubs and trees along waterways for food and for dam and lodge construction.[20]

For keystone ecological engineers like beavers, where they are found on the landscape can be more important than how many there are. On a large river system not subject to other stresses, large differences in the number of beavers may affect the growth of cottonwoods and willows (*Salix* spp.) but have little influence on river hydrology. In contrast, a few beavers on a small stream in semiarid grasslands can profoundly affect the ecosystem. Beavers can ecologically transform small upland streams from narrow

channels of water bordered by grass to ponds and marshes bordered by riparian forests, with far-reaching consequences for biodiversity. In semiarid western North America, riparian areas cover
only about 1% of the land area but support more species of breeding birds than upland areas.[21]

Many streams in the American Prairie–Russell Refuge region
could be transformed with the return of beavers. Most are intermittent streams, flowing when rains or snowmelt feed them
but with limited or no flow during dry periods. Beavers prefer
streams with perennial flows but will use intermittent streams,
especially during relatively wet periods. A single beaver colony
(family) may build several dams along a stream, creating a stair-
step profile that alternates between lotic (flowing water) and lentic
(still water) habitats that harbor distinct assemblages of plants, fish,
aquatic insects, and other organisms. The effects, however, extend
beyond the immediate stream. Beaver dams inundate floodplains
to create marshes with yet a different assembly of species. Beaver
removal in Wyoming resulted in a statewide loss of an estimated
680,000 acres of wetlands.[22] The sediments trapped behind beaver dams can slowly elevate the streambed and become new riparian habitat for plant growth when beaver dams are abandoned or
collapse. By storing water, recharging groundwater, and raising
the water table, beaver dams slowly feed the flow of streams that
may otherwise dry up in late summer and fall, thereby converting
an intermittent stream to one with more or less permanent flows.

The wider riparian areas created by beaver dams that support
the growth of willows, cottonwoods, and other moisture-loving
plants create woody habitat where otherwise none would exist. A
study in Wyoming found the average width of the area with riparian vegetation along streams with beavers was 111 feet versus 34 feet
in streams without beavers. One stream in the sagebrush steppe
habitat of south-central Wyoming had 52 beaver dams within
six-tenths of a mile. The resulting riparian area, dominated by
willows, supported 25 riparian bird species as well as numerous
species not necessarily associated with riparian habitats.[23] In the
American Prairie–Russell Refuge region these forested riparian

areas are also used by bats, white-tailed deer, bobcats, occasionally pumas, and other mammals. The combined effect of these processes is that beaver dams help restore the health of streams that have been deeply incised (their channels downcut) due to the loss of streamside vegetation caused by, among other things, intensive grazing and trampling by cattle.[24]

The influence of beaver dams can extend for miles beyond the riparian zone by providing year-round water for wildlife that inhabit the surrounding upland prairies. Bison and pronghorn come from miles away to drink. Elk and white-tailed deer shelter in the riparian forest by day and venture out at dusk to forage on the grassland. Flycatchers and raptors launch from perches of riparian trees to hunt. Other species move out on the ground from the forest to hunt in the prairie. I was reminded of this riparian–prairie connection a few years ago when, while staying at American Prairie's Enrico Education and Science Center, I heard researchers' excited voices when reviewing camera trap photos. There it was: a bobcat, a denizen of riparian forests, with a prairie dog, strictly a grassland inhabitant, in its jaws.

Beaver populations experience wide fluctuations in semiarid ecosystems. Streams in the American Prairie–Russell Refuge region, similar to streams in other semiarid regions, are notorious for large fluctuations in flow. A big thunderstorm can quickly convert a trickle to a torrent of water that knocks out beaver dams, or an especially dry year can leave beaver dams high and dry and abandoned. During wet years, streams may have sufficient water long enough for beavers to move up a stream, but when dry years return, beaver activity slides downstream. One study on an 11-mile stretch of a small stream in semiarid central Oregon found that over a period of 17 years the number of dams ranged from 9 to 103, and most dams were breached in 2 years or less.[25]

What beaver dam building provides in terms of more willows, cottonwoods, and other plants, beaver industriousness can take away. In the semiarid West, willows and cottonwoods are favorite food plants of beavers.[26] Beaver harvest willows and cottonwoods in the fall and store them in caches near their lodge or bank den as a food source for winter. The extent of these effects is limited because beavers seldom go farther than 300 feet from water to harvest plants.[27] Foraging on willows may increase willow coverage via coppicing, whereby the willows put out new growth from their roots. Cottonwoods sometimes respond to beaver cutting with dense, shrub-like growth. Long-term browsing of cottonwoods, however, can favor the growth of less palatable species that beavers avoid. This is of particular concern regarding two invasive tree species, salt cedar (*Tamarix ramosissima*) and Russian olive (*Elaeagus angustifolia*), found along rivers and streams in the American Prairie–Russell Refuge region. Research in eastern Montana found that beavers would intensively cut cottonwood trees while seldom using salt cedar and Russian olive, resulting in higher growth rates of the invasives.[28]

At 40–70 pounds and slow afoot when on land, the loss of beavers probably reduced prey options for large carnivores. Wolves in particular sometimes depend heavily on beavers as prey.[29] Cougar, bears, coyotes, and bobcats also occasionally dine on beavers.[30]

Beaver Recovery

The beaver population of the Upper Missouri River region appears to have recovered considerably by the 1850s.[31] The noted Smithsonian Institution biologist Spencer Fullerton Baird found them abundant in the Upper Missouri and Yellowstone Rivers in 1857.[32] The naturalist George Bird Grinnell also saw beavers frequently on these rivers in 1875.[33] Grinnell noted that beaver pelts from the muddy Missouri River were less valuable than those from mountain streams, offering a possible clue to why beavers recovered in the turbid rivers of eastern Montana (and perhaps similar rivers of the Great Plains) during the last half of the 1800s while populations elsewhere on the continent continued to be heavily trapped.

State and provincial wildlife agencies across North America began beaver restoration efforts in the late 1800s and early 1900s by curbing trapping and hunting and, where populations had been extirpated, reintroducing beavers.[34] Montana's territorial government instituted the first closed season on fur-bearing animals in 1876, although effective enforcement took several years to implement.[35]

While control of commercial trapping of beavers provided a chance for populations to recover, new barriers emerged to keep beaver numbers well below historic levels both continentally and in the American Prairie–Russell Refuge region.[36] Degradation of beaver habitat by livestock grazing, starting with the open-range era in the 1880s, would have extended from the Missouri River floodplains to dozens of smaller rivers and streams across the region.[37] In contrast to bison, which drink and leave and readily graze more than ten miles from water, cattle are reluctant to graze more than a mile or two from a water source.[38] Drive the region's roads in summer, and you'll see cattle hanging out near and standing in streams and stock ponds. Attracted to the water and shade of beaver ponds, cattle trampling and browsing would have exposed streams to rapid down-cutting of the channel during heavy runoff. Elimination of beavers and their dams further accelerates flows and downcutting. In a negative feedback loop, this lowers water tables below the reach of the roots of willows, cottonwoods, and other water-loving riparian vegetation. Gone is the beaver habitat, and bringing it back takes time.[39]

The construction of dams to create stock ponds and of water diversions and spreader dikes for irrigation began in the late 1800s, surged during the 1930s, and continues today. As noted in chapter 4, the American Prairie–Russell Refuge region, at 0.7–2.6 stock ponds per square mile, has one of the highest densities in the Great Plains.[40] These structures reduce stream flow and lower peak flood levels, thereby reducing the spread of sediments and cottonwood seeds across a stream's floodplain. The result is beavers are robbed of both water and vegetation.[41] The widespread impact of livestock use, stream diversions, stock ponds, and the loss of beavers was highlighted by a riparian assessment conducted on the Charles M. Russell National Wildlife Refuge in the mid-1990s that found nearly all streams to be "nonfunctional."[42]

Big river dams also degraded beaver habitat. Historically, the Missouri River was composed of multiple channels, sloughs, backwater areas, side channels, and islands and sandbars that shifted from year to year. Beavers were well adapted to the dynamics of the river, but Euro-American enterprises in the Great Plains were not. Rivers had to be tamed, and dams were the primary tool for taming them. The construction of dams and other diversions for irrigation on the Upper Missouri River and its tributaries have reduced peak flows through the Upper Missouri River Breaks National Monument by 40–50%.[43] This alters river dynamics and seed dispersal in ways that impede willow and cottonwood regeneration. Because of reduced flow, the channel width of the Missouri River in the east end of the Upper Missouri Monument declined between the 1890s and 2006 by more than 300 feet, from 871 feet to 566 feet.[44] River ecologist Mark Dixon and colleagues paint a grim scenario when they conclude, "In a sense, the large cottonwood forests remaining across much of the floodplain are a legacy of the past and could be thought of as the 'living dead,' currently helping support a high diversity of plants and animals, but unlikely to be replaced by regeneration in the future. Reversing this trend will require innovative thinking coupled with actions to restore and replicate the dynamic river processes that originally formed and sustained the cottonwood ecosystem."[45]

The best and most extensive beaver habitat in the entire region was irreversibly destroyed when the Fort Peck Dam, completed in 1940, inundated more than 100 miles of the Missouri River, including a one-to-four-mile-wide floodplain that, with islands and river meanders, probably offered 200–300 miles of shoreline habitat for beavers. The relatively steep, rocky, and barren shoreline of the reservoir is of little use to beavers. The 1942 annual report from the C. M. Russell Refuge describes the newly constructed dam's consequences for beavers: "The rise of Fort Peck Lake has had the same effect on beaver as has been noted on whitetail deer. They have been crowded up the river in quest of food. . . . A heavy concentration of beavers is evident above the point where the flood plain is submerged. Residents along the river have advised that many dead beavers were observed this spring."[46] I suspect the reservoir reduced the beaver population of the region by half. I'll have a lot more to say about dams and fish in chapter 10.

A persistent impediment to beaver recovery in the region's upland streams is the killing of beavers as pests. A June–April 1953 report from the C. M. Russell Refuge suggests a shift in attitude about beavers was occurring then as a result of low prices for beaver fur: "Throughout eastern Montana, beaver are fast changing from highly valued fur animals to general nuisances."[47] Nearly everyone enjoys beavers until their dam plugs a culvert or irrigation ditch and floods their road, yard, or cropland. And the beaver's sourcing of the construction material, often mature cottonwoods, may leave people without cherished shade trees. The result is that beavers are frequently killed in the region wherever they show up.

Aerial surveys of beavers show that the population on the Missouri River above the Fort Peck Reservoir was fairly healthy during the 1960s–80s. Surveys counted the number of food caches in the late fall after they had been compiled by beavers for winter use. Each colony constructs one food cache, so caches are a reliable indicator of colony numbers.[48] The surveys were conducted along 105 miles of river, from around Arrow Creek in the Upper Missouri Monument to where the river enters the headwaters of the Fort Peck Reservoir. Beaver colony densities ranged from about 0.6 per mile along the upper stretch of the river, where the river is less meandrous with limited riparian vegetation for beavers, to 1.7 per mile along the lower, more meandrous, cottonwood- and willow-rich stretch in the refuge.[49] That's within the range of colony densities reported for rivers across North America.[50] A beaver colony averages around six individuals—two parents, two young-of-the-year, and two yearlings, but the number can range from 1 to 10.[51] If the average was 6 beavers per colony, this stretch of the Missouri River may have averaged 400–800 beavers during the surveys.

As noted above, however, averages mask the boom-and-bust reality of beaver numbers in semiarid ecosystems. Counts on the river fluctuate widely—as much as sixfold from one year to the next. Aerial counts along 12 miles of the Musselshell River in the C. M. Russell Refuge found even greater fluctuations, ranging from no beavers some years to more than 40 colonies other years.

Over the long-term, the challenge on the Missouri River and its major tributaries is to at least maintain and hopefully improve conditions that currently support a healthy beaver population. This is going to require strong management measures on two fronts. One is the restoration of some semblance of natural flow to the Missouri and its tributaries by altering releases from upriver dams to support the regeneration of cottonwoods. A phalanx of powerful stakeholders who use or depend on what the dams provide—electricity, irrigation, flood control, river navigation, and recreation—will need to be satisfied with any changes in flow. On only a somewhat smaller scale, reversing years of upstream dewatering for irrigation on the Musselshell, Judith, and other major tributaries of the Missouri will also be important for the health of both these rivers and the Missouri River.

The other long-term threat to tackle is the displacement of cottonwoods, willows, and other native riparian plants by Russian olive and salt cedar, among other invasive plant species.[52] Physical and chemical control of invasive plants over such large areas is labor intensive and expensive. Biological control methods can be effective in some situations, but the introduction of nonnative biological agents always poses the risk of unintended consequences in an ecosystem.[53] Where Russian olive and salt cedar are well established, eradication is nearly impossible, and so continuous, long-term control will be necessary.

Not unlike the big rivers, improving the health of smaller prairie streams depends on restoring natural flows by removing diversion and stock pond dams. Progress can also be made by limiting browsing and trampling by livestock. The C. M. Russell Refuge's riparian assessment in 2009 found substantial improvements in the health of most streams compared to the mid-1990s assessment, primarily due to the refuge's reduction in cattle grazing along these streams. As the stream and its riparian area slowly recover—the process can take many years—they begin to attract beavers. Beaver dams then accelerate recovery by slowing stream flow, capturing sediments, raising water tables, and improving riparian health.[54]

Cutting and browsing by beavers and other wildlife such as elk and deer can also impede stream restoration. This presents a chicken-and-egg conundrum: good willow and cottonwood growth is important for attracting and sustaining beavers, but willow and cottonwood growth often depends on high water tables created by beaver ponds. In the early stages of stream recovery, it may be useful in some areas to fence out or in other ways prevent extensive browsing by beavers, elk, and deer to allow willows, cottonwoods, and other plants to become established first.[55]

One method for accelerating the restoration process is the construction of beaver analogue dams (BDAs). Artificial dams are used to mimic the function of beaver dams—slow the flow, create ponds, raise the water table, and trap sediments that eventually support riparian vegetation. BDAs are usually constructed by pounding in a few wooden posts across the stream channel and weaving branches of willows or similar material between the posts to create a temporary dam. Small rocks and organic material may be added to the dam to help hold the water. They are fairly easy and inexpensive to construct. In some areas, beavers have shown up shortly after the BDAs have been constructed to add their own engineering touch to the dam.[56]

River Otter Recovery

River otter populations of the Great Plains have been slow to recover. Although river otters are highly capable of dispersing long distances, including across land, according to otter biologist Wayne Melquist and colleagues, they had failed to recolonize any significant portion of the Great Plains, including the American Prairie–Russell Refuge region, by 1977.[57] About this time, state wildlife agencies across the United States began otter reintroduction programs.[58] As of 2016, 23 states had reintroduced more than 4,000 otters.[59]

Probably because river otters never entirely disappeared from the mountains of western Montana, the state never conducted river otter reintroductions in the plains. A map published by Melquist and colleagues shows river otters had recolonized the Missouri River of eastern Montana by 1988,[60] presumably by dispersal downriver from western Montana. However, reports from Montana's and North Dakota's fish and wildlife agencies show that otters remain extremely rare in the region. From 1974 to 2021, Montana Fish, Wildlife & Parks' fur harvest program recorded only one river otter taken, that one in 1984 above the Fort Peck reservoir.[61] Farther downriver, North Dakota's Game and Fish Department has only two verified records of river otters above the Garrison Dam since 2000.[62]

Reports to the Montana Natural Heritage Program and my informal survey of fish biologists, river guides, and others who have worked on the river and Fort Peck Reservoir for years, going as far back as 1992, resulted in about 10 confirmed otter sightings on the Missouri River between Fort Benton and the North Dakota border. Two of the most recent sightings were in 2020, when Montana Fish, Wildlife & Parks pallid sturgeon biologist Luke Holmquist observed two otters wrestling on the banks of the Missouri River in the C. M. Russell Refuge, the first he had seen in his seven years working on the river.[63]

Encouraging Signs of a Fast Recovery

Although the recovery of beavers and the lush riparian habitat they create can take decades, the recovery can be quick under the right conditions. Beaver Creek, a small stream that flows east out of the Little Rocky Mountains and through American Prairie's Dry Fork management unit, offers a glimpse of the future for other streams that may more slowly recover their beaver populations. According to American Prairie superintendent Damien Austin, before American Prairie acquired Dry Fork in 2009, beaver numbers were controlled and Beaver Creek was generally a five-foot-wide channel running through the property with very little aquatic vegetation and little-to-no flowing water during dry periods. After acquisition of the property, American Prairie protected beavers and, in 2016, replaced cattle with bison on the range surrounding the stream.[64] Figure 9 shows the results. A thriving beaver population and their dams have transformed long stretches of Beaver Creek into a marsh that retains water year-round and is lined with wet meadows. The first cottonwood saplings may soon emerge to slowly grow into a riparian forest.

FIG. 9. Part of a newly constructed 100-foot beaver dam, with me standing on it, and associated marsh that American Prairie superintendent Damien Austin and the author discovered on Beaver Creek in 2022. Six years ago only a narrow stream channel existed here. Courtesy Damien Austin.

As American Prairie, the C. M. Russell Refuge, and others work to restore streams and riparian areas, Beaver Creek and potentially dozens of other streams across the region will increasingly attract beavers, beaver engineering will capture water, and the water will nourish the growth of aquatic lifelines into the semiarid prairie uplands. Perhaps, in response, the elusive river otter will make more frequent appearances. Finally, more than 150 years after the beaver's demise, its landscape-altering role will have been restored on the prairie landscape.

Western tiger salamanders are seldom seen, as they hibernate underground—sometimes in prairie dog burrows—and are active only at night during breeding season. Drawing by Erica Freese.

SIX

Ungulates

It was late afternoon on a sunny October day in 2005 by the time the bison had been rounded up from the far corners of Wind Cave National Park and run through chutes for blood sampling and sorting. The 16 bison that we—personnel of World Wildlife Fund and American Prairie—and the Wind Cave staff herded into a separate corral now needed to be loaded into two trailers, eight in each. Convincing bison to go where they don't want to go requires patience. But before the sun set we were on the road for the 10-hour drive to American Prairie's Sun Prairie management unit. It was dark by the time we reached the bridge over the Missouri River on Highway 191, still two hours from our destination, and it was threatening rain. I was driving a truck owned by American Prairie employee Bill Wilcutt, who was riding shotgun, with the trailer and eight bison in tow. By the time we turned off the highway onto the gravel road, it was raining. "Damn!" I thought. We had 40 miles to go on a gravel road that turns into a dirt road, which the rain would quickly convert to greasy, sticky Montana gumbo. Before tackling the gumbo, I had to dodge cattle that suddenly emerged from the night in the middle of the road. What a public relations nightmare it would be if we hit and kill some cows while delivering bison to the American Prairie. Then the road turned slick, and especially on the steeply banked curves, Bill was worried about flipping both his truck and the trailer with eight bison into the ditch. Go too fast and we'd slide off over the top of the embankment; too slow and we'd slip off the bottom. Who knew that gumbo on a banked curve offers a physics lesson in centrifugal force versus gravity? But both we and the other crew with eight bison in tow made it. We backed the trailers up to the quarantine corral, opened the trailer gates, and watched the bison leap out through flashlight beams of rain-filtered light into the dark recesses of the corral.

A month later we celebrated the release of the bison from quarantine with scores of invited guests. Various speeches were given, but particularly memorable and moving was the blessing by George Horse Capture Jr., a spiritual leader of the Aaniiniin Nation on the Fort Belknap Reservation. Once the corral gates were opened, the bison emerged with a quick sprint across the prairie before settling down to graze. Despite a 120-year absence, they looked like they belonged.

So began American Prairie's reintroduction of the last missing ungulate, which had been the first to disappear from the landscape under the pressure of Euro-American settlement. In 1870 native ungulates—bison, elk, mule deer, white-tailed deer, bighorn sheep, pronghorn, and moose—constituted at least 99% of all ungulates, whether in number of individuals or biomass, in the plains of Montana. Less than 1% were livestock—cattle, domestic sheep, and horses. By 1895—in 25 years or less—the ratio had flipped: 99% livestock and 1% native ungulates. The imminent naturalist George Bird Grinnell presciently forecast the fate of the region's native ungulates based on his 1875 expedition: "It may not be out of place here, to call your attention to the terrible destruction of large game, for the hides alone, which is constantly going on in those portions of Montana and Wyoming through which we passed. Buffalo, elk, mule-deer, and antelope are being slaughtered by the thousands each year, without regard to age or sex, and at all seasons."[1] Theodore Roosevelt also hinted at this rapid transition when he wrote about the fate of bison: "Never before in all history were so many large wild animals of one species slain in so short a time."[2] This rapid wild-to-domestic ungulate swap had swept across the Great Plains to convert it into one vast livestock facility.

Most estimates for the historic bison population of North America are in the range of 20–60 million.[3] Within just the plains of eastern Montana, 1–2 million must have roamed, a number in line with the fact that about 1.5 million cattle currently graze the region.[4] Though nearly extirpated from the southern and central Great Plains by the 1870s, bison were still abundant at that time in eastern Montana. Around 1870 people living at the mouth of the Musselshell River, in the heart of the American Prairie–Russell Refuge region, commonly hunted bison. The Montana forester Elers Koch reported in 1870 that his father, during a spring trip across the prairie from the Musselshell River to the Little Rockies, "traveled for three days without getting out of rifle shot of herds of buffalo which blackened the prairie."[5] As late as 1882 a bison herd of 50,000–80,000 crossed the Yellowstone River near Miles City. Another report that year estimated 30,000–50,000 bison, perhaps of the same herd, just south of there.[6]

Then they were gone. I won't unpack here the multiple causes of, and debate about, the bison's demise throughout its range, a topic examined exhaustively from every angle in countless books and articles. Few would debate the general conclusion that there were multiple causes—the hide and meat market, wanton killing, killing bison to control Native nations, forage depletion by livestock, diseases contracted from livestock, and so on.[7]

By 1885 only a few stragglers remained. Desperate to obtain specimens before bison were gone, William T. Hornaday, then chief taxidermist at the Smithsonian Institution, launched an expedition from Miles City in the plains of eastern Montana in 1886 and by the end of the year had killed 26 bison. In his letter of December 21, 1886, to Spencer F. Baird, secretary of the Smithsonian, Hornaday wrote, "The opinion is quite generally held that our 'haul' of specimens could not be equaled again in Montana by anybody, no matter what their resources for the reason that the buffalo are not there. We killed nearly all we saw and I am confident there are not over thirty-head remaining in Montana, all told. By this time next year the cowboys will have destroyed about all of this remnant."[8] He may have been right. The Montana photographer Laton A. Huffman reported that in July 1887 he saw two bulls along the Tongue River in southeast Montana. He lamented that he would probably never again see wild bison, and he never did.[9] No one is reported to have seen another in eastern Montana or elsewhere in the northern plains after then.

In the 1890s the Montana legislature set bag limits and prohibited the sale of game. Liberal bag limits—such as eight bighorn sheep, eight pronghorn, and eight deer—combined with inadequate enforcement failed to check the decline of wildlife. Consequently, in 1901 the Board of Game Commissioners created the Montana Fish and Game Department (today's Montana Fish, Wildlife & Parks—MFWP), which proceeded to hire eight game wardens to cover the entire state. This may represent the first boots on the ground aimed at conserving eastern Montana's wildlife.[10]

But it was too little, too late. With bison gone, markets for the hides and meat of the remaining wild ungulates developed and fueled intensive hunting. Elk were extirpated in eastern Montana around the mid-1880s.[11] Next in line for the slaughter were the smallest ungulates left—bighorn sheep, deer, and pronghorn (fig. 10).[12]

Considered by some biologists as a separate subspecies, the historic range of Audubon's bighorn sheep included badlands and similar rugged habitats along river corridors across the prairies of Montana, North Dakota, South Dakota, Wyoming, and Nebraska.[13] Given that the bighorn population was concentrated along the Missouri River corridor in the American Prairie–Russell Refuge region, hunting by fur trappers and river travelers may have begun reducing the bighorn population during the early 1800s. By the 1880s a new threat to bighorn populations in Montana emerged when domestic sheep numbers surged, peaking at 6 million sheep statewide around 1910, with large numbers in the American Prairie–Russell Refuge region.[14] Domestic sheep brought the double threat of increased competition for forage and novel diseases—scabies, pink eye, anthrax, pneumonia—that are deadly for bighorns. A hunter, however, may have delivered the final blow; the last recorded bighorn in eastern Montana was shot in the Missouri River breaks in 1916.[15] The total bighorn population across the western United States plummeted from an estimated 1.5–2 million to 15,000–18,200 in 1960, a 99% collapse.[16]

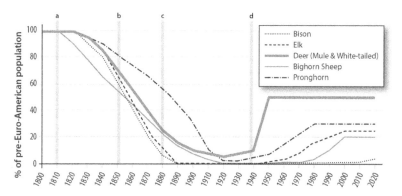

FIG. 10. Postulated population trends of six species of ungulates in the American
Prairie–Russell Refuge region from 1800 to 2020 as a percentage of population
levels before Euro-American colonization. Wide decade-to-decade fluctuations
are not shown. Vertical lines indicate the start of events with likely major effects
on the populations: (a) surge in hunting by fur trappers and traders and other
river travelers, (b) growth in hide and meat markets and unchecked slaughter,
(c) open-range livestock era followed by homesteading era, (d) previous decades'
extirpation of large carnivores followed by tighter hunting restrictions and
reintroduction of elk and bighorn sheep. Moose were likely always uncommon in
the region and thus are not shown. Created by author and Eric Cline.

Markets for both pronghorn hides and meat as well as unregulated hunting, including shooting pronghorn from trains,[17] caused
the total Great Plains population to plummet from tens of millions to an estimated 14,000 by about 1915. Montana's population
may have nose-dived from 2.5 million to 3,000 in 1922, a 99.9%
collapse.[18] Loss of forage to domestic sheep likely contributed to
the collapse in Montana. As a sign of the strength of Montana's
hide market, 12,000 pronghorn hides were exported from Bozeman in 1874. In 1924 the chairman of the Montana Fish and Game
Commission called the pronghorn's situation "precarious." The
state government recognized the peril by issuing a near total ban
on hunting of pronghorn from 1903 to 1943.[19]

White-tailed deer and mule deer were the last of the ungulate
populations to bottom out. The rugged and forested Missouri River
breaks and river bottomlands were probably their last stronghold,
but by the 1930s almost no deer remained there.[20]

The moose was the rarest ungulate in the plains of northeast Montana during pre-Euro-American times, and they remain rare today. Rather than the cool coniferous and aspen forests that moose typically prefer, the region offers marginal habitat in the forested corridors of the Missouri and Milk Rivers and the coniferous forest of the Little Rocky Mountains. Interestingly, one of the only two sightings of moose recorded by the Lewis and Clark Expedition during their entire journey was in or near the area now inundated by the Fort Peck Reservoir.[21] Moose likely met a fate similar to the other ungulates of the region, but they were always rare and information is too scarce to draw any conclusions.

Effects of Collapse on Biodiversity

One does not, without ecological consequences, delete such an eclectic mix of wild ungulate grazers and browsers and replace them with one domestic ungulate grazer.[22] Bison forage on open, rolling terrain and show a stronger preference than cattle for consuming grass rather than forbs.[23] White-tailed deer prefer forested riparian areas, where they browse primarily on woody plants. Mule deer are attracted to more open and rugged upland habitat with shrubs for browsing; this includes the Missouri River breaks, badlands, and rugged prairie terrain with brushy draws.[24] Elk are opportunistic feeders as they readily browse woody plants and graze grasses in both wooded and open habitats.[25] Pronghorn prefer sagebrush steppe habitat, where sagebrush is an important food, especially during winter, while grasses and forbs are commonly eaten during warmer months.[26] Bighorn sheep are also opportunists for which, depending on availability and season, forbs, grasses, or woody plants are important. Bighorns are highly adapted to the rugged terrain of the Missouri River breaks, resulting in little overlap in habitat use with other ungulates except mule deer.[27]

Six ungulate species with different foraging strategies make for complex interactions and effects on vegetation. (I leave moose out of this discussion because of their rarity in the region.) Historically, among ungulates, bison exerted the biggest influence on the grassland ecosystem. In addition to their effects as grazers, bison are sufficiently burly, rambunctious, and hairy to affect grassland habitat in other ways. By pawing the ground and rolling in the dirt, bison create dusty wallows up to 15 feet in diameter and a foot deep. The bare ground and water-catching depression of a wallow are ideal for the growth of forbs and, especially after heavy rains or spring snow melt, offer habitat for aquatic animals. The Great Plains toad uses wallows as breeding habitat.[28] Bison can create several wallows per acre, and thus the distinct plant and animal diversity of wallows results in greater biodiversity across the landscape than areas without wallows.[29] One estimate placed the density of presettlement wallows in the Great Pains at five per acre, or a total of 1.5 billion wallows.[30]

Bison also rub objects, typically shrubs or small trees or boulders, with their heads, horns, necks, and shoulders. The resulting damage to trees along grassland borders may have contributed to limiting the historic distribution of woody vegetation in the Great Plains.[31] Bison are also seed dispersers. Hair samples from 111 bison in a tallgrass prairie yielded 2,768 seeds representing at least 76 grass and forb species. Dung sampling yielded at least 70 species.[32] The thick hair of bison serves as nest-building material. Of 103 bird nests examined in the bison-inhabited Tallgrass Prairie Preserve of Oklahoma, 43%, representing 13 species, contained bison hair.[33]

A recent study in the tallgrass prairie of the Flint Hills of Kansas revealed how profoundly bison can affect plant biodiversity. Twenty-nine years after bison reintroduction, the number of plant species doubled in the study areas of a few hundred acres; new species appeared at the rate of about one per year. In contrast, seasonal grazing by cattle resulted in half as much of an increase. Bison wallows and bison grazing of dominant grasses likely combined to create room for the growth of new species of plants, especially forbs. Moreover, the results suggest that bison-grazed grasslands may be highly resilient to future climate changes in the Great Plains as plant species diversity on the bison-occupied study areas bounced back quickly after an intense two-year drought.[34]

Add five other ungulate species to interact with bison in the ecosystem and the picture gets more complicated. Depending on the circumstances, foraging by one species may be beneficial or detrimental to another species. Pronghorn browsing of sage-brush, for example, potentially makes room for increased grass production for bison, while grazing of grasses by bison favors increased growth of forbs and shrubs that benefits pronghorn.[35] The diverse diet of elk means that under some conditions elk graz-ing may reduce the grass available for bison, but in other cases intense browsing of shrubs by elk frees up light and space for the growth of grasses grazed by bison.[36] Elk and mule deer, espe-cially when forage is in short supply during winter, compete for browse. Browsing by large populations of elk and mule deer can, over years, eliminate woody growth and change a woodland used by white-tailed deer into a grass- and forb-dominated ecosystem that is not used by that species. Conversely, absence of browsing by these species may enable trees and shrubs to thrive and turn a grassland into a woodland.[37]

This complexity of ecological interactions among native ungu-lates is magnified by their interaction with fire and with other herbivores such as grasshoppers, jackrabbits, and prairie dogs. As mentioned in chapter 3, recently burned areas yield new plant growth that is more nutritious than that in unburned areas. This nutritious growth attracts intensive grazing by herbivores, such as bison and pronghorn, for a year or two, until they move on to eat plant growth on newly burned sites. Grasses and forbs continue to grow on the abandoned sites, creating tall and dense vegeta-tion that fuels the next lightning- or human-ignited fire, thereby starting a new cycle. This process of grazers following fire histor-ically played out over large landscapes of thousands of acres on the Great Plains. The result was a constantly shifting kaleidoscope of vegetation structure ranging from bare ground to tall and dense vegetation, a condition called "habitat heterogeneity."[38] Prairie dogs amplify habitat heterogeneity through their burrowing and by eat-ing and clipping vegetation that creates bare ground and, on the edges of their colonies, nutritious plant growth that attracts graz-ers.[39] These interactions were obliterated when native ungulate and prairie dog populations collapsed and fires were suppressed, to be replaced, today, by mostly one domestic ungulate, cattle, managed

under the heuristic noted earlier of "take half, leave half." This creates a homogeneous grassland, the antithesis of habitat heterogeneity, that erodes grassland biodiversity. The negative effect on
grassland birds, as we'll see in chapter 11, is of particular concern.[40]

To address this problem, the vast share of research and rancher
outreach programs aimed at restoring grassland biodiversity have
focused on managing livestock grazing—both with and without
fire—to create habitat heterogeneity, with bird diversity the main
metric for judging success.[41] Although livestock grazing can be
managed to create habitat heterogeneity while remaining equally
as profitable as traditional management, ranchers show widespread
resistance to adopting such practices.[42] In addition to misper-
ceptions about the costs to livestock production, this resistance
reflects ignorance about how habitat heterogeneity supports species diversity, negative attitudes toward fire and prairie dogs, and
social norms in ranch country that reject the visual appearance
of structurally diverse vegetation. Neighbors may think the last of
these conditions makes your ranch look mismanaged.[43]

The switch from native ungulates to livestock also lopped off the
role of ungulates in nourishing the food web. Largely gone were big,
nutrient-rich packages in the form of bison, elk, and other ungulates that fed predators, scavengers, decomposers, and other animal
and plant life. By the end of the 1800s, nearly all domestic ungulate
biomass production was being rounded up and loaded on trains
bound for distant markets to feed people.

Large carnivores are the most obvious losers when their ungulate prey disappear. Less appreciated are the cascading effects on
hundreds of species of smaller mammals, birds, invertebrates, and
plants. One study found 57 species of beetles and another recorded
39 species of birds and mammals feeding on elk carcasses, from
robins (*Turdus migratorious*) and least chipmunks (*Neotamias min-
imus*) to black-billed magpies (*Pica hudsonia*) and golden eagles.[44]

While scavengers are nourished aboveground, a chemical and
biological maelstrom is created under a large ungulate carcass.
Leachates from a decomposing carcass first create a toxic, nutrient-
rich hot spot that kills plant life under the carcass and alters the

biochemistry and microbes of the soil. Around the carcass, however, is a zone where the additional nutrients stimulate new plant growth and a change in plant species occupying the zone. As time passes, the bare ground under the carcass is also invaded by new plant growth. The first plant colonizers are often forbs rather than grasses, creating a plant community that is distinct from the surrounding grass-dominated prairie. Plant growth in the nutrient-rich ring around the decomposing carcass may create positive nutrient feedback by attracting grazers whose urine and dung expand the nutrient-rich patch. Decaying ungulate carcasses thereby contribute substantially to habitat heterogeneity and to species richness at diverse taxonomic levels—from plants to insects to soil microbes.[45]

Rotting ungulate carcasses also affected the aquatic realm. Pronghorn and bison swam in large numbers across the Missouri River during seasonal movements, exposing them to drowning and predation by wolves, grizzly bears, pumas, and humans waiting on the shore. Referring to pronghorn, on May 5, 1805, Meriwether Lewis wrote, "A great number of these goats are devowered by the wolves and bear at this season when they are poor and passing the river from S.W. to N.E. . . . The Indians take them in great numbers in the river at this season and in autumn when they repass to the S.W."[46] Early explorers encountered hundreds to thousands of dead bison in sections of the Missouri River. Montana pioneer Granville Stuart, during a trip up the Missouri, reported, "At one place the boat was forced to stop an hour and at another point an hour and a half for the buffalo to cross the river. Both above and below us the stream was covered with buffalo for half a mile."[47] As we'll explore in chapter 10, hundreds of thousands of bison may have drowned annually in Great Plains rivers, resulting in massive nutrient pulses affecting the rivers' ecosystems.[48]

There is much that livestock ranching could do to improve outcomes for biodiversity on grasslands across the Great Plains. The problem, as grassland ecologist Sam Fuhlendorf and colleagues note, is that "rangeland management continues to operate under the utilitarian paradigm appropriate to societal values of the 20th century and by and large has failed to provide management guidance to reverse degradation of several highly valued ecosystem ser-vices," of which biodiversity is one.[49] I see little evidence to sug-gest a sizeable shift in this paradigm in the foreseeable future. Moreover, even with the best of rancher intentions, there are lim-its to how well livestock can be managed to ecologically mimic the panoply of native ungulates and other herbivores interacting with each other, with fire, and with a complex food web of plants, decomposers, scavengers, and predators across large landscapes.[50] Restoring ecological conditions that enable prairie biodiversity to flourish and for which native ungulates are key players requires large protected areas whose management is not compromised by the exigencies of livestock production.

Bison Genetics

The near-extinction and subsequent history of plains bison have also raised concerns about the species' genetic health. Genetic variation provides the mechanism for evolutionary change and adaptation of populations to a changing environment—new dis-eases, climate change, and so on.[51] Because the bison population was reduced to around a thousand animals in the late 1800s and most of the bison herds at that time had fewer than 20 animals, some alleles were probably lost due to genetic drift. Nevertheless, plains bison appear to have retained good genetic variation at lev-els similar to other North American ungulates.[52] However, genetic conservation continues to be a concern because a large majority of the approximately 20,000 plains bison in conservation herds are in herds of fewer than 400 individuals and thus potentially sub-ject to genetic drift and inbreeding.[53]

As noted in chapter 1, artificial selection for traits in commer-cial herds raises additional genetic concerns. Both the physical characteristics and behavior of bison may be altered by produc-ers preferentially breeding animals that yield more meat and that are easier to handle. Cantankerous bulls—and their genes—are unwanted and culled from the herd. Producers generally keep a high ratio of females to males, which may alter bison genetics by reducing competition among bulls for breeding rights.[54]

Advances in genetic research uncovered another genetic issue during the 1990s—the introgression of cattle DNA in bison herds. While overlap between the range of cattle and bison before the latter's population collapse may have led to infrequent incidental hybridization between the two species (they don't interbreed readily), purposeful hybridization occurred at the turn of the 20th century when ranchers crossbred cattle with bison in hopes of creating a mixed breed—"beefalo"—with the commercial benefits of cattle and the hardiness of bison. Although the hybrids failed to yield the desired results, the legacy of these unsuccessful experiments and, possibly, incidental hybridization, is that low levels of cattle DNA likely exist in all bison herd genomes in North America. The conservation herds of Wind Cave National Park, Yellowstone National Park, and Elk Island National Park were thought to be free of cattle genes and, consequently, were preferred sources of bison for several Native nations' herds and other conservation herds, including American Prairie's. Great care has been given to maintaining the presumed genetic purity of these lineages, but recent research discovered that all of them have cattle ancestry.[55] Fortunately, the level of cattle introgression is generally less than 1% in these and other bison conservation herds, and no published research shows that cattle ancestry has affected bison morphology, physiology, or behavior.[56] Although there may be undetected subtle effects, as long as bison herds are managed to maintain low levels of cattle introgression and are allowed to behave and interact with their environment as wild bison, this genetic legacy from more than 100 years ago is of minor concern compared to other challenges facing bison restoration. The upside is that, without the need to maintain the genetic purity of some herds, there are more options for moving bison among herds to maintain and improve their genetic health.

Recovery

After decades of unregulated slaughter, public concern about game populations began to spur recovery efforts in the early 1900s. The field of wildlife management was in its earliest formative years and the state of Montana had little ability to enforce wildlife regulations and undertake other management actions. MFWP got a major boost to its management capacity when the U.S. Congress passed the 1937 Pittman-Robertson Act, which created an excise tax on firearms, archery equipment, and ammunition to generate funding for state wildlife conservation programs.[57]

Recovery of ungulate populations came in spurts in the American Prairie–Russell Refuge region during the 1900s.[58] Early recovery efforts for deer, elk, pronghorn, and bighorn sheep depended, first, on the state establishing and enforcing harvest bans and limits. Translocations of elk and bighorn sheep to repopulate the region were crucial. The creation of the Charles M. Russell National Wildlife Refuge in 1936 was instrumental in offering additional protection to wild ungulates and their habitats. These measures led to partial recovery of all ungulate species except one—bison. The recovery of wild ungulates, however, has been stymied by habitat loss and fragmentation, conflicts with farmers and ranchers, and in large part because of the latter, hunting quotas designed to keep populations sufficiently low to avoid such conflicts.

I provide below ballpark estimates of *potential* future population sizes for each species. I emphasize "potential" because my estimates are not predictions. Nature is far too unpredictable for that, as Yellowstone Park's elk and bison populations exemplify. Except for having mountain goats (a nonnative species), Yellowstone's Northern Range has the same assembly of ungulates and large predators that prey on them as the historic assembly of the American Prairie–Russell Refuge region. In the 1990s the Northern Range elk herd totaled around 15,000–20,000 and the bison herd about 400–600. By the 2010s the elk herd had declined to about 5,000 while the bison herd grew to 4,000 despite the removal some years of more than 1,000 bison.[59] These numbers will continue to change. Although the drop in elk numbers has been attributed to the reintroduction of wolves to Yellowstone in 1995, multiple causes—hunting, drought, and predation by grizzly bears, black bears, puma, and wolves—were probably involved.[60] This offers only a glimpse of the complex interactions and population fluctuations experienced by ungulates, predators, and plants in the

Northern Range.[61] The lesson is this: ungulate populations can and will unpredictably fluctuate widely due to often unpredictable and difficult-to-determine causes, especially once large carnivores are added to the mix.

With the above caveats, a few basic ecological principles guide population estimates. The size of an ungulate population, or of nearly any population, is determined by both bottom-up and top-down forces.[62] Bottom-up regulation occurs when the population's size is determined by food availability, mediated by competition for the same food from other species. Ecologists call this the carrying capacity of the habitat for a species.[63] Top-down regulation occurs when predators or parasites keep the population below what the habitat could otherwise support. Occasionally, factors that are neither bottom-up nor top-down, such as a catastrophic flood or immobilizing deep snow, kill large numbers in a population. Any one of these three types of population control may be dominant at different times, and they are usually interactive. For example, a drought may reduce plant productivity, resulting in undernourished elk that are more susceptible to predation or a harsh winter. Long, harsh winters themselves, a common occurrence in northeast Montana, can directly lead to ungulate deaths or render them more vulnerable to predation. Figuring out how these multiple interactive factors affect ungulate populations is mindbogglingly difficult.

Ecologists and rangeland managers generally start with a bottom-up approach to estimate the numbers of wild ungulates or livestock that a habitat can support. This approach involves two basic inputs: (1) the amount of aboveground plant tissue produced annually, called the annual net primary productivity (ANPP), and (2) the amount of ANPP consumed by each species of wild ungulate or livestock. Based on these inputs, and assuming bison are allowed to consume 25% of ANPP, the bison stocking rate on Bureau of Land Management (BLM) lands leased by American Prairie is 8.6 bison per square mile. The stocking rate is the same for domestic cows, since one bison and one cow are considered to have the same rate of plant consumption. Based on this, and knowing how much other ungulates consume compared to bison (or cows), one can estimate how much of the ANPP is being eaten by all the ungulates in a particular area. Compared to one bison, one elk consumes approximately 0.7 as much forage, mule deer and white-tailed deer 0.19, pronghorn 0.13, and bighorn sheep 0.16. Similar to guidelines used elsewhere in the West, for my ballpark estimates below, I assume that populations of wild ungulates would consume around 30–40% of ANPP.[64] The remaining 60–70% would be used by smaller herbivores, lost to trampling and other causes, and retained for plant growth and reproduction.

A source of uncertainty in making estimates of potential population sizes is how the six species of ungulates will divide up the ANPP. As explained above, depending on the circumstances, herbivory by one species may reduce, increase, or have no effect on plant production for another. Nonungulate herbivores—grasshoppers, jackrabbits, and so on—also have a say in this. Overlaying all these interactions is the fact that ANPP in any one locale in the mixed-grass prairie of the Northern Great Plains can regularly vary more than 50% from year to year, with large variation also among sites only a few miles apart.[65]

Human hunting, predation by carnivores, and disease will be the top-down forces limiting the future growth and size of ungulate populations in the region. As experiences in Yellowstone's Northern Range and other ecosystems demonstrate, putting numbers on how top-down forces will affect ungulate populations, especially in an ecosystem with several species of ungulates and of carnivores that prey on them, is a questionable exercise—even more so in an ecosystem such as the mixed-grass prairie, where ecologists have never had the chance to study the full suite of native ungulates and carnivores. My estimates of potential ungulate numbers therefore generally ignore top-down forces.

I based my estimates on a 3.2-million-acre landscape—American Prairie's goal for the total protected area—and assume it's all terrestrial (i.e., excludes the 360-square-mile Fort Peck Reservoir within the C. M. Russell Refuge).

Bison

In addition to bison from Wind Cave National Park, American Prairie has introduced bison from Elk Island National Park in Alberta, a herd whose history is especially relevant to bison restoration in eastern Montana. Around 1873 Walking Coyote, of the Kalispel (Pend d'Oreille) Nation, captured for safekeeping several bison from north-central Montana. Several years later Walking Coyote sold a few bison from his growing herd to Michel Pablo and Charles Allard, ranchers on the Flathead Indian Reservation. In 1907 bison from the Pablo-Allard herd were bought by the Canadian government and introduced to Elk Island National Park. Most of the genetic ancestry of Elk Island bison is probably from the Montana animals captured by Walking Coyote back in the early 1870s,[66] and thus their reintroduction to American Prairie constitutes something of a homecoming.

There is a glaring bison-shaped hole in Montana's efforts to restore populations of wild ungulates. The resistance to bison often begins with rancher concerns about transmission of diseases like brucellosis from bison to cattle, despite multiple layers of safeguards to ensure that bison are brucellosis-free when reintroduced onto American Prairie or elsewhere. More importantly, I believe, wild bison are symbols of wildness that are perceived as threats to rancher livelihoods and the ranch community way of life. Because of this resistance and strong rancher influence in Montana's political system, bison are legal outliers among the region's native ungulates. Bison in Montana are classified as either "domestic livestock" or "game animal." American Prairie–owned bison are legally "domestic bison," which, like other domestic livestock, fall under the regulatory jurisdiction of the Montana Department of Livestock.[67] This means that BLM and Montana's Department of Natural Resources and Conservation consider American Prairie's bison to be domestic livestock for American Prairie's grazing allotments on BLM and state lands. The upside of this is that the policies enable American Prairie to replace cattle with bison on BLM and state grazing lands.

In 2019 MFWP released the final environmental impact statement titled *Bison Conservation and Management in Montana*, which evaluated the feasibility of bison restoration in the state and presented alternatives for restoring bison under various land ownership options. Surveys found 70% of Montanan's support restoration of a public bison herd, including on and around the C. M. Russell Refuge.[68] However, because the agricultural community strongly opposes wild or free-roaming bison anywhere in the state, no on-the-ground progress has been made toward a state-sponsored program to restore wild bison to the plains of eastern Montana.

Bison are habitat generalists and could occupy nearly all the American Prairie–Russell Refuge region with the exception of extremely rugged terrain and densely forested areas with little grass such as the Little Rockies. As of 2023 American Prairie had roughly 1,000 bison, the number limited by grazing allotments approved to date by BLM for bison and the practicalities of fencing and managing bison on multiple management units. To keep bison numbers within the carrying capacity of the land, American Prairie employs a combination of hunting, translocation of bison to other herds, and birth control. There is currently no disease or nonhuman predator to inhibit population growth. In the future, predation by wolves is unlikely to be a significant limiting factor. Where bison populations are large and healthy, wolf predation by itself probably has little or no effect on bison population size.[69] We'll look at wolf predation on bison more in the next chapter.

Although the BLM-approved stocking rate for American Prairie's bison translates into more than 40,000 bison on 3.2 million acres (assuming bison consume 25% of ANPP), that's based on a formula catered to beef production. My estimate assumes bison will use somewhat less, perhaps 15–20% of ANPP, for a population of around 25,000–35,000. Given sufficient land and a 20% annual growth rate (roughly doubling every four years),[70] American Prairie's current bison herd could grow to more than 30,000 through natural reproduction in 20 years.

To help restore and maintain bison populations and their genetic integrity across North America, American Prairie has contributed hundreds of bison to multiple Native nations and state and federal herds, as well as to the Smithsonian Institution's National Zoo for educational purposes. With the right ironclad assurances by the state of Montana that it is prepared to build a wild, free-roaming bison population, American Prairie could consider placing its bison in the public trust for the state to manage. Until that time, American Prairie will retain ownership while managing bison as if they were a public trust resource managed for conservation purposes and for public benefit.[71] I'll return to the idea of free-roaming bison at the end of this chapter.

Elk

Because of their popularity among big game hunters, elk were first in line for state-level restoration efforts. After an absence of more than 50 years, in the early 1950s about 160 elk captured in Yellowstone National Park were translocated to the Missouri River breaks region, including the C. M. Russell Refuge. The breaks population grew quickly, perhaps aided by the scarcity of pumas and absence of wolves and grizzly bears, which had been extirpated from the region.[72]

As habitat generalists, elk may regularly use nearly all habitat types in the American Prairie–Russell Refuge region. Currently, however, elk are concentrated in the mostly forested breaks habitat of the C. M. Russell Refuge. Elk are scarce on the prairie uplands on the north and south sides of the refuge where MFWP limits their numbers because of landowner intolerance. MFWP's population goal is around 1 elk per square mile—about 5,000 elk—within an area of nearly 5,000 square miles in the region's breaks habitat.[73] The population has often been up to twice this size. From 2000 to 2012, elk densities in different regions of the C. M. Russell Refuge ranged from 1.2 to 6.9 per square mile.[74] Allowing elk to occupy upland prairies could greatly increase their numbers. A range of 3–5 elk per square mile seems reasonable for estimating future numbers on 3.2 million acres. That would yield 15,000–20,000 elk consuming 7–11% of ANPP.

While hunting is currently the primary top-down factor limiting the elk population, predation by wolves, pumas, and grizzly bears may become an important limiting factor in the future.[75] Elk behavior could also be affected. If elk respond to predation by pumas and wolves as they do in Yellowstone,[76] during the day elk will concentrate in riparian forests and the Missouri River breaks and avoid open grasslands where day-hunting wolves are found. By night, elk will concentrate in the open grasslands and avoid habitats conducive to the puma's ambush mode of hunting.

Chronic wasting disease, a neurodegenerative disease that is fatal in cervids (moose, elk, and deer) has emerged as a potential problem for elk recovery. It has not yet widely infected elk in eastern Montana, but could readily spread.[77] There is evidence, however, that elk populations may evolve some resistance to the disease.[78]

Deer

Mule deer of the American Prairie–Russell Refuge region are concentrated in and near the Missouri River breaks where they make extensive use of the rugged terrain, but they also use brushy draws across the upland prairie. The best habitat for white-tailed deer in the region is the bottomlands of the Missouri River and its major tributaries and a few other patches of forest/shrub habitat in the region, often in association with cropland. At least half of the American Prairie–Russell Refuge region is not suitable or occupied habitat for white-tailed deer.[79]

The recovery of mule and white-tailed deer populations came quickly during the 1940s and 1950s. In fact, from 1938 to 1948 mule deer exhibited what ecologists call "irruptive growth," when the population increases exponentially and overshoots the carrying capacity of the habitat. The classic long-term study of the two species by Montana biologist Richard Mackie and colleagues identifies several changes that may have helped the recovery of the Missouri River breaks mule deer population, including tighter hunting restrictions, restoration of natural habitat due to a dwindling human population, and reduced populations of predators.[80]

However, several factors have probably kept deer populations below their levels before Euro-American settlement. Tens of thousands of acres of forest and shrubland habitat were lost when the Fort Peck Dam flooded Missouri River bottomlands, and dewatering, livestock, and loss of beaver degraded upland streams and riparian areas. Predation by pumas and coyotes may be a factor under some conditions; Mackie and colleagues found that coyotes accounted for around 90% of fawn mortality in the Missouri River breaks.[81] Hunting will continue to be a primary top-down factor keeping mule and white-tailed deer populations below levels that the habitat could support. MFWP sets hunting quotas with the goal of maintaining deer populations high enough to satisfy hunters but low enough to avoid landowner complaints about deer eating hay and grain crops and to avert habitat degradation caused by excessive browsing of food plants.[82]

The American Prairie–Russell Refuge will be able to support more deer when forage competition with livestock and landowner complaints are reduced. Counts on the C. M. Russell Refuge from 2000 to 2014 averaged 4.1 mule deer per square mile, but lightly hunted areas had a density of around 6.4 per square mile.[83] Mackie and colleagues report an average density of 9.4 per square mile between 1960 and 1987 in the Missouri River breaks, but densities in open prairie and badlands habitat were usually less than half that.[84] Relatively good mule deer habitat exists throughout the region; thus, for a ballpark estimate, I assume 5,000 square miles could support an average of 4–6 mule deer per square mile, yielding a total population of 20,000–30,000. White-tailed deer will be a fraction of that, perhaps 4,000–6,000. This many deer would consume about 3–4% of ANPP.

Mule deer and white-tailed deer infected with chronic wasting disease have been found across much of the plains of eastern Montana. Controlling the disease is a top priority for MFWP and state wildlife agencies across the country. Unless effective methods are found to control or natural selection results in animals more resistant to the disease, substantially lower deer populations may result.[85]

Pronghorn

Pronghorn have made a modest comeback in the American Prairie–Russell Refuge region since their population nadir in the early 1900s. Perhaps more than any other ungulate, large fluctuations characterize the pronghorn population of eastern Montana. Aerial surveys in recent years indicate about 11,000–13,000 pronghorn inhabit a survey area of roughly 10,000 square miles—slightly more than 1 pronghorn per square mile—within the American Prairie–Russell Refuge region.[86] This is similar to nearby areas of western North Dakota where, from 1974 to 2013, pronghorn densities averaged less than 1 per square mile to 2 per square mile, with wide year-to-year fluctuations.[87] In contrast, pronghorn in northeast Wyoming have averaged about 8 per square mile, with some years well above 10 per square mile.[88]

Severe winters and other factors may be keeping numbers low in the American Prairie–Russell Refuge region despite an abundance of seemingly good habitat. The region's pronghorn are near the northern extent of their range in North America. They are well adapted to the heat and aridity of the region's summers, but severe winters can be demanding for them.[89] The severe winter of 1964–65 probably reduced the region's pronghorn population by half.[90] By the early 2000s the pronghorn population was relatively healthy, but then it was knocked back by at least 70% by blue-tongue virus and the severe winter of 2010–11.[91] More than 2,000 pronghorn that had moved south of the Fort Peck Reservoir during the winter were stranded on the south side by high waters in the spring and presumably died from drowning and after exhausting nearby forage.[92] Train strikes killed several hundred more as the pronghorn congregated on the tracks to avoid the deep snow.

Apparently as an adaptation to winter conditions, large numbers of pronghorn in the American Prairie–Russell Refuge region undertake spring migrations of 40 to more than 100 miles to southern Saskatchewan.[93] Migration routes and local movements, however, are impeded by fences, roads, railroads, irrigation canals, reservoirs, cropland, and other human activity. Because pronghorn are averse to jumping fences, the ubiquitous fences in the region are especially problematic. Some of their migration route is crisscrossed with four to eight miles of fence per square mile.[94] The result is pronghorn expend more energy avoiding these features, have less access to good habitat, and experience significant mortality.[95]

Because of their speed, pronghorn are subject to low predation levels once they reach a few weeks of age. Predators of pronghorn fawns range from golden eagles to badgers, but coyotes are by far the primary predators of fawns and in some cases have been a factor limiting population size.[96] Whether predation is at times limiting pronghorn numbers in the American Prairie–Russell Refuge region is not known.

Given how poorly we understand the diverse factors affecting pronghorn survival and reproduction, forecasting future pronghorn numbers is a fraught task. Perhaps a transition to biodiversity-driven management on 5,000 square miles of land can improve pronghorn habitat and, through defragmentation, their access to it. More work is needed to enable migratory pronghorn to move more freely across a vast region from Saskatchewan to south of the Missouri River in Montana. Conservation easements and other incentives are being used by The Nature Conservancy, U.S. Fish and Wildlife Service, and MFWP to conserve habitat on private lands along the pronghorn's migratory pathways. Fortunately, the migratory pathways of greater sage-grouse in the region (see chapter 11) overlap considerably with those of the pronghorn so that these conservation investments benefit both species.[97]

Though admittedly speculative (and hopeful), maybe such efforts would enable pronghorn to reach a density of 4 per square mile on suitable habitat. Assuming three-quarters of the 5,000 square miles is suitable habitat, that would yield a population of around 15,000–20,000 consuming less than 1% of ANPP. I expect, however, that pronghorn will continue to exhibit larger population fluctuations than any other ungulate in the region.

Bighorn Sheep

Bighorn sheep are the habitat specialist among Great Plains ungulates. They require very rugged terrain, such as the Missouri River breaks and isolated mountain ranges of eastern Montana. Currently, bighorn sheep occupy only 6% of their historic range in the plains of eastern Montana, and roughly half of that historic range is in the American Prairie–Russell Refuge region, where they mostly inhabit the rugged Missouri River breaks.[98]

Several reintroductions of bighorns from 1943 to 1980 created three relatively isolated herds in the American Prairie–Russell Refuge region. A small population of fewer than 100 inhabits the Little Rocky Mountains.[99] A second population, numbering about 1,000 animals, is primarily in the Upper Missouri Monument on both sides of the river. The third population, averaging a minimum of 255 animals in recent years, is on the north side of the Missouri River in mostly the C. M. Russell Refuge.[100] The combined total of about 1,300 animals makes this population one of the most important in Montana and the largest in the Northern Great Plains.

MFWP limits the size and range of these herds to avert die-offs caused by disease and to avoid bighorns eating grain crops. Disease problems are more likely under high bighorn densities, and any range expansion of bighorns increases the risk of disease transmission from local herds of domestic sheep.[101] Pneumonia, one of the diseases commonly transmitted, can trigger a die-off of 30–90% of a bighorn population. Outbreaks can continue in the herd for several years and recovery of the population can be slow, if it all. The main management approach is to keep bighorn population densities low and keep bighorn and domestic sheep widely separated on the landscape. Consequently, a buffer zone between bighorns and domestic sheep of at least 9 miles is recommended, but bighorn rams wander much farther than that and so 20 miles or more seems prudent.[102] Long term, the removal of a handful of domestic sheep herds could greatly diminish the risk of disease and free up tens of thousands of acres for expanding the bighorn populations on the American Prairie–Russell Refuge.

Based on suitable habitat located within areas of primarily public lands, five new bighorn reintroduction sites in the American Prairie–Russell Refuge region have been identified.[103] More suitable habitat for reintroduction exists on private lands. A population of 4,000–5,000 seems possible, especially if some private lands can be freed up for bighorn sheep occupation. Their consumption of ANPP in the region would be negligible.

Moose

While moose populations have been declining in much of their core areas in the forested mountain and hills of western Montana, their numbers have grown during the last two to three decades in northeast Montana and adjacent regions of Saskatchewan and North Dakota.[104] Probably a few dozen inhabit the American Prairie–Russell Refuge region. Although restoration of beavers, streams, and riparian areas will provide more moose habitat, their numbers will surely remain low.

Creating More Space to Roam

The above estimates suggest that up to roughly 100,000 native ungulates could inhabit the 3.2-million-acre American Prairie–Russell Refuge protected area. They would consume in the neighborhood of one-third of the area's annual net plant production. This is similar to estimates for total ungulate numbers in potential mixed-grass prairie reserves in nearby regions.[105] That number leaves plenty of plant resources for other wildlife and provides something of a buffer to the vicissitudes of the region's climate. The variable climate and a host of other factors will inevitably result in wide population fluctuations. Bison can be expected to occupy center stage by constituting more than half of total ungulate biomass, but elk, mule deer, and pronghorn may often be numerically as common and, like bison, will be widely dispersed across the landscape. White-tailed deer and bighorn sheep will be more restricted in range and fewer in number. Moose will be the rarity that elicits the wide-eyed look whenever someone is lucky enough to see one. To be clear, over the long term, I do not consider these population estimates to be management goals. Once the protected landscape is big enough, let the wildlife work it out among themselves.

A massive, long-term research program would be required to fully understand how this transition from livestock dominated by one species back to a multispecies system of grazers and browsers will contribute to restoring the natural diversity and rhythms of the region's ecosystems. As described in other chapters, it is sure to profoundly influence multiple trophic levels, from the plants they consume and resulting effects on habitat complexity to the predators, scavengers, and decomposers they nourish.

The final thought in this chapter is about bison and barriers, both physical and mental. Dams, fences, and highways are common barriers to movement by fish and wildlife. But in the Great Plains, and North America generally, these barriers are not built to intentionally confine wildlife—except for one species. Bison are the only wildlife species in North America that are habitually fenced in. The American bison—the Great Plains' most iconic species, an animal that exudes wildness, the U.S. National Mammal—is locked up. Look across public lands in the West and you'll find that livestock have more freedom to roam than bison. As two preeminent bison authorities, Keith Aune and Glenn Plumb, note in their book, *Theodore Roosevelt & Bison Restoration on the Great Plains*, the result is "a common public perception that bison no longer belong on intact grassland landscapes except behind a fence."[106] A severe form, I'd argue, of shifting baseline syndrome raising its ugly head.

For large-scale bison restoration to succeed, we have to tear down mental barriers to imagining what's possible. Aune and Plumb envision "shared stewardship" as a path toward that goal: "We have only just begun to reimagine the North American prairies and woodlands, painted with bison managed cooperatively under shared stewardship—with large herds grazing, wallowing, nourishing people and predators, sustaining the belief that we can work toward this large-scale, ambitious and long-term vision."[107]

What might such shared stewardship look like? One scenario might be to create one vast region for bison through cooperative management involving Grasslands National Park; the Bitter Creek region; American Prairie; C. M. Russell Refuge; Native nations of the Fort Belknap, Fort Peck, and Rocky Boy's Indian Reservations; and private ranchers who wish to cooperate (see figs. 1 and 2 in the introduction). The Bitter Creek region is in the center of these land jurisdictions and covers about a million acres of mostly intact prairie with substantial acreages of BLM and state trust lands interspersed with private landowners. Four bison herds already surround the Bitter Creek region, one in Grasslands National Park, one on American Prairie, and one each on the Fort Belknap and Fort Peck Indian Reservations. A little farther to the west, the Rocky Boy's Indian Reservation recently established a herd with bison contributed by American Prairie. Moreover, formal discussions have begun to explore the potential for reintroducing bison to the C. M. Russell Refuge. Shared stewardship among all or most of these land managers could open a vast region for a population of perhaps 50,000 or more bison that could roam more than 100 miles north and south, east and west. In some areas bison and livestock might graze the same land with a benefit sharing arrangement among landowners, as has been proposed for the Henry Mountains in Utah where bison and livestock coexist on BLM grazing lands.[108] Hundreds of miles of fence could be pulled as virtual fencing technology develops and renders physical fences obsolete.[109] Two or three wildlife overpasses or underpasses may need to be built on Highway 2. It will take time and tireless work, but the result could be a landscape transformed for bison, for other Great Plains wildlife, and for people. Imagine.

Pronghorn horns are unique among the world's ungulates for consisting of a bony core and an outer keratinous sheath that it sheds and grows back annually. Drawing by Erica Freese.

SEVEN

Carnivores

Aldo Leopold, in his inimitable and efficient way, wrote in 1944, "One gets the impression that wolves were incredibly abundant in the buffalo days, were severely decimated by commercialized poisoning for their fur in the 1870s, regained abundance in the 1880s when cattle and sheep replaced the buffalo as a dependable food supply, held their own for two more decades during a regime of graft-riddled bounty systems, and were finally wiped off the map when the U.S. Biological Survey, in 1914, began its federally supported predator-control campaign, during which bounties were discarded in favor of salaried trappers."[1] Leopold, who helped organize and later directed this campaign, confessed, "I personally believed, at least in 1914 when predator control began, that there could not be too much horned game, and that the extirpation of predators was a reasonable price to pay for better big game hunting."[2]

Not only did wolves pay the price for getting in the way of Euro-American values at the time, so did the grizzly bear and puma. The demise of a fourth carnivore, the diminutive swift fox, was like roadkill—more incidental than intentional. It was in the wrong place at the wrong time as the traffic of Euro-American settlement swept across the Great Plains. Two other carnivore collapses, the river otter (chapter 5) and black-footed ferret (chapter 9), are covered elsewhere.

The pre-Columbian range of grizzly bears extended across the mixed- and short-grass prairies of the Great Plains.[3] The grizzly bear is a generalist omnivore that opportunistically exploits a diversity of plant and animal foods in habitats ranging from grasslands to forests. Grizzly bears commonly feed on elk and bison if they are present.[4] Because abundant bison are considered an asset for supporting grizzly bear populations,[5] bison probably constituted a large share of the grizzly diet on the prairie as they preyed on calves and weakened animals and scavenged winter- and wolf-killed carcasses. The Lewis and Clark Expedition's frequent encounters with grizzlies along the Missouri River suggest the bears were finding food there as well, whether plant resources, beavers, fish stranded in backwaters, or ungulates crossing the river. With usually just one to five miles of rugged breaks habitat separating the upland prairies from the Missouri River, grizzlies could have readily moved between these habitats in search of food.

Based on Lewis and Clark observations, the density of grizzly bears along a one-mile-wide path of the expedition's entire route has been estimated at eight per 100 square miles.[6] But the estimated density would have been substantially higher in the American Prairie–Russell Refuge region, since many more bears were seen there than elsewhere along the expedition's route. We have no basis for estimating what grizzly bear densities may have been away from the river on the upland prairies.

Black bears were never common in the American Prairie–Russell Refuge region, as their preferred habitat is generally mid- to high-elevation coniferous forests. The few that inhabit the Little Rocky Mountains as well as other isolated mountain ranges in the plains of north-central Montana are infrequent visitors to the intervening valleys and plains.[7] Consequently, I don't attempt to assess black bear population trends.

As an ambush predator, pumas prefer the rugged and often forested habitats of the Missouri River breaks, riparian areas, and isolated mountain ranges of the American Prairie–Russell Refuge region. Their stealthy, nocturnal habits render them less visible, precluding any attempt to estimate their historic abundance based on observations by early explorers. However, given the abundance of their favorite prey—deer, elk, and bighorn sheep—a puma population of several hundred could have existed historically in the region.

Observations of early explorers and settlers and predator bounty records from eastern Montana in the late 1800s indicate that wolves were abundant in the American Prairie–Russell Refuge region.[8] Wolves are habitat generalists and may occur in almost any habitat with sufficient ungulate prey. Nearly the entire American Prairie–Russell Refuge region is suitable wolf habitat inhabited by prey such as deer, elk, and bison. Just how abundant wolves were historically depends in large part on their skill in harvesting the biggest potential protein source—the vast herds of bison. Journal entries from the Lewis and Clark Expedition suggest that wolves were up to the task. On May 5, 1805, on the eastern edge of the American Prairie–Russell Refuge region, Lewis wrote, "We scarcely see a gang of buffaloe without observing a parsel of those faithfull shepherds on their skirts in readiness to take care of the mamed and wounded."[9] Two weeks later, near Slaughter River (today's Arrow Creek, on American Prairie's westernmost management unit), where the party encountered the remains of more than 100 bison along the river, Lewis wrote, "We saw a great many wolves in the neighbourhood of these mangled carcasses they were fat and extremely gentle"[10]—so gentle that Clark killed one with a spear! With bison numbering in the thousands, at any one time there must have been plenty of animals vulnerable to wolf predation—wayward calves, injured or sick animals, weakened old cows and bulls.

The domestic-cat-sized swift fox, so named because of its sprinting speed of 25–35 miles per hour, was historically common in the plains of eastern Montana. Endemic to the short- and mixed-grass prairies of the Great Plains, its historic range extended from southern Alberta and Saskatchewan to northern Texas. It prefers areas of short vegetation and sparse shrub cover that give it long sight lines, perhaps to help it evade coyotes, its number-one killer. The fox's burrows provide safety from coyotes as well as golden eagles. It is an opportunistic hunter, feeding on insects, birds, small mammals, and occasionally carrion.[11]

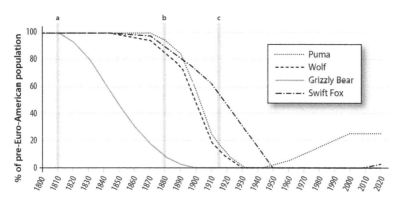

FIG. 11. Postulated population trends of four species of carnivores in the American Prairie–Russell Refuge region from 1800 to 2020 as a percentage of population levels before Euro-American colonization. Vertical lines indicate the start of events with likely major effects on the populations: (a) rapid growth in number of fur trappers and traders on Missouri River, which likely led to frequent encounters with, and high mortality of, grizzly bears; (b) collapse of native ungulate prey populations and initiation of state bounties for pumas and wolves; (c) start of U.S. government program to eradicate predators. Information about black bears is insufficient to estimate a trend line. Created by author and Eric Cline.

Four Carnivores Collapse

Leopold's words at the start of this chapter reveal not only the multiple layers of persecution suffered by wolves and other large carnivores but also that even such enlightened ecological thinkers as Leopold, before his conversion to "Thinking like a Mountain"—the oft-cited essay where he explained his realization that wolves also belong in the ecosystem—considered large predators expendable.[12]

Three waves of Euro-American influence—the fur trade, collapse of prey populations, and conflicts with humans and livestock—forced the collapse of plains populations of the wolf, puma, and grizzly bear (fig. 11). The rapid surge in beaver trappers and collapse of beaver populations in the early 1800s may have delivered the first glancing blows. All three large carnivores opportunistically prey on beavers, and in some cases, beavers are a significant part of their diet.[13] Moreover, trappers must have often encountered and killed the carnivores, especially those raiding their beaver traps. More would be shot as the number of gun-toting river travelers increased with steamboat access up the Missouri River.

The next blow was probably in the form of traps and poisoned baits set for wolves and for their smaller canid cousins, the coyote and swift fox, for the fur trade. From about 1840–1900 the recorded North American harvest of wolf pelts averaged roughly 10,000 annually.[14] The diary of C. M. Lee describes how wolves were killed for the fur trade while he lived at the mouth of the Musselshell River in the middle of the American Prairie–Russell Refuge region in 1868–72. Wolves were a nearly constant presence, as were bison, pronghorn, and other ungulates. Lee frequently described "wolfers" preparing strychnine-laced bison carcasses and returning later to find dozens of dead wolves. One wolfing party came back with 320 wolf skins after one outing.[15]

The combination of being highly intimidating, shot whenever encountered, and incidentally killed by poisoned baits, as well as steadily losing an important protein source in the form of bison, was too much for a slow-reproducing carnivore like the grizzly bear to withstand. It was gone from the American Prairie–Russell Refuge region by around 1880. The demise of the grizzly bear was widespread in the lower 48 U.S. states, where it suffered a 98% collapse in both the range it occupied and its population, from probably more than 50,000 in 1800 to fewer than 1,000 by 1975.[16]

Wolves and pumas in the plains of eastern Montana would hang on for a few more decades. Extirpation of bison from the plains of Montana by the early 1880s and the near total disappearance of the other native ungulates by the end of the century would have been devastating to wolves and pumas as well as to grizzly bears. Euro-American settlers, however, served up an alternative that was sure to create conflict: replace hard-to-catch and dangerous native prey with, as Leopold noted, a "dependable food supply" of slow and unformidable sheep and cattle.

Montana first placed a bounty on pumas in 1879. Bounty records are sporadic before 1900, but annual records for the period between 1900 and 1931 show a steady decline in bounties paid statewide, and by the mid-1920s only one or two were reported annually. Records for that period show only 42 puma bounties paid in counties of the American Prairie–Russell Refuge region.[17] The few bounties paid suggests a low puma population, perhaps because their prey base of deer and elk had collapsed by 1900. Except for a handful of stragglers that may have persisted in the most remote haunts of the Missouri River breaks and surrounding isolated mountain ranges, the puma was gone from northeastern Montana by 1930. The big cat met the same fate across the entire Great Plains.[18]

The wolf's demise is well documented. According to a 1907 report by Vernon Bailey to the U.S. Department of Agriculture describing his nationwide survey of large carnivores, wolves were widespread and common in the late 1800s across the plains of eastern Montana. He wrote that wolves were "common in 1893 around Alzada and Powderville (southeast corner of Montana) and were very destructive to stock, especially calves and colts." In "1894 wolf tracks were common" in various regions, including the "Musselshell River and around the Big Snowy Mountains, while packs of as many as 16 were reported 20 miles north of Great Falls."[19]

Montana instituted a bounty on wolves in 1884. Now in addition to being killed for the value of their pelts, wolves were shot, trapped, and poisoned for bounty payments. This meant more traps and strychnine-laced baits, which killed any number of scavenging species, from coyotes and swift foxes to golden eagles and black-billed magpies. Bounties on 5,450 wolf pelts were paid that first year, mostly in the plains of eastern Montana. Statewide, bounty payments for wolves declined from a high of about 4,000–6,000 annually around the turn of the century, to 1,000–2,000 annually around 1910, to none by the mid-1920s. At its peak in the late 1890s, roughly 1,500 wolves were killed annually for bounties in the American Prairie–Russell Refuge region. Wolves, as well as animus toward wolves, must have thrived in the plains of eastern Montana compared to the western mountains. Counties in the American Prairie–Russell Refuge region plus Musselshell and Rosebud counties to the south tallied 15,184 wolves killed from 1900 to 1931, or 45% of all wolves taken in Montana from an area representing just 25% of the state's land area.[20] The number killed may be considerably higher because, Bailey noted, many wolves were killed for which no bounty was reported.

But state-level efforts alone were not enough. And so, as Leopold lamented, in 1915 the U.S. Congress first appropriated funds for the eradication of wolves, coyotes, and other predators. This signaled the end for wolves across nearly the entire lower 48 states. Wolves were extinct in Montana by 1936, but the last ones in the eastern plains disappeared years earlier.[21]

The adaptable coyote survived and, in fact, probably thrived during this government-sponsored predator purge. A note from the chief of the U.S. Bureau of Biological Survey in its 1923 annual report is telling: "With the practical elimination of the gray or timber wolf over much of the range country of the Western United States, cattlemen have discovered that heavy losses of calves heretofore attributed to wolves have evidently been due to coyotes."[22] With wolves nearly gone but coyotes still abundant, the bureau had a new mission. It responded by churning out ever more predator poison. By 1924, 3,567,000 strychnine-laced baits were spread across 284,400 square miles.[23] But dogs also readily gulped down the baits and, as a result, in many areas puma hunters could no longer use hounds to hunt pumas. The thrill of the chase and promised bounty disappears quickly while watching your favorite hound violently convulse and die from strychnine poisoning. Michael J. Robinson, in his book *Predatory Bureaucracy*, concludes that the decision to rely so extensively on poison is the main reason wolves vanished from the mountains in the West while pumas did not.[24]

In the San Luis Valley of Colorado, coyote poisoning was hampered by black-billed magpies gulping down the baits first, and so the Bureau instituted a magpie eradication program with specially designed magpie baits.[25] Poisoning wolves leads to poisoning coyotes leads to poisoning magpies—a poisoning cascade.

In 1931 the U.S. Congress passed the National Animal Damage Control Act with the goal of destroying or controlling wildlife that cause damage to agricultural production.[26] Authority for implementing the act was eventually vested in the Division of

Predator and Rodent Control of the Department of the Interior. Government-funded control of coyotes by poisoning continued unabated through the 1930s and 1940s, including an intensive campaign by the newly created Charles M. Russell National Wildlife Refuge. Responding to pressure from sheep ranchers surrounding the refuge and reflecting the common attitude among wildlife managers at that time that too many predators make for too little game, the refuge conducted a mix of trapping, poisoning, aerial shooting, and public hunting to control coyote numbers from the 1940s to the early 1970s. The biggest effort may have been in 1946 when the refuge enlisted the help of the Division of Predator and Rodent Control to implement a coyote poisoning program that covered not only the entire refuge but also 1.2 million acres around it. The "poison pills," consisting of small cubes of strychnine wrapped in horse tallow and coated with sugar, were produced by the thousands and distributed across the landscape by plane. This was the year before Compound 1080 (sodium monofluoroacetate) became widely available as a new and better poison. The refuge reported that by 1948 the use of Compound 1080 had reduced the coyote population so that they were "no longer a serious menace to wildlife."[27] Refuge managers sometimes complained that golden eagles fed on the coyote carcasses and, in the process, ruined the coyote pelts. No reference was made to how many eagles and other nontarget animals may have been killed either directly by consuming the poison pill or indirectly by consuming the poisoned coyote carcasses.[28]

The C. M. Russell Refuge also often trapped bobcats that were killing its flock of captive geese or were speculated to be affecting deer fawn survival. In 1960 the refuge reported, "Bobcats continued to increase and as previously mentioned were known to take some of our geese. Despite our efforts to reduce the population they remain a problem and further extermination will be necessary to eliminate this predator."[29] The refuge, however, always expressed an interest in maintaining a bobcat population sufficient to control rodent numbers. I suspect bobcat numbers suffered a large decline in the late 1800s and first half of the 1900s due to excessive trapping for the fur trade, incidental killing in traps and poison baits set for coyotes and wolves, and loss of forested riparian habitat caused by stream dewatering, loss of beavers, and impacts of cattle. There is not sufficient evidence, however, to conclude their population collapsed by 90% or more in the American Prairie–Russell Refuge region.

Although federal- and state-sponsored coyote eradication programs continued across the West, coyote populations were never threatened. Biologists soon discovered that when more coyotes are killed, the females respond by having more pups, and more pups survive.[30] Consequently, lethal control measures often fail to reduce coyote numbers and livestock predation. Despite millions of coyotes being killed across the West, they have continued to thrive and even to expand their range to eastern North America. As we'll see later, wolves are far superior to humans in keeping coyote populations suppressed.

While the American Prairie–Russell Refuge region's midsized canid survived the Euro-American onslaught without trouble, its smallest canid went the way of the wolf. The last historical record of swift foxes in Montana was 1918, and the last one was seen in neighboring Saskatchewan in 1928. By this time they had been extirpated from most of the Northern Great Plains.[31] Trapping for the fur trade was an early assault on swift fox populations. From 1835 to 1838, the American Fur Company recorded 10,614 swift fox pelts taken from the Upper Missouri region;[32] from 1853 to 1877 the Hudson Bay Company sold 117,025 swift fox pelts in London.[33] Large numbers were incidentally killed by traps and poison baits set for wolves and coyotes. Loss of habitat to cropland and loss of prey (e.g., poisoning of ground squirrels and black-tailed prairie dogs) and of bison carcasses to scavenge likely contributed to the fox's decline.[34] Finally, several studies show that coyotes sometimes kill large numbers of swift foxes,[35] and thus a surge in coyote numbers in response to wolf eradication may have been a factor in the fox's collapse.

I suspect the population of one other carnivore, the American badger, suffered a steep decline during the first half of the 1900s when eradication programs annihilated the population of one of their favorite prey, the black-tailed prairie dog (more on this in chapter 9).[36] Their diverse diet of mice, voles, bird eggs, snakes, and other small animals, however, probably buffered the near total loss of one of their main foods.

Effects of Collapse on Biodiversity

In a process that ecologists call a "trophic cascade," the removal of top predators often has ripple effects down the food chain. Trophic cascades have been documented in several places in the American West. Extirpation of wolves, pumas, and/or grizzly bears in four western parks—Yellowstone, Zion, Yosemite, and Olympic—led to increased deer and/or elk populations, which, in turn, severely reduced numbers of trees and shrubs due to intensive browsing.[37] Forests became meadows. The possibility of a similar trophic cascade in the American Prairie–Russell Refuge region was precluded because all native ungulates were extirpated, or nearly so, before the large carnivores were.

Other pathways in the food chain, however, would have been affected by the loss of large carnivores. The killing of ungulates by carnivores leaves a year-round supply of carcasses for scavengers. Without predation, ungulate deaths are more sporadic—large winter die-offs, for instance—leaving scavengers to endure months of carcass scarcity.[38]

Puma predation may be an important source of protein for other animals. Wolves and bears benefit because they frequently drive off pumas from their kills. Moreover, unlike a pack of wolves that may polish off an elk in one day, the solitary puma takes several days to eat it. Consequently, pumas attempt to hide large prey they killed, but these prey caches are often discovered by scavengers. In one study each puma killed on average 22.3 pounds of prey per day and abandoned 8.6 pounds per day; that's more than 3,000 pounds per year that each puma supplied to scavengers in its territory.[39]

Wolf eradication may have released another trophic cascade via the coyote. Wolves and coyotes compete with each other for food. Since wolves are two to five times larger than coyotes, when the two species compete, wolves win. When the competition gets physical, the result is often a dead coyote. The coyote's response is to avoid areas occupied by wolves. Consequently, as wolves were eradicated, the coyote population appears to have boomed across the West in a process called "mesopredator release." ("Mesopredator"—the coyote in this case—is biologic-speak for midsized predators, from *mesos* in Greek, meaning "middle.") Various lines of evidence indicate that a bigger coyote population can have a cascading effect down the food chain. A decline in snowshoe hare (*Lepus americanus*), jackrabbit (*Lepus* spp.), and cottontail rabbit (*Sylvilagus* spp.) populations across much of the West may have been due to increased predation by coyotes after wolves were extirpated. Coyotes commonly prey on birds and their nests, including long-billed curlew (*Numenius americanus*), sandhill cranes (*Antigone canadensis*), and greater sage-grouse.[40] Coyotes are adept at finding pronghorn fawns and in some cases have significantly reduced the reproductive success of pronghorns. The reintroduction of wolves into Yellowstone National Park reduced the number of coyotes in areas inhabited by pronghorn, leading to less coyote predation on pronghorn fawns.[41]

It's not clear how this wolf–coyote interaction played out in the American Prairie–Russell Refuge region in the 1800s. Anecdotal reports are equivocal. D. M. Lee's diary from around 1870 lends support to the idea that wolves kept coyote numbers at bay. While he comments often on the abundance of wolves around the mouth of the Musselshell River, he never mentions hearing or seeing coyotes or finding them poisoned, although their fur would have been valued as well.[42] It's possible, however, that he lumped coyotes with wolves. In 1895 and 1897, when bounty records indicate that wolves were still abundant in northeast and north-central Montana, roughly four times more coyotes were bountied, suggesting that wolves were not significantly suppressing the coyote population.[43]

Regardless of how coyotes responded to wolf eradication more than 100 years ago, the question remains regarding what controls the number of coyotes on the American Prairie–Russell Refuge landscape today, what their ecological effect is as today's top

canine predator, and how their numbers and effect on the ecosystem will change as both prey and large carnivores, especially
wolves, return to the region.

Recovery

Recovery of grizzly bears, pumas, and wolves in the American
Prairie–Russell Refuge region primarily depends on four factors:
sufficient habitat, sufficient prey, secure recolonization routes, and
human tolerance. Plenty of intact habitat exists for each of the species. Native (nonlivestock) food resources should be sufficient,
especially if ungulate populations are allowed to grow beyond their
current levels. Habitat corridors and stepping stones between the
Rocky Mountain front and the American Prairie–Russell Refuge
region should be adequate both for recolonization and for maintaining genetic exchange between populations.

Intolerance by humans is—in the short term, at least—the biggest barrier. Nevertheless, a slight shift in attitude has occurred in
ranch country since pressure from ranchers led to the extirpation
of large carnivores 100 years ago. Some ranchers, as exemplified
by members of the Western Landowners Alliance, are working
with wildlife agencies and nonprofit conservation groups to find
innovative ways to coexist with large carnivores.[44] American Prairie's Wild Sky program pays ranchers whose land is used by bears,
pumas, or wolves. Given the wide-roaming nature of these species, creating predator-safe buffer zones around the American
Prairie–Russell Refuge and safe corridors for long-distance movements is crucial for long-term success.

My estimates for potential carnivore populations are based on a
fully restored prey base of ungulates. But as I said in the last chapter, how ungulate populations will respond to the return of all
native large carnivores is a big unknown. As in the other chapters,
I make these estimates with the caveat that nature is unpredictable.

Grizzly Bear

All habitats in the American Prairie–Russell Refuge region, from
forested floodplains and mountains to rolling prairies and badlands,

could be used by grizzly bears. Half of the protein consumed by grizzly bears in Yellowstone comes from elk and bison.[45] A combined population of 40,000–50,000 elk and bison, as estimated in the previous chapter, would be important for a robust grizzly bear population. I expect grizzly bears won't be far from wherever elk and bison are common to prey on vulnerable animals and scavenge carcasses.

Increasing movement by grizzly bears from the mountains of western Montana into the prairies in recent years has placed them at the doorstep of the American Prairie–Russell Refuge. So far, however, these adventurous bruins are either killed or trapped and moved back to the western mountains. The rugged terrain of the Missouri River breaks of the American Prairie–Russell Refuge, however, may offer an environment where bears have much less chance of being noticed and getting into trouble than on the open terrain of wheat fields and prairies. Regardless, managing human–bear conflict in the farm and ranch country of the Montana plains will be crucial to enable grizzly bears to recolonize and thrive in the region. Bear attractants such as spilled grain, livestock carcasses, and non-bear-proof garbage cans need to be removed. Scare devises, electric fences, guard dogs, and other livestock management practices can keep bears away from livestock, beehives, chicken coops, and human dwellings. Much can be gained by simply teaching people smart habits for living in bear country. In general, successful cases of coexistence with large predators elsewhere in the West, growing acceptance by the U.S. public toward large predators, and new mechanisms and policies that foster coexistence are encouraging signs for the recovery of grizzly bears on the American Prairie–Russell Refuge.[46]

The grizzly bear density in the Greater Yellowstone Ecosystem of about 3 bears/per 100 square miles provides a lower limit for estimating potential densities,[47] although densities in Yellowstone's Northern Range have been five times that level.[48] For the upper limit, I use 8 bears per 100 square miles, similar to the estimate based on Lewis and Clark observations and to grizzly density in and around Glacier National Park.[49] In round numbers, a density of 3–8 bears per 100 square miles on 3.2 million acres yields a population of 150–400 bears.

Puma

Displaying an impressive feat of recolonization, from 1960 to 1995 the puma's distribution in Montana tripled as it spread east from the mountains across the plains.[50] Their return to the America Prairie–Russell Refuge region was facilitated by populations of their favorite prey—deer and elk—recovering in the Missouri River breaks during the mid-1900s. As early as 1941 the C. M. Russell Refuge reported the sighting of a puma, although sightings remained scarce there through the 1940s and into the 1950s.[51] By 1961 the refuge reported, "Mountain lions are apparently on the increase and have been reported on three different occasions."[52] Reflecting some ambivalence about puma recovery, in 1960 the refuge reported, "A mountain lion was again reported on the West Unit. . . . The extreme range and flexibility of behavior of this animal makes control measures difficult." And later, it stated that the mountain lions were "not common enough to cause any serious threat to our game population except the possibility of their getting into our bighorn sheep enclosure."[53]

Roughly one million acres of good puma habitat exist in the floodplain and breaks of the Missouri River and its main tributaries through the Upper Missouri River Breaks National Monument and the C. M. Russell Refuge. The Little Rocky Mountains, as well as other isolated mountain ranges in the region, also provide puma habitat. Pumas use open grassland habitats also, though much less frequently. Subadult males in the Cypress Hills region of southern Alberta commonly established temporary home ranges in nearby grassland and shrub habitats.[54] Subadult pumas dispersing from the Black Hills of South Dakota successfully moved hundreds of miles—one traveled a straight-line distance of 663 miles—across open grassland habitat to colonize new areas.[55] The dispersal record, however, is a young male puma that traveled 1,500 miles from South Dakota to Connecticut, probably looking for a female, only to be killed by a vehicle.[56]

Conflict with landowners has not arisen as a problem as pumas seem to have blended into the American Prairie–Russell Refuge landscape largely unnoticed and with little or no livestock depredation.[57] Nevertheless, hunting and incidental human-caused mortality are keeping puma numbers suppressed. A study on the north side of the Missouri River in 2006 indicated too many pumas were being killed by hunters in the Bear's Paw and Little Rocky Mountains for the populations there to be self-sustaining. Puma numbers in these two areas probably depended on immigrants from a healthier population found on the nearby C. M. Russell Refuge.[58] Another study from 2010 to 2015 that was centered on the C. M. Russell Refuge offers a view of the risks pumas face. Of six documented deaths recorded by refuge biologist Randy Matchett and colleagues, one was legally killed by a hunter in Montana, two were nontarget mortalities associated with coyote snaring and bobcat trapping, one drowned in the Fort Peck Reservoir, one died from an elk predation attempt, and one was killed and consumed by another puma.[59]

This same study found pumas used the forested breaks of the Missouri River as a travel corridor for eastward dispersal.[60] Eastward expansion won't be easy, however, as pumas face a virtual firing line when they reach the North Dakota border. In 2021 the southwest corner of the state, from the Missouri River south, allowed 15 pumas to be killed annually while the rest of the state had no limit.[61] To wit, two of the dispersing pumas from the C. M. Russell Refuge that traveled to North Dakota were legally killed by hunters.[62]

Large elk and deer populations and the extensive rugged, forested landscapes of the American Prairie–Russell Refuge region should make for a healthy puma population in the future. Studies across the West and within the American Prairie–Russell Refuge region suggest a range of 5–10 pumas per 100 square miles, although this range includes populations that are probably limited by hunting.[63] Applying this range to the roughly 1 million acres of suitable habitat in the American Prairie–Russell Refuge region yields 75–150 pumas.

Among the many unknowns affecting puma numbers is how they might respond to recolonization by grizzly bears and wolves.

As noted above, pumas are subordinate to bears and wolves, especially when wolves show up in a pack. Research in the Yellowstone region found that when wolves recolonized areas inhabited by pumas, pumas shifted their ranges to more rugged and forested habitat infrequently used by wolves, which, in turn, resulted in pumas switching from elk to mule deer as their primary prey.[64] While wolves also directly kill pumas, harassment, kleptoparasitism, and displacement of pumas by wolves and bears may lead to lower survival and reproductive success and, ultimately, to fewer pumas.[65]

Wolf

Wolf recovery in western Montana began in the early 1980s through both natural dispersals from Canada and reintroductions to Yellowstone National Park and central Idaho in 1995 and 1996.[66] Wolf packs that inhabit the Rocky Mountain front from Glacier National Park to Yellowstone National Park are about 100–125 miles from the American Prairie–Russell Refuge region, but at least one pack has been spotted much closer, and the occasional lone wolf probably wanders into the region.[67] Average dispersal distance of wolves monitored in the Rocky Mountains was nearly 60 miles, but some dispersed more than 180 miles.[68] Wolves could readily recolonize the American Prairie–Russell Refuge if they can avoid heavy persecution while en route and once they arrive.

Like grizzly bears, the ability of wolves to recolonize and thrive on the American Prairie–Russell Refuge will depend on effectively managing the interaction of wolves, livestock, and people in the surrounding ranch country of eastern Montana. Ranchers and wildlife managers have been experimenting and applying a diversity of methods for minimizing wolf depredation on livestock. Guard dogs, range riders (people patrolling on horseback), electric fences and fences with fladry (flagging), more active herding (e.g., moving animals into enclosures at night), removal of livestock carcasses, and scare devices can keep wolves from getting into trouble. Livestock themselves can make a difference as some cattle breeds and cattle raised in wolf country are savvy at avoiding predation by wolves. None of these mitigation tactics, however, are 100% effective and once wolves are accustomed to preying on livestock, reconditioning is extremely difficult. In such cases, the only solution is to kill or, more rarely, translocate the problem wolves.[69]

Wolves arriving in the region will encounter ungulate species that are commonly their principal prey in other ecosystems. Where wolves have a choice of deer, elk, and bison, wolves show a strong preference for pursuing deer or elk.[70] Although bison are the wolf's primary prey in some areas where other species of ungulates are not abundant, they are difficult and dangerous prey for wolves to capture.[71] In Yellowstone National Park, elk capture success leveled off at 2–6 wolves involved in the pursuit whereas bison capture success leveled off at 9–13 wolves.[72] However, as bison abundance increased in the park, they became much more important in the wolves' diet, not because wolves killed more bison, but because wolves could scavenge more carcasses of bison that died from other causes.[73]

The three approaches I used for estimating the potential number of wolves that could inhabit the 3.2-million-acre American Prairie–Russell Refuge arrive at roughly the same answer. Estimates by pioneering wolf biologist Durwood Allen and national park ecologist Daniel Licht for two hypothetical mixed-grass prairie parks in the Northern Great Plains yield a range of 480–640 wolves on 3.2 million acres.[74] Such diverse areas as Algonquin National Park in Ontario, the northern forest of Minnesota, and northern Yellowstone National Park have had recent wolf densities that translate into roughly 300–800 wolves on 3.2 million acres.[75] These are ecosystems distinctly different from northeast Montana, although Yellowstone, representing the high end of wolf densities, has the same principal prey species—deer, elk, and bison. A third method is a formula developed by wolf biologists David Mech and Shannon Barber-Meyer for estimating wolf densities based on the biomass of ungulate prey.[76] If I plug in the range of ungulate numbers from chapter 6 and assume that wolves make full use, according to the formula, of deer and elk but just one-quarter to one-half of the bison, the result is 400–650 wolves on 3.2 million acres. The three approaches offer a range of about 300–800 wolves

(6–16 wolves per 100 square miles) in dozens of wolf packs dividing up the 3.2 million acres.

Swift Fox

Canada began reintroducing swift foxes into southern Alberta and Saskatchewan near the Montana border in 1983; the population has since expanded across the border into north-central Montana. The Fort Peck Indian Reservation began reintroductions in 2006. However, growth and expansion of the swift fox population resulting from these reintroductions has stalled, and as of 2020 swift foxes had not moved south across the Milk River and Highway 2 into the American Prairie–Russell Refuge. A gap of more than 200 miles exists between this population along the Canada–Montana border and the nearest population to the south in northeastern Wyoming and northwestern South Dakota.[77]

Research on the swift fox population on the Montana side of the border indicated that reproduction was not sufficiently high for the population to expand into new areas. While coyotes were the main cause of mortality, the research also found that swift foxes tended to avoid cropland and their survival was lower in areas with more cropland compared to native prairie. This may be due to competition with nonnative red foxes (*Vulpes vulpes*), which moved into the region during the 1960s and frequently inhabit croplands. The upshot is that the extensive cropland found along the Milk River corridor may be a barrier to swift fox range expansion south onto the American Prairie–Russell Refuge. Interestingly, swift foxes tend to concentrate near unpaved roads, perhaps using them for travel, for encountering road-killed animals to scavenge, and as a "human shield" against being killed by coyotes, since coyotes often avoid roads to avoid being shot.[78]

To establish a swift fox population between the Milk and Missouri Rivers, in 2020 a five-year reintroduction program began on the Fort Belknap Indian Reservation with help from the Smithsonian Conservation Biology Institute, American Prairie, Defenders of Wildlife, and World Wildlife Fund. During the first two years of the program a total of 75 swift foxes captured from healthy

FIG. 12. Radio-collared swift fox captured in Colorado and released on the Fort Belknap Indian Reservation in 2021. Courtesy Johnny Stutzman.

populations in Wyoming and Colorado were released and appear to be doing well (fig. 12).[79] The released animals and their descendants are expected to disperse and eventually occupy roughly 3.4 million acres of suitable habitat between the Milk and Missouri Rivers in the American Prairie–Russell Refuge region. Modeling for the reintroduction program suggests the region's fox population could total about 450–500 in 30 years.[80]

The bottom line for swift fox recovery on the American Prairie–Russell Refuge and beyond is that grassland corridors and large areas of intact grasslands will be crucial for enabling the population to grow and disperse to recolonize areas of their former range. Recovery of wolves may benefit swift foxes by reducing the number of coyotes, thereby decreasing the number of swift foxes killed and reducing competition for food by coyotes.

A Recovered Carnivore Community

Based on the above estimates, imagine 1,000 large carnivores— wolves, pumas, grizzly bears, and black bears—in a 3.2-million-acre Great Plains protected area. I expect wolves will be more abundant than the other three, hunting deer, elk, and bison over nearly the entire American Prairie–Russell Refuge. Visitors should have frequent views of wolves shadowing and pursuing elk and bison on the prairie. Grizzly bears may be second in abundance and will probably be encountered in any habitat with some seasonal shifts—perhaps hibernating in the rugged breaks or Little Rocky Mountains during winter and emerging, protein-starved, in the spring to feast on the abundance of elk and bison calves and carcasses. Maybe, if Lewis and Clark's observations are any indication, grizzly bears will gather near the Missouri River in late spring in search of beavers or nutritious plant growth or ungulates struggling to cross the high-flowing river. Pumas should be mostly sticking to the Missouri River breaks, badlands, and Little Rocky Mountains. Black bears will continue to concentrate in the Little Rocky Mountains and other nearby mountain ranges of the prairie and be infrequent visitors to the forested breaks and prairie. How coyotes respond to being kicked out of their top-dog position in the prairie by the return of wolves will be interesting to watch. They may find more carcass-scavenging opportunities, but that may be offset by their assiduous avoidance of wolves. With wolves potentially suppressing coyote numbers and vast expanses of unfragmented prairie restored, the swift fox may again become one of the region's most common carnivores.

Watching the top trophic level come to life in the prairie food web will be exciting for prairie visitors and scientists alike. Native people and a few early Euro-American explorers experienced this intact food web before ungulate and carnivore populations collapsed, but today's public and scientists have never had the chance to see or study it on the Great Plains. In light of the multifaceted ecological responses and enthusiastic tourist reactions to wolf restoration in Yellowstone National Park, one can only imagine the endless fascination and ecological questions that restoring the missing carnivores on a 3.2-million-acre American Prairie–Russell Refuge would provide.

Striking black-and-white banding is typical of this genus (*Triepeolus*) of cuckoo bees—so called because, like cuckoo birds, they deposit their eggs in the nest of other ground-nesting grassland bees. Drawing by Erica Freese.

EIGHT

Rocky Mountain Locust

I n the spring of 1876 the 60 acres of corn that the Finch boys
had planted on their Nebraska farm was about ready for harvest. Then

> one afternoon they discovered what appeared to be a prairie
> fire, a dense cloud of smoke arising in the northwest. . . . They
> watched it intently as it came nearer and nearer, until it obscured
> the sun and darkened the air like an eclipse. When it had come
> within a hundred yards of them they heard a continuous crack-
> ing and snapping sound, which increased to a perfect roar as
> it approached them, when they discovered to their horror that
> a cloud of grasshoppers were upon them. They alighted and
> in a few seconds every green thing in sight was literally cov-
> ered and hidden with a seething, crawling mass several inches
> in depth. . . . The hoppers ate up everything as if it had been
> swept with fire.[1]

Descriptions of similar scenes were common during the mid-
1870s from Manitoba to Texas as swarms of the Rocky Mountain
locust emerged from the Rocky Mountains and plains of Montana and neighboring regions to darken skies across the Great
Plains. The locusts consumed almost all plant life—native grasses
and forbs, corn and wheat, garden vegetables and fruit trees. They
ate curtains, clothes, and leather; munched the wooden fibers of
fence posts and the salty handles of axes and shovels; gnawed
wool on the backs of sheep; and fed on animal carcasses and one

another. Trains stopped running because the tracks became too
slick for traction due to the oils of locusts crushed on the tracks.
Poultry that feasted on the locusts yielded meat and eggs infused
by the insect's reddish-brown oil, which rendered them inedi-
ble. Streams and wells loaded with the rotting bodies and excrement of locusts became putrid and undrinkable to livestock and
humans alike. Livestock starved as their forage was consumed by
the munching hordes.[2] Soon people were starving too and aban-
doning their homesteads to head back east. An estimated 74% of
the total value of U.S. farm production was lost to locusts in 1874.
States and the federal governments launched relief programs to
help families left destitute by the locusts.[3]

Reflecting concerns about locust plagues impeding homesteading and development of agriculture in the West, in 1876 the U.S.
Congress created the U.S. Entomological Commission to study
and find ways to avert and manage locust plagues and appointed
three of the nation's leading scientists to lead it. A brilliant, inde-
fatigable, and eccentric entomologist named Charles V. Riley was
appointed chief scientist of the commission. Riley quickly published in 1877 a book making the case, in the introduction, for the
national importance of the locust plague and the commission's
work: "No insect has ever occupied a larger share of public attention in North America, or more injuriously affected our greatest national interest, than the subject of this treatise. Especially
during the past four years has it brought ruin and destitution to
thousands of our Western farmers, and it constitutes to-day the
greatest obstacle to the settlement of much of the fertile country between the Mississippi and Rocky Mountains. Knowledge is
power in protecting our crops against the ravages of a tiny insect."[4]

Due to Riley's leadership and doggedness, the Entomological Commission's research and voluminous reports left no stone
unturned to provide an invaluable foundation of knowledge about
the insect's biology, its plagues, and what worked and what didn't
to control it. By 1880 the Rocky Mountain locust was surely the
most studied pest insect in the world. Riley went on to become
the greatest U.S. entomologist of his time, pioneered the field of

biological pest control, and among a long list of other achieve-
ments, founded the U.S. National Insect Collection, now home to
25 million specimens, at the Smithsonian Institution.[5]

A little background on locusts and their biology before going
further. First, to clear up a common misconception: cicadas are not
locusts—not even close. Locusts are in the insect order Orthoptera
(grasshoppers, crickets, katydids) and cicadas are Hemiptera (true
bugs). All the world's 20 species of locusts, including the Rocky
Mountain locust, are grasshoppers (the taxonomic family Acrididae). Locusts occur on all continents except Antarctica.[6] North
America had or has (more about this below) only one species, the
Rocky Mountain locust.

What makes locusts different from other grasshoppers is their
dual-phase life history—a solitary, nonmigratory phase and a gregarious, migratory phase. At low densities and with plenty of food,
they lead a rather solitary life with no urge to aggregate and migrate.
But with the right environmental cues, such as high densities and
an impending food shortage, this changes. The locust nymphs
detect crowding by sensory hairs on their legs and a pheromone
released from the excrement. These cause a hormonal cascade
that triggers the "phase change" from the solitary to the migratory
form with longer wings and other morphological and physiological changes, adapting them to a new diet and long-distance migration. In addition, adult female locusts give their eggs a chemical
signal to develop into locusts that are gregarious and migratory.[7]

The female Rocky Mountain locust, after mating, usually deposited one to four pods with 20–35 eggs per pod over the course of
several weeks. Pods were deposited about an inch deep in the
soil, where they remained until hatching the next spring or summer (fig. 13). Egg densities could be as high as several dozen per
square inch. The newly hatched nymphs, which looked like small
wingless adult locusts, went through four or five instars (molts),
constantly consuming plants to fuel their growth, before becoming winged adults at about six to eight weeks.[8]

During the solitary phase the Rocky Mountain locust inhabited what the Entomological Commission called the "permanent

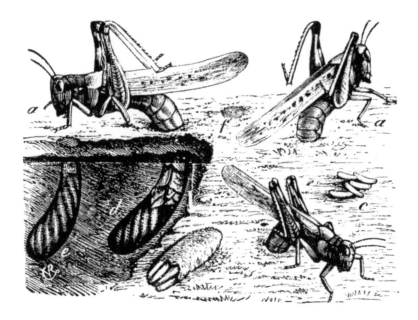

FIG. 13. Illustration of Rocky Mountain locust by Charles V. Riley, showing, as described by Riley, "a, female in different positions, ovipositing; b [letter not visible], egg-pod extracted from ground, with the end broken open; c, a few eggs lying loose on the ground; d, e, show the earth partially removed, to illustrate an egg-mass already in place and one being deposited; f, shows where such a mass has been covered up." Riley, *Destructive Locusts*, 61, fig. 1.

region" in the valleys of the Rocky Mountains and adjacent high plains from southern Alberta to central Colorado, including the American Prairie–Russell Refuge region (fig. 14). The permanent region was the origin of the largest and most devastating swarms.[9] It covered 500,000 square miles, the vast share of it on the east side of the continental divide. During any one year during their solitary phase, the locusts occupied maybe 25,000–30,000 square miles— 5–6% of the permanent region—among widely scattered reproductive sites. The number and specific location of egg-laying sites within this region are, at best, vaguely understood. It was simply too large an area for Entomological Commission investigators to adequately cover on horseback. In general, however, in Montana the primary concentration of locusts during the solitary phase was a swath of plains within 100 miles of the Rocky Mountain front,

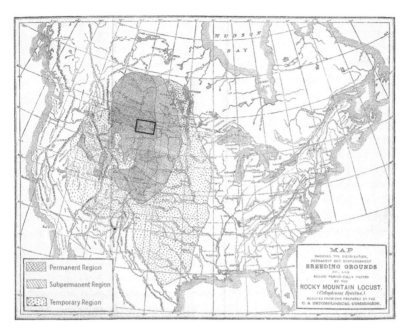

FIG. 14. Map published by the U.S. Entomological Commission showing
permanent, subpermanent, and temporary regions of the Rocky Mountain
locust. The black rectangle indicates the American Prairie–Russell Refuge region.
Created by Eric Cline (modified from U.S. Entomological Commission, *Map
Showing the Distribution, Permanent and Subpermanent Breeding Grounds of, and
Region Periodically Visited by the Rocky Mountain Locust* (Caloptenus spretus*).*).

with fingers into the mountains via major drainages, particularly
the Missouri and Yellowstone Rivers. The American Prairie–Russell
Refuge region was on the eastern margin of this swath.[10]

Although the locusts would lay eggs in a variety of terrains and
soils in the permanent region, they preferred sandy soils in river
bottoms, sunny slopes of uplands, and subalpine meadows. Egg-
laying sites in semiarid grasslands were generally at elevations
below 3,000–5,000 feet. Some of the Entomological Commission's accounts were ambiguous. In 1880 the commission reported
that the locusts never oviposited on "perfectly barren areas," but
in 1891 Riley noted that they "prefer bare, sandy places, especially
on high ground." Riley reported that the locust frequently used
"closely grazed" grasslands and avoided wet or moist areas.[11] Eggs

were commonly laid in the valleys of the Marias, Sun, Milk, Missouri, and Yellowstone Rivers and in the adjacent prairies bordering their tributaries. Since the floodplains of these rivers in the plains are generally forested or shrubland, and locusts avoided such habitat, presumably uplands next to the floodplain were used. Newly plowed land was avoided, but the locusts commonly laid eggs in cultivated cropland.[12]

During the migratory phase, the adult locusts emerging in Montana generally flew east or southeast, often catching air currents, toward the subpermanent region and temporary region of the central, eastern, and southern Great Plains while feasting on plant life along the way. Before the end of summer, the adults would feed more, oviposit their eggs, die, and the eggs would hibernate for the winter. The nymphs would emerge the next spring and feed and grow into winged adults to carry on the rampage of a locust swarm. This cycle might last for several years in the subpermanent region but for generally one to three years in the temporary region.

Of locust plagues documented around the world, those of the Rocky Mountain locust were the largest. Swarms could be both far-ranging and large. One swarm that left Montana in mid-July 1876 reached Texas by the end of September—eating its way across 1,500 miles of the Great Plains in 75 days.[13] During the 1870s locusts plagued 25 states and provinces, ranging into the plains of Canada; east to Minnesota, Iowa, and Missouri; and south to southern Texas.[14] The most epic swarm—the swarm that devoured the Finch brothers' corn—was the Albert Swarm, named after the self-made meteorologist Albert Child, who carefully documented the swarm's apocalyptic sweep across Nebraska. Child estimated the swarm to be one-quarter to one-half mile deep and, with a strong tail wind, to fly by at a rate of 15 miles per hour for five straight days. Based on this and reports from various residents, Child figured the swarm must have been 1,800 miles long and 110 miles wide. That yields 198,000 square miles of locusts—an area much larger than California—stacked one-quarter to one-half mile deep. The swarm may have contained 3.5 trillion locusts.[15] Much of Albert's swarm likely originated in the intermountain valleys and eastern plains of Montana.

Beating the locusts back by hand was fruitless. Following the maxim that necessity is the mother of invention, soon on the scene was an arsenal of contraptions for conquering the swarming locusts. There were horse-drawn devices to scoop up locusts and funnel them into bags; some, such as Robbins Hopperdozer, first ran the locusts through a chamber poisoned with kerosene or coal tar. There were the Hansberry, Hoos, and Simpson Locust-Crushers that employed rollers, wheels, and other methods to smash locusts into the ground. The King Suction-Machine sucked up locusts with a fan and dropped them into bags. Various types of flamethrowers and burning kerosene-soaked rags were dragged across fields. Fires were lit to smoke them out. Ditches were dug and filled with water and oil to drown the locust nymphs as they emerged and marched across the land. Arsenic insecticides were applied but probably did more damage to bird and mammal populations than to locusts. Riley even suggested harvesting locusts for their culinary attributes, noting that one day he ate nothing but several thousand half grown locusts prepared in various ways.[16] Although tens of millions of locusts were probably killed by these methods, they hardly made a dent in a population of billions or trillions.

A more targeted approach focused on killing locust eggs by plowing the soil or flooding fields. Farmers also began planting crops that were less susceptible to the infestation and converting cropland back to more resilient pastures. States passed legislation and governors issued proclamations protecting insect-eating birds, offering bounties for killing locusts, and requiring people to commit time to combatting the plague. Probably most effective were natural biological controls afforded by bird predation and parasitic infections of the locusts. In the end, however, outbreaks had a life span of usually three to five years and the swarms that emerged so ferociously in 1874 were largely gone by 1877.[17]

While Euro-Americans were planting crops and fighting locusts in the eastern and central Great Plains, Native people and Euro-Americans in the plains of Montana were still hunting bison and

Native nations still controlled much of the region. Large swarms were reported in the plains of Montana at those times, from the Milk River and Fort Benton on the Missouri River in the north, through the Judith and Musselshell River basins to the Yellowstone River region in the southeast. Interestingly, the large swarms that visited eastern Montana during the mid-1870s came from the east, apparently having hatched in Minnesota and other eastern states and then undertaking a reverse migration back west. However, because Euro-American settlements in the plains of eastern Montana during the 1870s were largely limited to places along the Missouri River, with almost no cropland in the region, reports of the swarms and their effects on the land are limited. As late as 1880, an Entomological Commission researcher avoided the Judith and Musselshell basins because he thought that Sitting Bull and his followers were in the region (though Sitting Bull lived in Canada at the time). The locust, however, caused considerable crop damage in the intermountain valleys of Montana, such as the Gallatin Valley around Bozeman, during the 1860s and the mid-1870s.[18]

To combat a main source of locust plagues—the permanent region in Montana—the Entomological Commission made an audacious proposal to the U.S. Congress. It suggested that the government donate to a railroad company a swath of land 50–60 miles wide extending from the Black Hills of South Dakota to the northwest, across the plains of Montana, to the Canadian border, skirting the eastern edge of the American Prairie–Russell Refuge region. The railroad company would have to agree to install irrigation to attract farmers. The locust eggs would be destroyed by the flooding and cultivation. The commission suggested that the area be settled by Russian peasants who were accustomed to fighting locusts. Moreover, the plan "would also help settle the troublesome Indian problem in this Section of the West."[19] Congress never acted on the proposal.

Then it ended (fig. 15). The locust outbreak of the mid-1870s was the last big one. The locust's vanishing act was particularly stark in the plains of Montana. In 1877 reports of large locust hatches ranged from the Marias River in the north to the Yellowstone

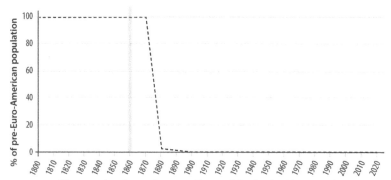

FIG. 15. The postulated population collapse of the Rocky Mountain locust to extinction or near-extinction. The vertical line indicates the first major surge of Euro-American settlements and agriculture in the locust's permanent region. Created by author and Eric Cline.

River in the south, with the swath encompassing the American Prairie–Russell Refuge region. Just two years later, in 1879, the intermountain valleys and plains of Montana were free of locusts for the first time since 1861. The region, the Entomological Commission noted, had been "the very citadel whence in former years hordes of locusts have invaded the regions East and South."[20] By 1880 only a few locusts could be found in Montana or elsewhere and numbers apparently continued to decline through the 1890s.[21] In 1904 a Montana entomologist reported not having seen the locust in five years.[22] The last record of live locusts is of one male and one female collected in 1902 in Manitoba, now part of the Smithsonian Institution's insect collection. The Rocky Mountain locust—the only locust species in North America, a natural ecological phenomenon like no other—seemed to have vanished.

Is It a Distinct Species and Really Gone?

Fear of another locust plague lingered for years, but slowly farmers and the Entomological Commission turned their attention to other insect pests and challenges of farming the Great Plains. However, the total disappearance of an insect that had once darkened the skies seemed impossible, and so while the Rocky Mountain locust faded from public consciousness, entomologists researched and debated the insect's fate during the first half of the 1900s. The debate primarily centered around whether the Rocky Mountain locust was, in fact, a distinct species or was hiding in plain site as another grasshopper species that, for whatever reason, had failed since the last swarms of the late 1800s to transform from the solitary phase to the gregarious migratory phase.

The leading candidate was the migratory grasshopper (*Melanoplus sanguinipes*), a species closely related and similar to the Rocky Mountain locust. The migratory grasshopper was common and often a crop pest that sometimes became migratory during outbreaks—though nothing on the scale of a Rocky Mountain locust outbreak. Some entomologists believed, due perhaps to changes in the grasshopper's habitat caused by agricultural practices, that an environmental cue that triggered the phase transformation to a longer-winged, migratory, swarming Rocky Mountain locust was missing.[23]

Grasshopper identification at the time was still based mostly on morphological features, and the single most reliable feature for telling species apart was the male grasshopper's penis, called the "aedeagus" by entomologists. Evolution's solution for avoiding interbreeding among grasshopper species was to create complex and elaborate male and female genitalia, unique to each species, that precisely fit each other for successful mating. The idea that the Rocky Mountain locust was a distinct species gained the upper hand in 1959 when two entomologists, Ashley B. Gurney and A. R. Brooks, published the results of their examination of the aedeagus in the prestigious Smithsonian Institution's Proceedings of the U.S. National Museum and concluded that the Rocky Mountain locust was a distinct species.[24]

Although doubts about its identification lingered, little further research on the question was done until 1989, when Jeffrey Lockwood, an entomologist at the University of Wyoming, published a reexamination of the question of whether it was a distinct species based on the aedeagus and other morphological features. Lockwood also concludes that the Rocky Mountain locust was a distinct species.[25] More importantly, Lockwood was smitten with the mystery of the Rocky Mountain locust and began a tireless quest to answer questions surrounding its status as a species and its disappearance. As a result, his research and publication of the fascinating *Locust: The Devastating Rise and Mysterious Disappearance of the Insect That Shaped the American Frontier* rescued the locust from the relative obscurity of research published in entomological journals to make it one of North America's great biological mysteries and stories. It leaves one wondering how a creature that blocked out the sun like the passenger pigeon and whose fall was equally swift and enigmatic had escaped from our consciousness for a century.

A major impediment to ending any reservations about the taxonomic status of the Rocky Mountain locust and to determining possible causes of its disappearance was that only dried, pinned specimens remained, nearly all collected in the late 1800s. Intact soft parts, like bodies preserved in ice, would be much better for investigating diet, analyzing proteins and DNA, and researching other features. The direction this story is going becomes evident if, as Lockwood did, one looks at a geological map of the Rocky Mountains of Montana and Wyoming and sees various glaciers named "Grasshopper Glacier." In fact, it was well known that grasshopper remains littered the surfaces of several glaciers in the region. During flights over the mountain ranges, grasshoppers were frequently caught in snowstorms and died on glaciers, creating sedimentary layers of grasshopper remains. Due to a warming climate, however, the glaciers were melting fast. So Lockwood and his colleagues wasted no time, and by 1992 several glaciers, especially from the Wind River Range in Wyoming, had yielded a bonanza of specimens of the Rocky Mountain locust, of migratory grasshoppers, and of other grasshoppers.[26]

A 1996 paper demonstrated that chemical fingerprints of the specimens strongly supported the recognition of the Rocky Mountain locust as a distinct species.[27] More definitively, a 2004 paper on the analysis of DNA from both dried museum specimens and 400-year-old glacial deposits confirmed the distinct species conclusion. The DNA analysis also found no evidence that population bottlenecks or inbreeding had compromised the locust's genetic health and led to its presumed extinction.[28] Another important finding, based on aging the glacial layers and carbon dating of specimens, was that the locust swarms had been occurring for hundreds of years; they were not an aberration caused by Euro-American colonization.[29]

With the question of the Rocky Mountain locust's status as a distinct species settled, the question remains "Is it extinct?" Entomologists unsuccessfully searched for the locust in grasshopper outbreaks in the early 1900s.[30] However, proving beyond a reasonable doubt the extinction of a grasshopper—the Rocky Mountain locust—that looks almost exactly like other grasshoppers except for its penis poses challenges unlike searching for, say, the ivory-billed woodpecker (*Campephilus principalis*). Moreover, a lot more ornithologists and bird watchers have looked for the ivory-billed than entomologists have looked for the locust. No one doubts that the gregarious, migratory phase of the locust has not resurfaced since the late 1800s, but some level of doubt remains that the locust isn't carrying on, undetected, in its solitary, don't-attract-attention-to-yourself phase in some intermountain meadow.[31]

The Elusive Cause

If the Rocky Mountain locust had been common in the region for hundreds of years and showed no sign of genetic deterioration causing its extinction or descent into rarity, what did? In their second report in 1880, the entomological commissioners state that "utter extermination of the pest is out of the question."[32] I doubt any conservation biologist today, knowing what the commissioners knew, would think differently. As the commissioners express in their reports, while eradication was considered impossible, controlling the locusts required focusing on the permanent region, where their populations retreated to and had endured for centuries between periodic outbreaks.

Lockwood, who has explored the possible causes of extinction more than anyone else, suggests that the ecological concept of "metapopulation" is the key to understanding the locust's disappearance. A metapopulation exists when the population of a species consists of several isolated subpopulations.[33] Locusts fit this definition well during their solitary, nonmigratory phase. Locust egg-laying sites were concentrated in intermountain and plains valleys during the solitary phase, and they preferred certain areas within these valleys, those that had the best habitat for egg laying. Valley bottoms are widely dispersed across the permanent region, separated by montane habitat in the Rocky Mountains and by hills and other uplands in the plains. Consequently, sites with reproducing adults, their eggs, and nymphs, while numerous, were patchily distributed across the landscape.[34]

The explanation for how the metapopulation of the Rocky Mountain locust seemingly vanished fits the general theory for other species, especially insects, that face the risk of extinction because of their metapopulation status.[35] During any given year the locusts' eggs or emerging nymphs in a few of their egg-laying sites may have all been killed by natural phenomena such as a local flood, late freeze or snowstorm, or a massive fungal infection (a common occurrence in humid conditions). But dispersing adult locusts from other valleys unaffected by the local disaster would have repopulated these areas in a year or two. In this way, while isolated subpopulations constantly winked out here and there, the entire metapopulation in the permanent region persisted. The extinction risk in this situation is closely tied to the theory of island biogeography introduced in chapter 1: in general, egg-laying sites where subpopulations have vanished are more readily found and repopulated if they are near, rather than far from, other sites with subpopulations.

Lockwood suggests that several changes to river valleys during the late 1800s could have increased the rate of locusts disappearing in egg-laying sites to the point where the valleys with surviving locusts that could recolonize those sites were too few and too widely separated to keep up. (Remember that eggs are the only form in which locusts survive the winter.) In short, if subpopulations of the locust were vanishing faster than they were being reestablished through recolonization, that's a downward spiral to extinction.

Eggs and nymphs, according to Lockwood, may have been destroyed by various factors, including cultivation, irrigation, livestock trampling of eggs, overgrazing by cattle, alteration of hydrological patterns, and/or planting of alfalfa (one of the few plants inimical to locusts). He also suggests, more speculatively, that rampant logging, large forest fires, depletion of beavers, and extirpation of large carnivores leading to irruptive growth of elk and deer populations, and consequent overbrowsing of riparian vegetation, could have led to more flooding and drowning of eggs and nymphs.

It is surely no coincidence that the locust's disappearance coincided with numerous changes in the permanent region's lands, plants, and animals caused by Euro-American settlement. No single change, however, stands out as the smoking gun. In Montana, for example, the surge in farming during the late 1860s in the intermountain valleys of Montana to feed the mining camps may have destroyed locust nesting habitat. In the plains, the biggest change would seem to be the wholesale swap of bison for livestock during roughly 1876–86 (detailed in chapter 6). But depending on how one looks at it, the timing is a little off. When locusts apparently vanished from the plains between 1878 and 1880, bison were still common and the cattle boom in the plains of Montana hadn't begun.[36] And farming was nearly nonexistent in Montana's plains then. Perhaps natural events or cycles caused the initial drop in the population during the late 1870s and then the switch from bison to cattle drove the numbers lower. Maybe a change in grazing patterns, including the propensity of cattle (unlike bison) to linger near water, ruined egg-laying habitat or resulted in the trampling of locust egg pods. Maybe the coup de grâce was delivered by irrigation and farming in the bottomlands of the Milk, Missouri, and Yellowstone Rivers in the late 1880s and 1990s.[37] There are far too many variables and unknowns to sort this out in any definitive way. What caused the locust's presumed extinction is, and likely always will be, a mystery.

Ecological Effects of a "Metabolic Wildfire"

The Rocky Mountain locust arguably deserves a place alongside fire and bison grazing as a historically dominant ecological force of the Great Plains. At their respective peak populations—tens of millions of bison and trillions of locusts—the total biomass of each may have tipped the scales in the neighborhood of 10 million tons.[38] Lockwood aptly calls the locust a "metabolic wildfire" as swarms of various sizes and locations cleared swaths of plant life across the plains at an average of 20 miles per day.[39] Records from the 1800s show the average interval between major outbreaks was three years, with the longest interval having been six years.[40] Perhaps any given area of the mixed-grass prairie was hit by a swarm every decade or two—similar to the return rate of grassland fires. If so, swarms of locusts must have interacted with grassland fires and grazing by bison and other native ungulates to create a constantly shifting mosaic of diverse grassland habitats across the Great Plains. The American Prairie–Russell Refuge region was in the midst of this ecological maelstrom.

While swarming, the locusts were notoriously polyphagous—nearly any plant was palatable. A large swarm could metabolically burn through 100 tons of vegetation per day.[41] Some plants, however, were preferred over others, resulting in large changes in the plant community following a plague. Like a prairie fire, the excrement and decaying bodies from a large swarm fertilized the soil, resulting in luxuriant plant growth.[42] Unlike a fire, the mass of locusts also directly nourished grassland animals. Invertebrates constituted the greatest diversity of species gorging on the locusts, especially the parasites and predators of the eggs and nymphs. Fifty pages of the first report of the Entomological Commission were needed to describe the locust-feasting invertebrates, including fungi, nematodes, mites, maggots, beetles, and ants.[43]

Locust-eating vertebrates ranged from frogs, snakes, and birds to ground squirrels, skunks, and even wolves. Birds, including the now rare mountain plover (*Charadrius montanus*) (see chapter 11), were the most obvious vertebrates attracted to the food bonanza and were profusely praised for their good deed by those submitting reports to the Entomological Commission. Dissection of several mountain plovers in Nebraska found 27–63 locusts per stomach.[44] While overhunting was the primary cause of the Eskimo curlew's (*Numenius borealis*) extinction, the disappearance of locusts, eaten by curlews during migration, may have been a contributing factor.[45] Some insectivorous bird species may have tracked locust plagues as a mobile source of reliable and abundant food. With a modicum of memory for the location of swarms of egg-laying adults, birds could return in the spring to gorge on the densely packed egg pods and emerging nymphs, a food bonanza that might sustain a population of birds throughout the nesting season.

Populations of herbivores surely paid a price if they happened to fall in the path of a large locust swarm. The closest competitors for plant food were other species of grasshoppers. The extinction of locust swarms may have provided an ecological release that resulted in several massive outbreaks of grasshoppers in the 1900s.[46] Native people in Montana reported that large swarms of locusts sometimes consumed so much vegetation in the valleys of the Yellowstone River and its tributaries that bison had to go elsewhere to find forage.[47] Pronghorn, elk, and other ungulates would have done the same. Less mobile herbivores, such as prairie dogs and ground squirrels, may have gone through lean periods after a swarm moved through.

Although we are ignorant of the true dimensions of the ecological effects of the locust on the America Prairie–Russell Refuge region and beyond, it seems safe to conclude that the Rocky Mountain locust, in both its numbers and its ecological effects, had an outsized role that epitomized the boom-and-bust nature of the Great Plains.

And now, 140 years after the locust's collapse, other grasshopper populations are in decline, with potentially rippling effects on grassland ecosystems. Evidence comes from long-term research at the Konza Prairie in Kansas, where the total population of 44 species of grasshoppers declined by one-third from 1998 to 2018. The "nutrient dilution" hypothesis seems to offer the best explanation:

The increase in atmospheric levels of carbon dioxide is causing greater plant growth that results in lower nutrient concentrations in plant tissue. Thus, grasshoppers—and other herbivores—get fewer nutrients per bite, resulting in lower levels of grasshopper reproduction and survival.[48] The implications of nutrient dilution obviously extend beyond grasshoppers to all herbivores, including humans, in natural and agricultural systems.

Recovery?

Speaking of recovery of the Rocky Mountain locust is probably akin, to some, to contemplating release of the smallpox virus from cold storage. The locust, however, as a former keystone species of the Great Plains, might provide societal benefits were it to return. The recovery of grassland birds, many in steep decline (as described in chapter 11), might benefit from both the periodically abundant food source and the heterogeneous grassland habitat the swarms created. Like the two other major ecological disturbances of Great Plains grasslands—fire and grazing—the locust may have been a third major disturbance that led to greater and more resilient grassland biodiversity.

I doubt that any of these or other potential benefits would convince most people today that the locust deserves another chance. But that's today. One hundred years ago society and wildlife managers were sufficiently convinced that wolves were such a plague on ranching and game animals that the U.S. government undertook their eradication. Later, however, based on changing societal attitudes and better ecological thinking, the U.S. government decided that the benefits of their recovery outweighed the costs. Though a wolf outbreak may be easier to control than a locust outbreak, my general point that "times change" holds.

Recovery could take various routes. If the species is, in fact, extinct and no surviving population is found between now and whenever society might decide to proceed with their recovery, the locust could be cloned using DNA from frozen specimens of the Rocky Mountain glaciers. That's probably the easy part. Two bigger questions would face the locust restoration authority and managers: Is there suitable habitat and to what degree, if any, should the species be contained? One extreme would be to contain it in a laboratory or in zoo-like conditions, in which case the species might as well be maintained as frozen DNA.

Somewhat more daring, if suitable habitat exists, would be to restore a "wild" population in the solitary, nonmigratory phase, perhaps through manipulation of its genome or managing the population and habitat to avoid cues that trigger the gregarious, migratory phase. Or perhaps, after more than 100 generations of living only in the solitary phase, the swarming instinct in the locust genome has diminished or disappeared.[49] The species would survive in a few valleys while being ecologically extinct—not displaying its full ecological potential as a keystone species.

That would be a holding pattern, waiting for times to change whereby society decides to restore the locust to its full ecological self. Like the wolf analogy, this may require thinking a hundred years out when, who knows, all our vegetables are hydroponically grown, most meat is cultured, and any number of other changes have reduced the threat locusts pose to food production. If most of the Great Plains is managed for biodiversity, there may be a welcome mat for locusts. To be clear, I don't expect cloning and reintroduction to happen any time soon—if ever.

Another route to recovery might be taken if the locust is discovered in the near future to still be living in its solitary phase in an isolated valley or two. Lockwood has pondered the question of what happens then.[50] Would it merit listing as a threatened or endangered species? Even if the population is found to be on the edge of extinction, the U.S. Endangered Species Act specifically excludes insects that are considered pests from being listed. What constitutes a "pest," however, is not defined. Is the locust a pest if it hasn't swarmed and damaged crops since the late 1800s? While some would propose protecting this last population, others may call for its extermination as a precaution against potential future outbreaks.

Lockwood suggests one more route for conserving any surviving locust population that is discovered. Lockwood often searched for the locust in Yellowstone National Park because its meadowed valleys have been spared the plow and livestock grazing. During one trip he captured several grasshoppers that looked slightly different from a closely related species he often found. "I think I know what they were," he opaquely writes, "so I released them back into the field." Since he didn't remove them from the park, there was no requirement to tell park authorities what they were or where they were found. And he didn't.[51]

In addition to cryptically blending in to its badland habitat, the greater short-horned lizard (*Phrynosoma hernandesi*) defends itself by shooting toxic blood from its eyes. Drawing by Erica Freese.

NINE

Black-Tailed Prairie Dog and Black-Footed Ferret

They are the sentinels of the Great Plains, their barks warning creatures large and small of an approaching snake, raptor, carnivore, or human. Historically, across tens of millions of acres of grasslands from Canada to Mexico, at any one moment millions of prairie dogs must have been perched on their mounds scanning the horizon and skies. At any one moment, like a crowd wave at a football game, tens of thousands must have been bouncing up on their hind legs and throwing their heads and front legs into the air to issue warning barks. Perhaps more than any sound, their yip indicated you were in the short- and mixed-grass prairies of the Great Plains.

Then, in a few decades, there was silence. With a historical population of three to five billion, the black-tailed prairie dog shares with the passenger pigeon the lamentable distinction of suffering one of the greatest population collapses of any wildlife species—among vertebrates at least—in the New World as a result of Euro-American settlement. Around the time that eastern forest cutting and market hunting were, by 1900, driving the passenger pigeon to extinction in the wild, westward Euro-American expansion was beginning the assault on the five species of prairie dogs in North America's semiarid western grasslands. The population of the black-tailed prairie dog—which inhabits the Great Plains, including the American Prairie–Russell Refuge, and is by far the most common of the four species—collapsed by 98% or more. The four other species of prairie dogs, mostly inhabitants of

FIG. 16. Black-tailed prairie dogs. Courtesy Dennis Lingohr.

intermountain grasslands of the West, underwent similar declines. Prairie dogs went from occupying an estimated 100 million acres of grasslands in the late 1800s to roughly 1.4 million highly fragmented acres 100 years later.[1]

The historic range of black-tailed prairie dogs spanned the short- and mixed-grass prairies and shrub-steppe ecosystems of the Great Plains from just north of the Canada–U.S. border to just south of the U.S.–Mexico border.[2] As a plump, two-to-three-pound rodent in an ecosystem with diverse predators—snakes, hawks, eagles, badgers, coyotes, black-footed ferrets, and others—much of a prairie dog's life is devoted to not being eaten (fig. 16). Black-tailed prairie dogs are social animals that are active aboveground during the day and live in a network of underground burrows they excavate. Family units, called coteries, consist of one adult male, two to four adult females, and all their young less than two years old. Coteries live together to create colonies, sometimes called towns, which may cover a few acres to thousands of acres. At a larger scale is the prairie dog complex, an area that contains multiple colonies separated by a few hundred yards to several miles. Some complexes described in the 1800s covered hundreds of thousands of acres. A complex in Texas measured 250 miles by 100–150 miles. One in Wyoming was 100 miles long, and another in Kansas was 60 miles long.[3]

The population collapses of the five species of prairie dogs were due primarily to three factors. First, starting in the late 1800s and particularly bad for black-tailed prairie dogs, was the destruction of prairie dog habitat as Great Plains grasslands were converted to croplands. This conversion was most intense in the eastern third of the black-tailed prairie dog's range in the Great Plains where, when cropland acreage peaked in the 1940s, nearly all counties had at least 25%, and some more than 75%, of their land in crops.[4]

Next, and more devastatingly, came government-funded eradication campaigns, urged by livestock producers who viewed prairie dogs as competing for forage. Persecution of prairie dogs by poisoning, shooting, and other lethal means employed by landowners and local and state agencies began in the late 1800s but gained its greatest head of steam starting around 1915, when the federal government stepped in. From 1912 to 1939 incomplete records show at least 70 million acres of prairie dogs and ground squirrels poisoned in the U.S. Great Plains and nearby intermountain grasslands.[5]

The third and final assault emerged when sylvatic plague, a nonnative, flea-borne disease, arrived in the United States around 1900 and first infected prairie dog colonies in the 1930s. The cause, *Yersinia pestis*, is a zoonotic bacterium, meaning it can spread between wildlife and humans. This is the same germ responsible for the plague pandemic—the so-called black death—that killed tens of millions of people during the Middle Ages. Though no longer a major public health threat in North America, plague is nearly 100% lethal to prairie dogs and has annihilated colonies across their historic range. Many species of mammals, especially rodents, are reservoirs of the disease. Plague can exist for years at a low level, in what's called an enzootic state, when it is relatively harmless to prairie dogs and ferrets. But then, for unknown reasons plague may explode into an epizootic state that can wipe out entire prairie dog colonies and any ferrets inhabiting the colonies in a week or two.[6]

Without a break between the three assaults—habitat destruction, poisoning, and plague—prairie dog populations were relentlessly hammered. The collapse of more than 98% of the populations of the five species was probably completed by the 1960s. It's a surprise, if one reflects on the passenger pigeon, that none of the five went extinct. The repercussions of the collapse, however, had become apparent years earlier.

The Ferret's "Extinctions" and Rediscoveries

The slender black-footed ferret weighs roughly two pounds, is primarily a nocturnal hunter, and is solitary except during mating and when mothers are with young (see drawing at the end of this chapter). Throughout their range, black-footed ferrets prey almost exclusively on prairie dogs and make their homes in prairie dog burrows. As a result, the ferret's historic distribution was nearly identical to the combined distribution of the black-tailed prairie dog in the Great Plains and the much smaller populations of the white-tailed prairie dog (*Cynomys leucurus*) and Gunnison's prairie dog (*Cynomys gunnisoni*) in the nearby intermountain grasslands to the west. Without prairie dogs there are no ferrets.

While the historic ferret population may have tallied 500,000–1,000,000,[7] by the early 1960s it was thought to be extinct. In 1964, however, a small population was discovered in Mellette County, South Dakota. A few ferrets from that population were captured for captive breeding, but that effort foundered. The last wild animals in the South Dakota population were observed in 1974, and the last captive animals from that population, having failed to breed, died in 1979. Once again, the ferret was presumed extinct.[8]

Meanwhile, during the late 1960s and the 1970s, massive efforts were launched to find black-footed ferrets. In 1967 the ferret was among the first species listed as endangered in the United States under the 1966 Endangered Species Preservation Act, the precursor to the U.S. Endangered Species Act of 1973 under which the ferret is now listed as endangered. Day and night searches involving thousands of person-hours were conducted on foot and by horseback, car, snowmobile, helicopter, and fixed-wing aircraft. Scent dogs, track stations, remote cameras, scat surveys, and scent attractants were employed. Press releases and thousands of "Ferret Wanted" posters, with a $250 reward, were sent to state and provinces across the range of the ferret. Hundreds of hopeful reports came in, but none panned out.[9]

Finally, a rancher's dog named Shep unintentionally proved up to task. In September 1981 near Meeteetse, Wyoming, Shep brought a dead black-footed ferret home and earned a $250 reward, marking the start of a surprising new chapter in the ferret's struggle for survival. A small population of ferrets inhabiting the white-tailed prairie dog colonies of the area was soon confirmed.[10] This discovery catalyzed new searches for other black-footed ferret populations, with the reward for finding one eventually reaching $10,000 in Montana. But none were found.[11] The future of black-footed ferrets rested entirely on the shoulders of the Meeteetse population. Then disaster struck in the form of canine distemper, a disease native to North America. The Meeteetse ferret population of around 125 in 1984 plummeted to roughly 16 in the fall of 1985. Six ferrets captured as a first attempt to restart a captive population died immediately of canine distemper. Simultaneously, a plague epizootic reduced white-tailed prairie dog numbers in the area, possibly contributing to the ferret's decline due to a reduced prey base.[12] Not discovered until later was the fact that, unlike many carnivores, black-footed ferrets also readily contract plague and suffer high mortality. Thus, in addition to reducing its prey base, the disease may also have killed ferrets directly.[13]

In a desperate move to save the species, the entire remaining population of 18 ferrets was captured from 1985 to 1987. This time, the right captive conditions avoided the early mistakes made with the South Dakota ferrets, helped by a big dose of good luck. Of those 18, 3 males and 4 females produced offspring, becoming the founder population for all ferrets alive today—except one, which I explain later.[14] Seven ferrets made the difference between extinction and renewed hope and efforts for saving the species. As we'll see, the road to recovery is still long, tortuous, and uncertain.

Collapse in the American Prairie–Russell Refuge Region

Prairie dogs and presumably ferrets were historically common in the American Prairie–Russell Refuge region. The English adventurer Charles Messiter described a prairie dog complex in the region in 1871 that was 30–40 miles long. As late as the 1930s, a string of prairie dog colonies called the "40-mile town" extended from the Little Rocky Mountains to the southeast. Evidence exists of another colony of similar size that stretched for tens of miles from the Fort Belknap Indian Reservation to the east.[15]

How many acres of prairie dogs were there, and how many ferrets did they support? To answer those and related questions, I sought advice from two colleagues, Steve Forrest and Randy Matchett, who have spent a combined 70 years working on ferret and prairie dog conservation. (Both patiently endured and replied to my repeated requests for information and advice throughout this chapter.) Steve was among the first to gather data in the 1980s on the newly discovered Meeteetse ferrets. Randy has been working on ferret restoration on the Charles M. Russell National Wildlife Refuge ever since he joined its staff in 1987. To estimate acres of prairie dogs, Steve used the lower end of Messiter's observation, a 30-mile-long complex, and figured if the complex was elliptical, it would have covered roughly 226,000 acres; a rounder shape would raise it to over 400,000 acres. There are often gaps between colonies that form a complex, so a minimum estimate of 200,000 acres of prairie-dog-occupied habitat seems reasonable.

Crop cultivation, shooting, and poisoning, which began as homesteaders surged into the region in the early 1900s, surely

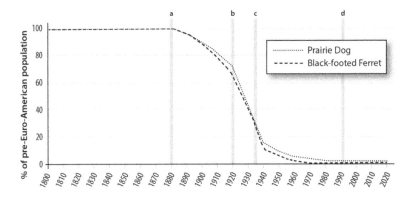

FIG. 17. Postulated population trends of the black-tailed prairie dog and black-footed ferret in the American Prairie–Russell Refuge region and across the ranges of the two species from 1800 to 2020 as a percentage of population levels before Euro-American colonization. Vertical lines indicate the start of events with likely major effects on the populations: (a) open-range livestock era followed by homesteading era, (b) U.S. government–sponsored prairie dog eradication program, (c) first documented plague epizootic in prairie dogs in North America, (d) first documented plague epizootic in prairie dogs in the American Prairie–Russell Refuge region and ongoing rancher intolerance. Created by author and Eric Cline.

began to whittle away the complex's size. This was followed by U.S. government–sponsored programs to eradicate prairie dogs. The result was that in southern Phillips County, located immediately to the east of the Fort Belknap Indian Reservation, 179,026 acres of prairie dogs were poisoned from 1924 to 1939.[16] This acreage may have included roughly one million prairie dogs based on densities observed elsewhere.[17] By 1988 prairie dog colonies in southern Phillips County had plummeted to around 27,000 acres. Then, starting in 1992 a series of die-offs reduced the colonies to just 8,000 acres by 1998.[18] Although not confirmed with antibody tests at the time, plague is the only disease known to cause such rapid and large-scale die-offs in prairie dogs. Assuming 200,000 acres as the minimum presettlement size of colonies, that's a population collapse of at least 96% (fig. 17).

How far did ferret numbers fall? An average of roughly 225 acres of black-tailed prairie dogs are required to support one adult female ferret. Territories of adult male ferrets overlap female territories, there are generally two adult females per male in a population, and three is the average litter size.[19] Using these figures, 200,000 acres of prairie dogs may have supported a population of about 4,000 ferrets—900 adult females, 450 adult males and 2,700 kits. The near total loss of its principal prey base alone would have caused a catastrophic nosedive in the ferret population. On top of that, ferrets probably also died from secondary poisoning by feeding on prairie dogs dead or dying from strychnine-laced baits. Ferret specimens from the American Prairie–Russell Refuge region are scarce after the 1920s.[20] The last reported sighting of a ferret in the region was noted in a C. M. Russell Refuge report in 1940.[21]

Other Effects of the Prairie Dog's Collapse

The ferret is not the only species to suffer the consequences of the prairie dog's collapse. At their pre-Columbian abundance, prairie dogs probably exerted a greater influence on grassland biodiversity than any other species—or at least on par with, and in combination with, bison. That keystone role is now nearly entirely missing from the Great Plains.[22]

Prairie dogs are pivotal in the grassland food web as nutrients move from the plants they eat, through the prairie dogs, and on to a diverse suite of reptilian, avian, and mammalian predators and scores of invertebrate decomposers. In addition to ferrets, populations of carnivores such as the swift fox and badger, as noted in chapter 7, surely suffered due to the collapse of prairie dog populations. Prairie rattlesnakes (*Crotalus viridus*) and bull snakes (*Pituophis catenifer*) commonly prey on prairie dogs, as do ferruginous hawks and golden eagles, among other raptors.[23] Populations of these and other predators must be a fraction of what they were before the prairie dog's collapse.

Prairie dogs have two major effects on habitat structure. By eating grasses and forbs and clipping vegetation to create clear sight lines, presumably for predator detection, prairie dogs create more bare ground and shorter vegetation with more forbs and reduced shrub cover compared to off-colony areas. In addition, their burrowing adds a third dimension to the mostly two-dimensional habitat of the prairie. The burrows provide protection from the elements and from predators for numerous species, from arthropods, tiger salamanders (*Ambystoma mavortium*), and rattlesnakes to burrowing owls, deer mice (*Peromyscus maniculatus*), swift foxes, and black-footed ferrets. According to one estimate, prairie dogs churn 440–500 pounds of soil per burrow system, resulting in potentially tens of thousands of pounds churned per acre, which enables deeper aeration and water penetration into the soil. Soils on burrow mounds are nutrient "hotspots" that store more nitrogen and organic carbon with greater nutrient-rich plant productivity than off-mound sites.[24] The result, compared to off-colony sites, is that prairie dog colonies tend to have higher soil nematode abundance, more bees and other pollinators, a distinctly different community of arthropods, and more grazing by bison, elk, and pronghorn, as well as by livestock.[25] Colonies also provide important nesting and foraging habitat for mountain plovers, thick-billed longspurs, and several other bird species.[26]

Research in Colorado indicates black-tailed prairie dog colonies are also important for feeding bats and other aerial insectivores. On average, nine species of bats tracked via echolocation calls were 2.4 times more active over prairie dog colonies than reference sites off prairie dog colonies. Open habitat specialists, such as the big brown bat (*Eptesicus fuscus*) and hoary bat (*Lasiurus cinereus*) as well as the forest-edge-inhabiting small-footed myotis (*Myotis ciliolabrum*)—all residents in the American Prairie–Russell Refuge region—showed especially strong attraction to prairie dog colonies.[27] These findings suggest it was not a coincidence when few years ago I watched an aggregation of nighthawks (*Chordeiles minor*) feeding over a prairie dog colony on American Prairie lands.

Although the prairie dog's population collapse has wide-ranging consequences for grassland biodiversity, no single impact has been more severe than driving the black-footed ferret to the edge of extinction. As a consequence, the black-footed ferret is a "conservation-reliant species," meaning its survival requires continual management interventions.[28] A vast array of tools of endangered species management—perhaps some yet to be invented—are needed to save the ferret.

Range-Wide Recovery Efforts

After their success in getting seven of the ferrets captured near Meeteetse to breed in captivity—no sure thing at the time—the ferret recovery team turned its attention to designing long-term recovery goals and strategies. A range-wide recovery plan for the black-footed ferret was first published in 1988 and last updated in 2013.[29] Recovery is an international effort involving cooperation among federal, state, and provincial agencies, Native nations, zoos with breeding facilities, and recovery sites in Canada, the United States, and Mexico.

Two overarching, interrelated goals shaped recovery planning. The first goal was to maintain as much genetic variation as possible. A century of ferret populations disappearing in the Great Plains and intermountain grasslands had resulted in the loss of 30–50% of the species' genetic variation, leaving the small, isolated Meeteetse population to represent the ferret's remaining genetic diversity. Moreover, the seven captive ferrets that bred to become the founders for ferret reintroductions to the wild represented only 70–85% of the genetic variation of the Meeteetse population. Decline in genetic variation due to genetic drift is inevitable in small populations, and so minimizing that decline was crucial for ferret managers.[30]

Second, to avoid the risk of placing all your eggs in one or very few baskets, multiple populations had to be created. These goals led to the establishment of six captive breeding facilities and to efforts to establish several populations of ferrets on prairie dog colonies across the Great Plains and nearby intermountain grasslands. The captive breeding facilities, with a total of about 280 adult ferrets, enable scientists to control who breeds with whom to minimize loss of genetic variation and to produce animals for introduction to the wild.[31]

Plans for establishing ferrets in the wild had to answer two basic questions: First, how many ferrets should a population have? Second, how many acres of prairie dogs are needed to support that many ferrets? The answer to the first question involves the genetics of small populations. As noted in chapter 1, the concept of minimum viable population (MVP) emerged in the 1980s as an approach to defining the smallest isolated population that had a good chance of surviving for a long time. One approach to determining the MVP based on genetics is the 50/500 rule.[32] Fifty is the effective population required to avoid extinction over the short term—a few generations—due to the effects of inbreeding. Five hundred is the effective population size required to avoid the long-term risk of extinction. "Effective" population means that the numbers 50 and 500 refer to an ideal population where mating is random, all individuals breed and produce the same number of offspring, and other stipulations that almost never occur in the wild. The actual number of adults needed (called the "census" population) to achieve this effective size is often much larger.

The recovery plan goal for "delisting" the ferret, which means it would no longer be officially listed as endangered or threatened, is at least 3,000 adults in 30 or more geographically widely distributed subpopulations. That means that 20 subpopulations must have at least 30 adults, and 10 or more subpopulations must have at least 100 adults. Because the target subpopulations are too small for long-term genetic health, the plan calls for periodic exchanges of animals, whether by natural ferret movements between sites, managers translocating ferrets between sites, or the introduction of captive-bred ferrets.[33]

The next task for the recovery team was to determine the acres of prairie dog colonies needed to support the ferret populations. For ferrets in black-tailed prairie dog areas, the recovery plan assumes an adult sex ratio of two females per male and that each female ferret requires 225 acres of prairie dogs.[34] Thus, to provide sufficient habitat for 30 adult ferrets, each reintroduction site should have a minimum of 20 × 225 = 4,500 acres of prairie dog colonies; 100 adult ferrets will need at least 15,000 acres of prairie dogs.

A brief history of ferret recovery efforts shows how diverse and relentless the obstacles are to meeting these recovery goals.

Starting with the four females and three males from the rescued Meeteetse population, the breeding program was soon yielding surplus ferrets. Reintroduction efforts began in 1991 with the release of ferrets onto white-tailed prairie dog colonies in the Shirley Basin in Wyoming. Since then, more than 5,100 captive-born ferrets and a few wild-born ones have been released on 29 sites ranging from Canada to Mexico, including three sites in the American Prairie–Russell Refuge region.[35]

Establishing a new wild population typically involves a fall release of 10–30 or more male and female ferrets annually over the course of three or more years. Before being released, all captive-born ferrets are vaccinated against canine distemper and plague, and to help track their movements and survival, a passive integrated transponder (PIT) tag is hypodermically implanted under the skin of each released ferret. All wild-born ferrets that are captured are also vaccinated and marked with PIT tags. For the highest level of protection, both vaccines require a booster injection two to four weeks after the first injection, making its use in wild-born ferrets a challenge.[36] Canine distemper has not been a problem since reintroduction efforts began in 1991.[37]

The program found early success in building the wild ferret populations to a total of around 600–700 animals from 2005 to 2010. But then the wild populations began to decline as plague decimated prairie dog colonies at several reintroduction sites.[38] As of fall 2019, only 14 of 29 reintroduction sites still had ferrets, with a total estimated population of about 315 animals.[39]

Despite forty years of recovery work since the discovery of the Meeteetse population, six captive breeding facilities, 29 reintroduction sites across three countries, more than 5,000 ferrets released into the wild, extensive flea control, vaccines, sophisticated monitoring, breeding and genetic technologies, millions of hours of professional and volunteer work, the ferret remains one of the world's most endangered species. What's the problem?

The overriding issue is too few prairie dogs. That problem distills down mostly to plague and intolerance by livestock producers to prairie dogs.[40] Also, although low genetic variation is not currently the choke point for ferret recovery, it remains a long-term concern. Let's look at each of these.

Plague

Currently the two main strategies for minimizing plague in prairie dogs focus on the use of flea-killing insecticides. One method, developed many years ago, is squirting insecticide dust (deltamethrin is currently the dust of choice) into every prairie dog burrow. Annual applications are the norm because the insecticide is effective for about 10 months. But dusting is labor intensive and requires more person-power and other resources than most reintroduction sites can afford. With annual applications, however, another problem arises: the fleas develop resistance to the insecticide after as few as five or six years.[41] A second concern about the use of deltamethrin is that it kills nontarget invertebrates, with negative consequences for animals that eat those invertebrates.[42]

A second, more recent and promising approach is the use of fipronil, the active ingredient in widely sold flea and tick treatments for domestic pets. Fipronil is used as a systemic in prairie dogs; prairie dogs eat a bait with fipronil, and the fleas die when they eat the prairie dog's blood. The first field tests showed fipronil to be effective in flea control on prairie dogs for one to two years. To make fipronil tasty to prairie dogs, Randy Matchett invented what he calls FipBits, which are fipronil-laced pellets composed of flour, molasses, peanut butter, and other ingredients. FipBits can be much more efficiently applied to a prairie dog colony than deltamethrin and may reduce the cost of flea control by more than 90%. Preliminary research found no toxicity to prairie dogs or ferrets, but this, as well as potential effects on nontarget species, is being further evaluated. The idea would be to regularly rotate the application of fipronil and deltamethrin to avoid fleas developing resistance to either.[43] FipBit has the potential to be a game changer in prairie dog and black-footed ferret conservation.

Long-term plague control in prairie dogs boils down to three potential options. One is to control the plague's vector, fleas, which will require a long-term battle between fleas evolving resistance to insecticides and biologists counterpunching with new formulations. The second is to perfect an oral vaccine against plague that confers long-term immunity and could be efficiently fed to prairie dogs. This, too, would involve ongoing evaluation and adjustments in response to the plague bacterium evolving resistance to the vaccine. The third option, genetic resistance to plague, could occur via two routes. Prairie dogs (and ferrets) might evolve resistance to plague through natural selection, but so far there is no evidence of this occurring. Using CRISPR/Cas 9 technology to edit the prairie dog genome may be a more promising approach to creating long-term immunity[44]—with occasional gene-editing adjustments as the plague bacterium's evolution dictates. Genetic modification of species we are trying to save, however, raises ethical considerations.[45]

Ranchers' Intolerance

Reflecting the attitude of livestock ranchers across the Great Plains, ranchers in the American Prairie–Russell Refuge region loathe prairie dogs nearly as much as they loathe wolves and grizzly bears.[46] Prairie dogs are viewed by most ranchers as competing with livestock for forage and being destructive to grassland health. Sometimes, especially during a drought, competition for forage occurs.[47] In other cases, although prairie dogs may reduce forage quantity, they enhance forage quality and thereby, in the balance, may benefit or have little effect on livestock production.[48] Even if livestock productivity is negatively affected by prairie dogs, control may not be cost-effective because poisoning is expensive and time consuming and prairie dogs can repopulate sites.[49]

Despite these uncertainties, rancher intolerance translates into state and federal decisions and policies that are stacked against restoring populations of prairie dogs. States, including Montana, generally designate prairie dogs as pests and allow ranchers and pest-control companies to employ poisoning, shooting, and other methods to control populations. Although the state of Montana classifies prairie dogs as a "species of concern," the state allows year-round shooting of prairie dogs. The Bureau of Land Management

(BLM) has the authority to prohibit prairie shooting, but nearly all BLM lands, including those in the American Prairie–Russell Refuge region, are open to shooting. A quick internet search shows numerous outfitters across the Great Plains advertising guided prairie dog hunts.

Shooting profoundly affects prairie dog behavior and survival beyond just the animals killed. A study in Wyoming found that, compared to prairie dog colonies with no shooting, animals in colonies subject to shooting increased alert behavior eightfold, reduced time aboveground and foraging by 66%, had 35% lower body condition, and suffered near-total reproductive collapse.[50] A more insidious effect of prairie dog shooting is the lead poisoning of eagles and hawks that eat lead-laced carcasses.[51] The end result of ranch-country intolerance is that poisoning and shooting, combined with plague, maintain a choke-hold on prairie dog populations in the American Prairie–Russell Refuge region and across the Great Plains.[52]

Ferret Genetics

Though not the main impediment to ferret recovery today, the ferret's low genetic variation requires ongoing attention to minimize further genetic erosion and for long-term evolutionary adaptability. Genetic variation has continued to decline since the start of captive breeding.[53] Kinked tails, malformed kidneys, abnormal sperm, and reduced reproductive success in the captive population suggest inbreeding depression.[54] Inbreeding, however, has not yet emerged as a problem in the reintroduced wild populations.[55]

Long term, the ferret's genetic health will require ongoing management by moving ferrets and their genes between wild and captive populations.[56] Ferret managers had the foresight more than 20 years ago to freeze the semen of male ferrets from the breeding program before they died. As the genetic lineage of some of those ferrets became underrepresented in the population, managers have successfully used artificial insemination of those frozen sperm to reintroduce genes from some long-dead males back into the gene pool.[57] But this still leaves the ferrets with a gene pool based on only the seven founders.

Fortunately, recent advances in cloning technology greatly expand the potential for diversifying the ferret genome.[58] Ferret biologists also had the foresight in 1985 to cryopreserve tissue samples from two captive Meeteetse ferrets that never bred. The technology is complicated and takes considerable luck, but using DNA from that tissue, in December 2020 the first cloned black-footed ferret, a female, was born. If she successfully breeds, she will become the eighth member of the founding population of all black-footed ferrets alive today. With three times more genetic diversity than the current population, she is genetically the most valuable black-footed ferret in existence.[59] Preserved tissue is also available from the first group of ferrets captured in the 1970s from the extinct population in Mellette County, South Dakota.

Recovery in the American Prairie–Russell Refuge Region

Rich in prairie dog habitat and with sizeable colonies, ferrets were introduced to three sites in and near the American Prairie–Russell Refuge region during the mid-1990s. One was on BLM lands, one on the UL Bend area of the C. M. Russell Refuge, and one on the Fort Belknap Indian Reservation.[60] The reintroduction on BLM lands was short-lived, as plague soon devastated the prairie dog colonies and the ferrets vanished.

The first ferrets were released onto prairie dog colonies of the Fort Belknap Indian Reservation in 1997.[61] The effort suffered a setback when in 1999 a plague epizootic swept through the release sites. After regrowth of the prairie dog colonies, ferrets were again reintroduced from 2013 to 2015. With careful management, a ferret population of about 15–20 animals has been maintained on the reservation in recent years.

No reintroduction site exemplifies the Sisyphean task of ferret recovery more than UL Bend in the C. M. Russell Refuge. As the second site in North America for ferret reintroduction, the UL Bend program met with early success. The release of 171 captive-reared ferrets between 1994 and 1999 resulted in at least 168 kits born in the wild from 1995 to 2000. By 2000 there were nearly 30 adults with 44 wild-born kits that spring. For Randy Matchett, the person with his shoulder to the boulder of ferret recovery on UL Bend, things were going well. With such success, Randy needed help, and so in the fall of 2000, Steve Forrest, who I introduced earlier; Bob Irvin, then head of the World Wildlife Fund's U.S. program; and I signed up to help him conduct the fall survey on UL Bend.

After a long drive on dusty roads and two-tracks, Steve, Bob, and I checked into field headquarters for the UL Bend ferret site, a collection of camp trailers and a wooden shed known fondly as "ferret camp." After dinner at the picnic tables and a brief nap, we chugged some coffee, got final instructions from Randy, and headed out shortly after sunset, Randy in a truck with me, to follow two-tracks crisscrossing the prairie to spotlight for ferrets. Spotlighting is done by driving slowly while scanning the dark expanses of prairie with a spotlight—"roller painting the prairie with light," as Randy describes it. When the light shines on the ferret's tapetum lucidum, the reflective tissue in the back of the eyes of most nocturnal animals, the animals' eyes show up as two bright, emerald-green gems. Ferrets spend most of their life underground in prairie dog burrows, so it takes luck to be at the right place at the right time and with the ferret facing the spotlight to see one during one of its brief forays aboveground.

Once a ferret is spotted, and it enters a burrow, the observers hustle to place a PIT tag reading ring over the burrow entrance. Ferrets are not particularly shy, and so the individual may soon poke its head out of the burrow to see what's happening. When it does, the reader ring is checked to see if it has read a PIT tag and, if so, recorded that particular ferret's number. If the reader does not register a number, its likely a wild-born ferret that should be captured for the first time. This involves inserting a trap into the burrow, wrapping it with a blanket so the ferret thinks it's still in the tunnel system when it crawls up into the trap, and returning periodically during the night to check the trap. If a ferret is captured for the first time, it gets a full treatment: transported back to the lab at ferret camp, anesthetized, weighed and measured, vaccinated, and implanted with a PIT tag, as well as having blood and hair samples taken. Once the anesthetic wears off, the ferret is released at the burrow where it was captured.

Spotlighting doesn't stop until sunup. By five in the morning my attempt to impress a still bright-eyed and talkative Randy with my field biologist's stamina was belied by my mumbling and bobbing head. Attempting a complete tally of ferrets means repeating these all-nighters for two or three consecutive nights over one to two weeks. In what has to rank high in the annals of beginner's luck for ferret counters, Bob, while taking a walk around ferret camp, looked down a burrow and saw a ferret with a prairie dog in its jaws! Ferret biologists work a lifetime without seeing this. We were lucky to have found so many ferrets in 2000 when ferret numbers were near their peak because the next 20 years at UL Bend would epitomize the struggle of ferret recovery at reintroduction sites across the species' range.

It began when a drought struck in 2001, and ferret numbers began a nosedive until one adult female remained in 2003. Sixty more captive-reared ferrets were released in 2003 and 2004. At the same time Randy began an intensive study to better understand what was killing ferrets despite a healthy prairie dog population that showed no sign of a plague epizootic. Randy and his collaborators found that the survival of ferrets vaccinated against plague was more than twice that of unvaccinated ferrets and that ferret survival was also twice as high on prairie dog colonies dusted with deltamethrin as on undusted colonies. It appeared that low-level plague (the "enzootic" state) was killing ferrets.

Another plague epizootic, however, struck in 2007 and eliminated 50% of the nondusted prairie dog colonies. Ferret numbers plummeted. The prairie dog colonies began to recover and 20 more ferrets were released in the fall of 2013, but only 1 survived to the next spring. Nevertheless, good reproduction among the handful of surviving wild ferrets began to grow the population, and by fall 2017 the count registered a minimum of 24 ferrets. But then, perhaps all to predictably, a plague epizootic reduced the prairie dog population by 70% and the number of ferrets fell to 4 by the fall of 2018, to 1 by the spring of 2019, and then none.[62]

The raw numbers at UL Bend tell a stark story: 25 years (1994–2019) of recovery work, tens of thousands of prairie dog burrows dusted, hundreds of ferrets vaccinated, 255 captive-born ferrets released, at least 328 ferrets born in the wild, four separate periods where good ferret reproduction gave hope that this time it would work, and yet today, zero ferrets and only 350 acres of prairie dogs remain on UL Bend. The UL Bend ferret population never achieved that minimum threshold of 30 breeding adults to count toward recovery. Randy concludes that more ferret reintroductions on UL Bend would be futile. The area's prairie dog habitat is too limited and, like other reintroduction sites, remains vulnerable to plague.[63]

A Transformational Future for Ferrets

The 2019 *Species Status Assessment Report for the Black-Footed Ferret* (Mustela nigripes*)* by the U.S. Fish and Wildlife Service (USFWS) proposes five future scenarios for ferret recovery, ranging from the worst, the "disastrous scenario," to the best, the "transformation scenario." The transformation scenario calls for five new reintroduction sites, each capable of supporting at least 100 breeding adults by the year 2029.[64]

Considering that historically there were at least 200,000 acres of prairie dogs between the Milk River and Missouri River in the core of the American Prairie–Russell Refuge region, there is no shortage of habitat for growing 15,000 acres of prairie dog colonies that could support 100 ferrets. As long as plague or a severe drought does not cause major setbacks, prairie dog colonies on good habitat can double in size every two years.[65] At that rate, prairie dog colonies of 1,000–2,000 acres found on American Prairie lands today could readily grow to more than 15,000 acres in less than 10 years.

The most important action for assisting population growth is assiduous treatment with insecticides to control plague-carrying fleas. The chances of long-term success, however, would greatly increase with new breakthroughs in plague control such as improved and more affordable flea control, an oral vaccine, or genome editing for resistance to plague. Colony growth can also be aided by introducing prairie dogs, captured from areas where they are not wanted or from low priority colonies, to start a new colony or augment existing colonies. Another method for growth that American Prairie and others use is to dig artificial burrows and mow vegetation close to the ground to help prairie dogs get established on reintroduction sites and, when done beyond the margins of existing colonies, to encourage their expansion.

While growing and maintaining 15,000 acres of prairie dogs would constitute a significant achievement, that shouldn't stop us from setting a bigger long-term goal. One hundred ferrets seems dangerously few. Especially if breakthroughs for controlling plague emerge, several hundred ferrets on 50,000 or more acres of prairie dogs seems prudent and doable. But we don't need to wait that long for ferret reintroduction.

American Prairie hopes to begin ferret reintroduction soon. While over the long term I assume that prairie dog and ferret recovery can be pursued without compromise over a vast landscape of the American Prairie–Russell Refuge, over the short term rancher intolerance and inscrutable, adverse government policies are a huge impediment to recovery. BLM is a federal agency with a multiple-use mandate that includes conserving biodiversity and supporting endangered species recovery. A sister agency of BLM in the Department of the Interior is USFWS, the lead federal agency spending millions of dollars to restore prairie dogs and prevent ferret extinction. BLM should be front and center in helping this effort. Instead, it undermines USFWS's recovery work by allowing unregulated shooting of prairie dogs on BLM lands. In basic scientific jargon, this is nuts!

State-level policies are no better. Although Montana's State Wildlife Action Plan calls for the right actions for restoring prairie dogs and black-footed ferrets, the Montana Department of Agriculture's designation of prairie dogs as vertebrate pests generally smothers any significant state-led prairie dog conservation efforts.

The bottom line is the livestock industry maintains its 100-year stranglehold on prairie dog—and thus black-footed ferret—conservation.

The Black-Footed Ferret as Umbrella Species

Among carnivores, the label "umbrella species," a species whose conservation will help conserve many other species,[66] is generally reserved for only the biggest—lions, wolves, and so on. But perhaps the two-pound ferret deserves the label as well because its survival depends on big populations of a keystone species, the black-tailed prairie dog. And big populations of prairie dogs are crucial for successful restoration of grassland biodiversity in the Great Plains. If the ferret was not listed as endangered or had gone extinct, the minimal protection afforded prairie dogs because of their importance to ferret recovery would not exist. That could spell the end for nearly all remaining prairie dog populations and for their keystone role.

I qualified the umbrella species label for the ferret with "perhaps" because meeting the goals for delisting the ferret will fall far short of restoring any semblance of the prairie dog's historic keystone role. To reach the delisting goal of at least 3,000 ferrets in 30 or more subpopulations, the recovery plan calls for roughly 500,000 acres of prairie dogs—just 0.05% of the estimated acreage 150 years ago. At a minimum we should aim for "decollapsing" prairie dog populations back to at least 10% of their historic numbers—10 million acres.

Restoring and conserving nature on North America's semiarid western grasslands without restoring and conserving a species that underpins the ecological integrity and biodiversity of those grasslands makes little sense. Cooperation among landowners—private, Native nations, and governments—will be crucial. The U.S. government could make a major and immediate contribution to this goal on tens of millions of acres by prohibiting prairie dog poisoning and shooting on all federal lands. If we succeed—even partially—in meeting this goal, not only will grassland biodiversity and dozens of species benefit, but we will avoid stopping at the minimalist goal for delisting the black-footed ferret. Rather than 3,000 ferrets, imagine 100,000. Then, by day, prairie visitors will again be greeted by the warning yips of prairie dogs. And those venturing out at night may encounter the gem-like green eye shine of black-footed ferrets and be thankful for a society with the ethics, wisdom, and commitment required to bring a species back from the edge of extinction.

A black-footed ferret eats one prairie dog every 3 or 4 days; a ferret family—a
mother and her kits—may eat more than 250 prairie dogs in a year.
Drawing by Erica Freese.

TEN

Pallid Sturgeon

U p to six feet long and 80 pounds, a top predator, a hold-
over from the age of dinosaurs, armored with bony plates,
loaded with electrosensors and long fleshy whiskers, sucking up prey while prowling the bottom of deep, muddy rivers:
maybe potential material for a science-fiction monster, but defi-
nitely a fascinating fish for biologists. Any species that has changed
little in 100 million years, like the pallid sturgeon, must have a
storied history. The Acipenseridae, the taxonomic family that the
world's 25 species of sturgeon belong to, has been around more
than 200 million years, one of the oldest lineages of vertebrates
living today.[1] The pallid sturgeon swam in Cretaceous rivers in the
company of the 35-foot *Deinosuchus* ("terrible crocodile") while
T. rex prowled the shorelines. It survived the massive extinction
event at the end of the Cretaceous, 66 million years ago. It experienced the rise of the Rocky Mountains and the resulting birth of
its new home, the Missouri River. Multiple ice ages and another
global extinction episode at the end of the Pleistocene didn't knock
it out, but human actions since Euro-American colonization nearly
have, especially in the American Prairie–Russell Refuge region of
the Upper Missouri River.

The pallid sturgeon and other native fish of the Missouri and
Mississippi River systems have been pummeled by physical, chemical, and biological changes in the rivers' ecosystems since Euro-
American colonization. Most noticeable has been the physical
alteration of the river, particularly dam construction during the

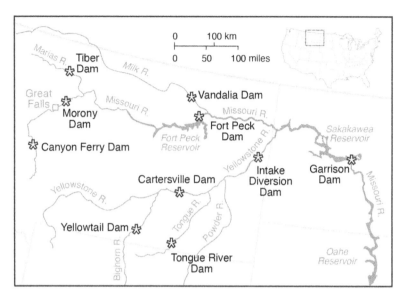

FIG. 18. Rivers and main dams of the region historically inhabited by Upper Missouri River pallid sturgeon population. Created by Eric Cline (modified from U.S. Fish and Wildlife Service, *Revised Recovery Plan for the Pallid Sturgeon* (Scaphirhynchus albus), fig. 7).

1930s–50s, as well as channelization and other projects to tame the river and use its waters. By the early 1900s fishermen had begun to heavily harvest the high-valued flesh and eggs (caviar) of the pallid sturgeon and its smaller cousin, the shovelnose sturgeon (*Scaphirhynchus platorynchus*).[2] Pollution and introduced nonnative fish species are other threats that arose during the last 100 years.[3] The population of wild pallid sturgeon in the Upper Missouri River region (fig. 18), the focus of this chapter, has collapsed more than 99%. In fact, by the time this book goes to press, wild-born fish of this population—fish not born in a hatchery—may be extinct.

The pallid sturgeon of the Upper Missouri River is the aquatic equivalent of the black-footed ferret, a conservation-reliant population that cannot survive without intensive management interventions for which captive breeding is essential. The pallid sturgeon and the world's other sturgeon species could serve as poster children for what ails fish and river systems globally. Of the world's 25 species of sturgeon, the IUCN Red List categorizes 64% as critically endangered and 8% as endangered, making Acipenseridae the most endangered taxonomic family in the world.[4]

Studying and keeping track of a fish living on the bottom of the turbid Missouri and Mississippi Rivers, even one as big as the pallid sturgeon, is not easy. Tellingly, the species wasn't described by science until 1905. Endemic to the Mississippi and Missouri River systems, the pallid sturgeon's range extends to the northwest in these river systems, into the plains of eastern Montana. A notable decline in pallid sturgeon numbers led to the species being listed as endangered under the U.S. Endangered Species Act in 1990. The official notice in the U.S. Federal Register justified the listing by noting the number of observations averaged 50 per year during the 1960s, 21 per year in the 1970s, and 7 per year in the 1980s over the entire 3,550 river miles of the fish's range. Habitat alteration, commercial fishing, and hybridization with the shovelnose sturgeon were listed as potential threats to the species' survival. Meanwhile, researchers began to notice another indicator of trouble: the pallid sturgeon population was growing old—recruitment of young sturgeon into the population was failing.[5]

The conservation importance of the pallid sturgeon in the Upper Missouri River was highlighted when research revealed this population to be genetically distinct from downstream populations.[6] The genetic difference between the Upper Missouri River population and that of the Atchafalaya River in the Lower Mississippi River basin is nearly as great as the difference between the pallid sturgeon and shovelnose sturgeon. Among other features, pallids in the Upper Missouri River attain a much larger size than other pallid populations. Given the vastly different ecological conditions between the Upper Missouri River system and the Lower Mississippi River system, evolution has surely honed the genome of each system's population to be highly adapted to local conditions.[7]

The listing of pallid sturgeon as endangered led the U.S. Fish and Wildlife Service (USFWS) to establish the Pallid Sturgeon Recovery Program and to expand research to better understand the fish's biology, threats to its survival, and how to restore its populations. Population surveys confirmed the dire status of the Upper

FIG. 19. Wild-born female pallid sturgeon captured in the Missouri River above
the Fort Peck Reservoir being held by Michael Schilz of Montana Fish, Wildlife
& Parks. Likely more than 65 years old, this fish must have hatched before
construction of the Fort Peck Dam choked off natural reproduction of this species
above the dam. Courtesy Michael Schilz.

Missouri River population. Moreover, the Fort Peck Dam and Garrison Dam in North Dakota had artificially fragmented the Upper
Missouri River system so that the population was divided into
two subpopulations. The Missouri-Marias subpopulation inhabits
waters above the Fort Peck Dam and includes a stretch of a Missouri River tributary, the Marias River. The Missouri-Yellowstone
subpopulation is between the Fort Peck Dam and the Garrison
Dam, and includes the Yellowstone River and Milk River. These
two subpopulations are genetically the same.[8]

Historically, several thousand adult pallid sturgeon probably
inhabited the Upper Missouri River. In 2021 the wild (hatched in
the river, not the hatchery) Missouri-Marias subpopulation was
estimated to number fewer than 20,[9] all them well over 60 years
old—old age for sturgeon (fig. 19). No natural reproduction in
this wild subpopulation has been observed in decades, and the extinction of wild-born pallids in this subpopulation is likely imminent.[10]

The status of the Missouri-Yellowstone wild subpopulation is
similarly precarious. In 1969 the subpopulation was estimated to

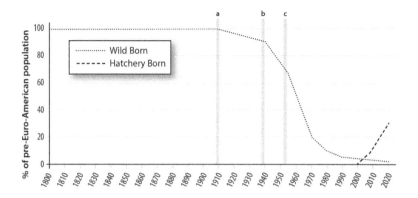

FIG. 20. Postulated population trends of the Upper Missouri River pallid
sturgeon, wild- and hatchery-born, from 1800 to 2020 as a percentage of
population levels before Euro-American colonization. Vertical lines indicate
the start of events with likely major effects on the wild-born population:
(a) construction of Intake Diversion Dam on the Yellowstone River,
(b) construction of Fort Peck Dam, (c) construction of Garrison, Canyon Ferry,
and Tiber Dams. Created by author and Eric Cline.

consist of about 1,000 adults.[11] In 2004 the subpopulation of wild-
born pallid sturgeon was estimated at 158 adults and, because the
remaining fish were old, the last of these were projected to die
between 2016 and 2024. Although wild- and hatchery-born adult
pallids have been reproductively active in recent years, evidence
indicates complete or nearly complete failure of any recruitment
into the juvenile or adult population since the mid-1950s.[12] The
bottom line is that the Upper Missouri River wild population, consisting of these two subpopulations, has severely collapsed and is
in critical condition (fig. 20).

The Pallid Sturgeon Recovery Plan, last updated in 2014, evaluated potential chemical, physical, and biological threats to pallid
sturgeon. The Missouri and Mississippi River systems are subject
to a panoply of agricultural, residential, and industrial chemicals.
Some of these have been shown to impact pallid sturgeon at various life cycle stages, but more research is needed to understand the
circumstances where pollution is a threat to pallid populations.[13]

Another threat is *entrainment*, the term fish biologists use when
fish get trapped, injured, or killed in artificial structures such as

irrigation canals, hydroelectric turbines, cooling intake structures for power plants, and boat propellers. Although it is well documented that entrainment injures and kills pallid sturgeon, the extent of its impact on populations is poorly understood.[14]

The plan also identifies nonnative fish as a threat. The Upper Missouri River alone has 27 introduced species of fish compared to 37 native species.[15] Five species of carp (Cyprinidae) from Eurasia that have been spreading throughout the pallid sturgeon's range are of particular concern. Carp and other nonnative fish may prey on young sturgeon and compete with sturgeon for food, as well as alter habitat and be potential vectors for diseases. Another introduced species, the Zebra mussel (*Dreissena polymorpha*), is spreading and altering pallid sturgeon habitat. Again, the recovery plan concludes that our current knowledge is inadequate to assess the degree of threat that diseases and nonnative species pose to pallid sturgeon.[16]

Crossbreeding between pallid sturgeon and shovelnose sturgeon is also a potential problem. Hybridization is relatively common in the Mississippi River but uncommon in the Upper Missouri River system. Scientists have yet to determine whether hybridization is a natural phenomenon or has been favored by human alteration of their populations and habitats that destroyed mechanisms, such as distinct spawning sites, that previously kept the two species reproductively isolated.[17] Because of fishing regulations—catching pallid sturgeon is illegal and fishing of shovelnose sturgeon is restricted to areas away from pallid sturgeon populations—commercial fishing is no longer a threat.[18]

As the recovery plan makes clear, the above threats pale in comparison to the one that stands out as the major cause of the pallid sturgeon's population collapse: dams. For the Missouri-Marias and Missouri-Yellowstone subpopulations, several dams are wreaking havoc with sturgeon habitat and movement.[19] A little knowledge of pallid sturgeon biology will help us understand why.

Referred to by fish biologists as "big-river fish," the pallid sturgeon's range is limited to the Missouri and Mississippi Rivers and their large tributaries. Lacking teeth and with tiny eyes, they feed along the bottom in highly turbid waters and swift currents using electroreceptors, taste-bud-studded lips, and whisker-like barbels to detect fish and other bottom-dwelling organisms, which they capture by sucking them into their mouth. Wild pallid sturgeon in the Upper Missouri River live an estimated 50–60 or more years, with females reaching reproductive age at about 15–20 years and males at around 7–9 years. Because pallids, like other fish, are ectothermic—cold-blooded—their growth rate, from egg incubation to reaching maturity, is slower at lower temperatures. Males may spawn annually, but females reproduce once every two or three years. Spawning occurs in the spring, generally after an upstream migration by the adults of sometimes hundreds of miles to suitable spawning sites. The exact substrate on which females deposit their eggs is difficult to determine but generally thought to be rock or gravel and perhaps sometimes sand.[20] Spawning behavior is probably cued by increasing water temperature, rising spring flows, increasing day length, and the presence of suitable mates, among other factors. The largest Missouri River fish can produce 150,000–170,000 eggs during spawning. Once fertilized the eggs quickly become adhesive and stick to the substrate. Eggs hatch in about a week, longer if water temperatures are low. The newly hatched fish, called free embryos, are about one-third of an inch long, have a big yolk sac for nutrition, and are weak swimmers, so in the Upper Missouri River region they drift in the current for several days as they grow. After drifting 100–300 or more miles downriver from where they hatched, the free embryos settle to the bottom of the river as free-swimming larvae and begin feeding on little bugs in the sediment.[21]

As this knowledge of the pallid's highly mobile life history emerged from research over the last decade or two, it became clear that dams were blocking pallid sturgeon reproduction. To understand how, let's start with an inventory of dams in the upper reaches of the Missouri River watershed and their influence on the Missouri-Marias subpopulation of pallid sturgeon.

Dams and the Missouri-Marias Subpopulation

Two large storage dams—the Canyon Ferry Dam on the Missouri River, built in 1954, and the Tiber Dam on the Marias River, completed in 1956—have potentially significant downriver effects on pallid sturgeon. Storage dams have large reservoirs for storing water for multiple purposes—usually flood control, hydropower, irrigation, and/or maintaining flow levels for navigation. These storage dams modulate downriver flows by holding back water during spring runoff and by releasing water later in the summer when river levels are low. Peak flows below these dams on the Missouri River are 40–50% lower than predam levels and are delayed from spring into summer.[22] Altered flows have narrowed the river's channel and destroyed habitat of pallid sturgeon and their prey. The dams also reduce water temperature of the river by releasing cold water from the bottom of the reservoirs and capture sediments in the still waters of the reservoirs, thereby reducing suspended sediments and increasing water clarity below the dams.

The altered flow regime, lower water temperature, and reduced turbidity may be scrambling cues for spawning by pallid sturgeon.[23] Increased water clarity may reduce the foraging efficiency of adult pallid sturgeon and favor big-eyed, visual predators such as walleye (*Sander vitreus*) that prey on drifting pallid embryos. The Canyon Ferry Dam is beyond the range of the pallid sturgeon, but pallids have recently been found in the Marias River below Tiber Dam and thus the dam may block pallid access to habitat, including possible historic spawning sites, above the dam.[24]

In addition to storage dams there are several diversion dams on the Upper Missouri River. Diversion dams, often referred to as run-of-the-river dams because they do not have reservoirs for water storage, divert water into a structure for hydroelectric generation or to supply irrigation systems. Compared to storage dams, they have generally minor to no effects on flow levels but are often significant barriers to upstream fish movement and contribute to changes in water temperature and sediments. Five diversion dams exist in the vicinity of Great Falls, of which the Morony Dam is furthest down river. Completed in 1930, the dam is located four miles below Big Falls, a natural waterfall of the river that was a historical barrier to upstream movement of pallid sturgeon. The dam completely blocks their upstream movement into the four-mile stretch to Big Falls.[25]

About 375 miles below Morony Dam is the mother of all Montana dams, the Fort Peck Dam. Completed in 1940, the four-mile-long dam dwarfs the upriver dams in size and impacts on the river and the pallid sturgeon. The dam's reservoir is 134 miles long and up to 120 feet deep, transforming the free-flowing, turbid, relatively shallow Missouri River into the still, deep, clear thermoclined waters of a lake, an aquatic ecosystem foreign to and uninhabitable by the pallid sturgeon and many other native fish. Between the Morony Dam and the headwaters of the Fort Peck Reservoir are 240 miles of uninterrupted flow of the Missouri River, the longest uninterrupted stretch of the entire river.

The first line of evidence that dams were the main problem was that pallid sturgeon reproduction began to fail shortly after the Fort Peck Dam's construction. Evidence was pointing at survival of the eggs, embryos, or larvae as the choke point. Nothing appeared to be killing off adults except old age. One- and two-year-old hatchery-reared pallid sturgeon were surviving well (more about hatcheries below). Radio-tagging showed that adults were aggregating during spawning periods within 50 miles of the Fort Peck reservoir, near the Fred Robinson Bridge where Highway 191 crosses the river.[26] The implication was that any free embryos resulting from spawning—if spawning was occurring—were drifting into the reservoir before completing their growth to the free-swimming larval stage. The question became, What happens when the free embryos enter the reservoir? A seminal paper in 2015 by Christopher Guy and colleagues provided the answer.[27] As the flow of the river slows upon entering the transition zone to the reservoir, both the organically rich sediments and the embryos settle to the bottom. The organic matter fuels a robust community of microbes that consume the water's oxygen. At the bottom, where the embryos have settled out, anoxic—no oxygen—conditions are created, and the embryos quickly asphyxiate. If a few manage to get past the transition zone, they enter the clear waters of the main reservoir to be greeted as prey by introduced predatory fish such as the walleye and lake trout (*Salvelinus namaycush*). The reservoir is, literally, a dead end for pallid sturgeon embryos and larvae.

If pallid sturgeon spawned just below the Morony Dam on the Missouri River or the Tiber Dam on the Marias River, the 200-some miles of free-flowing river before it enters the reservoir might offer a sufficient distance for the 11–17 days that the free embryos drift before settling to the bottom. However, despite years of searching, biologists had, until recently, never recorded spawning by either wild- or hatchery-born pallid sturgeon anywhere above the Fort Peck Reservoir. But then, in the world of pallid sturgeon recovery work, where even small victories seem all too rare, two important breakthroughs occurred. First, starting in 2018 and again in 2019, 2020, and 2021, biologists documented spawning for the first time in the Missouri-Marias subpopulation. Each year's spawnings were by two or three radio-tagged hatchery-born female pallids, all introduced as one-year-olds in 1998. Then the second breakthrough occurred: biologists found four newly hatched free embryos, at least two from the radio-tagged pallid females that spawned. As Montana Fish, Wildlife & Parks biologist Luke Holmquist told me, "This was a really huge finding because it shows that the hatchery pallid sturgeon will successfully spawn in the wild, thus checking a major box when it comes to conservation propagation efforts and the potential for recovery." This good news is tempered by the fact that all the spawnings occurred within 40–80 miles of the Fort Peck Reservoir. Free embryos would almost certainly drift into the anoxic death trap of the reservoir's headwaters before completing their development to free-swimming larvae.[28]

In short, the dams pose two problems for spawning and one problem for embryo survival. Spawning may be inhibited by dams blocking upstream migration to spawning sites and by creating water and habitat conditions below the dams that inhibit or create miscues for spawning and that reduce egg survival. If spawning does occur and eggs hatch, the Fort Peck Reservoir interrupts the free embryos' downstream drift before they grow to the free-swimming stage and suffocates them as they settle to the bottom. The triple threat posed by dams has clearly broken the reproductive cycle and caused the collapse—perhaps to extirpation—of wild-born pallid sturgeon above the Fort Peck Dam.

Dams and the Missouri-Yellowstone Subpopulation

The Missouri-Yellowstone pallid sturgeon subpopulation has a three-dam problem. The Fort Peck Dam, again, plays a central role. The Garrison Dam, completed in 1953, is the next main-stem dam on the Missouri River; it creates the Sakakawea Reservoir, whose headwaters are about 200 river miles below the Fort Peck Dam. Third, constructed in 1909, is the Intake Diversion Dam on the Yellowstone River, 70 river miles upstream from its confluence with the Missouri River, which is 189 miles below the Fort Peck Dam. A few other dams are found on tributaries of the Missouri River and Yellowstone River in this region, but have minor effects compared to these three.[29]

The roughly 200 miles of free-flowing river between the Fort Peck Dam and Sakakawea Reservoir are severely compromised by three changes the Fort Peck Dam makes to the waters it releases. First, rather than maintaining the natural spring peak flows, the U.S. Army Corps of Engineers (USACE), which is responsible for managing main-stem dams on the Missouri River, has generally released water from the dam to create a much lower peak flow. This artificial flow likely disrupts important cues for spawning. Reduced peak flows also result in less flooding of adjacent floodplains and disrupt processes that create the braided, ever-changing course of the river, which degrades habitat for sturgeon and for the organisms they feed on for up to 120 miles below the dam.[30]

Second, the deep waters of the Fort Peck Reservoir develop a strong thermocline during the summer as cold water settles to the bottom. Consequently, water drawn from the bottom of the reservoir to spin the hydropower turbines results in the river below the dam being 10–25°F colder than under damless conditions. The cold water generally inhibits spawning within 40–50 miles of the dam and, if there is spawning, may kill the eggs or delay their hatching and slow the growth of free embryos so that they drift into the deadly transition zone of the Sakakawea Reservoir before they have a chance to grow into free-swimming larvae.[31]

The third effect results from the Fort Peck Dam entrapping river sediments that enter the reservoir. Consequently, clear water is released from the reservoir and doesn't begin to regain some of the river's typical sediment load until the muddy waters of the Milk River enter nine miles below the dam, but the water remains much less turbid for miles downstream than would be the case under natural conditions. Clearer water may expose the eggs, drifting free embryos, and larvae to greater predation. Reduced sediment and lower peak flows also reduce dynamic changes in the floodplain and sandbars that are important for sturgeon and their prey as well as for other rare species such as the piping plover (*Charadrius melodus*) and least tern (*Sternula antillarum*).[32]

Research on habitat use and movement by pallid sturgeon in the early 1990s revealed the downstream effects of the Fort Peck Dam. During fall and winter pallid sturgeon concentrated in a 30-mile section of the Missouri River immediately below the confluence with the Yellowstone River, generally avoiding the entire 180 miles of river from the confluence to the Fort Peck Dam as well as a stretch near the headwaters of the Sakakawea Reservoir. During spring and summer most pallids moved into the lower 20 miles of the Yellowstone River, although some ventured upstream until they encountered the Intake Diversion Dam.[33]

The original Intake Diversion Dam was 700 feet long, 12 feet high, and made of wood and rock. It was recently replaced by a concrete dam of similar proportions. We'll look at the new dam later when discussing pallid sturgeon recovery efforts. For now, let's see how the old dam affected pallid sturgeon. With rare exceptions, the dam denied pallid sturgeon access to more than 200 miles of habitat of the Yellowstone River and its tributaries, although it is unknown if this includes spawning habitat that was historically important. During especially high flows, however, a few pallid sturgeon navigated a side channel to get above the dam. Some of these, as well as pallid sturgeon moved above the dam by biologists, have migrated far upriver, including into a Yellowstone tributary, the Powder River, apparently to spawn.[34] The only spawning verified for the Missouri-Yellowstone population, however, has occurred in a stretch of the Yellowstone River 5–10 miles above its confluence with the Missouri River.[35] Free embryos from this location have less than 50 miles of uninterrupted drift before entering the anoxic transition zone of the Sakakawea Reservoir. Regardless of spawning location, there is no evidence of pallid sturgeon surviving beyond the embryo stage in the Missouri-Yellowstone subpopulation.[36]

Conditions Farther Downriver

Though not directly influencing the two subpopulations in the American Prairie–Russell Refuge region, it's worth taking stock of habitat degradation downriver that affects pallid sturgeon and other fish. Below the Garrison Dam, the Missouri River is strangled by four more main-stem dams, by dikes and levees for flood control, and by channelization and engineered cutoffs that have shortened the river by 72 miles. The Upper Mississippi River has 29 locks and dams and hundreds of miles of dikes and levees, the Lower Mississippi alone has 3,500 miles of levees, and channelization and engineered cutoffs have shortened the river by 218 miles.[37] All told, of the 3,350 river miles of the pallid sturgeon's range, 28% is impounded behind dams, 51% is channelized into deep, uniform, faster-flowing channels, and the remaining 21% is downstream of dams that have altered the rivers' flow regime, temperature, and turbidity.[38]

Given this phalanx of engineered habitat alterations, it's not surprising that in the Missouri River below the Garrison Dam, recruitment of young pallid sturgeon from natural reproduction is too low to sustain the population.[39] Although natural recruitment into the adult population in the Mississippi River and its other tributaries is occurring, the long-term health of that population also faces major challenges such as hybridization with shovelnose sturgeon.[40]

Recovery

As research data grew and the pallid sturgeon's population shrunk, it became increasingly clear to researchers and managers that, without rapid action, the historic 100-million-year run of the pallid sturgeon was doomed. Saving the species, especially the Upper Missouri River population, would require extraordinary measures.

In drafting the first Pallid Sturgeon Recovery Plan, published in 1993, the recovery team faced the daunting fact that none of the priority conservation areas on the Missouri and Mississippi Rivers showed evidence of pallid sturgeon reproduction. If so, the species was in a free fall. The plan didn't mince words in stating the dire situation and what needed to be done fast: "The short-term recovery objective for the pallid sturgeon is to prevent species extinction by establishing three captive broodstock populations . . . by 1998."[41] Meanwhile, much more research would be required to better understand pallid sturgeon ecology and what needed to be done to get the wild population healthy and reproducing again. Involving collaboration among federal and state agencies, private organizations, and universities, the program marshaled resources for extensive research on pallid sturgeon and the development of an updated pallid sturgeon recovery plan in 2014.[42]

To move the pallid sturgeon from an "endangered" status to the more secure status of "threatened," the 2014 plan called for a genetically diverse population of 5,000 adult pallid sturgeon to be maintained through natural reproduction for two generations (20–30 years) in each of the plan's four management units. The uppermost recovery area is the Great Plains Management Unit, which encompasses the Missouri-Marias and Missouri-Yellowstone subpopulations and three other hatchery-maintained subpopulations that are divided by dams farther downriver to the Fort Randall Dam near the South Dakota–Nebraska border.

That goal was based on the same 50/500 effective population size guidelines applied to black-footed ferret recovery for maintaining genetic variation and avoiding inbreeding depression (see chapter 9).[43] Although the recovery plan doesn't specify a goal for each subpopulation, at least 1,000 adults would seem to be a minimum for each of the Missouri-Marias and Missouri-Yellowstone subpopulations.

Similar to black-footed ferret management, a captive-rearing program was initiated in the 1990s to avert extinction of the Missouri River population of the pallid sturgeon. Unlike the ferret, disease didn't threaten the last surviving sturgeon, and so captured adults were returned to the wild after their eggs and sperm were harvested for hatchery reproduction. The resulting newly hatched sturgeon are raised until one to two years of age, when they are released into the river. Captive breeding and reintroduction to the wild are closely guided by genetics. Males and females need to be carefully selected for hatchery breeding to maintain genetic variation in the hatchery population and in young released into the rivers. Because the Missouri-Marias and Missouri-Yellowstone subpopulations are genetically the same and have good genetic variation, hatchery reproduction and releases of young fish do not need to keep these subpopulations separate. They are managed genetically as one population. Great care, however, is taken to not introduce genetic material from genetically distinct pallid populations found farther downriver.[44]

Domestication is another concern, as the cushy but crowded conditions of hatchery-reared fish create a different set of evolutionary selection pressures compared to life in rivers. Studies of other fish species show that a single generation of hatchery breeding can result in heritable differences in the expression of hundreds of genes.[45]

Hatcheries are like a second home to many fish biologists, so it didn't take long to ramp up successful hatchery operations for pallid sturgeon. Since the first release in 1998, roughly 400,000 hatchery-born pallid sturgeon have been released into the Upper Missouri River. Young hatchery-raised fish show good survival rates after release and now number in the thousands. In fact, there is concern about the hatchery-origin population becoming too large relative to food resources and competition with other bottom-feeding fish. The first hatchery fish released are reaching reproductive age and are exhibiting spawning movement similar to wild pallids. However, these fish have shown unusually slow growth—80% of the 19-year-old stocked females were still immature.[46] More problematic are recent observations that both wild- and hatchery-born females, especially those of the Missouri-Marias subpopulation above the Fort Peck Reservoir, are often reabsorbing their eggs.[47] The cause has not been determined.

The big picture is that despite a highly successful hatchery program, good survival by hatchery-born fish introduced to the wild, and documented spawning by both subpopulations, there is no evidence of reproduction in the wild leading to the recruitment of young pallid sturgeon, much less to adults of reproductive age. Neither subpopulation is self-sustaining. If something doesn't change for the better, we face a future of only hatchery-born pallid sturgeon living in the Upper Missouri River.

Although dams are the main problem, options for removing dams or altering their operations to help pallid sturgeon are severely restricted by politically and economically powerful stakeholders who want tamed rivers and their services—power, irrigation water, navigation, recreation, flood control, and so on. Given that removing the Fort Peck Dam and draining the reservoir is not currently an option being considered to free up river miles for the Missouri-Marias subpopulation, the Canyon Ferry Dam on the Missouri River and the Tiber Dam on the Marias River are the next best candidates for change. Although dam removal would be the most effective change for restoring natural flows, extensive human infrastructure in the floodplain below the Canyon Ferry Dam nixes that option. Removal of the Tiber Dam has been raised as a possibility because of limited development in the floodplain of the Marias River,[48] but there is currently no serious proposal for doing so. Releases from these dams, however, have been altered to create what has been called a "quasi-natural" flow for the benefit of the downriver ecosystem and fish,[49] but the degree that releases can be altered is limited because of flood control needs and other purposes.[50] Reproductive failure of the Missouri-Marias subpopulation indicates that trying to improve flow regimes is not the solution. Even if the Tiber Dam were removed, we don't know if the Marias River has historically important spawning sites on the river above or below the dam and, if spawning would occur, if the drift distance would be sufficient for embryos before they encounter the death trap of the Fort Peck Reservoir.[51]

What about the Missouri-Yellowstone subpopulation? In 2018 USACE issued the final *Missouri River Recovery Management Plan and Environmental Impact Statement.*[52] Prepared in cooperation with the USFWS, the document proposes a suite of actions to meet Endangered Species Act responsibilities for the interior least tern (removed from the endangered species list in 2021), Northern Great Plains piping plover, and pallid sturgeon. Again, the best long-term solution for the species, removal of the Fort Peck and Garrison Dams, was not on the table for the USACE's consideration. The USACE's primary tool for benefiting the pallid sturgeon is regulating the amount and timing of water released from the Fort Peck Reservoir.

Competing demands for how fast and when waters are released through the dam are diverse and intense, made all the more complicated by the vagaries of Mother Nature that one year produces deep mountain snows, unusually warm and wet spring weather, and big runoffs, and the next year yields little snow, cold and dry spring weather, and drought-level runoff. Big releases during wet years can cause downstream flooding of towns and farmland and damage irrigation systems. Big releases during dry years drop the reservoir to levels that reduce power generation by the dam's turbines and curtail recreational uses of the reservoir. Let the river flow too low, and it drops below the intake for irrigation canals, municipal and industrial use, and other users that tap into the river's water, as well as affecting river navigation in the Lower Missouri River. It's a cascading effect, as the rate of water released from the Fort Peck Reservoir directly affects the level of the Sakakawea Reservoir and water releases from the Garrison Dam, and so on down through the next four main-stem dams and reservoirs.

The biological opinion of the plan by the USFWS offered this grim assessment:

As a result of project-related impacts from Missouri River Mainstem Reservoir System Operations that cause alterations to water temperature, flow regime, and sediment regime within the Action Area, we anticipate that all pallid sturgeon life stages will be adversely affected by the Proposed Action by the following: 1) inhibit spawning, 2) delay or inhibit incubation and hatching, 3) inhibit growth in all life stages of sturgeon and its prey base, 4) delay sexual maturity, 5) reduce primary production which affects all life stages and prey base, 6) reduce habitat availability for feeding, breeding, and sheltering for pallid sturgeon and its prey base.[53]

In 2021 USACE released a draft environmental impact statement for a plan to conduct test releases through the Fort Peck Dam in an attempt to improve spawning conditions for pallid sturgeon by creating flows that resemble the predam natural flow of the river.[54] Releases would be timed to create high flows in the late spring to potentially provide cues for upriver migration by fish to spawning sites and for spawning itself in the Missouri River. Warm waters from the top of the reservoir may be released through the spillway to dilute the cold waters released through the turbines from the bottom of the reservoir. After spawning, releases would be reduced to create low flows and a slower current that might provide sufficient drift time for the pallid free embryos to grow to the free-swimming stage before entering the anoxic zone at the head of the Sakakawea Reservoir. If spawning does occur in the river below the dam, near the mouth of the Milk River for example, free embryos would have roughly 200 miles to drift, a distance that recent research suggests may be sufficient for embryos to become free-swimming larvae.[55]

The wide year-to-year variation in the Missouri River's flow and the need for a minimum reservoir level for spillway releases will challenge USACE's ability to implement these changes because of competing user demands. To wit, in 2021 Montana's governor, Greg Gianforte, publicly opposed USACE's plan to alter flows to help the pallid sturgeon.[56] Nevertheless, the hope is that once every few years a big spring runoff may create conditions for spawning. Such conditions apparently occurred in 2011 when natural spawning and production of embryos was documented in the stretch of river above the Montana–North Dakota border.[57]

What about the Intake Diversion Dam on the Yellowstone River? The dam's permanent removal, a relatively easy task, was one option considered by USACE and the Bureau of Reclamation in their 2016 record of decision for the *Lower Yellowstone Intake Diversion Dam Fish Passage Project, Montana.*[58] But the influence of more than 400 farmers who irrigate 58,000 acres with water diverted by the dam was too much for fish conservationists to overcome. Removal of the dam and using pumps to draw water from the river for irrigation were deemed too expensive and too unreliable. Thus, the decision was to construct a new diversion dam and a two-mile-long bypass channel intended to enable pallid sturgeon and other fish to swim around the dam.[59] The dam and bypass channel were completed in the spring of 2022, and subsequent monitoring showed 15 radio-tagged pallids passing upstream through the channel by June 2. Given that less than 1% of the population is radio-tagged, many more likely used the channel for upstream migration.[60] However, whether the bypass channel is a solution to reproduction of pallid sturgeon in the Yellowstone River depends not only on reproductive adults using the structure for upstream movement but also on the existence of suitable spawning areas upstream from the dam, on the use of these areas to spawn, and on any resulting progeny surviving and reproducing in sufficient numbers for a self-sustaining wild population.[61] If any of these is not true, there is no plan B except to continue stocking the river with hatchery fish.

Pallid sturgeon of the Upper Missouri River are on life support. At present, no solutions appear to be at hand to enable the Missouri-Marias subpopulation to become self-sustaining through natural reproduction. The experimental water releases from the Fort Peck Dam and completion of the new Intake Diversion Dam and bypass channel offer hope for a management breakthrough for the Missouri-Yellowstone subpopulation. But the efficacy of both measures is highly uncertain, and years of research and monitoring will be required to adequately assess the results. A long-term solution for saving the wild pallid sturgeon may depend on a transformation in societal priorities for river biodiversity and river management. Meanwhile, the last of the wild-born pallid sturgeon—a few dozen at most by now—are dying of old age. Fortunately, the pallid sturgeon hatchery program offers a lifeline between these genetically unique old pallid sturgeon of the Upper Missouri River and a future when their descendants can again be fully wild.

Other Fish Stories

Like the pallid sturgeon, several other species that inhabit the Missouri River are benthic (bottom-dwelling) specialists that evolved similar adaptations—small eyes, external taste buds, and an array of electrosensory and chemosensory organs—to navigate, find food, and avoid predators in the turbid, swift waters and sand-silt bottom environment of the river.[62] Populations of most species, especially those of small body size and not popular in recreational fisheries, receive little or no monitoring to track population trends, and no baseline data exist regarding the size of pre-Euro-American populations. Although no population of other big-river fish species in the Missouri and Yellowstone Rivers is known to have collapsed like that of the pallid sturgeon, several are listed as species of concern by the state of Montana because they have suffered declines and/or their populations are small and potentially vulnerable.[63]

The two species of greatest concern are the sicklefin chub (*Macrhybopsis meeki*) and sturgeon chub (*Macrhybopsis gelida*), both members of the minnow family, Cyprinidae. Both were candidates in 2001 for listing under the U.S. Endangered Species Act and, though not listed, are still considered to be potentially at risk of extinction across their entire range, including Montana. The two species reach about four inches in length. The sicklefin is named for its long, pointed sickle-like fins and the sturgeon chub for its sturgeon-like bottom-feeding mouth overhung by a long snout. The distributions of both species are limited to the turbid, fast-flowing

waters of the Missouri and Mississippi Rivers and their large tributaries. The sicklefin chub is of particular concern in Montana where
it is known to occur in only two areas: one subpopulation in the
Missouri River from Cow Island downstream about 60 river miles
to the headwaters of Fort Peck Reservoir and the other upstream
several miles on both the Yellowstone and Missouri Rivers from
their confluence.[64] The Fort Peck Dam both fragments this population and creates downstream conditions—higher summer
flows and lower turbidity—that are inimical to sicklefin chub survival and reproduction.[65] Both species appear to do best when living in undammed stretches of river at least 185 miles in length.
River fragmentation is also a threat to several other species of min-
nows in the Great Plains.[66]

A close relative of the walleye, the sauger (*Sander canadensis*) is
a predatory fish that prefers turbid waters and has a broad distribution across the central and eastern United States and Canada.
It historically inhabited the Missouri and Yellowstone Rivers and
many of their tributaries, but its range in Montana has declined
by an estimated 53%, with much of the decline occurring before
the 1980s. The sauger is even more migratory than the pallid sturgeon, swimming upstream as much as 370 miles to spawn. Like the
pallid sturgeon, the sauger's larvae also drift downstream before
they become free swimming. By blocking sauger migrations and
degrading habitat, storage dams on major rivers and smaller diversion dams on tributaries are the major cause of the species' decline
in Montana. The species has experienced limited recovery.[67]

The blue sucker (*Cycleptus elongatus*) is a bottom-dwelling, big-
river fish with a distribution in Montana similar to the pallid sturgeon. Like the pallid sturgeon, it depends on spring surges in flow
to trigger spawning and large unfragmented reaches of rivers for
both spawning migration and embryo drift. Dam operations appear
to be taking a toll on their numbers. Recent surveys of the Missouri
River and its tributaries above the Fort Peck Dam found the population consists of mostly old fish, suggesting reproductive failure.[68]

Threats to pallid sturgeon and other big-river fish and the importance of big rivers and reservoirs for recreational fishing have led

researchers and managers to focus on the Missouri River and its large tributaries and reservoirs in the plains of eastern Montana. However, many small (usually less than six inches long) inconspicuous fish, especially those of the minnow family, that inhabit the small prairie streams as well as the large rivers of the region, have experienced significant population declines. One obvious cause (as discussed in chapter 5 about beavers) is widespread degradation of small prairie streams. A survey in 2008 and 2009 of prairie streams in eastern Montana, including the American Prairie–Russell Refuge region, rated 47% of in-stream fish habitat as "poor" condition and 35% as "good."[69] Another cause is the widespread introduction of northern pike (*Esox lucius*), a highly predatory fish not native to Montana's rivers and streams. Research in northeast Montana found the number of minnow species was 52% lower in streams with northern pike than in streams without them. Two minnow species at risk of extirpation in Montana, the northern pearl dace (*Margariscus nachtriebi*) and northern redbelly dace (*Chrosomus eos*), rarely occurred wherever northern pike and nonnative trout were present. Consequently, some check dams on prairie streams should be maintained to prevent upstream movement by northern pike into reaches of streams above dams where native fish still thrive.[70]

Fish are not the only organisms of prairie rivers and streams that may be threatened by destruction of their habitats. The spiny softshell turtle, for example, is a Montana species of concern. Although relatively common in the Missouri River above the Fort Peck Reservoir, the next closest population in the Missouri River is more than 370 miles downstream, the two populations fragmented by the Fort Peck and Garrison Dams and reservoirs.[71]

Recovery Role of the American Prairie–Russell Refuge

Restoration of beavers, prairie streams, and associated riparian areas by American Prairie and the Charles M. Russell National Wildlife Refuge will directly contribute to conserving the diverse species of fish that inhabit small prairie streams. Restoring natural flows and the health of the prairie streams that feed the Missouri

River will provide incremental support to restoring natural conditions in the river.

Less obvious, but perhaps significant, is the potential effect that restoration of a large population of bison and other ungulates could have on the Missouri River ecosystem and its fish. Commonly reported historic mass drownings of bison attempting to cross Great Plains rivers on thin ice in spring would have released tons of carbon, nitrogen, and phosphorus into the river systems. On the Mara River in Kenya, blue wildebeest (*Connochaetes taurinus*) mass drownings contributed an average of 1,096 tons of biomass to the river annually, representing 107 tons of carbon, 25 tons of nitrogen, and 13 tons of phosphorus distributed along several miles of river. (The equivalent would be the mass drowning of about 1,000 bison.) When wildebeest carcasses were present, their tissue accounted for 34–50% of the assimilated diet of three common fish species, and four months after the last drowning, biofilm (bacteria, fungi, and algae) growing on the bones accounted for 7–24% of the assimilated diet of the three fish species.[72] Bones take several years to decompose and release relatively high amounts of phosphorus. The total phosphorus released from the bones of a reported drowning in 1795 of 7,360 bison in Canada's Assiniboine River would have released an estimated 50% of the river's current median annual load of phosphorus.[73] Restoration of large populations of bison and other ungulates could again result in mass drownings that affect nutrient cycling, the food web, and fish and other organisms in the Missouri River.

Thoughts about Fort Peck Reservoir

When I stand on the rocky shore of the Fort Peck reservoir and look out over its miles of open water, I am victim to an Aldo Leopold lament: "One of the penalties of an ecological education is that one lives alone in a world of wounds. Much of the damage on land is quite invisible to laymen."[74] I don't think of big walleyes and lake trout lurking beneath the surface and taking my lure. I see, instead, a six-trillion-gallon aquarium, a relatively homogeneous, not-very-dynamic ecosystem with 21 species of nonnative fish. Biodiversity and ecological health lost out when we swapped the dynamic, wild river for a deep artificial lake. The bottom of the reservoir was once a massive floodplain—at one to four miles across, one of the widest on the Upper Missouri River. I imagine, standing there 150 years ago, a surging spring current gouging out a new channel and depositing cottonwood seeds on a high bench, offering the chance for a new generation. I see a braided, sinuous river with side channels and backwaters and sandbars and islands covered with willows and old cottonwoods and the wildlife they supported. In the now flooded lower canyons of the breaks, I imagine a herd of elk being stalked by a cougar or wolf pack. Beavers, waterfowl, and maybe the occasional otter are around every bend. And I imagine, moving silently along the bottom, six-foot pallid sturgeon making their annual upriver migration to spawn and renew the cycle of life. I also imagine that, someday, the dam will be gone.

Weighing as much as 150 pounds, the filter-feeding paddlefish uses its electrosensor-studded snout as an antenna to locate plankton in the murky waters of the Missouri River. Drawing by Erica Freese.

ELEVEN

Grassland Birds

I marvel every spring at the chorus and courtship displays of birds during early morning walks through prairies of the Great Plains. But what if, through a time warp, I could be joined on those walks by naturalists John James Audubon and Elliot Coues who ventured through the Great Plains in the 1800s? Would they be similarly awed by the birdlife? Or would they be underwhelmed and wonder why the massive numbers of prairie birds they used to see were missing? I suspect the latter. After getting up to date on more than a century of wildlife research and reading about the insidious effects of shifting baseline syndrome, they would conclude that I'm still not fully cured from the prairie strain of the syndrome, that my baseline for what constituted abundant prairie birdlife had been set far below theirs.

Springs are surely more silent on the prairie today because grassland birds are at the epicenter of a continent-wide plummet in bird populations. Of all native species in North America, 57% (303 of 529 species) are in decline with a net population loss of nearly 3 billion birds since 1970. Of birds that inhabit the 10 biomes of North America, grassland birds have experienced the largest population loss. Thirty-one species, representing 74% of all grassland species, declined by an estimated total of 717.5 million birds.[1] With 10–12 species of nesting grassland endemics (birds that breed only in or near the region) as well as many other grassland nesting species, northeast Montana and nearby areas of southern Canada and the western Dakotas are linchpins in the quest to save grassland bird populations.[2]

So many species undergoing such massive declines present an unwanted wealth of material to write about. I've narrowed it down to eight—five songbirds, one shorebird, one owl, one grouse. They're a diverse group, ranging in size from less than one ounce to seven pounds. They include seed eaters, leaf eaters, insect eaters, and vertebrate eaters. Some breed almost exclusively in the Northern Great Plains, others breed more broadly across North America, and one is hemispheric. I singled out these eight species because the Northern Great Plains represents a major center of their breeding populations and their populations may have suffered the greatest collapses among grassland birds.

While most of the five songbirds are "must sees" for bird watchers visiting the region, their names, what they look like, and their places in the grassland ecosystem are unfamiliar to most people: chestnut-collared longspur, thick-billed longspur, grasshopper sparrow (*Ammodramus savannarum*), lark bunting, and Sprague's pipit (figs. 21–25). All five are sparrow size, with males generally standing out more than females during breeding season because of their distinctive color patterns and/or melodious singing and elaborate courtship displays. Males of the chestnut-collared longspur (longspurs are named for the elongated claw on their hind toe) display a striking color pattern with a black crown, eyeline, and breast; chestnut-colored nape; and black shoulders with white trim. The black, white, gray, and chestnut color pattern of the male thick-billed longspur is only slightly less striking. The breeding males of grasshopper sparrows are somewhat of an exception to male distinctiveness; both the male and female are buffy brown overall and the male's common song is an insect-like buzz.[3] Breeding male lark buntings stand out with their velvety black body highlighted by bright-white wing coverts. Both the male and female Sprague's pipit have plain buffy plumage, but the male makes up for what it lacks in colorfulness with an energetic courtship display that takes it high above its territory for a half hour or more during a single aerial display—the longest known of any bird species—to sing a high-pitched song during short glides.

FIG. 21. Adult male chestnut-collared longspur. Courtesy Marky Mutchler.

FIG. 22. Adult male thick-billed longspur. Courtesy Greg Lavaty.

FIG. 23. Adult grasshopper sparrow. Courtesy Greg Lavaty.

FIG. 24. Adult male lark bunting. Courtesy Marky Mutchler.

FIG. 25. Adult Sprague's pipit. Courtesy Greg Lavaty.

The breeding ranges of the two longspur species and Sprague's pipit are almost exclusively in the Northern Great Plains. Lark buntings nest primarily there and in the central plains. These four species migrate for the winter to grasslands of the Southern Great Plains and Chihuahuan desert grasslands of the southwestern United States and northern Mexico. Grasshopper sparrow nesting is centered on the Great Plains but they can be found nesting in grasslands across eastern North America. They winter in the southern United States, Mexico, and the Caribbean.[4] All five species have sizeable breeding populations in the American Prairie–Russell Refuge region.

The five species are ground nesters and considered monogamous (one male and one female pair up to rear young), although there are exceptions such as occasional polygyny (one male mating with two or more females) in the lark bunting.[5] The young, usually three to five per nest, are altricial (born helpless, only able to open their mouths to beg and be fed). The two longspurs, lark bunting, and grasshopper sparrow consume both seeds and insects, with insects being especially important for the young during nesting season. Sprague's pipit is mostly insectivorous.[6]

The shorebird among the eight species—the drab, robin-sized mountain plover—inhabits neither the shore nor the mountains (fig. 26). It's strictly a species of flat to rolling mixed- and short-grass prairies where it occupies relatively barren ground created by intense grazing and prairie dog colonies to feed on insects and other arthropods. The American Prairie–Russell Refuge is near the northern edge of the mountain plover's breeding range, with most breeding occurring in the central Great Plains. It winters across the southwest and adjoining regions of Mexico. The nest is a scrape in the ground, often placed near a conspicuous object such as a cow pie. They have an unusual reproductive arrangement: the female will lay one clutch of usually two or three eggs that she leaves for the male to tend to and then lays and cares for a second clutch in another nest. The newly hatched mountain plovers are precocial, leaving the nest on foot and feeding on their own as soon as their down dries.[7]

Their striking, expressive faces with big yellow eyes and white eyebrows frequently land burrowing owls on the cover of nature magazines and in power point talks about grasslands (fig. 27). Both sexes are sandy colored with long legs and weigh up to a third of

FIG. 26. Adult mountain plover. Courtesy Greg Lavaty.

FIG. 27. Adult burrowing owl. Courtesy U.S. Geological Survey.

FIG. 28. Adult male greater sage-grouse in courtship display.
Courtesy Dennis Lingohr.

a pound. The western subspecies inhabits grasslands and deserts ranging from the Great Plains to California and from southern Canada to central Mexico. Other subspecies are found in Florida, the Caribbean Islands, and Central and South America. As the name suggests, they nest in burrows. The owls are monogamous, the female lays usually 6–10 eggs and does all the incubation, and newly hatched young are altricial.[8] Although they dig their own burrows in some regions, in the Great Plains they depend on mammal-dug burrows, particularly those of black-tailed prairie dogs.[9] Burrowing owls nesting in the Northern Great Plains migrate for the winter to southern Texas and northern Mexico.[10] They hunt any time of day or night in search of arthropods and small vertebrates.[11]

The eighth bird, the greater sage-grouse, is, at three to seven pounds (males weigh twice as much as females), the continent's largest grouse (fig. 28). Greater sage-grouse (hereafter sage-grouse) inhabit sagebrush steppe habitat of the Great Plains and Intermountain West. Sage-grouse are well known for their spring gatherings of 10–50 males in courtship arenas, called leks, where, in front of discerning females, they strut, puff out their chests, and inflate two yellow air sacs that, when deflated, create loud popping sounds. One male usually mates with several females, who incubate the eggs in a ground nest and take care of the precocial young.[12] Sage-grouse are generally nonmigratory or move only short distances between seasons.[13] An exception are sage-grouse that spend their winter in the American Prairie–Russell Refuge region and in the spring migrate on average 50–75 miles—and sometimes more than 100 miles—to nest as far north as southern Saskatchewan. This is the longest-known migration of any gallinaceous (grouse, turkeys, pheasants, etc.) bird in the world.[14] As noted in chapter 6, the migratory pathways of sage-grouse and pronghorn in the region are similar and thus investments in conserving migration habitats for one often benefit the other.[15] Sage-grouse require extensive stands of sagebrush for shelter and nesting, and sagebrush leaves are their only food during winter. Newly hatched chicks feed on forbs and insects to fuel rapid growth during their first few weeks of life when they prefer more open habitat with good herbaceous growth, often found in low-lying wet areas.[16]

My focus in this chapter is on grassland birds with ranges that strongly overlap the American Prairie–Russell Refuge region. Consequently, I do not cover the population collapses, including two extinctions, of five species—passenger pigeon, Eskimo curlew, whooping crane (*Grus americana*), interior least tern, and Northern Great Plains population of the piping plover—whose historic ranges were on the edge of the American Prairie–Russell Refuge region. Nor do I cover the insecticide-induced population collapses 60–70 years ago of the bald eagle (*Haliaeetus leucocephalus*) and peregrine falcon (*Falco peregrinus*) and their subsequent recoveries.[17]

How Far Did They Fall, and Why?

The cornerstone for assessing population changes of North American birds—the basis for the population statistics at the start of this chapter—is the North American Breeding Bird Survey (BBS).[18] Launched in 1966, the BBS is a joint program among Canadian,

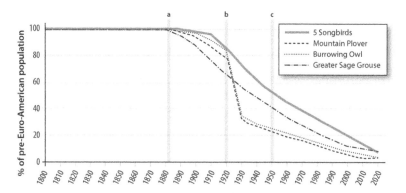

FIG. 29. Postulated population trends of eight species of grassland birds in the American Prairie–Russell Refuge region from 1800 to 2020 as a percentage of population levels before Euro-American colonization. Declines of the five songbirds—chestnut-collared longspur, thick-billed longspur, lark bunting, grasshopper sparrow, and Sprague's pipit—are assumed to be similar and thus are shown as a single trend line. Vertical lines indicate the start of events with likely major effects on the populations: (a) hunting of sage-grouse and mountain plover and prairie plow-up during homesteading era, (b) U.S. government–sponsored eradication of prairie dogs, (c) post–World War II pesticide use and recurring surges in prairie plow-up. Created by author and Eric Cline.

U.S., and Mexican research agencies. Involving thousands of skilled volunteer birders and survey routes across the continent, about 550 species of birds are surveyed annually, yielding a wealth of data for analyzing bird population trends on a species-by-species, region-by-region basis.

Estimating each species' decline since Euro-American colonization requires that one combine 50-some years of BBS data with more than 100 years of almost no trend data and mix that with what we know about habitat loss and other factors affecting the birds on their breeding grounds, wintering grounds, and migratory pathways. To explore how far the eight species have declined, the causes of those declines over the last 150 years, and pressures that continue to suppress or further drive down their populations, I'll begin with the five grassland songbirds (fig 29).

The Five Songbirds

The limited number of BBS survey routes in the American Prairie–Russell Refuge region renders statistical analyses of trends at that scale problematic. Moreover, most grassland songbirds are highly mobile, and consequently concentrations of nesting birds often shift across the landscape from year to year as they track food abundance.[19] I therefore assess the status of the five songbirds across their nesting ranges, with a focus on the Northern Great Plains.

Table 3 shows population trends based on BBS data and estimated current population sizes for the five songbirds. As data for the period of 1993–2019 show, there is no evidence that the rates of population decline have decreased compared to long-term trends since 1966. No other grassland songbird whose breeding population is centered on the north-central Great Plains has experienced BBS-documented declines as large as these five. Despite these troubling trends, none of the five is listed as threatened or endangered under the U.S. Endangered Species Act. In Canada, however, all except the grasshopper sparrow are listed as threatened under the Species at Risk Act.[20]

Several other grassland birds that nest in the American Prairie–Russell Refuge region are in trouble. The horned lark (*Eremophila alpestris*), with a nearly continent-wide nesting range and high nesting concentration in the Southern Great Plains, has declined by 64% since 1966. The loggerhead shrike (*Lanius ludovicianus*), which breeds coast-to-coast, has declined 74%. Lark sparrow (*Chondestes grammacus*), Baird's sparrow (*Centronyx bairdii*), Brewer's sparrow (*Spizella breweri*), vesper sparrow (*Pooecetes gramineus*), savannah sparrow (*Passerculus sandwichensis*), bobolink (*Dolichonyx oryzivorus*), and western meadowlark (*Sturnella neglecta*) have declined in the range of 35–55%.[21]

With populations of nearly all these species numbering in the millions, some might wonder, "Why worry?" The worry is that the rates of decline have been cutting the populations of the five focal species in half every 20–30 years. Or consider the focal species plus the nine species in the previous paragraph. If we multiply

Table 3. Range-wide population declines for five songbirds

Species	Average annual rate of decline, 1966–2019, 1993–2019 (%)	Population decline, 1966–2019 (%)	Estimated current population size
Thick-billed longspur	2.1, 1.9	68	840,000
Chestnut-collared longspur	2.6, 3.4	75	3,100,000
Lark bunting	3.7, 4.5	86	12,000,000
Grasshopper sparrow	2.5, 2.3	74	34,000,000
Sprague's pipit	3.2, 2.3	82	1,400,000

Sources: Sauer, Link, and Hines, "North American Breeding Bird"; Bird Conservancy of the Rockies, "Population Estimates Database"

the estimated population size of each species by its annual rate of decline since 1993 and add them up, the total is nearly 10 million fewer birds of these 14 grassland species every year. A good portion of that total is in the Northern Great Plains.

Though systematic survey data are lacking, it's recognized that populations of grassland birds underwent large declines before the BBS began in 1966.[22] In 1873 as he traveled in northwest North Dakota and northeast Montana, the pioneer ornithologist Elliot Coues reported all five of the focal songbirds to be abundant.[23] One hundred years later, Robert Stewart, in his *Breeding Birds of North Dakota*, noted large population declines in the state of three of the five focal species during the early Euro-American settlement period. Populations of the Sprague's pipit "apparently were much greater during the early pioneer days."[24] Regarding the thick-billed longspur, "It has been well documented that a drastic reduction in populations and marked constrictions of breeding range took place throughout the greater part of North Dakota during the period 1906–1930."[25] The "breeding populations of Chestnut-collared Longspurs have been greatly reduced" in the wake of agricultural development in the late 1800s.[26] The BBS shows populations of the five species have continued their tailspins since Stewart's accounts.

Pre-BBS population declines of the five songbirds likely began when the first wave of cropland expansion swept across the Great Plains in the late 1800s and early 1900s. Ongoing conversion of native grasslands to cropland and fields of tame grasses continue to hammer grassland birds. More recent declines may also be due to cropland expansion in the Chihuahuan Desert grasslands of northern Mexico, wintering habitat for 19 species of grassland birds, including the five focal songbirds, mountain plover, and burrowing owl.[27]

The five songbirds generally prefer native grasslands but sometimes nest in croplands, fallow fields, nonnative grasslands, and other areas of disturbed vegetation.[28] Nesting in nonnative vegetation, however, often results in what ecologists call a "population sink." The imagery of bird populations going down the drain is apt because birds nesting in such habitat often fail to produce enough young to sustain the population. In essence, the nonnative vegetation gives birds the right cues for nesting behavior but not the right conditions for nesting success.[29]

Habitat fragmentation also arrived in the Northern Great Plains well before the BBS began in the form of thousands of miles of roads, fences, utility poles and lines, and shelterbelts, as well as croplands, stock ponds, and farm and ranch buildings. Besides resulting in the direct loss of native prairie, these infringements on the landscape pose two basic problems: grassland birds tend to avoid nesting near them and, if they do nest near them, they often suffer lower nesting success and higher mortality.[30] Except for trees along rivers and streams, anything more than waist or chest high is novel in the evolutionary history of grassland birds of the Northern Great Plains. Vertical structures are warning signs that cause many species to avoid nesting near them.[31] Both species of longspurs and Sprague's pipit have an aversion to even modest shrub cover.[32] The likely reason is that raptors and the loggerhead shrike use vertical structures to perch while hunting, and grassland songbirds are often on the menu.[33] Edge habitat, such as the margin between prairie and cropland or a road, also causes elevated predation rates because it attracts raccoons, skunks, badgers, foxes, and other voracious predators of eggs and nestlings.[34] The birds have caught on. In native grasslands of southern Alberta, chestnut-collared longspurs were less common up to one mile or more from cropland and Sprague's pipit up to more than a half mile.[35]

The bottom line is that very large intact grassland landscapes of tens of thousands of acres, unfragmented by croplands or other unnatural features, are important for many grassland birds, but such areas are scarce across the Great Plains.[36]

The "take half, leave half" paradigm of livestock management that aims to uniformly graze the landscape and suppress fires has homogenized grassland habitat to the detriment of grassland birds and other wildlife. The habitat preferences of the five focal grassland species show why. Thick-billed longspurs prefer habitat of sparse and very short vegetation and lots of bare ground. The chestnut-collared longspur and Sprague's pipit, in contrast, seek out medium to tall grassland vegetation.[37] The lark bunting prefers vegetation height between these two extremes and welcomes the presence of shrubs.[38] In the Northern Great Plains the grasshopper sparrow prefers taller grasses with some bare ground for foraging.[39] Other grassland songbirds similarly display strong preferences for different types of grassland habitat.

In addition to disrupting the process whereby ungulates preferentially graze nutritious postfire plant growth, the suppression of grassland fires has enabled the invasion of fire-intolerant trees, rendering millions of acres, mostly in the central and southern plains, nearly useless to most grassland birds.[40] Though much less severe, this effect of fire suppression is seen on the Charles M. Russell National Wildlife Refuge, where fire intolerant shrubs such as big sagebrush and Rocky Mountain juniper (*Juniperus scopulorum*) have increased while fire-tolerant species have decreased.[41]

The post–World War II boom in pesticide treatment of both croplands and rangelands brought a new threat to grassland birds. Insecticides, because they are more directly toxic to nontarget animals than herbicides and because they reduce arthropod populations that birds prey on, are of greatest concern.[42] During a grasshopper outbreak in 2020, the U.S. Department of Agriculture contracted aerial spraying of an insecticide on 2.6 million acres of grasslands in eastern Montana with likely devastating effects on not only grasshoppers but also pollinators and other arthropods. The effects this had on insectivorous birds are unknown, although surely their prey populations were severely reduced.[43]

Tracking and responding to pesticide use is like playing whack-a-mole—as soon as one gets knocked down because of toxicity to wildlife, another pops up. It started with eggshell-thinning organochlorines such as DDT, followed by organophosphates and carbamates, and then pyrethroid insecticides, which remain in use today, all with various forms of toxicity to wildlife and ecosystems. Finally, neonicotinoids were introduced in the mid-1990s and rapidly grew to become the most-used insecticide in North American and around the world.[44]

With various formulations for both urban and agricultural applications, neonicotinoid use in the United States skyrocketed roughly 15-fold between 2000 and 2014.[45] In North America, virtually every planted seed of corn, wheat, cotton, and canola, and most seeds of soybean, are coated with neonicotinoids. However, only 2–20% is absorbed by the crop, leaving 80–98% to accumulate in the soil, dispersed as dust while planting, and transported elsewhere by surface and ground water.[46]

Research soon began to identify trouble. Nontarget insects, especially bees and butterflies, were affected.[47] Ingestion of field-realistic levels of a neonicotinoid insecticide by migrating white-crowned sparrows (*Zonotrichia leucophrys*) resulted in reduced food consumption, body mass, and fat, and delayed departure on their next migratory leg—all likely imposing costs on survival and reproductive success.[48] A U.S.-wide analysis for the years 2008–14 (the only years for which data were available) suggests that, whether via direct toxicity to birds or decline of their insect prey or both, neonicotinoids are having a devastating effect on grassland birds. Increased neonicotinoid use over this period was estimated to account for a 4% annual decline in grassland bird populations, including parts of the Northern Great Plains.[49] Meanwhile, evidence is accumulating on the ubiquity of neonicotinoids in the environment and the diverse toxic pathways by which they may affect human health.[50]

In 2018 the European Union halted the use of commonly used neonicotinoids on all field crops and Health Canada's Pest Management Regulatory Agency is phasing out use of some of them.[51] Interim decisions to control the use of neonicotinoids by the U.S. Environmental Protection Agency,[52] however, fall short of recognizing the insecticide's threats to both biodiversity and human health.

More grassland nesting habitat for the five focal species was plowed during the 100-year period before the BBS began in 1966 than after. If nesting habitat is a limiting factor, this suggests that their population declines before the BBS began were as large or larger than since then. Population collapses of more than 90%, maybe more than 95%, since the late 1800s seem probable. Other grassland species may have experienced similar collapses. Teasing apart what elements of habitat change have contributed most to the decline of each species is incredibly difficult. The potentially large role that insecticides, particularly neonicotinoids, have played in recent population declines further complicates attempts to single out any one or two causes. Perhaps what we can say with confidence is that there are multiple interacting causes that must be addressed to pull grassland birds out of their tailspin.

Mountain Plover

The BBS shows the mountain plover population in their breeding range declined by 78% since the late 1960s.[53] Survey data on their winter range confirm this decline. The annual Audubon Christmas Bird Count for California, which includes much of the species' winter range, shows average counts during the 2000s–2010s to be 90% lower than the averages during the 1940s–1950s.[54]

By far the rarest of this chapter's eight focal species, the mountain plover was listed as endangered in Canada in 1987.[55] The U.S. Fish and Wildlife Service (USFWS) first proposed listing the mountain plover as threatened or endangered in 1999 and then again in 2010. In 2011 the USFWS, believing the population was secure at an estimated 20,000 birds, withdrew its proposal.[56] An accurate estimate is lacking, but the population is likely less than 20,000 today.

The mountain plover population was estimated at more than 300,000 around 1970, suggesting a population collapse of more than 90% over the last 50 years.[57] Whatever the number was then, it was surely a remnant of what existed 150 years ago. Population declines were already being reported during the early and mid-1900s.[58] Again, the BBS has caught only the tail end of a much larger population collapse.

Naturalists' reports from the late 1800s and early 1900s indicate mountain plovers were once common in their breeding range of the Great Plains. In Montana, mountain plovers were reported to breed "in considerable numbers" in 1874 in the Milk River region and, in the early 1900s, to be "quite common" in the headwaters region of the Missouri River.[59] In the 1870s mountain plovers were "abundant" in western Nebraska and occurred with "considerable frequency" on grasslands from Kansas to the west.[60] As late as the 1950s, the imminent ornithologist Olin Pettingill Jr. found mountain plovers to be "fairly common" in southeast Wyoming.[61]

In their winter range, the ornithologist Elliot Coues reported mountain plovers to be "abundant" in New Mexico and southern California during the 1870s. Another pioneering ornithologist, Joseph Grinnell, wrote that mountain plovers were "often abundant" and "occurred in great numbers . . . within a few miles of Los Angeles." Grinnell mentioned the mountain plover's "fair size and consequent food value. In earlier years numbers were sold in the markets at least of Los Angeles."[62]

The first strike against mountain plovers may have been the loss of the massive swarms of Rocky Mountain locusts, a prey the plover seemed to relish.[63] The effects of market hunting were addressed when the Migratory Bird Treaty Act of 1918 abolished unregulated hunting of migratory birds. Around the same time, however, plover habitat was being lost as the first wave of cropland development swept across their nesting habitat in the Great Plains

and their winter range of southern California. Although mountain plovers commonly nest and forage on tilled or short-stature
cropland, nesting success in such areas may be lower.[64]

The most severe long-term blow to mountain plovers occurred
when their preferred habitat of barren ground and very short vegetation was severely reduced by the widespread elimination of grassland fires, prairie dog colonies, and intensive grazing by bison.[65]
In the American Prairie–Russell Refuge region, for example, one
study found three-quarters of prairie dog colonies were occupied
by plovers and three-quarters of breeding plovers inhabited active
prairie dog colonies.[66] The 98% collapse of prairie dog colonies
by the 1940s, due primarily to the government-sponsored prairie
dog eradication program, surely triggered a precipitous drop in
the mountain plover population.

Recent trends in mountain plover numbers on their breeding
range demonstrate the ongoing threats they face. Surveys in eastern Montana conducted by biologists Craig and Pamela Knowles
from 1992 to 2019 found that of nine mountain plover nesting areas
they initially identified, five no longer have plovers, and numbers in most of the other sites have declined. They identify several causes: decline in prairie dog colonies, conversion of prairie
to crops and tame grass, reduction in intensive grazing by livestock, and wind farms and snow fences constructed in nesting
areas, among others.[67]

The number of mountain plovers in the Pawnee National
Grasslands of northeast Colorado dropped from 77 in 1990 to
3 in 2007, with indications that the region's plover population
had been in decline since the late 1930s or early 1940s. Among
the obvious causes were the loss of prairie dogs, grassland fires,
and intensive grazing, as well as movement of plovers to other
areas. However, increased predation of plover eggs and young
by a growing swift fox population was also implicated, an example that recovery efforts for two imperiled species may not always
go hand in hand.[68]

The cumulative evidence is overwhelming. Mountain plovers
have undergone a massive population collapse. More than one

million may have populated the Great Plains before their 150-year descent to perhaps less than 2% of that number.

Threats to the mountain plover's survival have not abated. In addition to habitat destruction, the loss of insect prey due to insecticide applications and direct poisoning by neonicotinoids are poorly understood threats to mountain plovers.[69] Despite these ongoing perils, USFWS and the wildlife agencies of the states within the plover's range have put little effort into population monitoring since the 2011 decision to not list the species as threatened or endangered. Compare that to the large investments in sage-grouse conservation described below; though much needed, sage-grouse are far more abundant. The USFWS needs to revisit their 2011 decision to not list the plover as threatened or endangered. Moreover, we simply should not be satisfied with the remnants, now seldom seen, of what was once a common bird of the Great Plains.

Burrowing Owl

BBS counts suggest the western burrowing owl population in the United States has declined by at least 50% since 1966. The biggest decline in numbers occurred from 1966 to 1995 in the northernmost parts of its range in the plains of eastern Montana, North Dakota, and southern Alberta and Saskatchewan.[70] In Canada, where burrowing owls are designated as endangered, the population has plummeted by at least 95% since 1990.[71] Burrowing owl life history strongly suggests these BBS-documented population declines of the last 50 years are only the tip of the iceberg.

Burrowing owls cue in on three habitat needs: burrows for nesting, roosting, and security; short sparse vegetation; and plenty of nearby prey. In the Great Plains burrowing owls depend on black-tailed prairie dog colonies for creating burrows surrounded by sparse vegetation. North of the Milk River and into southern Alberta and Saskatchewan, Richardson's ground squirrels (*Urocitellus richardsonii*) are also a primary source of burrows.[72] Burrowing owl numbers generally decline in lockstep with declining prairie dog populations.[73] Thus, the collapse of prairie dog and probably ground squirrel populations from 1910 to 1940 due to the combination of conversion of prairie to cropland and government-sponsored eradication programs must have also caused a collapse of the burrowing owl population. The obvious conclusion is that burrowing owls suffered a far greater decline in numbers before 1966 than after. If so, I suspect the population collapsed by 95% or more in the Northern Great Plains and possibly across the West since Euro-American settlement.

One other relatively recent threat comes via the owl's food chain. Unlike most raptors, hunting seldom takes burrowing owls farther than a few hundred yards from their nests. Burrowing owls hunt wherever the most prey occur—cropland, tame pasture, native grassland, even golf courses—as long as the vegetation isn't too tall. Some of these habitats may expose burrowing owl prey, and thus burrowing owls, to a panoply of toxic chemicals. Application of insecticides and rodenticides, both of which are extensively used in areas inhabited by burrowing owls, not only reduce prey abundance but may lead to secondary poisoning of owls.[74]

The current population of the western burrowing owl in Canada and the United States is estimated at 990,000.[75] One hundred and fifty years ago 10–20 million or more must have been constant companions of prairie dogs, ground squirrels, badgers, and other burrowing mammals across the Great Plains and Inter-mountain West.

Greater Sage-Grouse

As early as 1916 William T. Hornaday predicted extinction of the greater sage-grouse due to unregulated hunting.[76] The species has survived, but the bird's numbers have tumbled and continue to do so. The sage-grouse is listed as endangered in Canada and had been proposed for listing as threatened in the United States, but in 2015 the USFWS determined that it did not warrant such protection.[77] To avoid potential listing as threatened in the future and because sage-grouse are a highly visible game species, state wildlife agencies have invested heavily in monitoring and conserving sage-grouse populations.

Sage-grouse populations are monitored by counting males when they congregate and are highly visible on leks, their spring court-ship sites.[78] Lek counts since 1966 show a range-wide population decline of 81%;[79] in 2015 the range-wide population was estimated at a minimum of 424,645.[80] In the eastern portion of its range—mainly the Great Plains of Montana and Wyoming—numbers are down 87%. Lek counts, however, have documented only the tail end of a long-term decline of likely more than 95% from a population that once probably numbered several million. One of the few encour-aging signs of this downward spiral being reversed is in northeast Montana, centered on the American Prairie–Russell Refuge region, where the population has grown during the last two decades.[81]

Sage-grouse populations could have recovered from intensive hunting after game regulations were developed and enforced in the early 1900s. They do not recover, however, from permanent habitat destruction. Since the first surge in plow-up of sagebrush habitat in the 1910s in eastern Montana, a primary cause of the sage-grouse's population decline across its range is the loss, fragmentation, and degradation of sage-grouse habitat. More than 80% of sagebrush rangelands across the West have been altered in some way. Millions of acres of this habitat were destroyed during the 1960s when it became popular to eliminate sagebrush by fire, spraying, and cut-ting to improve rangelands for cattle grazing.[82] Wet meadows that are important for brood rearing have disappeared due to stream dewatering and conversion to alfalfa.[83] Although fire was histor-ically part of the sagebrush ecosystem, the invasion of cheatgrass and other exotic, fire-tolerant grasses has increased fuel loads, leading to more frequent large-scale fires that destroy sagebrush habitat. At higher elevations, however, fire suppression has led to the invasion of conifers into sagebrush habitat.[84] The direct effect of livestock grazing on sage-grouse is little studied but unlikely to be a significant factor affecting population levels across most of their range.[85]

Predation is another potential cause of sage-grouse popula-tion declines. Adult sage-grouse are commonly killed by eagles, owls, coyotes, and red foxes. Sage-grouse eggs are eaten by ravens

(*Corvus corax*), badgers, and coyotes. While sage-grouse evolved with predation under natural conditions, human infrastructure and development may upset that predator-prey balance. Ravens, for example, thrive around human settlements, and consequently, their numbers have increased dramatically across the Intermountain West. The apparent increase in coyote numbers following wolf eradication and growing numbers of red foxes in the West may have increased predation pressure by these species.[86] Habitat fragmentation has reduced suitable nesting habitat because, like many grassland songbirds, sage-grouse are averse to nesting near vertical structures and habitat edges that expose them to increased predation risks.[87]

A recent problem for sage-grouse is West Nile virus, a mosquito-transmitted pathogen from Africa that infects many bird species as well as humans. The disease reduced sage-grouse reproduction by 25% after it first arrived in the West in 2002. Ponds associated with coalbed methane wells, irrigated fields, and stock ponds may increase the disease's prevalence by providing breeding habitat for mosquitos. Although sage-grouse have developed some resistance to West Nile, it continues to be a cause of mortality.[88]

Collisions with fences and powerlines are commonly cited as problems for sage-grouse, but these are not considered major factors contributing to population declines. Nevertheless, flagging the top wire of fences and providing escape ramps in water tanks are inexpensive solutions.[89]

The American Prairie–Russell Refuge region remains a stronghold for the species and is identified as one of the core areas for sage-grouse conservation. Moreover, the world-record migration of the region's sage-grouse and the need to conserve more than one million acres of their migratory pathway merit special attention.[90]

Effects of Collapses on Biodiversity

What are the ecological consequences of these population collapses in the Northern Great Plains? Considering the collective decline of all grassland birds, does anything in the ecosystem notice that there are several million fewer grassland songbirds every year?

To assess this, we need to consider the density of birds in their habitat. More or fewer birds per square mile should affect how many insects and seeds are eaten per square mile and how many birds, nestlings, and eggs are available for predators. It's not uncommon for current densities of each of the five focal songbirds to be in the range of 50–200 or more per square mile in good habitat.[91] To illustrate, let's use 100 birds per square mile. If 150 years ago the total population of the five songbirds was 10 times greater than today, but good habitat was only double what it is today (i.e., assuming 50% has been converted to cropland), then songbird density 150 years ago would have been 500 per square mile. Other songbirds that have undergone significant declines—especially the horned lark, savannah sparrow, and western meadowlark—often occur at similar or higher densities than the five focal songbirds. Although assessing changes in grassland bird densities over the last 150 years is fraught with uncertainties, these figures raise the possibility that grassland songbirds in the Northern Great Plains historically numbered in the thousands per square mile, whereas today they number in the hundreds. Would the loss of thousands of songbirds per square mile have ecological consequences, either down the food web as they forage for seeds and insects or up the food web as food for predators?

During the nesting season many grassland birds, including the five focal songbirds, are primarily insectivorous because nestlings require lots of protein. Songbird parents may make up to 10,000 food deliveries, sometimes with multiple prey per delivery, during the nestling phase alone.[92] Grasshoppers are favorite prey of grassland birds and are often a dominant herbivore in grassland ecosystems.[93] Experiments have shown that excluding grassland songbirds from grassland habitat can result in large increases in grasshopper numbers.[94] The grasshopper response to bird population collapses might be particularly strong in regions, such as much of the Northern Great Plains, where nonsongbirds—mountain plovers, burrowing owls, and broods of greater sage-grouse—also eat grasshoppers. The community of grasshoppers (and other arthropods), their predators, and the plants they eat is far too complex to predict how changes in the bird-grasshopper-plant food chain will affect the grassland ecosystem. Nevertheless, it's one component among myriad moving parts to consider.

Grassland songbirds are also granivorous, meaning they eat seeds of grasses and flowering plants, with two possible outcomes: the birds are seed predators because the seed is killed as it's digested, or the birds are seed dispersers because the seed passes through the gut intact and remains viable for germination. A decline in seed predators should favor an increase in the plants whose seeds are eaten. Again, a handful of experiments indicates that the loss of seed-eating grassland birds can affect the abundance of plants whose seeds they eat.[95] The decline of seed predation and dispersal by birds could have various effects, both positive and negative, on the recovery of native vegetation on former croplands and other disturbed sites.

Did the population collapses of the eight grassland bird species affect species that eat them? It's difficult to detect such effects because most predators are opportunists—they're adept at preying on whatever is around and most abundant. The most common victims of bird predation are generally eggs and nestlings, and so snakes, ground squirrels, swift foxes, and other ground-based predators would perhaps be most affected by grassland bird declines. Among raptors, the grassland-bird-hunting merlin (*Falco columbianus*) would seem most likely to show the effects. Studies in the Northern Great Plains have found several species of grassland songbirds with declining populations—horned larks, chestnut-collared longspurs, lark buntings, vesper sparrows, western meadowlarks—commonly occur in the merlin's diet.[96] Although BBS data suggest the merlin population is doing poorly in some parts of the Northern Great Plains, it is doing well in other parts of the region and across North America.[97]

At the other end of the size spectrum, the meaty sage-grouse and its large eggs are prey for eagles, hawks, owls, coyotes, foxes, badgers, snakes, and other predators.[98] BBS data indicate that golden eagles, gyrfalcons (*Falco rusticolus*), and most other large raptors that hunt sage-grouse are doing well.[99] How their populations fared before the BBS began in 1966 is not known.

Recovery

Compared to recovery of many other imperiled species, grassland birds require action at much larger scales with much larger population goals—hundreds of thousands to millions of birds. The result is that a description of measures needed to restore populations of the eight focal bird species reads like a to-do list for nearly all that ails grassland biodiversity: stop and reverse the plow-up of grasslands, including sagebrush steppe; bring back all the disturbances—fire, prairie dogs, and variable grazing—that create habitat heterogeneity; and stop poisoning grassland ecosystems with pesticides. Moreover, this must be done on their nesting, migratory, and winter habitats. Include several other grassland bird species undergoing significant population declines, and it becomes more apparent that a continent-wide effort to conserve and better manage grasslands is required.

Although continental action is needed, a logical focal point for restoration work is where the continent's highest concentration of imperiled grassland birds exists: the glaciated plains of northeast Montana and nearby regions of Alberta and Saskatchewan (see fig. 7 in chapter 3). The region's importance for grassland birds has been a major reason that government agencies, research institutions, and nonprofit organizations, including American Prairie, are working to identify and implement measures to restore and conserve the region's grassland bird habitats.

These collective efforts in the region can make a significant contribution to grassland bird conservation, but full annual-cycle conservation of the eight species requires international cooperation across the continent's central grasslands, from Canada to Mexico.[100] This task is becoming more complicated as climate change forces shifts in the birds' ranges. Under projected climate change scenarios, the current nesting ranges of the chestnut-collared longspur, thick-billed longspur, and Sprague's pipit could be reduced by more than 95%, and Baird's sparrow could lose all of its nesting habitat.[101] Climate change will also drive large shifts in sagebrush ecosystems.[102] Sagebrush may expand in the American Prairie–Russell

Refuge region—good for greater sage-grouse but bad for shrub-averse species such as Sprague's pipit.

While much can be done to improve management on government-owned lands in the breeding ranges of the eight species, most lands are privately owned. A vast range of actions and policy changes by government agencies, the corporate sector, and nonprofit organizations are needed to provide incentives and mechanisms for landowners to conserve and restore grasslands and grassland birds. Multiple government policies that create incentives for landowners to plow grasslands, such as crop subsidies and the ethanol mandate, need to be eliminated. Incentives for landowners to conserve grasslands—conservation easements, carbon credits, ecolabeling beef, and so on—need to be expanded.[103] The single most impactful measure would be for every corporation and government agency whose actions affect prairies to set a goal and policy of "no prairie conversion."[104]

Like the dire conditions facing so many species, we are at a crossroads with grassland birds. The road of inaction, of business as usual, portends catastrophe for the eight focal species and others like them. The alternative road toward the public giving higher value to grasslands and their wildlife—and to landowners, government agencies, corporations, and other institutions responding accordingly—can lead to a richer and more resilient and interesting Great Plains landscape of abundant birdlife. As Andy Boyce, a bird ecologist with the Smithsonian Institution told me, "Grassland birds should be among the easiest animals to conserve. No one opposes birds, they don't threaten livestock operations, they need less space than many mammals, and they voluntarily search far and wide for the best habitat each year. If we can't manage to arrest their decline, what hope is there for the harder stuff?"[105]

A predatory songbird, the loggerhead shrike impales its prey, ranging from insects to small mammals and birds, on thorns and other sharp objects. Drawing by Erica Freese.

TWELVE

Conclusion

G rasslands arrived late on the world's biome scene, appearing during the last 1% of the history of life on Earth. Grasses made up for a late start by radiating into 11,000 species, yielding the world's most important food crops, and displacing forests to dominate up to 40% of the Earth's land.[1] The Great Plains was part of this grassland surge, and the region's plants and animals reflect the evolutionary adaptations sculpted by the transition from forest to grassland living. Humans participated in this evolutionary journey as we adapted to the spread of African grasslands by becoming bipedal, long-legged, long-distance foragers.[2]

The evolution of the Great Plains, especially the Northern Great Plains, was a tumultuous, multi-hundred-million-year ride through shifting tectonic plates, fire and ice, inundations and droughts, chaos and calm, extinction, immigration, speciation, and multiple pathways of evolutionary experimentation and adaptation. The last species standing and present when Euro-Americans arrived represented diverse and fascinating ancestries and evolutionary histories. Some were homegrown; others came from far-off lands. Despite diverse origins, thousands of species coalesced and adapted to the lands and waters and to one another to form a thriving, rambunctious, complex, grassland-dominated ecosystem in the core of North America. This ecosystem and its biodiversity both challenged and nurtured Native peoples for thousands of years and elicited wonder by the first Euro-American explorers more than two centuries ago. The American Prairie–Russell Refuge region before Euro-American immigration exemplified this astonishing diversity and abundance of wildlife. But it didn't last. Wildlife populations withered as the Great Plains was "conquered" in the name of manifest destiny.

Within the American Prairie–Russel Refuge region, populations of at least 24 species—14 mammals, 8 birds, 1 fish, and 1 insect—have declined by at least 90% since 1800 (fig. 30). The collapses began with the beaver and river otter in the early 1800s and peaked with the annihilation of 11 species—ungulates, carnivores, and one insect—around 1880–1920. Every population of the region's 10 most common mammals of adult weights of more than 40 pounds collapsed. Next to fall were the prairie dog and black-footed ferret in the 1920s–30s. The pallid sturgeon soon followed with its decline likely beginning in the early 1900s and then accelerating during the 1940s–50s. Collapses of the 8 grassland bird species began more than 100 years ago and continue. Of the 24 animal species, a few populations have partially recovered, but most have not. One species, the Rocky Mountain locust, may be extinct and two, the black-footed ferret and Upper Missouri River pallid sturgeon, depend on captive propagation for their survival with no sign that either is ready to make it on its own.

I have surely missed some collapses. An especially quick and severe one, I fear, is underway as this book goes to press. White-nose syndrome, a deadly disease of hibernating bats, including little brown bats (*Myotis lucifugus*), is caused by a fungal pathogen (*Pseudogymnoascus destructans*) likely introduced from Eurasia. First reported in 2006 in the northeast United States, the fungus has since steadily spread westward across the continent with devastating effects on bat populations.[3] The disease was first reported in bats in eastern Montana, including Azure Cave in the Little Rocky Mountains, in 2020.[4] Based on surveys that began in 1993, Azure Cave has sheltered the largest known colony of little brown bats in the West. Around 1,700–1,900 bats, mostly little browns, hibernate annually in the cave. A May 2022 survey of the cave found about 40 bats, a 98% collapse of the population. Half of the remaining bats showed signs of white-nose syndrome.[5] There

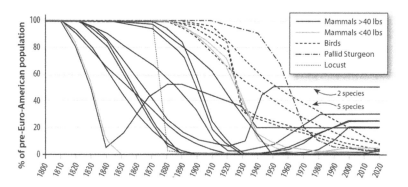

FIG. 30. Profile of the population collapses of 24 species, compiled from other graphs herein. Created by author and Eric Cline.

is no cure for the disease, so combatting it presents a formidable, continent-wide conservation challenge.

Though less dramatic and obvious, populations of other species have likely entered or are approaching collapse territory. Candidates among grassland birds include the horned lark, Baird's sparrow, and loggerhead shrike. The sicklefin chub and blue sucker—and perhaps other species of small, inconspicuous prairie fish—may exist as small fractions of their historic numbers. From beetles to badgers, populations of other species closely associated with prairie dogs may have suffered severe but undocumented declines. Populations and geographic ranges of white-tailed jackrabbits (*Lepus townsendii*) and long-tailed weasels are showing serious but poorly tracked shrinkage in portions of their ranges in the Great Plains and beyond.[6] The widespread decline of insect pollinators in North America makes one wonder if some of the 250 or more species of bees and butterflies of the American Prairie–Russell Refuge are at risk.

Figure 30 reflects what happened to wildlife not only in the American Prairie–Russell Refuge region but also across the 620 million acres of the Great Plains from Canada to Mexico. For example, none of the 14 mammal species studied, all with ranges that historically spanned all or nearly all of the Great Plains, escaped the same fate. As one expands into the central and southern Great Plains the list of documented collapses—blowout penstemon (*Penstemon haydenii*), American burying beetle (*Nicrophorus americanus*), Wyoming toad (*Anaxyrs baxteri*), lesser prairie chicken (*Tympanuchus pallidicinctus*), Arkansas River shiner (*Notropis girardi*), and others—grows. This list gets longer when considering species such as the Eskimo curlew and whooping crane, for which the Great Plains is a migratory pathway.

Without long-term population data for hundreds of species, we can only speculate about the scope of biotic devastation across the region. More systematic, continent-wide monitoring of plant and animal populations is urgently needed.

A population collapse implies much more than just adding to the raw tally of species affected. Each collapse sends waves of change through the ecosystem. Some, such as those experienced by grassland songbirds, may create only ripples. The collective collapse of others—such as beavers, bison, prairie dogs, and perhaps the Rocky Mountain locust—unleashed tidal waves of ecological degradation. Moreover, focusing on individual species ignores broader and more insidious ecological decay problems that are harder to track, such as the decline of pollinator populations and consequent effects on plant reproduction.[7]

Ecologists Gerardo Ceballos, Paul Ehrlich, and Rodolfo Dirzo caution that the focus on species extinctions tends to obscure the problems of contracting populations and ranges: "Dwindling population sizes and range shrinkages amount to a massive anthropogenic erosion of biodiversity and of the ecosystem services essential to civilization. This 'biological annihilation' underlines the seriousness for humanity of Earth's ongoing sixth mass extinction event."[8]

Mammals are useful indicators of the extent of biological annihilation because many are dominant ecological players, and compared to other taxonomic groups, we have a good handle on their distributions and numbers. Global mammalian population trends offer a context for what has happened in the Great Plains. Since around 1900, nearly half of the world's mammals for which we have adequate data—mostly medium- to large-sized mammals—experienced range contractions of more than 80%.[9] Their population declines must be even greater than 80% because the populations that inhabit the remaining 20% of their former ranges are likely reduced compared to historic levels. In contrast, global mammalian livestock numbers during that time have increased by roughly 320%, with cattle increasing 250% to 1.5 billion, outnumbering all other livestock categories.[10] The population of the third major mammalian category, humans, rose from 1.7 billion in 1900 to 8 billion today.[11]

While these population trends are daunting, an ecologically more meaningful measure is their effects on mammalian biomass. (The loss of a thousand 1,000-pound bison will reverberate through the food web much more than the loss of a thousand 3-pound rabbits.) A recent analysis provides a sobering estimate of how the world's mammalian biomass is now allocated: 60% in livestock, 36% in humans, and 4% in wild mammals.[12] Leave humans out, and livestock comprise 85% and wild mammals 15% of mammalian biomass. How does the Great Plains compare? I estimate that livestock (mostly cattle) comprise at least 95% and wild mammals (mostly rodents, lagomorphs, and deer) less than 5% of non-human mammalian biomass in the region's remaining grasslands.[13]

This sorry condition reminds me of biologist Kent Redford's 1992 paper, "The Empty Forest," a title reflecting how a seemingly intact tropical forest conveys a deceptive image of "all is well" even though the animals within the forest have been decimated.[14] We now have across most of the Great Plains the "empty grassland" or, considering ongoing declines of many species, the "emptying grassland." Urgent, large-scale action is needed to reverse these trends, to restore and reconnect grasslands and refill them with wildlife.

Whether in the Great Plains or in nearly any other ecosystem in the world, conserving the full sweep of a region's biodiversity—from viable populations and genetic variation of all native species to maintaining ecological and evolutionary processes—requires large protected areas.[15] With a long-term vision aimed at restoring all native biodiversity and a size 12 times larger than the next largest protected area in the Great Plains, a 3.2-million-acre American

Prairie–Russell Refuge offers our best chance to establish a new paradigm for Great Plains conservation.

The unfolding ecological scene promises to be unlike anything experienced on this continent in more than 150 years. When done, the reserve could potentially support more than 100,000 native ungulates, representing seven species and inhabiting every terrestrial habitat of the region. The combined populations of the gray wolf, puma, grizzly bear, and black bear could approach 1,000 animals and, in the process, unleash cascading effects up and down the predator-herbivore-plant food web. One hundred thousand acres of prairie dogs and scores of species that thrive when they thrive, including black-footed ferrets and swift foxes, will offer multitudes of fascinating wildlife interactions. Grassland birds will flourish in a landscape of heterogeneous grassland habitats unfragmented by fences and cropland and unpolluted by agrochemicals. Beaver ponds strung like pearls along restored prairie streams could again be magnets for wildlife in this semiarid land. And perhaps as the public is increasingly inspired by the restored biological richness of the region's terrestrial realm, it will demand that the Missouri River be unshackled for the benefit of the pallid sturgeon and other river life.

Even at 3.2 million acres the American Prairie–Russell Refuge will not be big enough to do the job by itself. Any protected area with species that are migratory, wide-roaming, or occur at low densities, with large-scale ecological processes such as fire and grazing, and with soil, precipitation, and other physical conditions that are highly variable across space and time—must operate within a larger framework of biodiversity-friendly lands and ecological connectivity to other protected habitats. The Serengeti-Mara Ecosystem in Kenya and Tanzania offers a cautionary example: though nearly 10 million acres in size, its biodiversity and ecosystem services have declined because the effects of surrounding agricultural practices extend into the ecosystem's core.[16] Whether the species of concern is pallid sturgeon, Sprague's pipit, bison, wolves, or insect pollinators, shared stewardship across multiple jurisdictions with diverse partners is fundamental to long-term, large-scale success.

Building community acceptance and a sense of shared stewardship is a challenge facing the development of large protected areas virtually anywhere in ranch country on the Great Plains. Northeast Montana is no exception. I won't attempt to unpack all the psychological, social, political, and economic factors that influence community attitudes about prairie dogs, bison, wolves, and American Prairie's mission. Steve Forrest captured part of the problem when he told me that "what the critics of American Prairie get wrong is that they see it as a return to the past, not a path to the future."[17] That path to the future is toward economic, cultural, and biological diversity as the key to adapting to the coming decades of economic and cultural uncertainties, much of it driven by climate change, facing the rural Great Plains.[18] Work by numerous Native nations to restore bison, driven not only by their cultural connections to bison but also by economic and food security based on the bison's capacity to adapt to climate change, exemplifies this forward-looking path.[19]

Although this book is about restoring biodiversity, it's worth noting the increasing cultural and socioeconomic diversity that American Prairie and its cooperation with the Charles M. Russell National Wildlife Refuge are bringing to the region. These benefits are substantial and slowly opening doors to community acceptance and support. Economic benefits flow primarily from direct expenditures by American Prairie and by people who come as visitors. In recent years American Prairie has spent locally more than $2 million annually on supplies, equipment, services, utilities, and vehicles. On top of this are the employment of staff and their expenditures as members of the community and American Prairie's Wild Sky program payments to landowners for biodiversity-friendly management practices.[20] Of much greater magnitude is the money spent on food, lodging, gas, and other goods and services by visiting tourists, hunters, researchers, artists, students, and educators. A recent analysis suggests the American Prairie–Russell Refuge could eventually generate $13.4–$56.3 million in additional nonresident expenditures and 163–683 additional jobs in the region.[21] Economic activity from two grassland national parks in the Northern Great Plains offer other data points. In 2015 The-odore Roosevelt National Park in North Dakota and Badlands National Park in South Dakota generated, respectively, 494 and 1,000 jobs, $35.9 million and $62.2 million in visitor expenditures, and $38.2 million and $77.5 million in economic output.[22]

Much less measurable are the social, cultural, educational, sci-entific, and spiritual benefits. Overnight stays at American Prairie's campgrounds and huts, constructed to expand opportunities to fully experience the prairie, grew from around 1,000 in 2019 to 5,000 in 2021. American Prairie's education and outreach pro-grams with Native nations and local towns and schools magnify these benefits. American Prairie staff collaborate with local com-munities, ranchers, and Native nations in projects ranging from weed control and installation of wildlife-friendly fences to res-toration of historic buildings and contributing bison to start or augment Native nations' herds. Hunters enjoy more opportuni-ties with greater access to lands with larger wildlife populations, including bison hunts reserved for members of local communi-ties, Native peoples, and wounded servicemen and women. Amer-ican Prairie's Enrico Education and Science Center, located in a remote prairie setting, attracts students, educators, and scientists from around the world. Recognizing the potential for large-scale, long-term research, the Smithsonian Institution selected Ameri-can Prairie as the base for its Great Plains Science Program. The most recent major investment in community outreach and edu-cation was the 2021 opening of American Prairie's National Dis-covery Center in the nearby town of Lewistown. The main street facility offers state-of-the art exhibits about the region's human and natural history. These and other benefits are establishing Ameri-can Prairie as an important contributor to community well-being in the region.

The American Prairie–Russell Refuge is changing the face of biodiversity conservation in the Great Plains. With nearly half of the long-term goal of 3.2 million acres secured for wildlife and more habitat being acquired nearly every year, wildlife and habitat restoration are proceeding on several fronts. The effort serves as a touchstone for others setting conservation goals and illuminates the scale of action needed to meet those goals in the Great Plains.

Building a Protected Area System

In 2010, parties to the Convention on Biological Diversity established Aichi Target 11, which called for 17% of the world's lands, by 2020, to be in protected areas dedicated to conserving biodiversity and ecosystem services.[23] When prairie conservationists gathered at the meeting in Bozeman in 2000 and launched the idea of the American Prairie project because they believed the Great Plains deserved more protected areas, 1% of the Great Plains and 10% of the world's lands were protected. Despite more lands being protected by American Prairie and a few other projects since then, Great Plains protected-area coverage has not yet reached 2%, while the rest of the world moved further ahead to achieve the Aichi Target 11 with a global average of 17% coverage.[24] Some regions have exceeded and others have fallen short of that goal, but no region has fallen shorter than the Great Plains. To reach the 17% goal, we need 100 million acres of new protected areas in the Great Plains.

Concern about this lack of progress is expressed in a 2016 report where the principal public land management agencies of Canada, the United States, and Mexico conclude, with respect to the continent's grasslands, that "sustained efforts . . . could allow North America to meet and potentially exceed the 17% protected area target established under the Convention on Biological Diversity."[25] I have yet to see evidence of any sustained efforts that will move us close to 17% in the foreseeable future.

For anyone who considers the Aichi Target 11 of 17% too ambitious or unnecessary for the Great Plains, recent analyses suggest that goal is far too modest. First proposed by the imminent biologist Edward O. Wilson and captured by the name "Nature Needs Half," scientists now widely believe that one-half of the Earth's terrestrial realm must be protected to avert a sixth mass extinction.[26] An interim goal of protecting 30% of the Earth's surface by 2030 has been proposed and widely endorsed by nations, including the U.S. and Canadian governments, and conservation organizations around the world.[27]

Instead of making significant progress by building new protected areas, the Great Plains as a whole is moving fast in the wrong direction. As noted in chapter 4, an estimated 120 million acres (19%) of the region's grasslands were plowed for use as cropland since 2000. Most of the plow-up is occurring in the semiarid western half of the Great Plains, where roughly 60% of the land remains in native and nonnative short- and mixed-grass prairies. Little remains to be plowed in the more moist eastern half, where only 10% of the tallgrass prairie remains intact.[28]

Although laudable progress has been made recently by institutions other than American Prairie in creating protected areas covering tens of thousands of acres in the Great Plains,[29] much more needs to be done. For that to happen we need a new paradigm for the Great Plains that elevates protected areas to the third major form of land use alongside cropland and livestock ranching. Crop and livestock production are not set in stone as the only two major types of land use in the Great Plains, especially for the short-grass and mixed-grass western regions. The dominance of these two land uses is not preordained but simply a contingency of history as agriculture swept across the Great Plains before a system of protected areas could be assembled.

Success in building a protected area system as the cornerstone for restoring and conserving Great Plains biodiversity will be affected by future management of the region's croplands and livestock grazing lands. Cropland expansion is the most serious threat to biodiversity and is the single biggest cause of destruction and fragmentation of prairie ecosystems, although woodland invasion rivals cropland as a threat in some regions. The conversion of prairie to cropland in the Great Plains is largely fueled by the approximately $10 billion in agricultural subsidies the region receives annually.[30] The American public, unfortunately, is largely uninformed about the scale and abuse of agricultural subsidies, how subsidies go primarily to the largest and wealthiest landowners, and how they are contributing to the loss of grasslands, wildlife, and ecosystem services that benefit millions of people. We urgently need to get to the goal of zero conversion of grasslands to croplands. Not only should state, provincial, and federal policies be reformed to reflect the goal of zero conversion, but corporations whose businesses affect grasslands need to embrace it.[31]

Unlike croplands, ranchlands can support substantial levels of native biodiversity. Nevertheless, as discussed in chapter 6, there are significant limits to how effectively livestock can be managed to ecologically mimic native ungulates and to rancher willingness to implement even modest management changes that could improve outcomes for wildlife.[32] This does not mean that ranchland coexistence with fire and species such as prairie dogs, bison, and wolves isn't possible and shouldn't be pursued. It is and should be. What it does mean is that we can't expect the livestock industry to provide core areas for large-scale, comprehensive recovery of grassland biodiversity. Large protected areas are the cornerstones for such efforts.

Unfortunately, while grassland conservationists in both the public and nonprofit sectors have focused on how to better manage livestock-grazed lands, scant attention has been given to building and connecting protected areas where all native grassland species could be restored. Contrast this with the nearby Rocky Mountains, where researchers and managers from diverse institutions work to conserve the full sweep of biodiversity, from wolves and grizzly bears to ecological connectivity among wildlands. While the prairie strain of shifting baseline syndrome may be at play by lowering visions of what could be, this less ambitious approach to grassland conservation also reflects the dominance of land ownership and political clout by the livestock industry in the Great Plains.

Despite this inattention to protected areas, several assessments have identified priority landscapes for conserving biodiversity in portions of or across the entire region.[33] Priority landscapes, many 1–4 million acres in size, represent around 10–20% of the areas assessed, a range in line with the Aichi 11 target of 17%.

A detailed review of these assessments is well beyond the scope of this chapter, but a couple of examples in the Northern Great Plains are worth noting. In addition to the region of the American Prairie–Russell Refuge, a nearby priority region identified by the assessments runs almost continuously for 300 miles from the foothills of the Rocky Mountains on the Alberta–Montana border east to Grasslands National Park along the Saskatchewan–Montana border. Especially notable is the potential for a large binational protected area in the region of Grasslands National Park that would incorporate more than one million acres of public lands on both sides of the border with private land acquisitions providing linkages to fill in the gaps. As I mentioned in chapter 6, the American Prairie–Russell Refuge lies a few miles to the south across the Milk River and Highway 2, where a few well-placed wildlife overpasses or underpasses could facilitate ecological connectivity for wildlife movement between these two high priority regions.

Other multi-million-acre priority regions where public lands could be linked by acquiring private lands include Theodore Roosevelt National Park and the Little Missouri National Grasslands in North Dakota; Buffalo Gap National Grassland and Badlands National Park, which includes part of the Pine Ridge Indian Reservation, in South Dakota; and the Oglala National Grassland in Nebraska and Thunder Basin National Grassland in Wyoming. Few large national parks, wildlife refuges, and national grasslands exist in the central and southern Great Plains to serve as anchors for building large protected areas. An exception is the 193,000-acre Pawnee National Grassland in a high priority region of the short-grass prairie of northeast Colorado. Nevertheless, the assessments identify several large grassland regions from Nebraska to Texas that are priorities for conserving the full range of Great Plains biodiversity.

How can protected area coverage grow to become the third major land-use category in the Great Plains? I won't attempt to predict how changes in public attitudes, Great Plains demographics and urbanization, food production, meat substitutes and dietary preferences, philanthropic funding, climate change, and numerous other variables will affect land use and prospects for protected area expansion during the coming decades. My general sense—admittedly influenced by hope—is that the winds of change will blow toward more protected areas and more wildlife. But it won't come easily and will involve tons of hard work. As former U.S. National Park Service ecologist Daniel Licht notes, "The obstacles to such public reserves are formidable and entrenched."[34]

Growing million-acre-plus protected areas will often require securing large acreages of both public and private lands for the primary purpose of biodiversity conservation. Numerous precedents exist for converting public lands to more formally protected areas in Canada and the United States. The most obvious option for incorporating private lands into protected areas is through their purchase by nonprofit organizations using philanthropic funds, as done by American Prairie, and by government agencies using public funds. Wealthy landowners with large land holdings—there are many in the Great Plains—could dedicate lands to the cause. Conservation easements and other methods of compensating landowners for conserving biodiversity and other ecosystem services are important, especially for protected-area buffer zones and wildlife corridors. Land exchanges between private and public lands could be used to consolidate Bureau of Land Management lands and National Grasslands into larger contiguous units for protected area management. Other approaches might be borrowed from eastern and southern Africa where conservancies consisting of communal or private lands have transitioned from livestock production to wildlife tourism and hunting as a more economically rewarding use of the land.[35]

A major financial commitment will be required to launch several large protected area projects in the Great Plains. Most of the funding for land acquisition and management will almost certainly have to come from government budgets. In the U.S. Great Plains, where the 2021 price for grasslands averaged about $1,000 per acre,[36] $1 billion annually could go a long way toward assembling and managing protected areas. If that seems like a lot of money, which it is, consider that it is roughly 10% of what is spent annually on farm subsidies in the region. Although other sources of governments funds such as the Land and Water Conservation Fund could potentially be tapped,[37] the scale of the farm subsidy budget and its negative effects on grasslands make it an attractive source. What's lacking is the public support and political will to reallocate a sizeable chunk of that budget to programs that save rather than destroy grassland biodiversity and its multiple benefits to society.

Not unlike the need to shatter the ossified mindset that pre-empts free-roaming wild bison, it's time to build and embrace a new vision for protected areas across the Great Plains. The status quo will neither enable us to restore wildlife populations that have collapsed across the region nor stop ongoing declines of other species. American Prairie's cooperation with the C. M. Russell Refuge and with other institutions and individuals to assemble a protected area for restoring Great Plains biodiversity is, in and of itself, an invaluable contribution to fulfilling this vision and to conserving North America's natural heritage. Beyond that, however, as the public increasingly experiences and comprehends the grandeur of its landscape and wildlife, the American Prairie–Russell Refuge also promises to provide the inspiration and will for aiming higher, for building a large network of protected areas in the quest to restore wildlife across the Great Plains. I can't predict how fast this will happen. But if the region's history teaches us anything, it's that big changes can come unexpectedly and quickly.

NOTES

Introduction

1. Pauly, "Anecdotes," 430.

2. Jones et al., "Investigating the Implications," 1131; Kahn, Severson, and Ruckert, "Human Relation," 37; Soga and Gaston, "Shifting Baseline Syndrome," 222–24.

3. Flores, *American Serengeti.*

4. IUCN, *North America's Northern Great Plains.*

5. American Prairie, "This Is American Prairie."

1. How It Started

1. Davy, *Historic Properties Survey*, 9–10, 9–17.

2. Journals of Lewis & Clark, May 8, 1805.

3. Northern Great Plains Steppe Ecoregional Planning Team, *Ecoregional Planning*, 42.

4. Knopf, *Prairie Legacies*, 137–38.

5. Kotliar et al., "Critical Review," 177; Proctor, "GIS Model," 24–26.

6. Licht, *Ecology and Economics*, 177–78.

7. Catlin, *Letters and Notes*, 261.

8. Catlin, *Letters and Notes*, 261–62.

9. Licht, *Ecology and Economics*, 20.

10. Commission for Environmental Cooperation and The Nature Conservancy, *North American Central Grasslands*, 17.

11. Malone, Roeder, and Lang, *Montana*, 153–58.

12. Carbutt, Henwood, and Gilfedder, "Global Plight," 2911.

13. Barnett, "U.S. Farm," 366–77; Parton et al., "Long-Term Trends," 740–44.

14. Popper and Popper, "Great Plains," 17.

15. Popper and Popper, "Great Plains," 18.

16. Popper and Popper, "Buffalo Commons," 1–3.

17. Michener, *Centennial*, 91.

18. Wheeler, *Buffalo Commons.*

19. Flynn, "Daybreak on the Land," 815–21.

20. *Time*, "Top 10."

21. Thompson, "First Sagebrush Rebellion."

22. Soulé, "What Is Conservation Biology?," 727.

23. Soulé, "What Is Conservation Biology?," 727–33.

24. Soulé and Noss, "Rewilding and Biodiversity," 21.

25. MacArthur and Wilson, *Theory*.

26. Diamond, "Island Dilemma," 129; Soulé and Simberloff, "Genetics and Ecology," 19.

27. Fahrig, "Effects of Habitat," 487.

28. Soulé and Simberloff, "Genetics and Ecology," 33–34.

29. Krummel et al., "Landscape Patterns," 321.

30. Boyce, "Population Viability," 481–82; Shaffer, "Minimum Population," 131.

31. Soulé and Simberloff, "Genetics and Ecology," 32–35.

32. Soulé and Noss, "Rewilding and Biodiversity," 22–24.

33. Miller et al., "Importance of Large Carnivores," 205–7.

34. Newmark, "Extinction of Mammal," 430.

35. Cahalane, "Proposed Great Plains," 126.

36. Allen, "Hole in the System," 5–6.

37. Licht, *Ecology and Economics*, 135.

38. Watson et al., "Performance and Potential," 68.

39. Olson et al., "Terrestrial Ecoregions," 933.

40. Forrest et al., "Population Attributes," 261.

41. Kotliar et al., "Critical Review," 177.

42. Samson and Knopf, *Prairie Conservation*.

43. Knopf and Samson, *Ecology and Conservation*, 177.

44. Claassen et al., *Grassland to Cropland*, iv–v.

45. Knopf, *Prairie Legacies*, 142.

46. Freese et al., "Second Chance," 177.

47. Knapp et al., "Keystone Role of Bison," 46–48.

48. Polziehn et al., "Bovine MtDNA," 1639–42.

49. Freese et al., "Second Chance," 175.

50. Dary, *Buffalo Book*; Geist, *Buffalo Nation*.

51. Ambrose, *Undaunted Courage*.

52. InterTribal Buffalo Council, "InterTribal Buffalo Council."

53. Newmark, "Extinction of Mammal," 518–21.

54. Lott, *American Bison*, 203.

55. Fuhlendorf et al., "Perspectives on Grassland Conservation," under "3. Herbivore Domain."

56. Noss et al., "Conservation Biology," 959–60.

57. American Prairie, "Building the Prairie."

58. Bureau of Land Management, "Our Mission."

59. Trust Lands Management Division, *Annual Report*.

60. U.S. Fish and Wildlife Service, *Final Comprehensive*, 133.

2. From Sea, Ice, and Forest Emerges a Prairie

1. Merdith et al., "Extending Full-Plate," fig. 9.
2. Merdith et al., "Extending Full-Plate," fig. 8.
3. Deep Time Maps, "North America."
4. University of California Museum of Paleontology, "Online Exhibits."
5. Fastovsky and Bercovici, "Hell Creek," 370.
6. Montana Department of Transportation, *Little Rocky Mountains.*
7. Burgess, Bowring, and Shen, "High-Precision Timeline," 3316, 3319–20; Penn et al., "Temperature-Dependent," under "Discussion."
8. University of California Museum of Paleontology, "Online Exhibits."
9. Deep Time Maps, "North America."
10. University of California Museum of Paleontology, "Online Exhibits."
11. Brusatte, O'Connor, and Jarvis, "Origin and Diversification," R888.
12. Sauquet et al., "Ancestral Flower," under "Discussion."
13. Cardinal and Danforth, "Bees Diversified," under "4(d) Estimated Ages in Relation to Angiosperm Divergence Events."
14. University of California Museum of Paleontology, "Online Exhibits."
15. English and Johnston, "Laramide Orogeny," 833–38.
16. Stein, "Taking Count," 1–2.
17. Hilton and Grande, "Review of the Fossil," 672; Murray et al., "Paddlefish," under "Introduction."
18. Chiarenza et al., "Asteroid Impact," 17084, 17088–91.
19. DePalma et al., "Seismically Induced," 8194–95.
20. Artemieva, Morgan, and Expedition 364 Science Party, "Quantifying the Release," 10180–81, 10184–85.
21. Fastovsky and Bercovici, "Hell Creek," 368.
22. Longrich, Tokaryk, and Field, "Mass Extinction," 1523.
23. Fastovsky and Bercovici, "Hell Creek," 368.
24. Deep Time Maps, "North America."
25. Figueirido et al., "Cenozoic Climate," 723.
26. English and Johnston, "Laramide Orogeny," 833–38.
27. Montana Department of Transportation, *Little Rocky Mountains.*
28. Brikiatis, "De Geer," 1036; Jiang et al., "Asymmetric Biotic," 739–40.
29. Jiang et al., "Asymmetric Biotic," 739–40.
30. Leite et al., "In the Wake of Invasion," under "Introduction"; Carrillo et al., "Disproportionate Extinction," 26285.
31. Beatty, Beasley, and Rhodes, "Habitat Selection," 43.
32. Batchelor et al., "Configuration of Northern Hemisphere," fig. 2.
33. Fullerton et al., *Map Showing Spatial,* 21–26; University of California Museum of Paleontology, "Online Exhibits."
34. Lacelle et al., "Buried Remnants," 2, 5–6.
35. Davis et al., "Glacial Lake Musselshell," 331.
36. Trimble, *Geologic Story,* 33.
37. Trimble, *Geologic Story,* 33.

38. Davis et al., "Glacial Lake Musselshell," 338–41.

39. Elias and Brigham-Grette, "Glaciations," 101–201.

40. Potter et al., "Current Evidence," under "Potential Migration Routes"; Heintzman et al., "Bison Phylogeography," 8057.

41. Yansa, "Lake Records," 120–30.

42. Strömberg, "Evolution of Grasses," 521–25, 534.

43. Friedman and Barrett, "Phylogenetic Analysis," 53.

44. Retallack, "Cenozoic Paleoclimate," 284–85.

45. Blumenthal et al., "Traits Link Drought," 2336; Coughenour, "Graminoid Responses," 853–56, 860.

46. Coughenour, "Graminoid Responses," 853–56, 860.

47. Blumenthal et al., "Traits Link Drought," 2337–38; Coughenour, "Graminoid Responses," 853–56, 860.

48. Osborne and Sack, "Evolution of C_4 Plants," 583.

49. Anderson, "Evolution and Origin," 627–28, 633.

50. Song et al., "Evolution, Diversification," 1–3, 14, 20–21.

51. Brusatte, O'Connor, and Jarvis, "Origin and Diversification," R894.

52. Emslie, "Fossil Passerines," 85; Klicka, Zink, and Winker, "Longspurs and Snow Buntings," 165.

53. Chester et al., "Oldest Known Euarchontan," 1487; Silcox et al., "Evolutionary Radiation," R894.

54. Mantilla et al., "Earliest Palaeocene Purgatoriids," under "Abstract."

55. Chester et al., "Oldest Known Euarchontan," 1491.

56. Mantilla et al., "Earliest Palaeocene Purgatoriids," under "Introduction."

57. Samuels, Albright, and Fremd, "Last Fossil Primate," 43.

58. Figueirido et al., "Cenozoic Climate," 725–26.

59. Ge et al., "Evolutionary History," under "Abstract"; Churakov et al., "Rodent Evolution," 1323.

60. Forrest et al., "Ocean of Grass," 150–52.

61. Forrest et al., 150–52; Samuels and Hopkins, "Impacts of Cenozoic," 45–48.

62. Samuels and Hopkins, "Impacts of Cenozoic," 36–39.

63. Samuels and Hopkins, "Impacts of Cenozoic," 36–39.

64. Davidson, Detling, and Brown, "Ecological Roles," 477–81.

65. Samuels and Hopkins, "Impacts of Cenozoic," 43–48.

66. Lovegrove and Mowoe, "Evolution of Mammal," 1318.

67. Janis, "Evolutionary History," 25.

68. Lovegrove and Mowoe, "Evolution of Mammal," 1318.

69. Janis, Damuth, and Theodor, "Origins and Evolution," 193.

70. Heffelfinger et al., "Bestiary," 91–98.

71. Janis, Damuth, and Theodor, "Origins and Evolution," 189.

72. Lovegrove and Mowoe, "Evolution of Mammal," 1320.

73. Alexander, "Relative Merits," 391–92, 399–400.

74. Chen et al., "Large-Scale Ruminant," 1152.

75. Alexander, "Relative Merits," 391–92.

76. Strömberg, "Evolution of Hypsodonty," 249–54.

77. Solounias et al., "Hypsodont Crowns," under "Abstract."

78. Harris et al., "Global Decline," 57; Ofstad et al., "Home Ranges," under "Abstract."

79. Bowyer et al., "Evolution of Ungulates," 5162–64.

80. Kubo et al., "Transitions between Foot," 2618–20; McHorse, Biewener, and Pierce, "Evolution of a Single Toe," 638–42.

81. University of California Museum of Paleontology, "Online Exhibits."

82. Malhi et al., "Megafauna and Ecosystem Function," 840–43.

83. Hill, "Stratigraphic and Geochronologic," 102–3.

84. Gilbert, Ropiquet, and Hassanin, "Mitochondrial and Nuclear," 113–14; Gustafson, *Early Pliocene*, 1, 54.

85. Hansen, "Desert Bighorn," 133–34; Wang, "Systematics and Population," 173, 180.

86. Froese et al., "Fossil and Genomic Evidence," 3460.

87. Hundertmark et al., "Mitochondrial Phylogeography," 382–85; Meiri et al., "Faunal Record," under "Discussion."

88. Pires, Silvestro, and Quental, "Continental Faunal Exchange," fig. 1.

89. Koepfli et al., "Multigene Phylogeny," under "Tempo and Mode of Mustelid Diversification"; Sato et al., "Evolutionary and Biogeographic," 753–54.

90. McLellan and Reiner, "Review of Bear," 91.

91. Mitchell et al., "Ancient Mitochondrial DNA," under "1. Introduction," "3. Results."

92. Salis et al., "Lions and Brown Bears," fig. 3.

93. Figueirido et al., "Habitat Changes," under "Discussion"; Janis and Wilhelm, "Were There Mammalian Pursuit Predators?," 115–22.

94. Ersmark et al., "Past to the Present," under "Introduction."

95. Dundas, "Quaternary Records," 381; Perri et al., "Dire Wolves," 87.

96. Meachen, Brannick, and Fry, "Extinct Beringian Wolf," 3430, 3435–36.

97. Barnett et al., "Genomic Adaptations," 5019–20; Salis et al., "Lions and Brown Bears," under "Results."

98. Johnson et al., "Late Miocene Radiation," 74.

99. Barnett et al., "Evolution of Extinct Sabre-Tooths," R2.

100. Saremi et al., "Puma Genomes," under "Discussion"; Werdelin et al., "Phylogeny," 71–72.

101. Bennett et al., "Evidence of Humans," 1528–31.

102. Malhi et al., "Megafauna and Ecosystem Function," 839.

103. Koch and Barnosky, "Late Quaternary Extinctions," 217–18.

104. Broughton and Weitzel, "Population Reconstructions" under "Results," "Discussion"; Meltzer, "Overkill," 28556.

105. Broughton and Weitzel, "Population Reconstructions," under "Discussion."

106. Koch and Barnosky, "Late Quaternary Extinctions," 217–21.

107. Martin, "Discovery of America," 969–74; Surovell et al., "Test of Martin's Overkill," 889–90.

108. Malhi et al., "Megafauna and Ecosystem Function," 840–45; Meltzer, "Overkill," 28555–60.

109. Broughton and Weitzel, "Population Reconstructions," under "Discussion"; Koch and Barnosky, "Late Quaternary Extinctions," 222–43.

110. Frison, "Paleoindian Large Mammal," 14577–80.

3. Holocene Wildlife Settle In

1. Perri et al., "New Evidence," 79–81.

2. Barnosky et al., "Variable Impact," 858–60; Tóth et al., "Reorganization of Surviving," 1305–7.

3. Dyke, "Late Quaternary Vegetation," 220–30; Yansa, "Lake Records," 120–30.

4. Malhi et al., "Megafauna and Ecosystem Function," 841.

5. Anderson, "Evolution and Origin," 631.

6. Broughton and Weitzel, "Population Reconstructions," under "Discussion."

7. Hill, Hill, and Widga, "Late Quaternary Bison," 1767; Martin, Mead, and Barboza, "Bison Body Size," 4569–71.

8. Meachen, Brannick, and Fry, "Extinct Beringian Wolf," 3434–36.

9. Meachen et al., "Ecological Changes," under "Conclusions."

10. Steffen and Fulton, "On the Association," 70–71.

11. Saremi et al., "Puma Genomes," under "Discussion."

12. Hill, Hill, and Widga, "Late Quaternary Bison," 1753–54.

13. Wisely, Statham, and Fleischer, "Pleistocene Refugia," 92–93.

14. Gherghel and Martin, "Postglacial Recolonization," 1503–7.

15. Samson, Knopf, and Ostlie, "Great Plains Ecosystems," 8.

16. National Centers for Environmental Information, "National Climatic Extremes."

17. Barnosky, "Postglacial Vegetation," 69–72; Yansa, "Timing and Nature," 278–79.

18. Brown et al., "Fire Cycles," 8867–69.

19. Fuhlendorf et al., "Should Heterogeneity," 1714.

20. Craine et al., "Global Diversity," 65–66.

21. Richards and Caldwell, "Hydraulic Lift," 487–88.

22. Wilson, Smith, and Naujokaitis-Lewis, "Opposing Responses to Drought," 1691–95.

23. Watson et al., "Migration Patterns," 271–75.

24. Tack et al., "Greater Sage-Grouse," 65–67.

25. Jakes et al., "Classifying the Migration," 1235–37; Kauffman et al., *Ungulate Migrations*, 4, 80, 84, 106.

26. Bragg, "Spadefoot Toad," 53–58.

27. Seipel, "Plant Species Diversity," 46–47.

28. Charles M. Russell National Wildlife Refuge, "Wildlife and Habitat."

29. Charboneau, Nelson, and Hartman, "Floristic Inventory," 853, 864–75.

30. Knopf, *Prairie Legacies*, 138–39.

31. Montana Field Guide, *Animals*.

32. Kimoto et al., "Investigating Temporal Patterns," 22, table 6.

33. Forrest, "Getting the Story," 526–29; Kay, "Were Native People Keystone Predators?," 10–13; Shaw, "How Many Bison?," 148–50.

34. Berger, "Undetected Species Losses," 139–41; Beschta and Ripple, "Large Predators," 2407–10.

4. From Euro-American Arrival to Today

1. Adams and Dood, *Background Information*, 5–20.

2. Journals of Lewis & Clark, August 29, 1806.

3. Martin and Szuter, "War Zones," 40–44.

4. Kay, "Were Native People Keystone Predators?," 1; Martin and Szuter, "War Zones," 40–44.

5. Haines, "Northward Spread of Horses," 430–36.

6. Hämäläinen, "Horse."

7. Laliberte and Ripple, "Wildlife Encounters," 1001–2.

8. Campbell, "Health."

9. Patterson and Runge, "Smallpox," 221.

10. Kay, "Were Native People Keystone Predators?," 12.

11. Daschuk, *Clearing the Plains*, 26.

12. Martin and Szuter, "War Zones," 42; Worcester and Schilz, "Spread of Firearms," 109–14.

13. Malone, Roeder, and Lang, *Montana*, 47–57.

14. Obbard et al., "Furbearer Harvests," 1013–31.

15. Gordon, "Steamboats," 33–41.

16. Gordon, "Steamboats," 38.

17. Lee and Hampton, *Life and Death*.

18. Malone, Roeder, and Lang, *Montana*, 178–81.

19. Campbell, "Health"; Patterson and Runge, "Smallpox," 221.

20. Fletcher, "End of the Open Range," 190.

21. Malone, Roeder, and Lang, *Montana*, 114–44.

22. Malone, Roeder, and Lang, *Montana*, 123–39.

23. Governor's Office of Indian Affairs, "Tribal Nations."

24. Malone, Roeder, and Lang, *Montana*, 237–38.

25. Malone, Roeder, and Lang, *Montana*, 154–55.

26. Malone, Roeder, and Lang, *Montana*, 145–58.

27. Mitchell and Hart, "Winter of 1886–87," 5.

28. Malone, Roeder, and Lang, *Montana*, 157.

29. Malone, Roeder, and Lang, *Montana*, 151–67.

30. Bureau of Agriculture, Labor and Industry of Montana, *Third Annual Report*, 162.

31. Bureau of Agriculture, Labor and Industry of Montana, *Thirteenth Annual Report*, 167.

32. Wildlife Society, *Lacey Act*.

33. Twidwell et al., "Rising Great Plains," e66.

34. Malone, Roeder, and Lang, *Montana*, 233–34.

35. Malone, Roeder, and Lang, *Montana*, 232–53.

36. Department of Commerce, *Fourteenth Census*, 70–71.

37. Malone, Roeder, and Lang, *Montana*, 280–84, 292–93.

38. Knowles, Proctor, and Forrest, "Black-Tailed Prairie Dog," 227–30.

39. Dimitri, Effland, and Conklin, *20th Century Transformation*, 9–11.

40. Ross, "Managing the Public Rangelands," 147–54.

41. Wiedenfeld, "Development of a New Deal," 2; Wooten, *Land Utilization Program*, 1–13.

42. Gaskin et al., "Managing Invasive Plants," 236; Lesica and Cooper, "Choosing Native Species," 327–28.

43. Pokorny and Mangold, *Montana's Noxious Weeds*, 6–9; Seipel, "Plant Species Diversity," 79–86.

44. Malone, Roeder, and Lang, *Montana*, 300–302.

45. U.S. Fish and Wildlife Service, *Final Comprehensive*, 21–29.

46. U.S. Fish and Wildlife Service, "Bowdoin."

47. Renwick et al., "Role of Impoundments," 99–101; Wooten, *Land Utilization Program*, 53.

48. Renwick et al., "Role of Impoundments," 100–101.

49. Legislative Environmental Quality Council, *Pittman-Robertson*.

50. Brain and Anderson, "Agro-Enabled Urban Revolution," 21725.

51. Evans, "Status Reports," 1.

52. Claassen et al., *Grassland to Cropland*, 1, 45; Lark et al., "Cropland Expansion," under "3. Policy Opportunities."

53. Environmental Working Group, "EWG's Farm Subsidy Database."

54. Augustine et al., "Thinking like a Grassland," 291–92.

55. Farm Service Agency, *Conservation Reserve*.

56. Schechinger and Cox, *"Retired" Sensitive Cropland*, 4.

57. Fargione et al., "Bioenergy and Wildlife," 768–71; Wright et al., "Recent Grassland Losses," under "Abstract."

58. Gutmann, "Beyond Social Science History," 7.

59. Willms, Adams, and McKenzie, "Overview: Anthropogenic Changes," 7.

60. Lark et al., "Cropland Expansion," under "Results"; World Wildlife Fund, *2016 Plowprint*.

61. Bauman et al., *Quantifying Undisturbed (Native) Lands*, 7–20.

62. Olimb et al., "Prairie or Planted?," 820–23.

63. World Wildlife Fund, *2016 Plowprint*; and *2021 Plowprint*.

64. Calculated using World Wildlife Fund, "Plowprint Report Map."

65. World Wildlife Fund, *2021 Plowprint*.

66. U.S. Department of Agriculture, "1950 Census Publications."

67. U.S. Department of Agriculture, "2017 Census of Agriculture."

68. Briske et al., "Rotational Grazing," 3; Budd and Thorpe, "Benefits of Managed Grazing," 11–14.

69. Briske et al., "Rotational Grazing," 5–11; Fuhlendorf and Engle, "Restoring Heterogeneity," 625–31; Fuhlendorf et al., "Conservation of Pattern and Process," 585–87.

70. Toombs and Roberts, "Natural Resources," 352–59.

71. Poor et al., "Modeling Fence Location," under "Model Accuracy Assessment."

72. Allred et al., "Ecosystem Services Lost," 401.

73. Ott et al., "Energy Development," 258–63.

74. Whitlock et al., *2017 Montana Climate*, xxvii–xxix.

75. Parks Canada, "Grasslands National Park."

76. Montana State Library, "Conservation Easements."

77. Martin, *Assessing and Implementing Ranch Management*, 1–4.

5. American Beaver and River Otter

1. Morgan, "Beaver Ecology," 41–65.

2. Naiman, Johnston, and Kelley, "Alteration of North American Streams," 753.

3. Journals of Lewis & Clark, April 27, 1805; and April 28, 1805.

4. Journals of Lewis & Clark, May 24, 1805.

5. Mattison, "Upper Missouri River," 1–5.

6. Obbard et al., "Furbearer Harvests," 1014.

7. Wishart, *Fur Trade*, 41–65.

8. Mattison, "Upper Missouri River," 7, 10; Wishart, *Fur Trade*, 33, 65–66.

9. Obbard et al., "Furbearer Harvests," 1014.

10. Naiman, Johnston, and Kelley, "Alteration of North American Streams," 753.

11. Melquist, Polechla, and Toweill, "River Otter," 708–10.

12. Wishart, *Fur Trade*, 42.

13. Journals of Lewis & Clark, July 12, 1805.

14. Melquist and Hornocker, "Ecology of River Otters," 20.

15. Melquist and Hornocker, "Ecology of River Otters," 39.

16. South Dakota Department of Game, Fish and Parks, *South Dakota River Otter*, 12–13.

17. Melquist, Polechla, and Toweill, "River Otter," 710.

18. Obbard et al., "Furbearer Harvests," 1015, 1023.

19. Pollock et al., *Beaver Restoration Guidebook*, 13.

20. Gibson and Olden, "Ecology, Management," 392, 395–403.

21. Knopf et al., "Conservation of Riparian," 273–74.

22. McKinstry, Caffrey, and Anderson, "Importance of Beaver," 1573–75.

23. Cooke and Zack, "Influence of Beaver," 368–70.

24. Gibson and Olden, "Ecology, Management," 395–403; Naiman, Johnston, and Kelley, "Alteration of North American Streams," 754–61; Pollock et al., *Beaver Restoration Guidebook*, 2–19, 116.

25. Gibson and Olden, "Ecology, Management," 398.

26. Gibson and Olden, "Ecology, Management," 401.

27. Pollock et al., *Beaver Restoration Guidebook*, 117.

28. Lesica and Miles, "Beavers Indirectly Enhance," 96–97.

29. Gable et al., "Forgotten Prey," 125–34.

30. Pollock et al., *Beaver Restoration Guidebook*, 116.

31. Schullery, *Documentary Record*, 1–23, 1–141; Wishart, *Fur Trade*, 66.

32. Hayden, "On the Geology," 146.

33. Grinnell, "Zoological Report," 67–68.

34. Baker and Hill, "Beaver," 288.

35. Brownell, "Genesis of Wildlife," 19.

36. Naiman, Johnston, and Kelley, "Alteration of North American Streams," 753–54.

37. Scott, Skagen, and Merigliano, "Relating Geomorphic Change," 290–95.

38. Kohl et al., "Bison versus Cattle," 729.

39. Ecological Solutions Group, *Riparian Health Assessment*, 18–19.

40. Renwick et al., "Role of Impoundments," 101–2.

41. Smith et al., "Distribution and Significance," 31, 35.

42. Ecological Solutions Group, *Riparian Health Assessment*, 3–4.

43. Bowen, Bovee, and Waddle, "Effects of Flow Regulation," 287.

44. Scott et al., "Long-Term Cottonwood," 1029.

45. Dixon et al., "Status and Trend," 2.

46. Horn, *Fort Peck Game Range: May–August 1942*, 3.

47. Aldous, *Fort Peck Game Range*, 6.

48. Pollock et al., *Beaver Restoration Guidebook*, 30–31.

49. Bown, "Beaver Habitat," 76–78; Randy Matchett, Charles M. Russell National Wildlife Refuge, unpublished data, email to author, June 24, 2019.

50. Pollock et al., *Beaver Restoration Guidebook*, 31.

51. Pollock et al., *Beaver Restoration Guidebook*, 29.

52. Lesica and Miles, "Beavers Indirectly Enhance," 93–98.

53. Nagler et al., "Distribution and Abundance," 520.

54. Ecological Solutions Group, *Riparian Health Assessment*, 2–3, 77–105.

55. Ecological Solutions Group, *Riparian Health Assessment*, 101.

56. Pollock et al., *Beaver Restoration Guidebook*, 85–95.

57. Melquist, Polechla, and Toweill, "River Otter," 710.

58. Raesly, "Status of River Otter," 859.

59. Roberts, Lovallo, and Crimmins, "River Otter Status," 281.

60. Melquist, Polechla, and Toweill, "River Otter," 708–10.

61. Scott Thompson, email to author, November 9, 2021.

62. Stephanie Tucker, North Dakota Game and Fish Department, unpublished data, email to author, November 12, 2021.

63. Luke Holmquist, email to author, November 15, 2021.

64. Damien Austin, text message to author, June 21, 2022.

6. Ungulates

1. Grinnell, "Zoological Report," under "Letter of Transmittal."

2. Roosevelt, *Hunting Trips*, 262.

3. Shaw, "How Many Bison?," 148–50.

4. U.S. Department of Agriculture, "USDA NASS Census."

5. Koch, "Big Game," 364.

6. Adams and Dood, *Background Information*, 25.

7. Adams and Dood, *Background Information*, 21–26.

8. Hornaday, letter to Baird.

9. Trexler, "Buffalo Range," 362.

10. Ericson, "Legislative and Political," 5.

11. Montana Fish, Wildlife & Parks, *Montana Statewide Elk*, 4.

12. Picton and Lonner, *Montana's Wildlife Legacy*, 13–26.

13. Garrott et al., *Role of Disease*, 49.

14. Bureau of Agriculture, Labor and Industry of Montana, *Thirteenth Annual Report*, 167.

15. Couey, *Rocky Mountain Bighorn*, 4.

16. Buechner, "Bighorn Sheep," 73–74.

17. McCabe, Reeves, and O'Gara, *Prairie Ghost*, 119.

18. Beer, "Distribution and Status," 43–44.

19. Picton and Lonner, *Montana's Wildlife Legacy*, 17.

20. Mackie et al., *Ecology and Management*, 16.

21. Journals of Lewis & Clark, May 10, 1805.

22. O'Connor, Taylor, and Nippert, "Browsing and Fire," under "Introduction."

23. Kohl et al., "Bison versus Cattle," 726–29.

24. Mackie et al., *Ecology and Management*, 49–53.

25. Mao et al., "Habitat Selection by Elk," 1691.

26. Gates et al., "Influence of Land Use," 278–81.

27. Garrott et al., *Role of Disease*, 49–53.

28. Bragg, "Observations on the Ecology," 333–34.

29. Knapp et al., "Keystone Role of Bison," 44.

30. National Park Service, "Bison Wallows."

31. Coppedge and Shaw, "Effects of Horning," 189.

32. Rosas et al., "Seed Dispersal," 769.

33. Coppedge, "Effects of Bison Hair," 110.

34. Ratajczak et al., "Reintroducing Bison," under "Abstract," "Discussion."

35. Truett et al., "Managing Bison," 130–31.

36. Hobbs et al., "Ungulate Grazing," 200; Weisberg et al., "Ecosystem Approach," 193–94.

37. Beschta and Ripple, "Large Predators," 2406–10; O'Connor, Taylor, and Nippert, "Browsing and Fire," under "Introduction."

38. Fuhlendorf et al., "Pyric Herbivory," 593–96.

39. Fuhlendorf et al., "Perspectives on Grassland Conservation," under "3. Herbivore Domain," "4. Biophysical Domain."

40. Fuhlendorf et al., "Should Heterogeneity," 1706.

41. Davis et al., "Adaptive Rangeland Management," under "Abstract"; Derner et al., "Livestock as Ecosystem Engineers," 111.

42. Becerra et al., "Preference for Grassland Heterogeneity," 606–10; Limb et al., "Pyric-Herbivory and Cattle," 659; Sliwinski et al., "Factors Influencing Ranchers' Intentions," under "Abstract."

43. Becerra et al., "Preference for Grassland Heterogeneity," 606–10; Fuhlendorf et al., "Perspectives on Grassland Conservation," under "5. Current and Future Conservation Landscape."

44. Elbroch et al., "Recolonizing Wolves," 125; Sikes, "Hidden Biodiversity," 12.

45. Bump et al., "Ungulate Carcasses," 996; Towne, "Prairie Vegetation," 232.

46. Journals of Lewis & Clark, May 5, 1805.

47. Trexler, "Buffalo Range," 352.

48. Wenger, Subalusky, and Freeman, "Missing Dead," under "6. Bison and Caribou."

49. Fuhlendorf et al., "Conservation of Pattern and Process," 579.

50. Freese, Fuhlendorf, and Kunkel, "Management Framework," 358; Freilich et al., "Ecological Effects," 760–63.

51. Allendorf, Hohenlohe, and Luikart, "Genomics and the Future," 703–4.

52. Halbert and Derr, "Patterns of Genetic Variation," 4963.

53. Freese et al., "Second Chance," 177–78; Hedrick, "Conservation Genetics," 417, 419.

54. Hedrick, "Conservation Genetics," 412.

55. Stroupe et al., "Genomic Evaluation of Hybridization," under "Results."

56. Hedrick, "Conservation Genetics," 412–15.

57. Ericson, "Legislative and Political," 42–43.

58. Picton and Lonner, Montana's Wildlife Legacy, 27–40.

59. Beschta et al., "Bison Limit Ecosystem," under "5.2 Ungulates," fig. 5; Mosely and Mundinger, "History and Status," 191, 198.

60. Peterson et al., "Trophic Cascades," 329.

61. Beschta et al., "Bison Limit Ecosystem," under "1. Introduction"; Peterson et al., "Trophic Cascades," 326–31.

62. Sinclair and Krebs, "Complex Numerical Responses," 1221.

63. Chapman and Byron, "Flexible Application," under "Abstract."

64. Wockner et al., Modeling Elk and Bison, 3.

65. Reeves et al., "Assessment of Production Trends," 172, 176.

66. Markewicz and Parks Canada, Like Distant Thunder, 22–36.

67. Adams and Dood, Background Information, 109–10.

68. Montana Fish, Wildlife & Parks, Bison Conservation, 55–57.

69. Joly and Messier, "Testing Hypotheses," 1165; Shave et al., "Seasonal and Interannual," under "Discussion."

70. Gogan et al., "General Biology," 53–54.

71. Freese et al., Bison Management, 11.

72. Picton and Lonner, Montana's Wildlife Legacy, 115–34.

73. Montana Fish, Wildlife & Parks, Montana Statewide Elk, 373.

74. Randy Matchett, Charles M. Russell National Wildlife Refuge, unpublished data, email to author, December 8, 2021.

75. Lukacs et al., "Factors Influencing Elk," 698; Proffitt et al., "Integrated Carnivore-Ungulate Management," 1–2.

76. Kohl et al., "Diel Predator Activity," 728–31.

77. Montana Fish, Wildlife & Parks, *Chronic Wasting*.

78. Monello et al., "Pathogen-Mediated Selection," 12208.

79. Mackie et al., *Ecology and Management*, 77–80, 138–42.

80. Mackie et al., *Ecology and Management*, 2, 110–12.

81. Mackie et al., *Ecology and Management*, 101.

82. Dickson, "Monitoring Muleys," 24–26.

83. Randy Matchett, Charles M. Russell National Wildlife Refuge, unpublished data, email to author, December 18, 2021.

84. Mackie et al., *Ecology and Management*, 77.

85. Montana Fish, Wildlife & Parks, *Chronic Wasting*, 2–3.

86. Montana Fish, Wildlife & Parks, "Pronghorn."

87. Christie, Jensen, and Boyce, *Pronghorn Abundance*, fig. 3.

88. Ellenberger and Byrne, *Population Status*, 132–81.

89. Millspaugh, DeVoe, and Proffitt, *Pronghorn Movement*, 4–5.

90. Martinka, "Mortality," 161–63.

91. Jones et al., "Annual Pronghorn," 1122–23.

92. Millspaugh, DeVoe, and Proffitt, *Pronghorn Movement*, 5.

93. Jakes et al., "Classifying the Migration," 1235–37.

94. Poor et al., "Modeling Fence Location," under "Results," figs. 2, 3.

95. Gates et al., "Influence of Land Use," 282–87; Jones et al., "Fences Reduce Habitat," under "Abstract."

96. Barnowe-Meyer et al., "Predator-Specific Mortality," 190–92.

97. Tack et al., "Beyond Protected Areas," 18.

98. DeVoe et al., "Restoration Potential," 1260–62.

99. Montana Fish, Wildlife & Parks, *Montana Bighorn*, 269.

100. Garrott et al., *Role of Disease*, 14–15.

101. Montana Fish, Wildlife & Parks, *Montana Bighorn*, 268–79.

102. Krehbiel, *Bighorns, Big Risks*, 11; Montana Fish, Wildlife & Parks, *Montana Bighorn*, 53.

103. Garrott et al., *Role of Disease*, 51–55.

104. Nadeau et al., "Status and Trends," 106.

105. Licht, *Ecology and Economics*, 162–71.

106. Aune and Plumb, "Looking Forward," 124.

107. Aune and Plumb, "Looking Forward," 126.

108. Ranglack and Du Toit, "Bison with Benefits," 552–53.

109. Campbell et al., "Virtual Fencing," under "Abstract."

7. Carnivores

1. Leopold, "Review of the Wolves," 928.

2. Leopold, "Review of the Wolves," 929.

3. Mattson and Merrill, "Extirpations of Grizzly Bears," 1125–28.

4. Gunther et al., "Dietary Breadth of Grizzly," 60–69.

5. Mattson and Merrill, "Extirpations of Grizzly Bears," 1128–35.

6. Laliberte and Ripple, "Wildlife Encounters," 1000.

7. Mace and Chilton-Radandt, *Black Bear*, 25–26.

8. Lee and Hampton, *Life and Death*; Bureau of Agriculture, Labor and Industry of Montana, *Third Annual Report*, 161; and *Sixth Annual Report*, 130; Journals of Lewis & Clark, May 5–June 12, 1805.

9. Journals of Lewis & Clark, May 5, 2005.

10. Journals of Lewis & Clark, May 29, 2005.

11. Sovada, Woodward, and Igl, "Historical Range," 356–59.

12. Leopold, *Sand County Almanac*, 129–32.

13. Gable et al., "Forgotten Prey," 123.

14. Obbard et al., "Furbearer Harvests," 1015–16.

15. Lee and Hampton, *Life and Death*, 39, 42, 45, and elsewhere.

16. Servheen, "Grizzly Bear," 9, 17.

17. Riley, "Integration," 137–38.

18. LaRue et al., "Cougars Are Recolonizing," 1364–65.

19. Bailey, *Destruction of Wolves*, 10.

20. Riley, "Integration," 136–40.

21. Montana Fish, Wildlife & Parks, *Montana Wolf Conservation*, 4.

22. Nelson, *Report of the Chief*, 5.

23. Robinson, *Predatory Bureaucracy*, 170.

24. Robinson, *Predatory Bureaucracy*, 170–71.

25. Robinson, *Predatory Bureaucracy*, 170–71.

26. Feldman, "Public Opinion," 113.

27. Horn, *Fort Peck Game Range: September–December 1946*, 8.

28. Horn, *Fort Peck Game Range: January–April 1945*, 6.

29. Staunton, *Fort Peck Game Range: May–August 1960*, 11.

30. Knowlton, Gese, and Jaeger, "Coyote Depredation Control," 401.

31. Sovada, Woodward, and Igl, "Historical Range," 356.

32. Johnson, "Returns," 837.

33. Sovada, Woodward, and Igl, "Historical Range," 347.

34. Sovada, Woodward, and Igl, "Historical Range," 347.

35. Kamler et al., "Impacts of Coyotes," 317.

36. Eads et al., "American Badgers," 1364.

37. Beschta and Ripple, "Large Predators," 2406–10.

38. Sikes, "Hidden Biodiversity," 12; Wilmers et al., "Trophic Facilitation," 914–15.

39. Elbroch et al., "Recolonizing Wolves," 125.

40. Ripple et al., "Widespread Mesopredator," 72–74.

41. Berger, Gese, and Berger, "Indirect Effects," 818.

42. Lee and Hampton, *Life and Death*.

43. Bureau of Agriculture, Labor and Industry of Montana, *Third Annual Report*, 161; and *Thirteenth Annual Report*, 130.

44. Western Landowners Alliance, *Reducing Conflict*.

45. Mattson and Merrill, "Extirpations of Grizzly Bears," 1135.

46. Carter, Nelson, and Easter, "Call for a National," 789–92; George et al., "Change in Attitudes," 237–38.

47. White, Gunther, and Wyman, "Population," 7.

48. Peterson et al., "Trophic Cascades," 328.

49. Kendall et al., "Grizzly Bear Density," 1693; Laliberte and Ripple, "Wildlife Encounters," 1000.

50. Riley and Malecki, "Landscape Analysis of Cougar," 317.

51. Pulling, *Fort Peck Game Range: May–August 1941*, 5.

52. Staunton, *Fort Peck Game Range: May–August 1961*, 9.

53. Staunton, *Fort Peck Game Range: September–December 1960*, 13.

54. Morrison, Boyce, and Nielsen, "Space-Use, Movement," under "Discussion."

55. Thompson and Jenks, "Dispersal Movements," under "Results."

56. Hawley et al., "Long-Distance Dispersal," 1435.

57. Kunkel, Vosburgh, and Robinson, *Ecology of Cougars*, 12.

58. Kunkel, Vosburgh, and Robinson, *Ecology of Cougars*, 13.

59. Randy Matchett, Charles M. Russell National Wildlife Refuge, unpublished data, email to author, February 18, 2022.

60. Gigliotti, Matchett, and Jachowski, "Mountain Lions on the Prairie," 4–8.

61. North Dakota Game and Fish Department, *Status of Mountain Lion*, 4.

62. Johnson et al., "Mountain Lion," 212–13.

63. Kunkel, Vosburgh, and Robinson, *Ecology of Cougars*, 12; Robinson et al., "Linking Resource Selection," 16.

64. Elbroch et al., "Recolonizing Wolves," under "Abstract."

65. Robinson et al., "Linking Resource Selection," 23.

66. Jimenez et al., "Wolf Dispersal," 581.

67. Sells et al., *Improving Estimation of Wolf*, 24.

68. Jimenez et al., "Wolf Dispersal," 581.

69. Inman et al., *Montana Gray Wolf*, 11–12; Western Landowners Alliance, *Reducing Conflict*.

70. Shave et al., "Seasonal and Inter-annual," under "Abstract"; Tallian et al., "Predator Foraging," 1418.

71. Jalkotzy and Ossenbrug, "Summer Food Habits," 160–63; O'Donovan et al., "Intrapopulation Variability," under "Abstract."

72. MacNulty et al., "Influence of Group Size," under "Abstract."

73. Tallian et al., "Predator Foraging," 1418.

74. Allen, "Hole in the System," 6–7; Licht, *Ecology and Economics*, 162–63.

75. Erb, Humpal, and Sampson, *Distribution and Abundance*, 5; Patterson et al., "Estimating Wolf Densities," 938; Peterson et al., "Trophic Cascades," 327; Smith et al., *Yellowstone National Park Wolf*, 4.

76. Mech and Barber-Meyer, "Yellowstone Wolf," 500–501.

77. Butler et al., "Home Range Size," 684, 691–93; Montana Fish, Wildlife & Parks, *Draft Montana Swift Fox*, 4, 7–8.

78. Butler et al., "Home Range Size," 684, 691–93; Butler et al., "Life on the Edge," 113–16.

79. Hila Shamon, email to author, June 21, 2022.

80. Miller, *Reintroduction of Swift Fox*, 4, 18.

8. Rocky Mountain Locust

1. Wagner, "Grasshoppered," 157.

2. Lockwood, *Locust*, 3–6; Wagner, "Grasshoppered," 156.

3. Lockwood, *Locust*, 65–84; Wagner, "Grasshoppered," 158–66.

4. Riley, *Locust Plague*, 9.

5. Lockwood, *Locust*, 87–124.

6. Le Gall, Overson, and Cease, "Global Review of Locusts," under "Abstract."

7. Lockwood, *Locust*, 146–47.

8. Riley, *Locust Plague*, 69–79.

9. U.S. Entomological Commission, *Third Report*, 30.

10. U.S. Entomological Commission, *Second Report*, 15–23.

11. Riley, *Destructive Locusts*, 10; U.S. Entomological Commission, *Second Report*, 16.

12. U.S. Entomological Commission, *First Annual Report*, 131–33; U.S. Entomological Commission, *Second Report*, 15–23, 161; U.S. Entomological Commission, *Third Report*, 8–20.

13. Riley, *Locust Plague*, 95–101.

14. Lockwood, "Fate of Rocky Mountain Locust," 129, 134–35.

15. Riley, *Locust Plague*, 19–21.

16. Riley, *Locust Plague*, 155–65, 221–27; Wagner, "Grasshoppered," 156.

17. Lockwood, *Locust*, 53–59, 239; Wagner, "Grasshoppered," 158–66.

18. U.S. Entomological Commission, *Third Report*, 8–20, 23.

19. U.S. Entomological Commission, *Second Report*, 21.

20. U.S. Entomological Commission, *Second Report*, 161–63.

21. Lockwood and DeBrey, "Solution for the Sudden," 1894; U.S. Entomological Commission, *Third Report*, 8–20.

22. Lockwood, *Locust*, 135.

23. Lockwood, *Locust*, 143–55.

24. Gurney and Brooks, "Grasshoppers," 1–2.

25. Lockwood, "Taxonomic Status," 1103–8.

26. Lockwood et al., "Preserved Insect Fauna," 228–34.

27. Lockwood, *Locust*, 220–22; Sutton et al., "Cuticular Hydrocarbons," 10–11.

28. Chapco and Litzenberger, "DNA Investigation," 810; Lockwood, *Locust*, 222–24.

29. Lockwood, *Locust*, 217–18.

30. Lockwood, "Fate of Rocky Mountain Locust," 147–48.

31. Lockwood, "Fate of Rocky Mountain Locust," 147–48.

32. U.S. Entomological Commission, *Second Report*, xv.

33. Hanski et al., "Ecological and Genetic Basis," under "Introduction."

34. Lockwood, "Fate of Rocky Mountain Locust," 137–41; Lockwood and DeBrey, "Solution for the Sudden," 1198–204.

35. Hanski et al., "Metapopulation Persistence," 27.

36. Malone, Roeder, and Lang, *Montana*, 154–55.

37. Malone, Roeder, and Lang, *Montana*, 232–33.

38. Lockwood, *Locust*, 164.

39. Lockwood, "Death of the Super Hopper."

40. Lockwood, "Fate of Rocky Mountain Locust," 133.

41. Lockwood, *Locust*, 142.

42. Riley, *Locust Plague*, 108–12.

43. U.S. Entomological Commission, *First Annual Report*, 284–334.

44. U.S. Entomological Commission, *First Annual Report*, 334–48.

45. Gill, Canevari, and Iversen, "Eskimo Curlew," 19–20.

46. Lockwood, *Locust*, 251.

47. U.S. Entomological Commission, *Third Report*, 23.

48. Welti et al., "Nutrient Dilution and Climate Cycles," 7271.

49. Lockwood, "Fate of Rocky Mountain Locust," 150.

50. Lockwood, "Fate of Rocky Mountain Locust," 148–54.

51. Lockwood, *Locust*, 262.

9. Black-Tailed Prairie Dog and Black-Footed Ferret

1. U.S. Fish and Wildlife Service, *Recovery for Black-Footed Ferret*, 16, 24.

2. U.S. Fish and Wildlife Service, *Recovery for Black-Footed Ferret*, 18.

3. Knowles, Proctor, and Forrest, "Black-Tailed Prairie Dog," 231.

4. Gutmann, "Beyond Social Science History," 7.

5. Knowles, Proctor, and Forrest, "Black-Tailed Prairie Dog," 228–29.

6. Antolin et al., *Influence of Sylvatic Plague*, 105–9.

7. Anderson et al., "Paleobiology, Biogeography," 58.

8. U.S. Fish and Wildlife Service, *Recovery for Black-Footed Ferret*, 42.

9. Hanebury and Biggins, "History of Searches," 47–52.

10. Livieri et al., "Conserving Endangered Black-Footed Ferrets," 5.

11. Hanebury and Biggins, "History of Searches," 47–52.

12. Forrest et al., "Population Attributes," 264–69.

13. Livieri et al., "Conserving Endangered Black-Footed Ferrets," 9.

14. Santymire et al., "Inbreeding Causes Decreased," 332.

15. Knowles, Proctor, and Forrest, "Black-Tailed Prairie Dog," 233.

16. Knowles, Proctor, and Forest, "Black-Tailed Prairie Dog," 229.

17. Severson and Plumb, "Estimating Population Densities," 861–62.

18. Knowles, Proctor, and Forrest, "Black-Tailed Prairie Dog," 236.

19. U.S. Fish and Wildlife Service, *Recovery for Black-Footed Ferret*, 66.

20. Anderson et al., "Paleobiology, Biogeography," 30.

21. Pulling, *Fort Peck Game Range: August–October 1940*, 3.

22. Kotliar et al., "Critical Review," 177; Miller et al., "Prairie Dogs," 2807.

23. Kotliar et al., "Critical Review," 186–90.

24. Barth et al., "Soil Change," 2054; Miller et al., "Prairie Dogs," 2807; Whicker and Detling, "Ecological Consequences," 778–82.

25. Bangert and Slobodchikoff, "Conservation of Prairie Dog," 100; Sierra-Corona et al., "Black-Tailed Prairie Dogs," under "Abstract"; Whicker and Detling, "Ecological Consequences," 779–83.

26. Augustine and Baker, "Associations of Grassland Bird," 324.

27. Adams, "Black-Tailed Prairie Dog," 156.

28. Scott et al., "Conservation-Reliant Species," 91.

29. U.S. Fish and Wildlife Service, Recovery for Black-Footed Ferret.

30. Wisely et al., "Road Map for 21st Century," 585.

31. U.S. Fish and Wildlife Service, Recovery for Black-Footed Ferret, 73.

32. Frankham, Bradshaw, and Brooks, "Genetics in Conservation," 57.

33. U.S. Fish and Wildlife Service, Recovery for Black-Footed Ferret, 61–62, 70–81.

34. U.S. Fish and Wildlife Service, Recovery for Black-Footed Ferret, 73.

35. Livieri et al., "Conserving Endangered Black-Footed Ferrets," 6.

36. U.S. Fish and Wildlife Service, U.S. FWS Black-Footed Ferret, 134, 138.

37. U.S. Fish and Wildlife Service, Special Status Assessment, 15–16.

38. U.S. Fish and Wildlife Service, Special Status Assessment, 16–21.

39. Livieri et al., "Conserving Endangered Black-Footed Ferrets," 7–8.

40. Miller and Reading, "Challenges to Black-Footed Ferret," 234–35; Titus and Jachowski, "Persistent Negative," under "Abstract."

41. Eads et al., "Resistance to Deltamethrin," 745.

42. Dinsmore, "Mountain Plover Responses to Deltamethrin," 415.

43. Eads et al., "Evaluation of Five Pulicides," 405; Eads et al., "Fipronil Pellets," 434, 437; Matchett et al., "Flea Control," under "Discussion,"

44. Islam et al., "Improvement of Disease," under "Abstract."

45. Sandler, Moses, and Wisely, "Ethical Analysis," under "Abstract."

46. Titus and Jachowski, "Persistent Negative," under "Abstract."

47. Augustine and Springer, "Competition and Facilitation," 850; Derner, Detling, and Antolin, "Livestock Weight Gains," 459.

48. Augustine and Springer, "Competition and Facilitation," 850; Brennan, "Grazing Behavior," 12; Connell, Porensky, and Scasta, "Prairie Dog," 360.

49. Crow, "Ranch-Level Economic Impacts," 87–88; Miller and Reading, "Challenges to Black-Footed Ferret," 234.

50. Pauli and Buskirk, "Risk-Disturbance Overrides," 1219.

51. McTee, Hiller, and Ramsey, "Free Lunch," 1469–70.

52. Miller and Reading, "Challenges to Black-Footed Ferret," 233–35.

53. Wisely et al., "Road Map for 21st Century," 585.

54. U.S. Fish and Wildlife Service, Recovery for Black-Footed Ferret, 50.

55. U.S. Fish and Wildlife Service, Special Status Assessment, 23.

56. U.S. Fish and Wildlife Service, Recovery for Black-Footed Ferret, 73–77.

57. Howard et al., "Recovery of Gene Diversity," 102.

58. Wisely et al., "Road Map for 21st Century," 581.

59. Revive and Restore, "Black-Footed Ferret."

60. Lockhart, Thorne, and Gober, "Historical Perspective," 10.

61. Vosburgh, "Ferret Restoration," 18.

62. Randy Matchett, Charles M. Russell National Wildlife Refuge, unpublished data, email to author, July 13, 2021.

63. Randy Matchett, Charles M. Russell National Wildlife Refuge, unpublished data, email to author, May 21, 2022.

64. U.S. Fish and Wildlife Service, *Special Status Assessment*, 70–80.

65. Derner, Detling, and Antolin, "Livestock Weight Gains," 461–62; Morrison, Boyce, and Nielsen, "Space-Use, Movement," 50–52.

66. Roberge and Angelstam, "Usefulness of the Umbrella Species," 76.

10. Pallid Sturgeon

1. Shen et al., "Phylogenetic Perspective," 3511.

2. Federal Register, "Endangered and Threatened," 36645–46.

3. U.S. Fish and Wildlife Service, *Revised Recovery Plan*, 26–28, 42–43.

4. Haxton and Cano, "Global Perspective of Fragmentation," 206.

5. Federal Register, "Endangered and Threatened," 36641–645.

6. Schrey and Heist, "Stock Structure," 297.

7. U.S. Fish and Wildlife Service, *Revised Recovery Plan*, 10–11.

8. U.S. Fish and Wildlife Service, *Revised Recovery Plan*, 10.

9. Luke Holmquist, email to author, November 15, 2021.

10. Holmquist et al., "Reproductive Ecology," 1069.

11. Braaten et al., "Estimate of the Historic Population," 2; Klungle and Baxter, *Lower Missouri*, cited in Braaten, "Estimate of the Historic Population," 3.

12. Braaten et al., "Age Estimation of Wild Pallid," 827–28.

13. Jordan et al., "Status of Knowledge," 199; U.S. Fish and Wildlife Service, *Revised Recovery Plan*, 26–29.

14. U.S. Fish and Wildlife Service, *Revised Recovery Plan*, 29–31.

15. Galat et al., "Spatiotemporal Patterns," 262.

16. U.S. Fish and Wildlife Service, *Revised Recovery Plan*, 33–34, 42–43.

17. Schrey, Boley, and Heist, "Hybridization between Pallid Sturgeon," 1836–40.

18. U.S. Fish and Wildlife Service, *Revised Recovery Plan*, 33.

19. U.S. Fish and Wildlife Service, *Revised Recovery Plan*, 118.

20. DeLonay et al., *Ecological Requirements for Pallid Sturgeon*, 14, 124.

21. Braaten et al., "Experimental Test and Models," 386–90.

22. Bovee and Scott, "Implications of Flood Pulse," 287.

23. Holmquist et al., "Reproductive Ecology," 1080–81; U.S. Fish and Wildlife Service, *Revised Recovery Plan*, 11–14.

24. Holmquist, "Native Endangered Species," 23–24.

25. Holmquist et al., "First Maturity and Spawning Periodicity," 140.

26. Holmquist et al., "Reproductive Ecology," 1081–82.

27. Guy et al., "Broadening the Regulated-River," 11–12.

28. Luke Holmquist, email to author, November 15, 2021.

29. Braaten et al., "Estimate of the Historic Population," 4; U.S. Army Corps of Engineers, *Missouri River Recovery Management Plan*, 262–63.

30. Bowen, Bovee, and Waddle, "Effects of Flow Regulation," 816–20.

31. Braaten et al., "Experimental Test and Models," 379, 390; DeLonay et al., *Ecological Requirements for Pallid Sturgeon*, 39–41.

32. Bowen, Bovee, and Waddle, "Effects of Flow Regulation," 820; U.S. Army Corps of Engineers, "Fort Peck Dam Test Releases," viii, 3-350-3-355, 3-357-3-361.

33. Bramblett and White, "Habitat Use and Movements," 1016–22.

34. DeLonay et al., *Ecological Requirements for Pallid Sturgeon*, 31–36.

35. Chojnacki et al., "Physical Characteristics," 74.

36. DeLonay et al., *Ecological Requirements for Pallid Sturgeon*, 113.

37. Alexander, Wilson, and Green, *Brief History and Summary*, 9–15.

38. Jordan et al., "Status of Knowledge," 198.

39. Steffensen et al., "Evidence of Limited Recruitment," 341–43.

40. Jordan et al., "Status of Knowledge," 201–3; Schrey, Boley, and Heist, "Hybridization between Pallid Sturgeon," 1836–40.

41. Dryer and Sandvol, *Recovery Plan*, 16.

42. U.S. Fish and Wildlife Service, *Revised Recovery Plan*.

43. Frankham, Bradshaw, and Brooks, "Genetics in Conservation," 57.

44. Heist et al., *Population Genetics Management Plan*, 9–10; Schrey and Heist, "Stock Structure," 297.

45. Christie et al., "Single Generation of Domestication," under "Discussion"; Teletchea, "Fish Domestication," 7.

46. Holmquist et al., "First Maturity and Spawning Periodicity," 144–46.

47. Holmquist et al., "Reproductive Ecology," 1081.

48. National Research Council, *Missouri River Ecosystem*, 118–19.

49. Tornabene et al., "Trends in River Discharge," 152.

50. Bovee and Scott, "Implications of Flood Pulse," 296–97.

51. Guy et al., "Broadening the Regulated-River," 13–14.

52. U.S. Army Corps of Engineers, *Missouri River Recovery Management Plan*.

53. U.S. Fish and Wildlife Service, *Biological Opinion*, 67.

54. U.S. Army Corps of Engineers, "Fort Peck Dam Test Releases," xi–xv.

55. Marotz and Lorang, "Pallid Sturgeon Larvae," 380–81.

56. Brown, "Governor Opposes Fort Peck Dam."

57. McKean, "Finding a Pulse," 39–40.

58. U.S. Army Corps of Engineers and U.S. Department of the Interior, *Lower Yellowstone Intake Diversion Dam*, 12–75.

59. U.S. Army Corps of Engineers and U.S. Department of the Interior, *Lower Yellowstone Intake Diversion Dam*, i–iv.

60. Herbaugh, "New Fish Bypass Channel."

61. DeLonay et al., *Ecological Requirements for Pallid Sturgeon*, 36.

62. Galat et al., "Spatiotemporal Patterns," 20.

63. Montana Field Guide, *Animals.*

64. Grisak, "Sickle Fin Chub."

65. Dieterman and Galat, "Large-Scale Factors," 584–85.

66. Dieterman and Galat, "Large-Scale Factors," 584–85; Perkin and Gido, "Stream Fragmentation Thresholds," 378–81.

67. McMahon and Gardner, "Status of Sauger," 1; Jaeger, "Sauger," under "Status."

68. Tornabene et al., "Trends in River Discharge," 158–59.

69. Teply, *Montana Rivers,* 15.

70. Stringer, "Status of Northern Pearl Dace," xi, 33.

71. Tornabene et al., "Spatiotemporal Ecology," 266–67.

72. Subalusky et al., "Annual Mass Drownings," 7647.

73. Wenger, Subalusky, and Freeman, "Missing Dead," under "6. Bison and Caribou."

74. Leopold, *Round River,* 165.

11. Grassland Birds

1. Correll et al., "Quantifying Specialist Avifaunal Decline," under "Discussion"; Rosenberg et al., "Decline," 1213.

2. Knopf, *Prairie Legacies,* 135–39.

3. Cornell Lab of Ornithology, "All about Birds."

4. Cornell Lab of Ornithology, "All about Birds."

5. Pleszczynska, "Microgeographic Prediction," 935–37.

6. Cornell Lab of Ornithology, "All about Birds."

7. Cornell Lab of Ornithology, "All about Birds."

8. Cornell Lab of Ornithology, "All about Birds."

9. Dechant et al., *Effects of Management—Burrowing Owl,* 2.

10. Holroyd, Trefry, and Duxbury, "Winter Destinations," 295–97.

11. Poulin and Todd, "Sex and Nest Stage," 861.

12. Cornell Lab of Ornithology, "All about Birds."

13. Rowland, *Effects of Management—Greater Sage-Grouse,* 12.

14. Tack et al., "Greater Sage-Grouse," 11; Newton et al., "Longest Sage-Grouse Migratory Behavior," 966–70.

15. Tack et al., "Greater Sage-Grouse," 18.

16. Rowland, *Effects of Management—Greater Sage-Grouse,* 8–10.

17. Evans, "Status Reports," 1.

18. U.S. Geological Survey, "North American Breeding Bird Survey."

19. Somershoe, *Full Annual-Cycle Conservation,* 22–23.

20. Government of Canada, "Species at Risk."

21. Sauer, Link and Hines, *North American Breeding Bird.*

22. U.S. Geological Survey, "McCown's Longspur."

23. Coues, "Field Notes on Birds," 546–97.

24. Stewart, *Breeding Birds,* 210.

25. Stewart, *Breeding Birds,* 267.

26. Stewart, *Breeding Birds*, 269–70.

27. Ceballos et al., "Rapid Decline of Grassland System," under "Abstract"; Pool et al., "Rapid Expansion of Croplands," 274.

28. Davis et al., "Songbird Abundance," 908; Ruth, *Status Assessment*, 22–27; Shaffer and DeLong, *Effects of Management—Introduction*, 20–25; Somershoe, *Full Annual-Cycle Conservation*, 28–31.

29. Davis et al., "Songbird Abundance," 913–14; Lloyd and Martin, "Reproductive Success," 363; Shaffer and DeLong, *Effects of Management—Introduction*, 21–22.

30. Somershoe, *Full Annual-Cycle Conservation*, 26–27; Shaffer and DeLong, *Effects of Management—Introduction*, 14.

31. Nenninger and Koper, "Effects of Conventional Oil," 124; Shaffer and Buhl, "Effects of Wind-Energy," 59; Thompson et al., "Avoidance of Unconventional Oil Wells," 82.

32. Somershoe, *Full Annual-Cycle Conservation*, 29–30.

33. Becker, "Food Habits," 227–29; Ruth, *Status Assessment*, 44; Strasser et al., *Identifying Limiting Factors*, 1.

34. Shaffer and DeLong, *Effects of Management—Introduction*, 40.

35. Sliwinski and Koper, "Grassland Bird Responses," under "Abstract."

36. Augustine et al., "Thinking like a Grassland," 285–89; Lipsey et al., "Extending Utility," 787–89; Somershoe, *Full Annual-Cycle Conservation*, 26.

37. Somershoe, *Full Annual-Cycle Conservation*, 28–31.

38. Shaffer et al., *Effects of Management—Lark Bunting*, 1.

39. Ruth, *Status Assessment*, 22–23.

40. Twidwell et al., "Rising Great Plains," e64–e66.

41. Reid and Fuhlendorf, "Fire Management," 17.

42. Mineau and Whiteside, "Pesticide Acute Toxicity," under "Abstract"; Xerces, "Feds Plan Insecticide."

43. Xerces, "Feds Plan Insecticide."

44. Brain and Anderson, "Agro-Enabled Urban Revolution," 21722–23.

45. Li, Miao, and Khanna, "Neonicotinoids and Decline," 1028.

46. Thompson et al., "Critical Review on the Potential Impacts," 1318–19.

47. Forister et al., "Increasing Neonicotinoid Use," under "Abstract"; Woodcock et al., "Country-Specific Effects," 1393.

48. Eng, Stutchbury, and Morrissey, "Neonicotinoid Insecticide Reduces," 1177.

49. Li, Miao, and Khanna, "Neonicotinoids and Decline," 1027.

50. Thompson et al., "Critical Review on the Potential Impacts," 1315.

51. Thompson et al., "Critical Review on the Potential Impacts," 1316, 1319.

52. U.S. Environmental Protection Agency, "Proposed Interim Registration."

53. Sauer, Link, and Hines, *North American Breeding Bird*.

54. Audubon Christmas Bird Count, "Historical Results."

55. Committee on the Status of Endangered Wildlife in Canada, *Assessment on Mountain Plover*.

56. U.S. Fish and Wildlife Service, *FWS Determines*.

57. Graul and Webster, "Breeding Status," 266.

58. Graul and Webster, "Breeding Status," 265.

59. Coues, "Field Notes on Birds," 635; Saunders, "Preliminary List," 28.

60. Coues, *Birds of the Northwest*, 457–59; U.S. Entomological Commission, *First Annual Report*, appendix 2, 50.

61. Pettingill, *Guide to Bird Finding*, 30–31.

62. Grinnell, Bryant, and Stores, *Game Birds*, 483–85.

63. U.S. Entomological Commission, *First Annual Report*, appendix 2, 50.

64. Knopf and Rupert, "Use of Cultivated Fields," 81; Shaffer et al., *Effects of Management—Mountain Plover*, 2–4.

65. Augustine and Baker, "Associations of Grassland Bird," 324; Augustine and Derner, "Disturbance Regimes," 927; Duchardt, Beck, and Augustine, "Mountain Plover Habitat Selection," 1; Shaffer et al., *Effects of Management—Mountain Plover*, 4.

66. Dinsmore and Smith, "Mountain Plover Responses to Plague," 37; Childers and Dinsmore, "Density and Abundance," 700.

67. Knowles and Knowles, *Mountain Plover Population*, 3, 23.

68. Knopf, *Mountain Plover Studies*, 60–77.

69. Andres and Stone, *Conservation Plan*, 30; Li, Miao, and Khanna, "Neonicotinoids and Decline," 1032–33; Shaffer et al., *Effects of Management—Mountain Plover*, 6.

70. Conway, "Spatial and Temporal Patterns," 129.

71. Committee on the Status of Endangered Wildlife in Canada, *Assessment on Burrowing Owl*, under "Executive Summary."

72. Conway, "Spatial and Temporal Patterns," 129.

73. Alverson and Dinsmore, "Factors Affecting Burrowing Owl," 247–48; Desmond, Savidge, and Eskridge, "Correlations," 1067.

74. Justice-Allen and Loyd, "Mortality of Western Burrowing Owl," 165.

75. Bird Conservancy of the Rockies, "Population Estimates Database."

76. Hornaday, *Save the Sage Grouse*, 179.

77. Committee on the Status of Endangered Wildlife in Canada, *Assessment on Greater Sage Grouse*, under "Executive Summary."

78. Western Association of Fish and Wildlife Agencies, *Greater Sage-Grouse*, 1.

79. Coates et al., *Range-Wide Greater Sage-Grouse*, 33.

80. Western Association of Fish and Wildlife Agencies, *Greater Sage-Grouse*, 1.

81. Coates et al., *Range-Wide Greater Sage-Grouse*, 33.

82. Rowland, *Effects of Management—Greater Sage-Grouse*, 15–17.

83. Conover and Roberts, "Declining Populations," 221; Rowland, *Effects of Management—Greater Sage-Grouse*, 20–21.

84. Boyd, Beck, and Tanaka, "Livestock Grazing," 63.

85. Boyd, Beck, and Tanaka, "Livestock Grazing," 64–65; Rowland, *Effects of Management—Greater Sage-Grouse*, 19–20.

86. Conover and Roberts, "Declining Populations," 217–18.

87. Conover and Roberts, "Declining Populations," 221; Conover and Roberts, "Predators, Predator Removal," 12–13; Kohl et al., "Effects of Electric Power," under "Abstract."

88. Conover and Roberts, "Declining Populations," 218–19.

89. Boyd, Beck, and Tanaka, "Livestock Grazing," 65.

90. Newton et al., "Longest Sage-Grouse Migratory Behavior," 966–70; Tack et al., "Greater Sage-Grouse," 64–65.

91. Ahlering, Johnson, and Faaborg, "Factors Associated," 609–11; Golding and Dreitz, "Songbird Response," 609–11; Jones, "Sprague's Pipit," 15–16; Yackel, Skagen, and Savidge, "Modeling Post-Fledging Survival," 183.

92. Martin, "Polygyny in the Bobolink," 72–73; Tallamy and Shriver, "Are Declines Related?," 2.

93. Song et al., "Evolution, Diversification," 1.

94. Bock, Bock, and Grant, "Effects of Bird Predation," 1706; Fowler et al., "Effects of Avian Predation," 1775; Joern, "Experimental Study," 243.

95. Guo et al., "Effects of Vertebrate Granivores," 251; Howe and Brown, "Effects of Birds," 1776.

96. Becker, "Food Habits," 228–29; Konrad, *Effects of Management—Merlin*, under "Prey Habitat."

97. Sauer, Link, and Hines, *North American Breeding Bird*.

98. Conover and Roberts, "Predators, Predator Removal," 8–10.

99. Sauer, Link, and Hines, *North American Breeding Bird*.

100. Somershoe, *Full Annual-Cycle Conservation*, 5–6.

101. Wilsey et al., "Climate Policy Action," under "Results."

102. Kleinhesselink and Adler, "Response of Big Sagebrush," 8–9.

103. Augustine et al., "Thinking like a Grassland," 293–95; Lark, "Protecting Our Prairies," under "3. Policy Opportunities," "4. Public-Driven Support."

104. Lark, "Protecting Our Prairies," under "5. Setting a Common Goal and Priorities."

105. Andy Boyce, email to author, January 13, 2022.

12. Conclusion

1. Strömberg, "Evolution of Grasses," 518.

2. Domínguez-Rodrigo, "Is the 'Savanna Hypothesis' Dead?," 59; Uno et al., "Neogene Biomarker Record," 6355.

3. Cheng et al., "Scope and Severity," 1587–88.

4. Montana Fish, Wildlife & Parks, *Montana FWP's White-Nose Syndrome*.

5. Kristina Smucker, email to author, August 9, 2022.

6. Brown et al., "Review of the Ongoing Decline," 343–46; Jachowski et al., "Tracking the Decline," under Abstract, table 4, fig. 6.

7. Niemuth et al., "Conservation Planning for Pollinators," under "Abstract."

8. Ceballos, Ehrlich, and Dirzo, "Biological Annihilation," E6089.

9. Ceballos, Ehrlich, and Dirzo, "Biological Annihilation," E6093.

10. Food and Agricultural Organization of the United Nations, "Livestock Systems"; Smith et al., "Exploring the Influence," 875.

11. Population Reference Bureau, "How Many People?"

12. Bar-On, Phillips, and Milo, "Biomass Distribution," 6507.

13. Dieter and Schaible, "Distribution and Population," 130–32; Ernest and Brown, "Homeostasis," 2128; Klemm and Briske, "Retrospective Assessment," 275; Lightfoot et al., "Bottom-Up Regulation," 1020; Mule Deer Working Group, *2021 Range-Wide Status*, 1–2; Olson et al., "Predicting Above-Ground," 9, 15; Rebollo et al., "Disproportionate Effects," 1759; Rogowitz and Wolfe, "Intraspecific Variation," 797.

14. Redford, "Empty Forest," 421.

15. Dinerstein et al., "Ecoregion-Based Approach," 535; Noss and Cooperrider, *Saving Nature's Legacy*, 89; Noss et al., "Conservation Biology," 959–60.

16. Veldhuis et al., "Cross-Boundary Human Impacts," 1424–25.

17. Steve Forrest, email to author, February 1, 2022.

18. Adams et al., *Climate Change and Human Health*, 50; Holechek et al., "Climate Change, Rangelands," under "Abstract."

19. Allred et al., "Conservation Implications," 1875; Shamon et al., "Potential of Bison Restoration," under "Abstract."

20. American Prairie, "Community Impact."

21. Sage and Nickerson, *Analyzing Economic*, 53.

22. Cullinane and Koontz, *National Park Visitor Spending*, 19–30.

23. Convention on Biological Diversity, "Aichi Targets."

24. Comer et al., "Continent-Scale Landscape Conservation Design," 201; *Protected Planet Report 2020*, chap. 1; Watson et al., "Performance and Potential," 68.

25. NAWPA Committee, *Conservation in North America*, 32.

26. Dinerstein et al., "Ecoregion-Based Approach," 534–35; Wilson, *Half-Earth*.

27. Dinerstein et al., "Global Deal," under "Theme 1: Protecting Biodiversity."

28. Comer et al., "Continent-Scale Landscape Conservation Design," 206.

29. Government of Canada, "Canadian Forces Base Suffield"; Government of Canada, "News Release"; Southern Plains Land Trust, "Our Preserves."

30. Environmental Working Group, "EWG's Farm Subsidy Database."

31. Lark, "Protecting Our Prairies," under "6. Conclusion: A Role for All."

32. Lamb et al., "Ecology of Human-Carnivore," 17876; Lute and Carter, "Are We Coexisting?," under "Abstract."

33. Commission for Environmental Cooperation and The Nature Conservancy, *North American Central Grasslands*; Comer et al., "Continent-Scale Landscape Conservation Design"; Forrest et al., "Ocean of Grass"; NAWPA Committee, *Conservation in North America*; Northern Great Plains Steppe Ecoregional Planning Team, *Ecoregional Planning*; Riley, Green, and Brodribb, *Conservation Blueprint*.

34. Licht, *Ecology and Economics*, 152.

35. Naidoo et al., "Effect of Biodiversity," 310; Nelson and Cooney, "Communities Hold the Key."

36. U.S. Department of Agriculture, *Land Values 2021*.

37. Licht, *Ecology and Economics*, 156–57.

BIBLIOGRAPHY

Adams, Alexandra, Robert Byron, Bruce Maxwell, Susan Higgins, Margaret Eggers, Lori Byron, and Cathy Whitlock. *Climate Change and Human Health in Montana: A Special Report of the Montana Climate Assessment.* Bozeman: Montana State University, Institute of Ecosystems, Center for American Indian and Rural Health Equity, 2021.

Adams, Rick A. "Do Black-Tailed Prairie Dog (*Cynomys ludovicianus*) Colonies Attract Foraging Bats?" *Journal of Zoology* 316, no. 2 (2021): 156–63.

Adams, Stephanie M., and Arnold R. Dood. *Background Information on Issues of Concern for Montana: Plains Bison Ecology, Management, and Conservation.* Bozeman: Montana Fish, Wildlife & Parks, June 2011.

Ahlering, Marissa A., Douglas H. Johnson, and John Faaborg. "Factors Associated with Arrival Densities of Grasshopper Sparrow (*Ammodramus savannarum*) and Baird's Sparrow (*A. Bairdii*) in the Upper Great Plains." *Auk* 126, no. 4 (October 2009): 799–808.

Aldous, M. Clair. *Fort Peck Game Range: Narrative Report: January, February, March, April 1953.* Fort Peck MT: U.S. Fish and Wildlife Service, 1953.

Alexander, J. S., R. C. Wilson, and W. R. Green. *A Brief History and Summary of the Effects of River Engineering and Dams on the Mississippi River System and Delta.* Circular. U.S. Geological Survey, 2012.

Alexander, R. McN. "The Relative Merits of Foregut and Hindgut Fermentation." *Journal of Zoology* 231, no. 3 (November 1993): 391–401.

Allen, Durwood L. "The Hole in the System: A Great Plains National Park." In *Proceedings of the First Conference on Scientific Research in the National Parks*, ed. Robert M. Linn, 1:5–8. New Orleans: National Park Service and American Institute of Biological Science, 1976.

Allendorf, Fred W., Paul A. Hohenlohe, and Gordon Luikart. "Genomics and the Future of Conservation Genetics." *Nature Reviews Genetics* 11, no. 10 (October 2010): 697–709.

Allred, Brady W., Samuel D. Fuhlendorf, Torre H. Hovick, R. Dwayne Elmore, David M. Engle, and Anthony Joern. "Conservation Implications of Native and Introduced Ungulates in a Changing Climate." *Global Change Biology* 19, no. 6 (June 2013): 1875–83.

Allred, Brady W., W. Kolby Smith, Dirac Twidwell, Julia H. Haggerty, Steven W. Running, David E. Naugle, and Samuel D. Fuhlendorf. "Ecosystem Services Lost to Oil and Gas in North America." *Science* 348, no. 6223 (April 24, 2015): 401–2.

Alverson, Kristen M., and Stephen J. Dinsmore. "Factors Affecting Burrowing Owl Occupancy of Prairie Dog Colonies." *Condor* 116, no. 2 (May 2014): 242–50.

Ambrose, Stephen E. *Undaunted Courage: Meriwether Lewis, Thomas Jefferson, and the Opening of the American West*. New York: Simon & Schuster, 1996.

American Prairie. "Building the Prairie." Accessed September 2021. https://www.americanprairie.org/building-the-reserve.

———. "Community Impact." Accessed January 2022. https://www.americanprairie.org.

———. "This Is American Prairie." Video. Accessed May 9, 2022. https://www.americanprairie.org/mission-and-values.

Anderson, Elaine, Steven C. Forrest, Tim W. Clark, and Louise Richardson. "Paleobiology, Biogeography, and Systematics of the Black-Footed Ferret, *Mustela nigripes* (Audubon and Bachman), 1851." *Great Basin Naturalist Memoirs* 8, no. 3 (1986): 11–62.

Anderson, Roger C. "Evolution and Origin of the Central Grassland of North America: Climate, Fire, and Mammalian Grazers." *Journal of the Torrey Botanical Society* 133, no. 4 (October 2006): 626–47.

Andres, Brad A., and Kelli L. Stone. *Conservation Plan for the Mountain Plover (Charadrius montanus)*. Manomet MA: Manomet Center for Conservation Sciences, 2009.

Antolin, Michael F., Pete Gober, Bob Luce, Dean E. Biggins, William E. Van Pelt, David B. Seery, Michael Lockhart, and Mark Ball. *The Influence of Sylvatic Plague on North American Wildlife at the Landscape Level, with Special Emphasis on Black-Footed Ferret and Prairie Dog Conservation*. U.S. Fish and Wildlife Publications, U.S. Fish and Wildlife Service, 2002.

Artemieva, Natalia, Joanna Morgan, and Expedition 364 Science Party. "Quantifying the Release of Climate-Active Gases by Large Meteorite Impacts with a Case Study of Chicxulub: Release of Climate-Active Gases." *Geophysical Research Letters* 44, no. 20 (October 28, 2017): 10180–88.

Audubon Christmas Bird Count. "Historical Results by Species." National Audubon Society. Accessed November 15, 2021. https://netapp.audubon.org/cbcobservation/Historical/ResultsBySpecies.aspx?1.

Augustine, David, and Bruce W. Baker. "Associations of Grassland Bird Communities with Black-Tailed Prairie Dogs in the North American Great Plains: Prairie Dogs and Grassland Bird Conservation." *Conservation Biology* 27, no. 2 (April 2013): 324–34.

Augustine, David, Ana Davidson, Kristin Dickinson, and Bill Van Pelt. "Thinking like a Grassland: Challenges and Opportunities for Biodiversity Conservation in the Great Plains of North America." *Rangeland Ecology & Management* 78, no. 1 (September 2021): 281–95.

Augustine, David, and Justin D. Derner. "Disturbance Regimes and Mountain Plover Habitat in Shortgrass Steppe: Large Herbivore Grazing Does Not Substitute for Prairie Dog Grazing or Fire." *Journal of Wildlife Management* 76, no. 4 (May 2012): 721–28.

Augustine, David, and Tim L. Springer. "Competition and Facilitation between a Native and a Domestic Herbivore: Trade-Offs between Forage Quantity and Quality." *Ecological Applications* 23, no. 4 (June 2013): 850–63.

Aune, Keith, and Glenn Plumb. "Looking Forward." In *Theodore Roosevelt & Bison Restoration on the Great Plains*, 108–31. Charleston NC: History Press, 2019.

Bailey, Vernon. *Destruction of Wolves and Coyotes: Results during 1907*. Circular no. 63. Bureau of Biological Survey, U.S. Department of Agriculture, April 29, 1908.

Baker, B. W., and E. P. Hill. "Beaver." In *Wild Mammals of North America: Biology, Management, and Conservation*, edited by G. A. Feldhamer, B. C. Thompson, and J. A. Chapman, 288–310. Baltimore: Johns Hopkins University Press, 2003.

Bangert, R. K., and C. N. Slobodchikoff. "Conservation of Prairie Dog Ecosystem Engineering May Support Arthropod Beta and Gamma Diversity." *Journal of Arid Environments* 67 (2006): 100–115.

Barnett, Barry J. "U.S. Farm Financial Crisis of the 1980s." *Agricultural History* 74, no. 2 (Spring 2000): 366–80.

Barnett, Ross, Ian Barnes, Matthew J. Phillips, Larry D. Martin, C. Richard Harington, Jennifer A. Leonard, and Alan Cooper. "Evolution of the Extinct Sabre-Tooths and the American Cheetah-like Cat." *Current Biology* 15, no. 15 (August 9, 2005): R1–R2.

Barnett, Ross, Michael V. Westbury, Marcela Sandoval-Velasco, Filipe Garrett Vieira, Sungwon Jeon, Grant Zazula, Michael D. Martin, et al. "Genomic Adaptations and Evolutionary History of the Extinct Scimitar-Toothed Cat, *Homotherium latidens*." *Current Biology* 30, no. 24 (December 21, 2020): 5018–25.

Barnosky, Anthony D., Emily L. Lindsey, Natalia A. Villavicencio, Enrique Bostelmann, Elizabeth A. Hadly, James Wanket, and Charles R. Marshall. "Variable Impact of Late-Quaternary Megafaunal Extinction in Causing Ecological State Shifts in North and South America." *Proceedings of the National Academy of Sciences* 113, no. 4 (January 26, 2016): 856–61.

Barnosky, Cathy W. "Postglacial Vegetation and Climate in the Northwestern Great Plains of Montana." *Quaternary Research* 31, no. 1 (January 1989): 57–73.

Barnowe-Meyer, Kerey K., P. J. White, Troy L. Davis, and John A. Byers. "Predator-Specific Mortality of Pronghorn on Yellowstone's Northern Range." *Western North American Naturalist* 69, no. 2 (June 2009): 186–94.

Bar-On, Yinon M., Rob Phillips, and Ron Milo. "The Biomass Distribution on Earth." *Proceedings of the National Academy of Sciences* 115, no. 25 (June 19, 2018): 6506–11.

Barth, C. J., M. A. Liebig, J. R. Hendrickson, K. K. Sedivec, and G. Halvorson. "Soil Change Induced by Prairie Dogs across Three Ecological Sites." *Soil Science Society of American Journal* 78, no. 6 (November–December 2014): 2054–60.

Batchelor, Christine L., Martin Margold, Mario Krapp, Della K. Murton, April S. Dalton, Philip L. Gibbard, Chris R. Stokes, Julian B. Murton, and Andrea Manica.

"The Configuration of Northern Hemisphere Ice Sheets through the Quaternary." *Nature Communications* 10, no. 1 (December 2019): 3713.

Bauman, Pete, Benjamin Carlson, Tanner Butler, and Brad Richardson. *Quantifying Undisturbed (Native) Lands in Northwestern South Dakota: 2013.* Natural Resource Management Department, South Dakota State University, 2018. https://openprairie.sdstate.edu/cgi/viewcontent.cgi?article=1000&context =data_land-northwestsd.

Beatty, William S., James C. Beasley, and Olin E. Rhodes. "Habitat Selection by a Generalist Mesopredator near Its Historical Range Boundary." *Canadian Journal of Zoology* 92, no. 1 (January 2014): 41–48.

Becerra, Terrie A., David M. Engle, Samuel D. Fuhlendorf, and R. Dwayne Elmore. "Preference for Grassland Heterogeneity: Implications for Biodiversity in the Great Plains." *Society & Natural Resources* 30, no. 5 (2017): 601–12.

Becker, Dale M. "Food Habits of Richardson's Merlins in Southeastern Montana." *Wilson Bulletin* 97, no. 2 (June 1985): 226–30.

Beer, James. "Distribution and Status of Pronghorn Antelope in Montana." *Journal of Mammalogy* 25, no. 1 (February 1944): 43–46.

Bennett, Matthew R., David Bustos, Jeffrey S. Pigati, Kathleen B. Springer, Thomas M. Urban, Vance T. Holliday, Sally C. Reynolds, et al. "Evidence of Humans in North America during the Last Glacial Maximum." *Science* 373, no. 6562 (September 24, 2021): 1528–31.

Berger, Joel. "Undetected Species Losses, Food Webs, and Ecological Baselines: A Cautionary Tale from the Greater Yellowstone Ecosystem, USA." *Oryx* 42, no. 1 (January 2008): 139–42.

Berger, Kim Murray, Eric M. Gese, and Joel Berger. "Indirect Effects and Traditional Trophic Cascades: A Test Involving Wolves, Coyotes, and Pronghorn." *Ecology* 89, no. 3 (March 2008): 818–28.

Berlanga, H., J. A. Kennedy, T. D. Rich, M. C. Arizmendi, C. J. Beardmore, P. J. Blancher, G. S. Butcher, et al. *Saving Our Shared Birds: Partners in Flight Trinational Vision for Landbird Conservation.* Ithaca NY: Cornell Lab of Ornithology, 2010. https://www.birds.cornell.edu/home/wp-content/uploads/2019/12/ PIF2010_Overview-Handout_English.pdf.

Beschta, Robert L., and William J. Ripple. "Large Predators and Trophic Cascades in Terrestrial Ecosystems of the Western United States." *Biological Conservation* 142, no. 11 (November 2009): 2401–14.

Beschta, Robert L., William J. Ripple, J. Boone Kauffman, and Luke E. Painter. "Bison Limit Ecosystem Recovery in Northern Yellowstone." *Food Webs* 23 (2020): e00142.

Bird Conservancy of the Rockies. "Population Estimates Database." Accessed December 1, 2021. https://pif.birdconservancy.org/population-estimates-database/.

Blumenthal, Dana M., Kevin E. Mueller, Julie A. Kray, Troy W. Ocheltree, David J. Augustine, and Kevin R. Wilcox. "Traits Link Drought Resistance with Herbivore Defence and Plant Economics in Semi-arid Grasslands: The Central Roles of Phenology and Leaf Dry Matter Content." Edited by Hans Cornelissen. *Journal of Ecology* 108, no. 6 (November 2020): 2336–51.

Bock, Carl E., Jane H. Bock, and Michael C. Grant. "Effects of Bird Predation on Grasshopper Densities in an Arizona Grassland." *Ecology* 73, no. 5 (October 1992): 1706–17.

Bovee, Ken D., and Michael L. Scott. "Implications of Flood Pulse Restoration for *Populus* Regeneration on the Upper Missouri River." *River Research and Applications* 18, no. 3 (May 2002): 287–98.

Bowen, Zachary H., Ken D. Bovee, and Terry J. Waddle. "Effects of Flow Regulation on Shallow-Water Habitat Dynamics and Floodplain Connectivity." *Transactions of the American Fisheries Society* 132 (2003): 809–23.

Bown, Robin. "Beaver Habitat along Rivers and Reservoirs in Central Montana." Master's thesis, University of Montana, 1988.

Bowyer, R. Terry, Dale R. McCullough, Janet L. Rachlow, Simone Ciuti, and Jericho C. Whiting. "Evolution of Ungulates Mating Systems: Integrating Social and Environmental Factors." *Ecology and Evolution* 10, no. 11 (June 2020): 5160–78.

Boyce, Mark S. "Population Viability Analysis." *Annual Review of Ecology and Systematics* 23, no. 1 (1992): 481–506.

Boyd, Chad S., Jeffrey L. Beck, and John A. Tanaka. "Livestock Grazing and Sage-Grouse Habitat: Impacts and Opportunities." *Journal of Rangeland Applications* 1 (2014): 58–77.

Braaten, P. J., S. E. Campana, D. B. Fuller, R. D. Lott, R. M. Bruch, and G. R. Jordan. "Age Estimation of Wild Pallid Sturgeon (*Scaphirhynchus albus*, Forbes & Richardson 1905) Based on Pectoral Fin Spines, Otoliths and Bomb Radiocarbon: Inferences on Recruitment in the Dam-Fragmented Missouri River." *Journal of Applied Ichthyology* 31, no. 5 (October 2015): 821–929.

Braaten, P. J., D. B. Fuller, R. D. Lott, and G. R. Jordan. "An Estimate of the Historic Population Size of Adult Pallid Sturgeon in the Upper Missouri River Basin, Montana and North Dakota." Supplement, *Journal of Applied Ichthyology* 25, no. s2 (2009): s2–7.

Braaten, Patrick J., David B. Fuller, Ryan D. Lott, Michael P. Ruggles, Tyrel F. Brandt, Robert G. Legare, and Robert J. Holm. "An Experimental Test and Models of Drift and Dispersal Processes of Pallid Sturgeon (*Scaphirhynchus albus*) Free Embryos in the Missouri River." *Environmental Biology of Fishes* 93, no. 3 (February 2012): 377–92.

Bragg, Arthur. "Observations on the Ecology and Natural History of Anura. I. Habits, Habitat and Breeding of *Bufo cognatus* Say." *American Naturalist* 74, no. 753 (July–August 1949): 322–49.

———. "The Spadefoot Toad in Oklahoma with a Summary of Our Knowledge of the Group. II." *American Naturalist* 79, no. 780 (January–February 1945): 52–72.

Brain, Richard A., and Julie C. Anderson. "The Agro-Enabled Urban Revolution, Pesticides, Politics, and Popular Culture: A Case Study of Land Use, Birds, and Insecticides in the USA." *Environmental Science and Pollution Research* 26, no. 21 (July 2019): 21717–35.

Bramblett, Robert G., and Robert G. White. "Habitat Use and Movements of Pallid and Shovelnose Sturgeon in the Yellowstone and Missouri Rivers in Montana and North Dakota." *Transactions of the American Fisheries Society* 130 (2001): 1006–25.

Brennan, Jameson, Kenneth Olson, Patricia Johnson, Janna Block, and Christopher Schauer. "Grazing Behavior, Forage Quality, and Intake Rates of Livestock Grazing Pastures Occupied by Prairie Dogs." *Rangeland Ecology & Management* 76, no. 1 (May 2021): 12–21.

Brikiatis, Leonidas. "The De Geer, Thulean and Beringia Routes: Key Concepts for Understanding Early Cenozoic Biogeography." *Journal of Biogeography* 41, no. 6 (June 2014): 1036–54.

Briske, D. D., J. D. Derner, J. R. Brown, S. D. Fuhlendorf, W. R. Teague, K. M. Havstad, R. L. Gillen, A. J. Ash, and W. D. Willms. "Rotational Grazing on Rangelands: Reconciliation of Perception and Experimental Evidence." *Rangeland Ecology & Management* 61, no. 1 (January 2008): 3–17.

Broughton, Jack M., and Elic M. Weitzel. "Population Reconstructions for Humans and Megafauna Suggest Mixed Causes for North American Pleistocene Extinctions." *Nature Communications* 9, no. 1 (December 2018): 5441.

Brown, David E., Andrew T. Smith, Jennifer K. Frey, and Brittany R. Schweiger. "A Review of the Ongoing Decline of the White-Tailed Jackrabbit." *Journal of Fish and Wildlife Management* 11, no. 1 (June 2020): 341–52.

Brown, K. J., J. S. Clark, E. C. Grimm, J. J. Donovan, P. G. Mueller, B. C. S. Hansen, and I. Stefanova. "Fire Cycles in North American Interior Grasslands and Their Relation to Prairie Drought." *Proceedings of the National Academy of Sciences* 102, no. 25 (June 21, 2005): 8865–70.

Brown, Matthew. "Governor Opposes Fort Peck Dam Changes to Aid Imperiled Fish." *AP News*, May 27, 2021. https://apnews.com/article/mt-state-wire-michael-brown-technology-dams-fish-8ad5495d4fcab1e795617ffd5811d4e4.

Brownell, Joan L. "The Genesis of Wildlife Conservation in Montana." Master's thesis, Montana State University, 1987.

Brusatte, Stephen L., Jingmai K. O'Connor, and Erich D. Jarvis. "The Origin and Diversification of Birds." *Current Biology* 25, no. 19 (October 2015): R888–98.

Budd, Bob, and Jim Thorpe. "Benefits of Managed Grazing: A Manager's Perspective." *Rangelands*, October 2009, 11–14.

Buechner, H. K. "The Bighorn Sheep in the United States, Its Past, Present, and Future." *Wildlife Monographs* 4 (1960): 3–174.

Bump, Joseph K., Christopher R. Webster, John A. Vucetich, Rolf O. Peterson, Joshua M. Shields, and Matthew D. Powers. "Ungulate Carcasses Perforate Ecological Filters and Create Biogeochemical Hotspots in Forest Herbaceous Layers Allowing Trees a Competitive Advantage." *Ecosystems* 12, no. 6 (September 2009): 996–1007.

Bureau of Agriculture, Labor and Industry of Montana. *Third Annual Report of the Bureau of Agriculture, Labor and Industry of Montana for the Year Ended November 30, 1895.* Helena: Bureau of Agriculture, Labor and Industry of Montana, 1896.

———. *Sixth Annual Report of the Bureau of Agriculture, Labor and Industry for the State of Montana for the Year Ending November 30, 1897.* Helena: Bureau of Agriculture, Labor and Industry of Montana, 1898.

———. *Thirteenth Annual Report of the Bureau of Agriculture, Labor and Industry of the State of Montana for the Years 1911 and 1912.* Helena: Bureau of Agriculture, Labor and Industry of Montana, 1913.

Bureau of Land Management. "Our Mission." Accessed January 21, 2022. https://www.blm.gov/about/our-mission.

Burgess, Seth D., Samuel Bowring, and Shu-zhong Shen. "High-Precision Timeline for Earth's Most Severe Extinction." *Proceedings of the National Academy of Sciences* 111, no. 9 (March 4, 2014): 3316–21.

Butler, Andrew R., Kristy L. S. Bly, Heather Harris, Robert M. Inman, Axel Moehrenschlager, Donelle Schwalm, and David S. Jachowski. "Home Range Size and Resource Use by Swift Foxes in Northeastern Montana." *Journal of Mammalogy* 101, no. 3 (2020): 684–96.

———. "Life on the Edge: Habitat Fragmentation Limits Expansion of a Restored Carnivore." *Animal Conservation* 24, no. 1 (February 2021): 108–19.

Cahalane, Victor H. "A Proposed Great Plains National Monument." *Scientific Monthly* 51, no. 2 (1940): 125–39.

Campbell, Dana L. M., J. M. Lea, Hamideh Kishavarzi, and Caroline Lee. "Virtual Fencing Is Comparable to Electric Tape Fencing for Cattle Behavior and Welfare." *Frontiers in Veterinary Science* 6 (December 11, 2019): article 445.

Campbell, Gregory. "Health." Encyclopedia of the Great Plains. University of Nebraska–Lincoln, 2011. http://plainshumanities.unl.edu/encyclopedia/doc/egp.na.034.

Carbutt, Clinton, William D. Henwood, and Louise A. Gilfedder. "Global Plight of Native Temperate Grasslands: Going, Going, Gone?" *Biodiversity and Conservation* 26, no. 12 (November 2017): 2911–32.

Cardinal, Sophie, and Bryan N. Danforth. "Bees Diversified in the Age of Eudicots." *Proceedings of the Royal Society B: Biological Sciences* 280, no. 1755 (March 22, 2013): 20122686.

Carrillo, Juan D., Søren Faurby, Daniele Silvestro, Alexander Zizka, Carlos Jaramillo, Christine D. Bacon, and Alexandre Antonelli. "Disproportionate Extinction of South American Mammals Drove the Asymmetry of the Great American Biotic Interchange." *Proceedings of the National Academy of Sciences* 117, no. 42 (October 20, 2020): 26281–87.

Carter, Neil H., Peter Nelson, and Tara Easter. "A Call for a National Collaborative Coexistence Programme." *People and Nature* 3, no. 4 (August 2021): 788–94.

Catlin, Geo. *Letters and Notes on the Manners, Customs, and Condition of the North American Indians*, London: printed by the author at the Egyptian Hall, Piccadilly, 1841.

Ceballos, Gerardo, Ana Davidson, Rurik List, Jesús Pacheco, Patricia Manzano-Fischer, Georgina Santos-Barrera, and Juan Cruzado. "Rapid Decline of a Grassland System and Its Ecological and Conservation Implications." *PLOS ONE* 5, no. 1 (January 6, 2010): e8562.

Ceballos, Gerardo, Paul R. Ehrlich, and Rodolfo Dirzo. "Biological Annihilation via the Ongoing Sixth Mass Extinction Signaled by Vertebrate Population Losses and Declines." *Proceedings of the National Academy of Sciences* 114 (2017): E6089–E6096.

Chapco, W., and G. Litzenberger. "A DNA Investigation into the Mysterious Disappearance of the Rocky Mountain Grasshopper, Mega-pest of the 1800s." *Molecular Phylogenetics and Evolution* 30, no. 3 (March 2004): 810–14.

Chapman, Eric J., and Carrie J. Byron. "The Flexible Application of Carrying Capacity in Ecology." *Global Ecology and Conservation* 13 (January 2018): e00365.

Charboneau, Joseph L. M., B. E. Nelson, and Ronald L. Hartman. "A Floristic Inventory of Phillips and Valley Counties, Montana (U.S.A.)." *Journal of the Floristic Research Institute of Texas* 7, no. 2 (December 2013): 847–78.

Charles M. Russell National Wildlife Refuge. "Wildlife and Habitat." U.S. Fish and Wildlife Service, May 20, 2013. https://www.fws.gov/refuge/Charles_M_Russell/Wildlife_and_Habitat/.html. Page discontinued.

Chen, Lei, Qiang Qiu, Yu Jiang, Kun Wang, Zeshan Lin, Zhipeng Li, Faysal Bibi, et al. "Large-Scale Ruminant Genome Sequencing Provides Insights into Their Evolution and Distinct Traits." *Science* 364, no. 6446 (June 21, 2019): 1152.

Cheng, Tina L., Jonathan D. Reichard, Jeremy T. H. Coleman, Theodore J. Weller, Wayne E. Thogmartin, Brian E. Reichert, Alyssa B. Bennett, et al. "The Scope and Severity of White-Nose Syndrome on Hibernating Bats in North America." *Conservation Biology* 35, no. 5 (October 2021): 1586–97.

Chester, Stephen G. B., Jonathan I. Bloch, Doug M. Boyer, and William A. Clemens. "Oldest Known Euarchontan Tarsals and Affinities of Paleocene *Purgatorius* to Primates." *Proceedings of the National Academy of Sciences* 112, no. 5 (February 3, 2015): 1487–92.

Chiarenza, Alfio Alessandro, Alexander Farnsworth, Philip D. Mannion, Daniel J. Lunt, Paul J. Valdes, Joanna V. Morgan, and Peter A. Allison. "Asteroid Impact, Not Volcanism, Caused the End-Cretaceous Dinosaur Extinction." *Proceedings of the National Academy of Sciences* 117, no. 29 (July 21, 2020): 17084–93.

Childers, Theresa M., and Stephen J. Dinsmore. "Density and Abundance of Mountain Plovers in Northeastern Montana." *Wilson Journal of Ornithology* 120, no. 4 (December 2008): 700–707.

Chojnacki, Kimberly A., Susannah O. Erwin, Amy E. George, James S. Candrl, Robert B. Jacobson, and Aaron J. DeLonay. "Physical Characteristics and Simulated Transport of Pallid Sturgeon and Shovelnose Sturgeon Eggs." *Journal of Freshwater Ecology* 35, no. 1 (January 1, 2020): 73–94.

Christie, Katie, Bill Jensen, and Mark Boyce. *Pronghorn Abundance and Habitat Selection in North Dakota*. Final report. Bismarck ND: North Dakota Game and Fish Department, December 2015.

Christie, Mark R., Melanie L. Marine, Samuel E. Fox, Rod A. French, and Michael S. Blouin. "A Single Generation of Domestication Heritably Alters the Expression of Hundreds of Genes." *Nature Communications* 7, no. 1 (April 2016): 10676.

Churakov, Gennady, Manoj K. Sadasivuni, Kate R. Rosenbloom, Dorothée Huchon, Jürgen Brosius, and Jürgen Schmitz. "Rodent Evolution: Back to the Root." *Molecular Biology and Evolution* 27, no. 6 (January 25, 2010): 1315–26.

Claassen, Roger, Fernando Carriazo, Joseph C. Cooper, Daniel Hellerstein, and Kohei Udea. *Grassland to Cropland Conversion in the Northern Plains: The Role of Crop Insurance, Commodity, and Disaster Payments*. U.S. Department of Agriculture, Economic Research Service, June 2011.

Coates, Peter S., Brian G. Prochazka, Michael S. O'Donnell, Cameron L. Aldridge, David R. Edmunds, Adrian P. Monroe, Mark A. Ricca, et al. *Range-Wide Greater Sage-Grouse Hierarchical Monitoring Framework—Implications for Defining Population Boundaries, Trend Estimation, and a Targeted Annual Warning System*. USGS Numbered Series. Open-file report. Reston VA: U.S. Geological Survey, 2021. http://pubs.er.usgs.gov/publication/ofr20201154.

Comer, Patrick J., Jon C. Hak, Kelly Kindscher, Esteban Muldavin, and Jason Singhurst. "Continent-Scale Landscape Conservation Design for Temperate Grasslands of the Great Plains and Chihuahuan Desert." *Natural Areas Journal* 38, no. 2 (2018): 196–210.

Commission for Environmental Cooperation and The Nature Conservancy. *North American Central Grasslands Priority Conservation Areas: Technical Report and Documentation*. Montreal: Commission for Environmental Cooperation and The Nature Conservancy, 2005.

Committee on the Status of Endangered Wildlife in Canada. *COSEWIC Assessment and Status Report on the Burrowing Owl* Athene cunicularia *in Canada*. Ottawa: Committee on the Status of Endangered Wildlife in Canada, 2017.

———. *COSEWIC Assessment and Status Report on the Greater Sage Grouse* Centrocercus urophasianus *in Canada*. Ottawa: Committee on the Status of Endangered Wildlife in Canada, 2000.

———. *COSEWIC Assessment and Status Report on the Mountain Plover* Charadrius montanus *in Canada*. Ottawa: Committee on the Status of Endangered Wildlife in Canada, 2009.

Connell, Lauren C., Lauren M. Porensky, and John Derek Scasta. "Prairie Dog (*Cynomys ludovicianus*) Influence on Forage Quantity and Quality in a Grazed Grassland-Shrubland Ecotone." *Rangeland Ecology & Management* 72, no. 2 (March 2019): 360–73.

Conover, Michael R., and Anthony J. Roberts. "Declining Populations of Greater Sage-Grouse: Where and Why." *Human-Wildlife Interactions* 10, no. 2 (Fall 2016): 217–29.

———. "Predators, Predator Removal, and Sage-Grouse: A Review: Sage-Grouse and Predators." *Journal of Wildlife Management* 81, no. 1 (January 2017): 7–15.

Convention of Biological Diversity. "Aichi Targets." Accessed January 18, 2022. https://www.cbd.int/aichi-targets/target/11.

Conway, Courtney J. "Spatial and Temporal Patterns in Population Trends and Burrow Usage of Burrowing Owls in North America." *Journal of Raptor Research* 52, no. 2 (June 2018): 129–42.

Cooke, Hilary A., and Steve Zack. "Influence of Beaver Dam Density on Riparian Areas and Riparian Birds in Shrubsteppe of Wyoming." *Western North American Naturalist* 68, no. 3 (September 2008): 365–73.

Coppedge, Bryan R. "Effects of Bison Hair Use in Nests of Tallgrass Prairie Birds." *Prairie Naturalist* 41, nos. 3/4 (December 2009): 110–15.

Coppedge, Bryan R., and James H. Shaw. "Effects of Horning and Rubbing Behavior by Bison (*Bison bison*) on Woody Vegetation in a Tallgrass Prairie Landscape." *American Midland Naturalist* 138, no. 1 (July 1997): 189.

Cornell Lab of Ornithology. "All about Birds." Accessed January 24, 2022. https://www.birds.cornell.edu/home/.

Correll, Maureen D., Erin H. Strasser, Adam W. Green, and Arvind O. Panjabi. "Quantifying Specialist Avifaunal Decline in Grassland Birds of the Northern Great Plains." *Ecosphere* 10, no. 1 (January 2019): e02523.

Coues, Elliott. *Birds of the Northwest: A Handbook of the Ornithology of the Region Drained by the Missouri River and Its Tributaries.* Miscellaneous publication no. 3. Washington DC: Department of the Interior, 1874.

———. "Field Notes on Birds Observed in Dakota and Montana along the Forty-Ninth Parallel during the Seasons of 1873 and 1874." In *Bulletin of the United States Geological and Geographical Survey of the Territories*, vol. 4, no. 3, Washington DC: Department of the Interior, July 29, 1878.

Couey, Faye M. *Rocky Mountain Bighorn Sheep of Montana.* Surveys and Investigations of Montana's Wildlife Resources under Federal Aid in Wildlife Restoration Act, Project 1-R. Helena: Montana Fish and Game Commission, 1950.

Coughenour, Michael B. "Graminoid Responses to Grazing by Large Herbivores: Adaptations, Exaptations, and Interacting Processes." *Annals of the Missouri Botanical Garden* 72, no. 4 (1985): 852.

Craine, Joseph M., Troy W. Ocheltree, Jesse B. Nippert, E. Gene Towne, Adam M. Skibbe, Steven W. Kembel, and Joseph E. Fargione. "Global Diversity of Drought Tolerance and Grassland Climate-Change Resilience." *Nature Climate Change* 3, no. 1 (January 2013): 63–67.

Crow, Lewis E. "Ranch-Level Economic Impacts of Prairie Dog Conservation in the Thunder Basin Ecoregion of Wyoming." Master's thesis, University of Wyoming, 2020.

Cullinane Thomas, Catherine, and Lynne L. Koontz. *National Park Visitor Spending Effects: Economic Contributions to Local Communities, States, and the Nation.*

Natural Resource Report NPS/NRSS/EQD/NRR-2016/1200. Fort Collins CO: National Park Service, 2016.

Dary, David. *The Buffalo Book: The Full Saga of the American Animal*. Rev. ed. Athens: Swallow Press / Ohio University Press, 1989.

Daschuk, James W. *Clearing the Plains: Disease, Politics of Starvation, and the Loss of Aboriginal Life*. Canadian Plains Studies 65. Regina, Saskatchewan, Canada: University of Regina Press, 2013.

Davidson, Ana D., James K. Detling, and James H. Brown. "Ecological Roles and Conservation Challenges of Social, Burrowing, Herbivorous Mammals in the World's Grasslands." *Frontiers in Ecology and the Environment* 10, no. 9 (September 2012): 477–86.

Davis, Kristin P., David J. Augustine, Adrian P. Monroe, Justin D. Derner, and Cameron L. Aldridge. "Adaptive Rangeland Management Benefits Grassland Birds Utilizing Opposing Vegetation Structure in the Shortgrass Steppe." *Ecological Applications* 30, no. 1 (January 2020): e02020.

Davis, Nicole K., William W. Locke, Kenneth L. Pierce, and Robert C. Finkel. "Glacial Lake Musselshell: Late Wisconsin Slackwater on the Laurentide Ice Margin in Central Montana, USA." *Geomorphology* 75, nos. 3–4 (May 2006): 330–45.

Davis, Stephen K., Ryan J. Fisher, Susan L. Skinner, Terry L. Shaffer, and R. Mark Brigham. "Songbird Abundance in Native and Planted Grassland Varies with Type and Amount of Grassland in the Surrounding Landscape: Songbirds in Native and Planted Grasslands." *Journal of Wildlife Management* 77, no. 5 (July 2013): 908–19.

Davy, Douglas M., Evan Franke, Connie Anderson, Larry Lahren, Peggy Scully, and Signe Lahren. *Historic Properties Survey of Selected Areas at Fort Peck Lake, Montana*. Environmental Impact Report for the Missouri River Master Water Control Manual Review and Update. Prepared for U.S. Army Corps of Engineers, Contract DACW45-91-C-0044, Task 12. Sacramento: Ebasco Environmental, August 1992.

Dechant, Jill A., Marriah L. Sondreal, Douglas H. Johnson, Lawrence D. Igl, Christopher M. Goldade, Paul A. Rabie, and Betty R. Euliss. *Effects of Management Practices on Grassland Birds—Burrowing Owl*. Jamestown ND: Northern Prairie Wildlife Research Center, 2002.

Deep Time Maps. "North America." 2020. https://deeptimemaps.com/north-america/.

DeLonay, Aaron J., Kimberly A. Chojnacki, Robert B. Jacobson, Patrick J. Braaten, Kevin J. Buhl, Caroline M. Elliott, Susannah O. Erwin, et al. *Ecological Requirements for Pallid Sturgeon Reproduction and Recruitment in the Missouri River—Annual Report 2014*. USGS Numbered Series. Open-file report. Reston VA: U.S. Geological Survey, 2016. http://pubs.er.usgs.gov/publication/ofr20161013.

DePalma, Robert A., Jan Smit, David A. Burnham, Klaudia Kuiper, Phillip L. Manning, Anton Oleinik, Peter Larson, et al. "A Seismically Induced Onshore Surge Deposit at the KPg Boundary, North Dakota." *Proceedings of the National Academy of Sciences* 116, no. 17 (April 23, 2019): 8190–99.

Department of Commerce. *Fourteenth Census of the United States Taken in the Year 1920*. Vol. 5, *Agriculture*. Washington DC: Department of Commerce, 1922.

Derner, Justin D., James K. Detling, and Michael F. Antolin. "Are Livestock Weight Gains Affected by Black-Tailed Prairie Dogs?" *Frontiers in Ecology and the Environment* 4, no. 9 (November 2006): 459–64.

Derner, Justin D., William K. Lauenroth, Paul Stapp, and David J. Augustine. "Livestock as Ecosystem Engineers for Grassland Bird Habitat in the Western Great Plains of North America." *Rangeland Ecology & Management* 62, no. 2 (March 2009): 111–18.

Desmond, Martha J., Julie A. Savidge, and Kent M. Eskridge. "Correlations between Burrowing Owl and Black-Tailed Prairie Dog Declines: A 7-Year Analysis." *Journal of Wildlife Management* 64, no. 4 (October 2000): 1067–75.

Devoe, Jesse D., Blake Lowrey, Kelly M. Proffitt, and Robert A. Garrott. "Restoration Potential of Bighorn Sheep in a Prairie Region." *Journal of Wildlife Management* 84, no. 7 (September 2020): 1256–67.

Diamond, Jared M. "The Island Dilemma: Lessons of Modern Biogeographic Studies for the Design of Natural Reserves." *Biological Conservation* 7, no. 2 (February 1975): 129–46.

Dickson, Tom. "Monitoring Muleys." *Montana Outdoors Magazine*, October 2016, 21–26.

Dieter, Charles D., and Dustin J. Schaible. "Distribution and Population Density of Jackrabbits in South Dakota." *Great Plains Research* 24, no. 2 (Fall 2014): 127–34.

Dieterman, Douglas J., and David L. Galat. "Large-Scale Factors Associated with Sicklefin Chub Distribution in the Missouri and Lower Yellowstone Rivers." *Transactions of the American Fisheries Society* 133 (2004): 577–87.

Dimitri, Carolyn, Anne Effland, and Neilson Conklin. *The 20th Century Transformation of U.S. Agriculture and Farm Policy*. Economic Information Bulletin no. 3. Electronic report. Economic Research Service, U.S. Department of Agriculture, June 2005. https://www.ers.usda.gov/publications/pub-details/?pubid=44198.

Dinerstein, Eric, David Olson, Anup Joshi, Carly Vynne, Neil D. Burgess, Eric Wikramanayake, Nathan Hahn, et al. "An Ecoregion-Based Approach to Protecting Half the Terrestrial Realm." *BioScience* 67, no. 6 (June 2017): 534–45.

Dinerstein, Eric, Carly Vynne, Enric Sala, Anup R. Joshi, Senura Fernando, Thomas E. Lovejoy, Juan Mayorga, et al. "A Global Deal for Nature: Guiding Principles, Milestones, and Targets." *Science Advances* 5 (April 19, 2019): eaaw2869.

Dinsmore, Stephen J. "Mountain Plover Responses to Deltamethrin Treatments on Prairie Dog Colonies in Montana." *Ecotoxicology* 22, no. 2 (March 2013): 415–24.

Dinsmore, Stephen J., and Mark D. Smith. "Mountain Plover Responses to Plague in Montana." *Vector-Borne and Zoonotic Diseases* 10, no. 1 (February 2010): 37–45.

Dixon, Mark D., W. Carter Johnson, Michael L. Scott, and Daniel Bowen. "Status and Trend of Cottonwood Forests along the Missouri River." U.S. Army Corps of Engineers, 2010. http://digitalcommons.unl.edu/usarmyceomaha/78.

Domínguez-Rodrigo, M. "Is the 'Savanna Hypothesis' a Dead Concept for Explaining the Emergence of Earliest Hominins?" *Current Anthropology* 55, no. 1 (February 2014): 59–81.

Dryer, Mark P., and A. J. Sandvol. *Recovery Plan for the Pallid Sturgeon (*Scaphirhynchus albus*).* Denver: U.S. Fish and Wildlife Service, 1993.

Duchardt, Courtney J., Jeffrey L. Beck, and David J. Augustine. "Mountain Plover Habitat Selection and Nest Survival in Relation to Weather Variability and Spatial Attributes of Black-Tailed Prairie Dog Disturbance." *Condor* 122, no. 1 (2020): 1–15.

Dundas, Robert G. "Quaternary Records of the Dire Wolf, *Canis dirus*, in North and South America." *Boreas* 28, no. 3 (January 1999): 375–85.

Dyke, Arthur S. "Late Quaternary Vegetation History of Northern North America Based on Pollen, Macrofossil, and Faunal Remains." *Géographie Physique et Quaternaire* 59, nos. 2–3 (April 4, 2007): 211–62.

Eads, David A., Dean E. Biggins, Jonathan Bowser, Kristina Broerman, Travis M. Livieri, Eddie Childers, Phillip Dobesh, and Randall L. Griebel. "Evaluation of Five Pulicides to Suppress Fleas on Black-Tailed Prairie Dogs: Encouraging Long-Term Results with Systemic 0.005% Fipronil." *Vector-Borne and Zoonotic Diseases* 19, no. 6 (2019): 400–406.

Eads, David A., Dean E. Biggins, Jonathan Bowser, Janet C. McAllister, Randall L. Griebel, Eddie Childers, Travis M. Livieri, Cristi Painter, Lindsey Sterling Krank, and Kristy Bly. "Resistance to Deltamethrin in Prairie Dog (*Cynomys ludovicianus*) Fleas in the Field and in the Laboratory." *Journal of Wildlife Diseases* 54, no. 4 (October 1, 2018): 745–54.

Eads, David A., Dean E. Biggins, Travis M. Livieri, and Joshua J. Millspaugh. "American Badgers Selectively Excavate Burrows in Areas Used by Black-Footed Ferrets: Implications for Predator Avoidance." *Journal of Mammalogy* 94, no. 6 (December 16, 2013): 1364–70.

Eads, David A., Travis M. Livieri, Phillip Dobesh, Eddie Childers, Lauren E. Noble, Michele C. Vasquez, and Dean E. Biggins. "Fipronil Pellets Reduce Flea Abundance on Black-Tailed Prairie Dogs: Potential Tool for Plague Management and Black-Footed Ferret Conservation." *Journal of Wildlife Diseases* 57, no. 2 (2021): 434–38.

Ecological Solutions Group. *Riparian Health Assessment of the Charles M. Russell National Wildlife Refuge and UL Bend National Wildlife Refuge: Analysis of Change from 1995 1996, and 1997 to 2009.* Prepared for USDI Fish and Wildlife Service, Contract GS10F0002V. Stevensville MT: Ecological Solutions Group, September 2010.

Elbroch, L. Mark, Patrick E. Lendrum, Jesse Newby, Howard Quigley, and Daniel J. Thompson. "Recolonizing Wolves Influence the Realized Niche of Resident Cougars." *Zoological Studies* 54 (2015): 41.

Elias, S. A., and J. Brigham-Grette. "Glaciations | Late Pleistocene Glacial Events in Beringia." In *Encyclopedia of Quaternary Science*, edited by Scott Elias, 191–201. Amsterdam: Elsevier, 2013.

Ellenberger, John H., and A. Eugene Byrne. *Population Status and Trends of Big Game and Greater Sage-Grouse in Southeast Montana and Northeast Wyoming.* Prepared for National Wildlife Federation and Natural Resources Defense Council. Palisade CO: Wildlife Management Consultants and Associates, July 2015.

Emslie, Steven D. "Fossil Passerines from the Early Pliocene of Kansas and the Evolution of Songbirds in North America." *Auk* 124, no. 1 (January 1, 2007): 85–95.

Eng, Margaret L., Bridget J. M. Stutchbury, and Christy A. Morrissey. "A Neonicotinoid Insecticide Reduces Fueling and Delays Migration in Songbirds." *Science* 365, no. 6458 (September 13, 2019): 1177–80.

English, Joseph M., and Stephen T. Johnston. "The Laramide Orogeny: What Were the Driving Forces?" *International Geology Review* 46, no. 9 (September 2004): 833–38.

Environmental Working Group. "EWG's Farm Subsidy Database." Accessed February 9, 2022. https://farm.ewg.org/index.php.

Erb, John, Carolin Humpal, and Barry Sampson. *Distribution and Abundance of Wolves in Minnesota, 2017–2018.* Minneapolis: Minnesota Department of Natural Resources, n.d.

Ericson, Diann. "The Legislative and Political Development of the Montana Department of Fish, Wildlife, and Parks (1895–1921): A Case of Cultural Heritage." Master's thesis, University of Montana, 1994.

Ernest, S. K. Morgan, and James H. Brown. "Homeostasis and Compensation: The Role of Species and Resources in Ecosystem Stability." *Ecology* 82, no. 8 (August 2001): 2118–32.

Ersmark, Erik, Cornelya F. C. Klütsch, Yvonne L. Chan, Mikkel-Holger S. Sinding, Steven R. Fain, Natalia A. Illarionova, Mattias Oskarsson, et al. "From the Past to the Present: Wolf Phylogeography and Demographic History Based on the Mitochondrial Control Region." *Frontiers in Ecology and Evolution* 4 (December 2, 2016): article 134.

Evans, David L. "Status Reports on Twelve Raptors." Special Scientific Report—Wildlife. Washington DC: U.S. Fish and Wildlife Service, 1982.

Fahrig, Lenore. "Effects of Habitat Fragmentation on Biodiversity." *Annual Review of Ecology, Evolution, and Systematics* 34, no. 1 (November 2003): 487–515.

Fargione, Joseph E., Thomas R. Cooper, David J. Flaspohler, Jason Hill, Clarence Lehman, David Tilman, Tim McCoy, Scott McLeod, Erik J. Nelson, and Karen S. Oberhauser. "Bioenergy and Wildlife: Threats and Opportunities for Grassland Conservation." *BioScience* 59, no. 9 (October 2009): 767–77.

Farm Service Agency. *Conservation Reserve Program Statistics.* U.S. Department of Agriculture. Accessed October 2021. https://www.fsa.usda.gov/programs-and-services/conservation-programs/reports-and-statistics/conservation-reserve-program-statistics/index.

Fastovsky, David E., and Antoine Bercovici. "The Hell Creek Formation and Its Contribution to the Cretaceous–Paleogene Extinction: A Short Primer." *Cretaceous Research* 57 (January 2016): 368–90.

Federal Register. "Endangered and Threatened Wildlife and Plants: Determination of Endangered Status for the Pallid Sturgeon." *Federal Register* 55, no. 173 (September 6, 1990): 36641–47.

Feldman, James W. "Public Opinion, the Leopold Report, and the Reform of Federal Predator Control Policy." *Human-Wildlife Interactions* 1, no. 1 (Spring 2007): 112–24.

Figueirido, B., C. M. Janis, J. A. Perez-Claros, M. De Renzi, and P. Palmqvist. "Cenozoic Climate Change Influences Mammalian Evolutionary Dynamics." *Proceedings of the National Academy of Sciences* 109, no. 3 (January 17, 2012): 722–27.

Figueirido, B., A. Martín-Serra, Z. J. Tseng, and C. M. Janis. "Habitat Changes and Changing Predatory Habits in North American Fossil Canids." *Nature Communications* 6, no. 1 (November 2015): 7976.

Fletcher, Robert S. "The End of the Open Range in Eastern Montana." *Mississippi Valley Historical Review* 16, no. 2 (September 1929): 188–211.

Flores, Dan L. *American Serengeti: The Last Big Animals of the Great Plains.* Lawrence: University Press of Kansas, 2016.

Flynn, Roger. "Daybreak on the Land: The Coming of Age of the Federal Land Policy and Management Act of 1976." *Vermont Law Review* 29, no. 3 (2005): 815–45.

Food and Agricultural Organization of the United Nations. "Livestock Systems." Accessed May 2022. https://www.fao.org/livestock-systems/global-distributions/sheep/en/.

Forister, Matthew L., Bruce Cousens, Joshua G. Harrison, Kayce Anderson, James H. Thorne, Dave Waetjen, Chris C. Nice, et al. "Increasing Neonicotinoid Use and the Declining Butterfly Fauna of Lowland California." *Biology Letters* 12, no. 8 (August 2016): 20160475.

Forrest, S. C., H. Strand, W. H. Haskins, C. Freese, J. Proctor, and E. Dinerstein. "Ocean of Grass: A Conservation Assessment for the Northern Great Plains." Bozeman MT: Northern Plains Conservation Network and World Wildlife Fund–U.S., 2004.

Forrest, Steve. "Getting the Story Right: A Response to Vermeire and Colleagues." *BioScience* 55, no. 6 (June 2005): 526–30.

Forrest, Steve, Dean E. Biggins, Louise Richardson, Tim W. Clark, Thomas M. Campbell III, Kathleen A. Fagerstone, and E. Tom Thorne. "Population Attributes for the Black-Footed Ferret (*Mustela nigripes*) at Meeteetse, Wyoming, 1981–1985." *Journal of Mammalogy* 69, no. 2 (May 1988): 261–73.

Fowler, Ada C., Richard L. Knight, T. Luke George, and Lowell C. McEwen. "Effects of Avian Predation on Grasshopper Populations in North Dakota Grasslands." *Ecology* 72, no. 5 (October 1991): 1775–81.

Frankham, Richard, Corey J. A. Bradshaw, and Barry W. Brook. "Genetics in Conservation Management: Revised Recommendations for the 50/500 Rules, Red List Criteria and Population Viability Analyses." *Biological Conservation* 170 (February 2014): 56–63.

Freese, Curtis H., Keith E. Aune, Delaney P. Boyd, James N. Derr, Steve C. Forrest, C. Cormack Gates, Peter J. P. Gogan, et al. "Second Chance for the Plains Bison." *Biological Conservation* 136, no. 2 (April 2007): 175–84.

Freese, Curtis H., Samuel D. Fuhlendorf, and Kyran Kunkel. "A Management Framework for the Transition from Livestock Production toward Biodiversity Conservation on Great Plains Rangelands." *Ecological Restoration* 32, no. 4 (December 2014): 358–63.

Freese, Curtis H., Kyran Kunkel, Damien Austin, and Betty Holder. *Bison Management Plan.* Bozeman MT: American Prairie Reserve, n.d.

Freilich, Jerome E., John M. Emlen, Jeffrey J. Duda, Carl Freeman, and Philip J. Cafaro. "Ecological Effects of Ranching: A Six-Point Critique." *BioScience* 53, no. 8 (August 2003): 759–65.

Friedman, Jannice, and Spencer C. H. Barrett. "A Phylogenetic Analysis of the Evolution of Wind Pollination in the Angiosperms." *International Journal of Plant Sciences* 169, no. 1 (January 2008): 49–58.

Frison, G. C. "Paleoindian Large Mammal Hunters on the Plains of North America." *Proceedings of the National Academy of Sciences* 95, no. 24 (November 24, 1998): 14576–83.

Froese, Duane, Mathias Stiller, Peter D. Heintzman, Alberto V. Reyes, Grant D. Zazula, André E. R. Soares, Matthias Meyer, et al. "Fossil and Genomic Evidence Constrains the Timing of Bison Arrival in North America." *Proceedings of the National Academy of Sciences* 114, no. 13 (March 28, 2017): 3457–62.

Fuhlendorf, Samuel D., Craig A. Davis, R. Dwayne Elmore, Laura E. Goodman, and Robert G. Hamilton. "Perspectives on Grassland Conservation Efforts: Should We Rewild to the Past or Conserve for the Future?" *Philosophical Transactions of the Royal Society B: Biological Sciences* 373, no. 1761 (December 5, 2018): 20170438.

Fuhlendorf, Samuel D., and David M. Engle. "Restoring Heterogeneity on Rangelands: Ecosystem Management Based on Evolutionary Grazing Patterns." *BioScience* 51, no. 8 (August 2001): 625–32.

Fuhlendorf, Samuel D., David M. Engle, R. Dwayne Elmore, Ryan F. Limb, and Terrence G. Bidwell. "Conservation of Pattern and Process: Developing an Alternative Paradigm of Rangeland Management." *Rangeland Ecology & Management* 65 (November 2012): 579–89.

Fuhlendorf, Samuel D., David M. Engle, Jay Kerby, and Robert Hamilton. "Pyric Herbivory: Rewilding Landscapes through the Recoupling of Fire and Grazing." *Conservation Biology* 23, no. 3 (June 2009): 588–98.

Fuhlendorf, Samuel D., Wade C. Harrell, David M. Engle, Robert G. Hamilton, Craig A. Davis, and David M. Leslie. "Should Heterogeneity Be the Basis for Conservation? Grassland Bird Response to Fire and Grazing." *Ecological Applications* 16, no. 5 (October 2006): 1706–16.

Fullerton, David. S., Roger B. Colton, Charles A. Bush, and Arthur W. Straub. *Map Showing Spatial and Temporal Relations of Mountain and Continental Glaciations on the Northern Plains, Primarily Northern Montana and Northwestern North Dakota.* U.S. Geological Survey, 2004.

Gable, Thomas D., Steve K. Windels, Mark C. Romanski, and Frank Rosell. "The Forgotten Prey of an Iconic Predator: A Review of Interactions between Grey Wolves *Canis lupus* and Beavers *Castor* spp." *Mammal Review* 48, no. 2 (April 2018): 123–38.

Galat, David L., Charles R. Berry, William M. Gardner, Jeff C. Hendrickson, Gerald E. Mestl, Greg J. Power, Clifton Stone, and Matthew R. Winston. "Spatiotemporal Patterns and Changes in Missouri River Fishes." *American Fisheries Society Symposium* 45 (2005): 249–91.

Garrott, R. K., K. Proffitt, J. Rotella, E. Flesch, E. Lula, C. Butler, B. Lowrey, J. T. Paterson, and J. DeVoe. *The Role of Disease, Habitat, Individual Condition, and Population Attributes on Bighorn Sheep Recruitment and Population Dynamics in Montana.* Final report for the Federal Aid in Wildlife Restoration Grant #W-159-R. Helena: Montana Fish, Wildlife & Parks, 2020.

Gaskin, John F., Erin Espeland, Casey D. Johnson, Diane L. Larson, Jane M. Mangold, Rachel A. McGee, Chuck Milner, et al. "Managing Invasive Plants on Great Plains Grasslands: A Discussion of Current Challenges." *Rangeland Ecology & Management* 78 (September 2021): 235–49.

Gates, Charles Cormack, Paul Jones, Michael Suitor, Andrew Jakes, Mark S. Boyce, Kyran Kunkel, and Kevin Wilson. "The Influence of Land Use and Fences on Habitat Effectiveness, Movements and Distribution of Pronghorn in the Grasslands of North America." In *Fencing for Conservation: Restoration of Evolutionary Potential or a Riposte to Threatening Processes*, edited by Michael J. Somers and Matthew Hayward, 277–98. New York: Springer, 2012.

Ge, Deyan, Zhixin Wen, Lin Xia, Zhaoqun Zhang, Margarita Erbajeva, Chengming Huang, and Qisen Yang. "Evolutionary History of Lagomorphs in Response to Global Environmental Change." *PLOS ONE* 8, no. 4 (April 3, 2013): e59668.

Geist, Valerius. *Buffalo Nation: History and Legend of the North American Bison.* Stillwater MN: Voyageur Press, 1998.

George, Kelly A., Kristina M. Slagle, Robyn S. Wilson, Steven J. Moeller, and Jeremy T. Bruskotter. "Changes in Attitudes toward Animals in the United States from 1978 to 2014." *Biological Conservation* 201 (2016): 237–42.

Gherghel, Iulian, and Ryan Andrew Martin. "Postglacial Recolonization of North America by Spadefoot Toads: Integrating Niche and Corridor Modeling to Study Species' Range Dynamics over Geologic Time." *Ecography* 43, no. 10 (October 2020): 1499–509.

Gibson, Polly P., and Julian D. Olden. "Ecology, Management, and Conservation Implications of North American Beaver (*Castor canadensis*) in Dryland Streams." *Aquatic Conservation: Marine and Freshwater Ecosystems* 24, no. 3 (June 2014): 391–409.

Gigliotti, Laura C., Marc R. Matchett, and David S. Jachowski. "Mountain Lions on the Prairie: Habitat Selection by Recolonizing Mountain Lions at the Edge of Their Range." *Restoration Ecology* 27, no. 5 (September 2019): 1032–40.

Gilbert, Clément, Anne Ropiquet, and Alexandre Hassanin. "Mitochondrial and Nuclear Phylogenies of Cervidae (Mammalia, Ruminantia): Systematics, Morphology, and Biogeography." *Molecular Phylogenetics and Evolution* 40, no. 1 (July 2006): 101–17.

Gill, Robert E., Jr., Pablo Canevari, and Eve H. Iversen. "Eskimo Curlew (*Numenius borealis*)." In *The Birds of North America*, edited by A. Poole and F. Gill, 1–27. Philadelphia: Birds of North America, 1998.

Gogan, Peter J. P., Nicholas C. Larter, James H. Shaw, and John E. Gross. "General Biology, Ecology and Demographics." In *American Bison: Status Survey and Conservation Guidelines 2010*, edited by Charles C. Gates, Curtis H. Freese, Peter J. P. Gogan, and Mandy Kotzman, 39–54. Gland, Switzerland: IUCN/SSC American Bison Specialist Group and International Union for Conservation of Nature, 2010.

Golding, Jessie D., and Victoria J. Dreitz. "Songbird Response to Rest-Rotation and Season-Long Cattle Grazing in a Grassland Sagebrush Ecosystem." *Journal of Environmental Management* 204, no. 1 (December 2017): 605–12.

Gordon, Greg. "Steamboats, Woodhawks, and War on the Upper Missouri River." *Montana, the Magazine of Western History*, Summer 2011, 31–47.

Government of Canada. "Canadian Forces Base Suffield National Wildlife Area." May 5, 2021. https://www.canada.ca/en/environment-climate-change/services/national-wildlife-areas/locations/canadian-forces-base-suffield.html.

———. "News Release." March 7, 2019. https://www.canada.ca/en/environment-climate-change/news/2019/03/the-governments-of-canada-and-manitoba-work-together-to-protect-nature-at-canadian-forces-base-shilo.html.

———. "Species at Risk Public Registry." Accessed December 1, 2021. https://www.canada.ca/en/environment-climate-change/services/species-risk-public-registry.html.

Governor's Office of Indian Affairs. "Tribal Nations." Accessed June 24, 2022. https://tribalnations.mt.gov/tribalnations.

Graul, Walter D., and Lois E. Webster. "Breeding Status of the Mountain Plover." *Condor* 78, no. 2 (1976): 265–67.

Grinnell, George Bird. "Zoological Report: List of Mammals and Birds." In *Report of the Reconnaissance from Carroll, Montana Territory, on the Upper Missouri River, to the Yellowstone National Park, and Return, Made in the Summer of 1875 by William Ludlow*. Washington DC: War Department, 1876.

Grinnell, Joseph, Harold C. Bryant, and Tracy I. Stores. *The Game Birds of California*. Berkeley: University of California Press, 1918.

Grisak, Grant. "Sickle Fin Chub." Montana Chapter of the American Fisheries Society, June 1998. https://units.fisheries.org/montana/science/species-of-concern/species-status/sicklefin-chub/.

Gunther, Kerry A., Rebecca R. Shoemaker, Kevin L. Frey, Mark A. Haroldson, Steven L. Cain, Frank T. van Manen, and Jennifer K. Fortin. "Dietary Breadth of Grizzly Bears in the Greater Yellowstone Ecosystem." *Ursus* 25, no. 1 (May 1, 2014): 60–72.

Guo, Qinfeng, Daniel B. Thompson, Thomas J. Valone, and James H. Brown. "The Effects of Vertebrate Granivores and Folivores on Plant Community Structure in the Chihuahuan Desert." *Oikos* 73, no. 2 (June 1995): 251–59.

Gurney, Ashley B., and A. R. Brooks. "Grasshoppers of the Mexicanus Group, Genus *Melanoplus* (Orthoptera: Acrididae)." *Proceedings of the United States National Museum* 110, no. 3416 (1959): 1–93.

Gustafson, Eric P. *An Early Pliocene North American Deer:* Bretzia pseudalces, *Its Osteology, Biology, and Place in Cervid History.* Eugene: Museum of Natural History, University of Oregon, May 2015.

Gutmann, Myron P. "Beyond Social Science History: Population and Environment in the US Great Plains." *Social Science History* 42, no. 1 (Spring 2018): 1–27.

Guy, Christopher S., Hilary B. Treanor, Kevin M. Kappenman, Eric A. Scholl, Jason E. Ilgen, and Molly A. H. Webb. "Broadening the Regulated-River Management Paradigm: A Case Study of the Forgotten Dead Zone Hindering Pallid Sturgeon Recovery." *Fisheries* 40, no. 1 (January 2, 2015): 6–14.

Haines, Francis. "The Northward Spread of Horses among the Plains Indians." *American Anthropologist* 40, no. 3 (July 1938): 429–37.

Halbert, Natalie D., and James N. Derr. "Patterns of Genetic Variation in US Federal Bison Herds." *Molecular Ecology* 17, no. 23 (December 2008): 4963–77.

Hämäläinen, Pekka. "Horse." Encyclopedia of the Great Plains. University of Nebraska–Lincoln, 2011. http://plainshumanities.unl.edu/encyclopedia/doc/egp.na.038.xml.

Hanebury, Louis R., and Dean E. Biggins. "A History of Searches for Black-Footed Ferrets." In *Recovery of the Black-Footed Ferret—Progress and Continuing Challenges,* Scientific Investigations Report 2005-5293, edited by J. E. Roelle, B. J. Miller, J. L. Godbey, and D. E. Biggins, 47–65. U.S. Geological Survey, 2006.

Hansen, Michael C. "Desert Bighorn Sheep: Another View." *Wildlife Society Bulletin* 10 (1982): 133–40.

Hanski, Ilkka, Timo Pakkala, Mikko Kuussaari, and Guangchun Lei. "Metapopulation Persistence of an Endangered Butterfly in a Fragmented Landscape." *Oikos* 72, no. 1 (1995): 21–28.

Hanski, Ilkka, Torsti Schulz, Swee Chong Wong, Virpi Ahola, Annukka Ruokolainen, and Sami P. Ojanen. "Ecological and Genetic Basis of Metapopulation Persistence of the Glanville Fritillary Butterfly in Fragmented Landscapes." *Nature Communications* 8 (February 2017): 14504.

Harris, G. S. Thirgood, J. G. C. Hopcraft, J. P. G. M. Cromsigt, and J. Berger. "Global Decline in Aggregated Migrations of Large Terrestrial Mammals." *Endangered Species Research* 7 (April 21, 2009): 55–76.

Hawley, Jason E., Paul W. Rego, Adrian P. Wydeven, Michael K. Schwartz, Tabitha C. Viner, Roland Kays, Kristine L. Pilgrim, and Jonathan A. Jenks. "Long-Distance Dispersal of a Subadult Male Cougar from South Dakota to Connecticut Documented with DNA Evidence." *Journal of Mammalogy* 97, no. 5 (May 17, 2016): 1435–40.

Haxton, T. J., and T. M. Cano. "A Global Perspective of Fragmentation on a Declining Taxon—the Sturgeon (Acipenseriformes)." *Endangered Species Research* 31 (October 31, 2016): 203–10.

Hayden, F. V. "On the Geology and Natural History of the Upper Missouri." *Transactions of the American Philosophical Society* 12, no. 1 (1862): 1–218.

Hedrick, P. W. "Conservation Genetics and North American Bison (*Bison bison*)." *Journal of Heredity* 100, no. 4 (July 1, 2009): 411–20.

Heffelfinger, James R., Bart W. O'Gara, Christine M. Janis, and Randall Babb. "A Bestiary of Ancestral Antilocaprids." *Proceedings of the 20th Biennial Pronghorn Workshop* 20 (2002): 87–111.

Heintzman, Peter D., Duane Froese, John W. Ives, André E. R. Soares, Grant D. Zazula, Brandon Letts, Thomas D. Andrews, et al. "Bison Phylogeography Constrains Dispersal and Viability of the Ice Free Corridor in Western Canada." *Proceedings of the National Academy of Sciences* 113, no. 29 (July 19, 2016): 8057–63.

Heist, Ed, Meredith Bartron, Jeff Kalie, and Robb Leary. *Population Genetics Management Plan for Pallid Sturgeon in the Upper Missouri River Basin*. Final report for Western Power Authority. Carbondale: Southern Illinois University, Fisheries and Illinois Aquaculture Center, January 30, 2013.

Herbaugh, Hunter. "New Fish Bypass Channel Working as Intended." *Glendive Ranger Review*, June 9, 2022. https://www.rangerreview.com/new-fish-bypass -channel-working-intended.

Hill, Christopher L. "Stratigraphic and Geochronologic Contexts of Mammoth (*Mammuthus*) and Other Pleistocene Fauna, Upper Missouri Basin (Northern Great Plains and Rocky Mountains), U.S.A." *Quaternary International* 142–43 (January 2006): 87–106.

Hill, Matthew E., Matthew G. Hill, and Christopher C. Widga. "Late Quaternary Bison Diminution on the Great Plains of North America: Evaluating the Role of Human Hunting versus Climate Change." *Quaternary Science Reviews* 27, nos. 17–18 (September 2008): 1752–71.

Hilton, Eric J., and Lance Grande. "Review of the Fossil Record of Sturgeons, Family Acipenseridae (Actinopterygii: Acipenseriformes), from North America." *Journal of Paleontology* 80, no. 4 (July 2006): 672–83.

Hobbs, N. Thompson, Dan L. Baker, George D. Bear, and David C. Bowden. "Ungulate Grazing in Sagebrush Grassland: Mechanisms of Resource Competition." *Ecological Applications* 6, no. 1 (February 1996): 200–17.

Holechek, Jerry L., Hatim M. E. Geli, Andres F. Cibils, and Mohammed N. Sawalhah. "Climate Change, Rangelands, and Sustainability of Ranching in the Western United States." *Sustainability* 12 (June 2020): 4942.

Holmquist, Luke. "Native Endangered Species Recovery (Pallid Sturgeon)." Permit report. In *Upper Basin Pallid Sturgeon Workgroup Annual Report for Work Completed in 2018*, 20–36. Upper Missouri River Basin Pallid Sturgeon Workgroup, 2019. http://www.pallidsturgeon.org/wp-content/uploads/2019/09/2019-Upper-Basin -Pallid-Sturgeon-Workgroup-Annual-Report-for-work-completed-in-2018.pdf.

Holmquist, Luke, Christopher S. Guy, Anne Tews, David J. Trimpe, and Molly A. H. Webb. "Reproductive Ecology and Movement of Pallid Sturgeon in the Upper Missouri River, Montana." *Journal of Applied Ichthyology* 35, no. 5 (October 2019): 1069–83.

Holmquist, Luke, Christopher S. Guy, Anne Tews, and Molly A. H. Webb. "First Maturity and Spawning Periodicity of Hatchery-Origin Pallid Sturgeon in the Upper Missouri River above Fort Peck Reservoir, Montana." *Journal of Applied Ichthyology* 35, no. 1 (February 2019): 138–48.

Holroyd, Geoffrey L., Helen E. Trefry, and Jason M. Duxbury. "Winter Destinations and Habitats of Canadian Burrowing Owls." *Journal of Raptor Research* 44, no. 4 (December 2010): 294–99.

Horn, Thomas C. *Fort Peck Game Range: Narrative Report: May, June, June, August 1942.* Fort Peck Game Range MT, 1942.

———. *Fort Peck Game Range: Narrative Report: January–April 1945.* Fort Peck National Wildlife Refuge, 1945.

———. *Fort Peck Game Range: Narrative Report: September–December 1946.* Fort Peck National Wildlife Refuge, 1947.

Hornaday, William. Letter to Professor Spencer F. Baird, Secretary of the Smithsonian, about Collecting Bison Specimens for Exhibit, dated December 21, 1886. Smithsonian Archives. Smithsonian Institution, December 21, 1886. https://siarchives.si.edu/history/featured-topics/stories/letter-dated-december-21-1886-professor-spencer-f-baird-secretary-smithsoni.

———. *Save the Sage Grouse from Extinction; a Demand from Civilization to the Western States.* Permanent Wild Life Protection Fund Bulletin no. 6. New York: New York Zoological Park, December 1, 1916. https://www.biodiversitylibrary.org/bibliography/156927.

Howard, J. G., C. Lynch, R. M. Santymire, P. E. Marinari, and D. E. Wildt. "Recovery of Gene Diversity Using Long-Term Cryopreserved Spermatozoa and Artificial Insemination in the Endangered Black-Footed Ferret: Black-Footed Ferret Gene Restoration." *Animal Conservation* 19, no. 2 (April 2016): 102–11.

Howe, H. F., and J. S. Brown. "Effects of Birds and Rodents on Synthetic Tallgrass Communities." *Ecology* 80, no. 5 (July 1999): 1776–81.

Hundertmark, Kris J., Gerald F. Shields, Irina G. Udina, R. Terry Bowyer, Alexei A. Danilkin, and Charles C. Schwartz. "Mitochondrial Phylogeography of Moose (*Alces alces*): Late Pleistocene Divergence and Population Expansion." *Molecular Phylogenetics and Evolution* 22, no. 3 (March 2002): 375–87.

Inman, B. K., K. Podruzny, A. Nelson, D. Boyd, T. Parks, T. Smucker, M. Ross, et al. *Montana Gray Wolf Conservation and Management 2019 Annual Report.* Helena: Montana Fish, Wildlife & Parks, 2020.

InterTribal Buffalo Council. "InterTribal Buffalo Council." Accessed August 2021. https://itbcbuffalonation.org.

Islam, Md. Aminul, Sharmin Aqter Rony, Mohammad Bozlur Rahman, Mehmet Ulas Cinar, Julio Villena, Muhammad Jasim Uddin, and Haruki Kitazawa.

"Improvement of Disease Resistance in Livestock: Application of Immunogenomics and CRISPR/Cas9 Technology." *Animals* 10, no. 12 (November 28, 2020): 2236.

IUCN. *North America's Northern Great Plains.* Accessed June 2022. https://www.iucn.org/sites/default/files/import/downloads/us_size_n_great_plains_final_note_apr_1.pdf.

Jachowski, David, Roland Kays, Andrew Butler, Anne M. Hoylman, and Matthew E. Gompper. "Tracking the Decline of Weasels in North America." *PLOS ONE* 16, no. 7 (2021): e0254387.

Jaeger, Matthew. "Sauger." Montana Chapter of the American Fisheries Society, January 2004. https://units.fisheries.org/montana/science/species-of-concern/species-status/sauger/.

Jakes, Andrew F., C. Cormack Gates, Nicholas J. DeCesare, Paul F. Jones, Joshua F. Goldberg, Kyran E. Kunkel, and Mark Hebblewhite. "Classifying the Migration Behaviors of Pronghorn on Their Northern Range: Migration Behaviors of Pronghorn." *Journal of Wildlife Management* 82, no. 6 (August 2018): 1229–42.

Jalkotzy, Peter, and Sebastian Ossenbrug. "Summer Food Habits of Wolves in Wood Buffalo National Park, Summer 1980." *Canadian Field-Naturalist* 12, no. 4 (1982): 157–67.

Janis, Christine. "An Evolutionary History of Browsing and Grazing Ungulates." In *The Ecology of Browsing and Grazing,* edited by I. J. Gordon and H. H. T. Prins, 21–45. Ecological Studies 195. Berlin: Springer-Verlag, 2008.

Janis, Christine, John Damuth, and Jessica M. Theodor. "The Origins and Evolution of the North American Grassland Biome: The Story from the Hoofed Mammals." *Palaeogeography, Palaeoclimatology, Palaeoecology* 177, nos. 1–2 (January 2002): 183–98.

Janis, Christine, and Patricia Brady Wilhelm. "Were There Mammalian Pursuit Predators in the Tertiary? Dances with Wolf Avatars." *Journal of Mammalian Evolution* 1, no. 2 (June 1993): 103–25.

Jiang, Dechun, Sebastian Klaus, Ya-Ping Zhang, David M. Hillis, and Jia-Tang Li. "Asymmetric Biotic Interchange across the Bering Land Bridge between Eurasia and North America." *National Science Review* 6 (March 15, 2019): 739–45.

Jimenez, Michael D., Edward E. Bangs, Diane K. Boyd, Douglas W. Smith, Scott A. Becker, David E. Ausband, Susannah P. Woodruff, Elizabeth H. Bradley, Jim Holyan, and Kent Laudon. "Wolf Dispersal in the Rocky Mountains, Western United States: 1993–2008." *Journal of Wildlife Management* 81, no. 4 (2017): 581–92.

Joern, Anthony. "Experimental Study of Avian Predation on Coexisting Grasshopper Populations (Orthoptera: Acrididae) in a Sandhills Grassland." *Oikos* 46, no. 2 (April 1986): 243–49.

Johnson, Donald R. "Returns of the American Fur Company, 1835–1839." *Journal of Mammalogy* 50, no. 4 (1969): 836–39.

Johnson, Randy D., Jonathan A. Jenks, Stephanie A. Tucker, and David T. Wilckens. "Mountain Lion (*Puma concolor*) Population Characteristics in the Little

Missouri Badlands of North Dakota." *American Midland Naturalist* 181, no. 2 (May 2019): 207–24.

Johnson, Warren E., Eduardo Eizirik, Jill Pecon-Slattery, William J. Murphy, Agostinho Antunes, Emma Teeling, and Stephen J. O'Brien. "The Late Miocene Radiation of Modern Felidae: A Genetic Assessment." *Science* 311, no. 5757 (January 6, 2006): 73–77.

Joly, D. O., and F. Messier. "Testing Hypotheses of Bison Population Decline (1970–1999) in Wood Buffalo National Park: Synergism between Exotic Disease and Predation." *Canadian Journal of Zoology* 82, no. 7 (July 2004): 1165–76.

Jones, Lizzie P., Samuel T. Turvey, Dario Massimino, and Sarah K. Papworth. "Investigating the Implications of Shifting Baseline Syndrome on Conservation." *People and Nature* 2, no. 4 (December 2020): 1131–44.

Jones, Paul F., Andrew F. Jakes, Daniel R. Eacker, and Mark Hebblewhite. "Annual Pronghorn Survival of a Partially Migratory Population." *Journal of Wildlife Management* 84, no. 6 (August 2020): 1114–26.

Jones, Paul F., Andrew F. Jakes, Andrew C. Telander, Hall Sawyer, Brian H. Martin, and Mark Hebblewhite. "Fences Reduce Habitat for a Partially Migratory Ungulate in the Northern Sagebrush Steppe." *Ecosphere* 10, no. 7 (July 2019): e02782.

Jones, Stephanie L. "Sprague's Pipit (*Anthus spragueii*) Conservation Plan." Denver: U.S. Fish and Wildlife Service, 2010.

Jordan, G. R., E. J. Heist, P. J. Braaten, A. J. DeLonay, P. Hartfield, D. P. Herzog, K. M. Kappenman, and M. A. H. Webb. "Status of Knowledge of the Pallid Sturgeon (*Scaphirhynchus albus* Forbes and Richardson, 1905)." Supplement, *Journal of Applied Ichthyology* 32, no. s1 (December 2016): s191–207.

Journals of the Lewis & Clark Expedition. University of Nebraska–Lincoln. Accessed August 2021. https://lewisandclarkjournals.unl.edu/journals.

Justice-Allen, Anne, and Kerrie Anne Loyd. "Mortality of Western Burrowing Owls (*Athene cunicularia hypugaea*) Associated with Brodifacoum Exposure." *Journal of Wildlife Diseases* 53, no. 1 (January 2017): 165–69.

Kahn, Peter H., Rachel L. Severson, and Jolina H. Ruckert. "The Human Relation with Nature and Technological Nature." *Current Directions in Psychological Science* 18, no. 1 (2009): 37–42.

Kamler, Jan F., Warren B. Ballard, Rickey L. Gilliland, Patrick R. Lemons II, and Kevin Mote. "Impacts of Coyotes on Swift Foxes in Northwestern Texas." *Journal of Wildlife Management* 67, no. 2 (April 2003): 317–23.

Kauffman, Matthew J., Holly Copeland, Eric Cole, Matt Cuzzocreo, Sarah Dewey, Julien Fattebert, Jeff Gagnon, et al. *Ungulate Migrations of the Western United States*. Vol. 1. U.S. Geological Survey, 2020.

Kay, Charles E. "Were Native People Keystone Predators? A Continuous-Time Analysis of Wildlife Observations Made by Lewis and Clark in 1804–6." *Canadian Field-Naturalist* 121, no. 1 (January–March 2007): 1–16.

Kendall, Katherine C., Jeffrey B. Stetz, David A. Roon, Lisette P. Waits, John B. Boulanger, and David Paetkau. "Grizzly Bear Density in Glacier National Park, Montana." *Journal of Wildlife Management* 72, no. 8 (December 2010): 1693–705.

Kimoto, Chiho, Sandra J. DeBano, Robbin W. Thorp, Sujaya Rao, and William P. Stephen. "Investigating Temporal Patterns of a Native Bee Community in a Remnant North American Bunchgrass Prairie Using Blue Vane Traps." *Journal of Insect Science* 12, no. 108 (September 2012): 1–23.

Kleinhesselink, Andrew R., and Peter B. Adler. "The Response of Big Sagebrush (*Artemisia tridentata*) to Interannual Climate Variation Changes across Its Range." *Ecology* 99, no. 5 (May 2018): 1139–49.

Klemm, Toni, and David D. Briske. "Retrospective Assessment of Beef Cow Numbers to Climate Variability throughout the U.S. Great Plains." *Rangeland Ecology & Management* 78, no. 1 (September 2021): 273–80.

Klicka, John, Robert M. Zink, and K. Winker. "Longspurs and Snow Buntings: Phylogeny and Biogeography of a High-Latitude Clade (*Calcarius*)." *Molecular Phylogenetics and Evolution* 26, no. 2 (February 2003): 165–75.

Klungle, M. M., and M. W. Baxter, 2005. *Lower Missouri and Yellowstone Rivers Pallid Sturgeon Study*. Report submitted to Western Area Power Administration. Fort Peck: Montana Fish, Wildlife & Parks, 2005.

Knapp, Alan K., John M. Blair, John M. Briggs, Scott L. Collins, David C. Hartnett, Loretta C. Johnson, and E. Gene Towne. "The Keystone Role of Bison in North American Tallgrass Prairie." *BioScience* 49, no. 1 (January 1999): 39–50.

Knopf, Fritz L. *Mountain Plover Studies: Pawnee National Grasslands, 1985–2007*. U.S. Forest Service, October 13, 2008. https://www.denveraudubon.org/wp-content/uploads/2011/03/Knopf2008_PNG_Plover_Studies.pdf.

———. *Prairie Legacies—Birds*. Washington DC: Island Press, 1996.

Knopf, Fritz L., R. Roy Johnson, Terrell Rich, Fred B. Samson, and Robert C. Szaro. "Conservation of Riparian Ecosystems in the United States." *Wilson Bulletin* 100, no. 2 (June 1988): 272–84.

Knopf, Fritz L., and Jeffery R. Rupert. "Use of Cultivated Fields by Breeding Mountain Plovers in Colorado." *Studies in Avian Biology* 19 (1999): 81–86.

Knopf, Fritz L., and Fred B. Samson, eds. *Ecology and Conservation of Great Plains Vertebrates*. Ecological Studies 125. New York: Springer, 1997.

Knowles, Craig J., and Pamela R. Knowles. *Mountain Plover Population Trends in Central and Northeastern Montana*. Prepared for Bureau of Land Management, Fanwood Foundation, and Montana Fish, Wildlife & Parks. Townsend MT: FaunaWest Wildlife Consultants, July 17, 2019.

Knowles, Craig J., Jonathan D. Proctor, and Steven C. Forrest. "Black-Tailed Prairie Dog Abundance and Distribution in the Great Plains Based on Historic and Contemporary Information." *Great Plains Research* 12 (Fall 2002): 219–54.

Knowlton, Frederick F., Eric M. Gese, and Michael M. Jaeger. "Coyote Depredation Control: An Interface between Biology and Management." *Journal of Range Management* 52, no. 5 (September 1999): 398–412.

Koch, Elers. "Big Game in Montana from Early Historical Records." *Journal of Wildlife Management* 5, no. 4 (October 1941): 357–70.

Koch, Paul L., and Anthony D. Barnosky. "Late Quaternary Extinctions: State of the Debate." *Annual Review of Ecology, Evolution, and Systematics* 37, no. 1 (December 2006): 215–50.

Koepfli, Klaus-Peter, Kerry A. Deere, Graham J. Slater, Colleen Begg, Keith Begg, Lon Grassman, Mauro Lucherini, Geraldine Veron, and Robert K. Wayne. "Multigene Phylogeny of the Mustelidae: Resolving Relationships, Tempo and Biogeographic History of a Mammalian Adaptive Radiation." *BMC Biology* 6 (December 2008): 10.

Kohl, Michel T., Paul R. Krausman, Kyran Kunkel, and David M. Williams. "Bison versus Cattle: Are They Ecologically Synonymous?" *Rangeland Ecology & Management* 66, no. 6 (November 2013): 721–31.

Kohl, Michel T., Terry A. Messmer, Benjamin A. Crabb, Michael R. Guttery, David K. Dahlgren, Randy T. Larsen, Shandra N. Frey, Sherry Liguori, and Rick J. Baxter. "The Effects of Electric Power Lines on the Breeding Ecology of Greater Sage-Grouse." *PLOS ONE* 14, no. 1 (January 30, 2019): e0209968.

Kohl, Michel T., Daniel R. Stahler, Matthew C. Metz, James D. Forester, Matthew J. Kauffman, Nathan Varley, P. J. White, Douglas W. Smith, and Daniel R. MacNulty. "Diel Predator Activity Drives a Dynamic Landscape of Fear." *Ecological Monographs* 88, no. 4 (November 2018): 638–52.

Konrad, Paul M. *Effects of Management Practices on Grassland Birds—Merlin.* Jamestown ND: Northern Prairie Wildlife Research Center, 2004.

Kotliar, Natasha B., Bruce W. Baker, April D. Whicker, and Glenn Plumb. "A Critical Review of Assumptions about the Prairie Dog as a Keystone Species." *Environmental Management* 24, no. 2 (September 1, 1999): 177–92.

Krehbiel, Robb. *Bighorns, Big Risks: Identifying Risks Posed by Domestic Sheep.* National Wildlife Federation. Accessed January 24, 2022. https://www.nwf.org/~/media/pdfs/Regional/Northern-Rockies/BighornsBigRisk.ashx.

Krummel, J. R., R. H. Gardner, G. Sugihara, R. V. O'Neill, and P. R. Coleman. "Landscape Patterns in a Disturbed Environment." *Oikos* 48, no. 3 (March 1987): 321–24.

Kubo, Tai, Manabu Sakamoto, Andrew Meade, and Chris Venditti. "Transitions between Foot Postures Are Associated with Elevated Rates of Body Size Evolution in Mammals." *Proceedings of the National Academy of Sciences* 116, no. 7 (February 12, 2019): 2618–23.

Kunkel, Kyran, Tim Vosburgh, and Hugh Robinson. *Ecology of Cougars (*Puma concolor*) in North-Central Montana: Distribution, Resource Selection, Dynamics, Harvest, and Conservation Design.* Final report for U.S. Fish and Wildlife Service. Bozeman MT: World Wildlife Fund, April 2012.

Lacelle, Denis, David A. Fisher, Stéphanie Coulombe, Daniel Fortier, and Roxanne Frappier. "Buried Remnants of the Laurentide Ice Sheet and Connections to Its Surface Elevation." *Scientific Reports* 8, no. 1 (December 2018): 13286.

Laliberte, Andrea S., and William J. Ripple. "Wildlife Encounters by Lewis and Clark: A Spatial Analysis of Interactions between Native Americans and Wildlife." *Bio-Science* 53, no. 10 (October 2003): 994–1003.

Lamb, Clayton T., Adam T. Ford, Bruce N. McLellan, Michael F. Proctor, Garth Mowat, Lana Ciarniello, Scott E. Nielsen, and Stan Boutin. "The Ecology of Human-Carnivore Coexistence." *Proceedings of the National Academy of Sciences* 117, no. 30 (July 28, 2020): 17876–83.

Lark, Tyler J. "Protecting Our Prairies: Research and Policy Actions for Conserving America's Grasslands." *Land Use Policy* 97 (September 2020): 104727.

Lark, Tyler J., Seth A. Spawn, Matthew Bougie, and Holly K. Gibbs. "Cropland Expansion in the United States Produces Marginal Yields at High Costs to Wildlife." *Nature Communications* 11, no. 1 (December 2020): 4295.

LaRue, Michelle A., Clayton K. Nielsen, Mark Dowling, Bob Wilson, Harley Shaw, and Charles Anderson Jr. "Cougars Are Recolonizing the Midwest: Analysis of Cougar Confirmations during 1990–2008." *Journal of Wildlife Management* 76, no. 7 (September 2012): 1364–69.

Le Gall, Marion, Rick Overson, and Arianne Cease. "A Global Review on Locusts (Orthoptera: Acrididae) and Their Interactions with Livestock Grazing Practices." *Frontiers in Ecology and Evolution* 7 (July 23, 2019): 263.

Lee, Corwin M., and H. Duane Hampton. *Life and Death at the Mouth of the Musselshell: Montana Territory, 1868–1872: Featuring the Diary of C. M. Lee, Gunsmith, Merchant.* Stevensville MT: Stoneydale Press, 2011.

Legislative Environmental Quality Council. *Pittman-Robertson Funding.* Accessed October 2021. https://leg.mt.gov/content/Publications/Environmental/2014 -pittman-robertson-brochure.pdf.

Leite, Rafael N., Sergios-Orestis Kolokotronis, Francisca C. Almeida, Fernanda P. Werneck, Duke S. Rogers, and Marcelo Weksler. "In the Wake of Invasion: Tracing the Historical Biogeography of the South American Cricetid Radiation (Rodentia, Sigmodontinae)." *PLOS ONE* 9, no. 6 (June 25, 2014): e100687.

Leopold, Aldo. "Review of the Wolves of North America." *Journal of Forestry* 42 (1944): 928–29.

———. *Round River.* New York: Oxford University Press, 1993.

———. *A Sand County Almanac, and Sketches Here and There.* New York: Oxford University Press, 1949.

Lesica, Peter, and Stephen V. Cooper. "Choosing Native Species for Restoring Crested Wheatgrass Fields on the Great Plains of Northeast Montana." *American Midland Naturalist* 181, no. 2 (May 6, 2019): 327–34.

Lesica, Peter, and Scott Miles. "Beavers Indirectly Enhance the Growth of Russian Olive and Tamarisk along Eastern Montana Rivers." *Western North American Naturalist* 64, no. 1 (2004): 93–100.

Li, Yijia, Ruiqing Miao, and Madhu Khanna. "Neonicotinoids and Decline in Bird Biodiversity in the United States." *Nature Sustainability* 3, no. 12 (December 2020): 1027–35.

Licht, Daniel S. *Ecology and Economics of the Great Plains.* Lincoln: University of Nebraska Press, 1997.

Lightfoot, David C., Ana D. Davidson, Dara G. Parker, Lucina Hernández, and John W. Laundré. "Bottom-Up Regulation of Desert Grassland and Shrubland Rodent Communities: Implications of Species-Specific Reproductive Potentials." *Journal of Mammalogy* 93, no. 4 (2012): 1017–28.

Limb, Ryan F., Samuel D. Fuhlendorf, David M. Engle, John R. Weir, R. Dwayne Elmore, and Terrence G. Bidwell. "Pyric-Herbivory and Cattle Performance in Grassland Ecosystems." *Rangeland Ecology & Management* 64, no. 6 (November 2011): 659–63.

Lipsey, Marisa K., David E. Naugle, Joshua Nowak, and Paul M. Lukacs. "Extending Utility of Hierarchical Models to Multi-Scale Habitat Selection." Edited by Thomas Albright. *Diversity and Distributions* 23, no. 7 (July 2017): 783–93.

Livieri, Travis M., Steven C. Forrest, Marc R. Matchett, and Stewart W. Breck. "Conserving Endangered Black-Footed Ferrets: Biological Threats, Political Challenges, and Lessons Learned." In *Imperiled: The Encyclopedia of Conservation,* edited by Dominick A. DellaSala and Michael I. Goldstein, 458–70. Elsevier, 2022. B978-0-12-821139-7.00061-1.

Lloyd, John D., and Thomas E. Martin. "Reproductive Success of Chestnut-Collared Longspurs in Native and Exotic Grassland." *Condor* 107, no. 2 (May 1, 2005): 363–74.

Lockhart, J. Michael, E. Tom Thorne, and Donald R. Gober. "A Historical Perspective on Recovery of the Black-Footed Ferret and the Biological and Political Challenges Affecting Its Future." In *Recovery of the Black-Footed Ferret—Progress and Continuing Challenges,* U.S. Geological Survey Scientific Investigations Report, edited by J. E. Roelle, B. J. Miller, and D. E. Biggins, 6–19. U.S. Geological Survey, 2006.

Lockwood, Jeffrey A. "The Death of the Super Hopper." *High Country News,* February 3, 2003.

———. "The Fate of the Rocky Mountain Locust, *Melanoplus spretus* Walsh: Implications for Conservation Biology." *Terrestrial Arthropod Reviews* 3, no. 2 (2010): 129–60.

———. *Locust: The Devastating Rise and Mysterious Disappearance of the Insect That Shaped the American Frontier.* 1st ed. New York: Basic Books, 2004.

———. "Taxonomic Status of the Rocky Mountain Locust: Morphometric Comparisons of *Melanoplus spretus* (Walsh) with Solitary and Migratory *Melanoplus sanguinipes* (F.)." *Canadian Entomologist* 121, no. 12 (December 1989): 1103–9.

Lockwood, Jeffrey A., and Larry D. DeBrey. "A Solution for the Sudden and Unexplained Extinction of the Rocky Mountain Grasshopper (Orthoptera: Acrididae)." *Environmental Entomology* 19, no. 5 (October 1, 1990): 1194–205.

Lockwood, Jeffrey A., L. D. DeBrey, C. D. Thompson, C. M. Love, R. A. Nunamaker, S. R. Shaw, S. P. Schell, and C. R. Bomar. "Preserved Insect Fauna of Glaciers of Fremont County in Wyoming: Insights into the Ecology of the

Extinct Rocky Mountain Locust." *Environmental Entomology* 23, no. 2 (April 1994): 220–35.

Longrich, N. R., T. Tokaryk, and D. J. Field. "Mass Extinction of Birds at the Cretaceous-Paleogene (K-Pg) Boundary." *Proceedings of the National Academy of Sciences* 108, no. 37 (September 13, 2011): 15253–57.

Lott, Dale F. *American Bison: A Natural History.* Organisms and Environments 6. Berkeley: University of California Press, 2002.

Lovegrove, B. G., and M. O. Mowoe. "The Evolution of Mammal Body Sizes: Responses to Cenozoic Climate Change in North American Mammals." *Journal of Evolutionary Biology* 26, no. 6 (June 2013): 1317–29.

Lukacs, Paul M., Michael S. Mitchell, Mark Hebblewhite, Bruce K. Johnson, Heather Johnson, Matthew Kauffman, Kelly M. Proffitt, et al. "Factors Influencing Elk Recruitment across Ecotypes in the Western United States." *Journal of Wildlife Management* 82, no. 4 (May 2018): 698–710.

Lute, Michelle L., and Neil H. Carter. "Are We Coexisting with Carnivores in the American West?" *Frontiers in Ecology and Evolution* 8 (March 6, 2020): 48.

MacArthur, Robert H., and Edward O. Wilson. *The Theory of Island Biogeography.* Princeton NJ: Princeton University Press, 2001.

Mace, R. D., and T. Chilton-Radandt. *Black Bear Harvest Research and Management in Montana: Final Report.* Helena: Montana Fish, Wildlife & Parks, 2011.

Mackie, Richard J., David F. Pac, Kenneth L. Hamlin, and Gary L. Dusek. *Ecology and Management of Mule Deer and White-Tailed Deer in Montana.* Helena: Montana Fish, Wildlife & Parks, 1998.

MacNulty, Daniel R., Aimee Tallian, Daniel R. Stahler, and Douglas W. Smith. "Influence of Group Size on the Success of Wolves Hunting Bison." *PLOS ONE* 9, no. 11 (November 12, 2014): e112884.

Malhi, Yadvinder, Christopher E. Doughty, Mauro Galetti, Felisa A. Smith, Jens-Christian Svenning, and John W. Terborgh. "Megafauna and Ecosystem Function from the Pleistocene to the Anthropocene." *Proceedings of the National Academy of Sciences* 113, no. 4 (January 26, 2016): 838–46.

Malone, Michael P., Richard B. Roeder, and William L. Lang. *Montana: A History of Two Centuries.* Rev. ed. Seattle: University of Washington Press, 1991.

Mantilla, Gregory P. Wilson, Stephen G. B. Chester, William A. Clemens, Jason R. Moore, Courtney J. Sprain, Brody T. Hovatter, William S. Mitchell, Wade W. Mans, Roland Mundil, and Paul R. Renne. "Earliest Palaeocene Purgatorrids and the Initial Radiation of Stem Primates." *Royal Society Open Science* 8 (2021): 210050.

Mao, Julie S., Mark S. Boyce, Douglas W. Smith, Francis J. Singer, David J. Vales, John M. Vore, and Evelyn H. Merrill. "Habitat Selection by Elk before and after Wolf Reintroduction in Yellowstone National Park." *Journal of Wildlife Management* 69, no. 4 (October 2005): 1691–707.

Markewicz, Lauren, and Parks Canada. *Like Distant Thunder: Canada's Bison Conservation Story.* Parks Canada, 2017.

Marotz, B. L., and M. S. Lorang. "Pallid Sturgeon Larvae: The Drift Dispersion Hypothesis." *Journal of Applied Ichthyology* 34, no. 2 (April 2018): 373–81.

Martin, Brian. *Assessing and Implementing Ranch Management Planning at Scale through the Matador Ranch Grassbank.* Helena: The Nature Conservancy, November 23, 2015.

Martin, Jeff M., Jim I. Mead, and Perry S. Barboza. "Bison Body Size and Climate Change." *Ecology and Evolution* 8, no. 9 (May 2018): 4564–74.

Martin, P. S. "The Discovery of America: The First Americans May Have Swept the Western Hemisphere and Decimated Its Fauna within 1000 Years." *Science* 179, no. 4077 (March 9, 1973): 969–74.

Martin, Paul S., and Christine R. Szuter. "War Zones and Game Sinks in Lewis and Clark's West." *Conservation Biology* 13, no. 1 (February 1999): 36–45.

Martin, Stephen M. "Polygyny in the Bobolink: Habitat Quality and the Adaptive Complex." PhD diss., Oregon State University, 1971.

Martinka, C. J. "Mortality of Northern Montana Pronghorns in a Severe Winter." *Journal of Wildlife Management* 31, no. 1 (January 1967): 159–64.

Matchett, Marc R., David A. Eads, Jennifer Cordova, Travis M. Livieri, Holly Hicks, and Dean E. Biggins. "Flea Control on Prairie Dogs with Fipronil Bait Pellets: Potential Plague Mitigation Tool for Rapid Field Application and Wildlife Conservation." *Journal of Wildlife Diseases* (forthcoming).

Mattison, Ray H. "The Upper Missouri River Fur Trade: Its Methods of Operation." *Nebraska History* 42 (1961): 1–28.

Mattson, David J., and Troy Merrill. "Extirpations of Grizzly Bears in the Contiguous United States, 1850–2000." *Conservation Biology* 16, no. 4 (August 2002): 1123–36.

McCabe, Richard E., Henry M. Reeves, and Bart W. O'Gara. *Prairie Ghost: Pronghorn and Human Interaction in Early America.* Sebastopol: University Press of Colorado, 2010.

McHorse, Brianna K., Andrew A. Biewener, and Stephanie E. Pierce. "The Evolution of a Single Toe in Horses: Causes, Consequences, and the Way Forward." *Integrative and Comparative Biology* 59, no. 3 (September 1, 2019): 638–55.

McKean, Andrew. "Finding a Pulse for Pallids." *Montana Outdoors,* June 2021, 35–41.

McKinstry, Mark C., Paul Caffrey, and Stanley H. Anderson. "The Importance of Beaver to Wetland Habitats and Waterfowl in Wyoming." *Journal of the American Water Resources Association* 37, no. 6 (December 2001): 1571–77.

McLellan, Bruce, and David C. Reiner. "A Review of Bear Evolution." *Bears: Their Biology and Management* 9, no. 1 (1994): 85–96.

McMahon, T. E., and W. M. Gardner. "Status of Sauger in Montana." *Intermountain Journal of Sciences* 7, no. 1 (March 2001): 1–21.

McTee, Michael, Brian Hiller, and Philip Ramsey. "Free Lunch, May Contain Lead: Scavenging Shot Small Mammals." *Journal of Wildlife Management* 83, no. 6 (August 2019): 1466–73.

Meachen, Julie A., Alexandria L. Brannick, and Trent J. Fry. "Extinct Beringian Wolf Morphotype Found in the Continental U.S. Has Implications for Wolf

Migration and Evolution." *Ecology and Evolution* 6, no. 10 (May 2016): 3430–38.

Meachen, Julie A., Adrianna C. Janowicz, Jori E. Avery, and Rudyard W. Sadleir. "Ecological Changes in Coyotes (*Canis latrans*) in Response to the Ice Age Megafaunal Extinctions." *PLOS ONE* 9, no. 12 (December 31, 2014): e116041.

Mech, L. David, and Shannon Barber-Meyer. "Yellowstone Wolf (*Canis lupus*) Density Predicted by Elk (*Cervus elaphus*) Biomass." *Canadian Journal of Zoology* 93, no. 6 (June 2015): 499–502.

Meiri, Meirav, Adrian M. Lister, Matthew J. Collins, Noreen Tuross, Ted Goebel, Simon Blockley, Grant D. Zazula, et al. "Faunal Record Identifies Bering Isthmus Conditions as Constraint to End-Pleistocene Migration to the New World." *Proceedings of the Royal Society B: Biological Sciences* 281, no. 1776 (February 7, 2014): 20132167.

Melquist, Wayne E., and Maurice G. Hornocker. "Ecology of River Otters in West Central Idaho." *Wildlife Monographs* 83 (April 1983): 3–60.

Melquist, Wayne E., Paul J. Polechla, and Dale Toweill. "River Otter, *Lutra canadensis*." In *Wild Mammals of North America: Biology, Management, and Conservation*, 2nd ed., edited by George A. Feldhamer, Bruce C. Thompson, and Joseph A. Chapman, 708–34 Baltimore: Johns Hopkins University Press, 2003.

Meltzer, David J. "Overkill, Glacial History, and the Extinction of North America's Ice Age Megafauna." *Proceedings of the National Academy of Sciences* 117, no. 46 (November 17, 2020): 28555–63.

Merdith, Andrew S., Simon E. Williams, Alan S. Collins, Michael G. Tetley, Jacob A. Mulder, Morgan L. Blades, Alexander Young, et al. "Extending Full-Plate Tectonic Models into Deep Time: Linking the Neoproterozoic and the Phanerozoic." *Earth-Science Reviews* 214 (March 2021): 103477.

Michener, James A. *Centennial*. 1st ed. New York: Random House, 1974.

Miller, Brian, Barb Dugelby, Dave Foreman, Carlos Martinez del Rio, Reed Noss, Mike Phillips, Rich Reading, John Terborgh, and Louisa Willcox. "The Importance of Large Carnivores to Healthy Ecosystems." *Endangered Species Update* 18, no. 5 (2001): 202–10.

Miller, Brian, and Richard P. Reading. "Challenges to Black-Footed Ferret Recovery: Protecting Prairie Dogs." *Western North American Naturalist* 72, no. 2 (August 2012): 228–40.

Miller, Brian, Richard P. Reading, Dean E. Biggins, James K. Detling, Steve C. Forrest, John L. Hoogland, Jody Javersak, et al. "Prairie Dogs: An Ecological Review and Current Politics." *Journal of Wildlife Management* 71, no. 8 (November 2007): 2801–10.

Miller, Phillip S. *Reintroduction of Swift Fox (Vulpes velox) to Fort Belknap Indian Reservation, Montana: An Assessment of Options Using Population Viability Analysis. Draft Report*. Apple Valley MN: IUCN/SSC Conservation Planning Specialist Group, 2020.

Millspaugh, Joshua, Jesse DeVoe, and Kelly Proffitt. *Pronghorn Movement and Population Ecology*. Annual interim report. Federal Aid in Wildlife Restoration

Great w-176-R, September 2021. https://fwp.mt.gov/binaries/content/assets/fwp/conservation/pronghorn/p-r-report---montana-pronghorn-project---2021.pdf.

Mineau, Pierre, and Mélanie Whiteside. "Pesticide Acute Toxicity Is a Better Correlate of U.S. Grassland Bird Declines Than Agricultural Intensification." *PLOS ONE* 8, no. 2 (February 20, 2013): e57457.

Mitchell, John E., and Richard H. Hart. "The Winter of 1886–87: The Death Knell of Open Range." *Rangelands* 9, no. 1 (1987): 3–8.

Mitchell, Kieren J., Sarah C. Bray, Pere Bover, Leopoldo Soibelzon, Blaine W. Schubert, Francisco Prevosti, Alfredo Prieto, Fabiana Martin, Jeremy J. Austin, and Alan Cooper. "Ancient Mitochondrial DNA Reveals Convergent Evolution of Giant Short-Faced Bears (Tremarctinae) in North and South America." *Biology Letters* 12, no. 4 (April 30, 2016): 20160062.

Monello, Ryan J., Nathan L. Galloway, Jenny G. Powers, Sally A. Madsen-Bouterse, William H. Edwards, Mary E. Wood, Katherine I. O'Rourke, and Margaret A. Wild. "Pathogen-Mediated Selection in Free-Ranging Elk Populations Infected by Chronic Wasting Disease." *Proceedings of the National Academy of Sciences* 114, no. 46 (November 14, 2017): 12208–12.

Montana Department of Transportation. *The Little Rocky Mountains.* Accessed September 2021. https://www.mdt.mt.gov/travinfo/docs/roadsigns/littleRockies.pdf.

Montana Field Guide. *Animals.* Accessed October 2021. https://fieldguide.mt.gov/default.aspx.

Montana Fish, Wildlife & Parks. *Bison Conservation and Management in Montana.* Final Programmatic Environmental Impact Statement. Helena: Montana Fish, Wildlife & Parks, 2019.

———. *Chronic Wasting Disease in Montana: Frequently Asked Questions.* Helena: Montana Fish, Wildlife & Parks, 2021.

———. *Draft Montana Swift Fox Conservation Strategy.* Helena: Montana Fish, Wildlife & Parks, 2019.

———. *Montana Bighorn Sheep Conservation Strategy.* Helena: Montana Fish, Wildlife & Parks, 2010.

———. *Montana Fish, Wildlife and Parks' White-Nose Syndrome Surveillance and Management.* Accessed July 19, 2022. https://fwp.mt.gov/binaries/content/assets/fwp/aboutfwp/legislature/wns-fact-sheet.pdf.

———. *Montana Statewide Elk Management Plan 2004.* Helena: Montana Fish, Wildlife & Parks, 2004.

———. *Montana Wolf Conservation and Management Planning Document.* Rocky Mountain Wolf Recovery Annual Reports. Helena: Montana Fish, Wildlife & Parks, 2002.

———. "Pronghorn (Antelope)" Accessed January 2021. https://fwp.mt.gov/conservation/wildlife-management/antelope.

Montana State Library. "Conservation Easements." Accessed October 2021. https://mslservices.mt.gov/geographic_information/data/datalist/datalist_Details.aspx?did=%7b9d69b262-b766-11e2-bc7e-f23c91aec05e%7d.

Morgan, Rosalind Grace. "Beaver Ecology / Beaver Mythology." PhD diss., University of Alberta, 1991.

Morrison, Carl D., Mark S. Boyce, and Scott E. Nielsen. "Space-Use, Movement and Dispersal of Sub-adult Cougars in a Geographically Isolated Population." *PeerJ* 3, no. 2 (August 6, 2015): e1118.

Mosely, Jeffrey C., and John G. Mundinger. "History and Status of Wild Ungulate Populations on the Northern Yellowstone Range." *Rangelands* (December 2018): 189–201.

Mule Deer Working Group. *2021 Range-Wide Status of Black-Tailed and Mule Deer.* Boise: Western Association of Fish and Wildlife Agencies, 2021.

Murray, Alison M., Donald B. Brinkman, David G. DeMar, and Gregory P. Wilson. "Paddlefish and Sturgeon (Chondrostei: Acipenseriformes: Polyodontidae and Acipenseridae) from Lower Paleocene Deposits of Montana, U.S.A." *Journal of Vertebrate Paleontology* 40, no. 2 (March 3, 2020): e1775091.

Nadeau, M. Steven, Nicholas J. DeCesare, Douglas G. Brimeyer, Eric J. Bergman, B. Harris, Kent R. Hersey, Kari K. Huebner, Patrick E. Matthews, and Timothy P. Thomas. "Status and Trends of Moose Populations and Hunting Opportunity in the Western United States." *Alces* 53 (2017): 99–112.

Nagler, Pamela L., Edward P. Glenn, Catherine S. Jarnevich, and Patrick B. Shafroth. "Distribution and Abundance of Saltcedar and Russian Olive in the Western United States." *Critical Reviews in Plant Sciences* 30, no. 6 (November 2011): 508–23.

Naidoo, Robin, L. Chris Weaver, Greg Stuart-Hill, and Jo Tagg. "Effect of Biodiversity on Economic Benefits from Communal Lands in Namibia." *Journal of Applied Ecology* 48, no. 2 (April 2011): 310–16.

Naiman, Robert J., Carol A. Johnston, and James C. Kelley. "Alteration of North American Streams by Beaver." *BioScience* 38, no. 11 (December 1988): 753–62.

National Centers for Environmental Information. "National Climatic Extremes Committee (NCEC)." Accessed October 2021. https://www.ncdc.noaa.gov/extremes/ncec/records.

National Park Service. "Bison Wallows: What's Wallowing All About?" Accessed November 26, 2021. https://www.nps.gov/articles/bison-bellow-1-28-16.htm.

———. "NPspecies." Accessed February 20, 2022. https://irma.nps.gov/npspecies/.

National Research Council (U.S.), ed. *The Missouri River Ecosystem: Exploring the Prospects for Recovery.* Washington DC: National Academy Press, 2002.

NAWPA Committee. *Conservation in North America: An Analysis of Land-Based Conservation in Canada, Mexico, and the United States by NAWPA Agencies.* North American Intergovernmental Committee on Cooperation for Wilderness and Protected Area Conservation, 2016. http://nawpacommittee.org/wp-content/uploads/2016/08/Conservation-in-North-America.pdf.

Nelson, E. W. *Report of Chief of Bureau of Biological Survey.* Washington DC: Biological Survey, U.S. Department of Agriculture, September 12, 1923.

Nelson, Fred, and Rosie Cooney, "Communities Hold the Key to Expanding Conservation Impact in Africa." *Crossroads* (blog), October 12, 2018. https://www.iucn

.org/crossroads-blog/201810/communities-hold-key-expanding-conservation
-impact-africa.

Nenninger, Heather R., and Nicola Koper. "Effects of Conventional Oil Wells on
Grassland Songbird Abundance Are Caused by Presence of Infrastructure, Not
Noise." *Biological Conservation* 218 (February 2018): 124–33.

Newmark, William D. "Extinction of Mammal Populations in Western North American National Parks." *Conservation Biology* 9, no. 3 (June 1995): 512–26.

Newton, Rebecca E., Jason D. Tack, John C. Carlson, Marc R. Matchett, Pat J. Fargey,
and David Naugle. "Longest Sage-Grouse Migratory Behavior Sustained by
Intact Pathway." *Journal of Wildlife Management* 81, no. 6 (2017): 962–72.

Niemuth, N. D., B. Wangler, J. J. LeBrun, D. Dewald, S. Larson, T. Schwagler, C. W.
Bradbury, R. D. Pritchert, and R. Iovanna. "Conservation Planning for Polli-
nators in the U.S. Great Plains: Considerations of Context, Treatments, and
Scale." *Ecosphere* 12, no. 7 (2021): e03556.

North Dakota Game and Fish Department. *Status of Mountain Lion Management
in North Dakota, 2021.* Bismarck: North Dakota Game and Fish Department,
October 2021.

Northern Great Plains Steppe Ecoregional Planning Team. *Ecoregional Planning in
the Northern Great Plains Steppe.* The Nature Conservancy, February 5, 1999.
https://www.conservationgateway.org/ConservationPlanning/SettingPriorities/
EcoregionalReports/Documents/ngps_final_feb99.pdf.

Noss, Reed F., and Allen Cooperrider. *Saving Nature's Legacy: Protecting and Restoring Biodiversity.* Washington DC: Island Press, 1994.

Noss, Reed F., Howard B. Quigley, Maurice G. Hornocker, Troy Merrill, and Paul C.
Paquet. "Conservation Biology and Carnivore Conservation in the Rocky Mountains." *Conservation Biology* 10, no. 4 (August 1996): 949–63.

Obbard, Martyn E., James G. Jones, Robert Newman, Annie Booth, Andrew J. Sat-
terthwaite, and Greg Linscombe. "Furbearer Harvests in North America." In
Wild Furbearer Management and Conservation in North America, edited by
Milan Novak, 1007–34. Toronto: Ontario Trapper's Association, 1987.

O'Connor, Rory C., Jeffrey H. Taylor, and Jesse B. Nippert. "Browsing and Fire
Decreases Dominance of a Resprouting Shrub in Woody Encroached Grassland." *Ecology* 101, no. 2 (2020): e02935.

O'Donovan, Sean A., Suzanne M. Budge, Keith A. Hobson, Allicia P. Kelly, and
Andrew E. Derocher. "Intrapopulation Variability in Wolf Diet Revealed Using
a Combined Stable Isotope and Fatty Acid Approach." *Ecosphere* 9, no. 9 (September 2018): e02420.

Ofstad, Endre Grüner, Ivar Herfindal, Erling Johan Solberg, and Bernt-Erik Sæther.
"Home Ranges, Habitat and Body Mass: Simple Correlates of Home Range Size
in Ungulates." *Proceedings of the Royal Society B: Biological Sciences* 283, no. 1845
(December 28, 2016): 20161234.

Olimb, Sarah K., Adam P. Dixon, Emmalee Dolfi, Ryan Engstrom, and Kate Anderson. "Prairie or Planted? Using Time-Series NDVI to Determine Grassland Characteristics in Montana." *GeoJournal* 83, no. 4 (August 2018): 819–34.

Olson, David M., Eric Dinerstein, Eric D. Wikramanayake, Neil D. Burgess, George V. N. Powell, Emma C. Underwood, Jennifer A. D'amico, et al. "Terrestrial Ecoregions of the World: A New Map of Life on Earth." *BioScience* 51, no. 11 (2001): 933–38.

Olson, Lucretia E., John R. Squires, Robert J. Oakleaf, Zachary P. Wallace, and Patricia L. Kennedy. "Predicting Above-Ground Density and Distribution of Small Mammal Prey Species at Large Spatial Scales." *PLOS ONE* 12, no. 5 (May 17, 2017): e0177165.

Osborne, Colin P., and Lawren Sack. "Evolution of c_4 Plants: A New Hypothesis for an Interaction of CO_2 and Water Relations Mediated by Plant Hydraulics." *Philosophical Transactions of the Royal Society B: Biological Sciences* 367, no. 1588 (February 19, 2012): 583–600.

Ott, Jacqueline P., Brice B. Hanberry, Mona Khalil, Mark W. Paschke, Max Post van der Burg, and Anthony J. Prenni. "Energy Development and Production in the Great Plains: Implications and Mitigation Opportunities." *Rangeland Ecology & Management* 78, no. 1 (September 2021): 257–72.

Parks Canada. "Grasslands National Park of Canada Management Plan, 2022." 2022. https://www.pc.gc.ca/en/pn-np/sk/grasslands/info/plan/plan-2022.

Parton, William J., Myron P. Gutmann, and Dennis Ojima. "Long-Term Trends in Population, Farm Income, and Crop Production in the Great Plains." *BioScience* 57, no. 9 (October 1, 2007): 737–47.

Patterson, Brent R., Norman W. S. Quinn, Earl F. Becker, and Derek B. Meier. "Estimating Wolf Densities in Forested Areas Using Network Sampling of Tracks in Snow." *Wildlife Society Bulletin* 32, no. 3 (September 2004): 938–47.

Patterson, Kristine B., and Thomas Runge. "Smallpox and the Native American." *American Journal of the Medical Sciences* 323, no. 4 (April 2002): 216–22.

Pauli, Jonathan N., and Steven W. Buskirk. "Risk-Disturbance Overrides Density Dependence in a Hunted Colonial Rodent, the Black-Tailed Prairie Dog *Cynomys ludovicianus*: Risk-Disturbance and Density Dependence in the Black-Tailed Prairie Dog." *Journal of Applied Ecology* 44, no. 6 (June 16, 2007): 1219–30.

Pauly, Daniel. "Anecdotes and the Shifting Baseline Syndrome of Fisheries." *Trends in Ecology and Evolution* 10, no. 10 (October 1995): 430.

Penn, Justin L., Curtis Deutsch, Jonathan L. Payne, and Erik A. Sperling. "Temperature-Dependent Hypoxia Explains Biogeography and Severity of End-Permian Marine Mass Extinction." *Science* 362, no. 6419 (December 7, 2018): eaat1327.

Perkin, Joshuah, and Keith B. Gido. "Stream Fragmentation Thresholds for a Reproductive Guild of Great Plains Fishes." *Fisheries* 38, no. 8 (2011): 371–83.

Perri, Angela R., Kieren J. Mitchell, Alice Mouton, Sandra Álavarez-Carretero, Arden Hulme-Beaman, James Haile, Alexandra Jameison, et al. "Dire Wolves Were the Last of an Ancient New World Canid Lineage." *Nature* 591, no. 7848 (January 2021): 87–91.

Perri, Angela R., Chris Widga, Dennis Lawler, Terrance Martin, Thomas Loebel, Kenneth Farnsworth, Luci Kohn, and Brent Buenger. "New Evidence of the

Earliest Domestic Dogs in the Americas." *American Antiquity* 84, no. 1 (December 26, 2018): 68–87.

Peterson, Rolf O., John A. Vucetich, Joseph M. Bump, and Douglas W. Smith. "Trophic Cascades in a Multicausal World: Isle Royale and Yellowstone." *Annual Review of Ecology and Systematics* 45 (November 2014): 325–45.

Pettingill, Olin Sewall, Jr. *A Guide to Bird Finding West of the Mississippi*. New York: Oxford University Press, 1953.

Picton, Harold D., and Terry N. Lonner. *Montana's Wildlife Legacy: Decimation to Restoration*. Bozeman MT: Media Works, 2008.

Pires, Mathias M., Daniele Silvestro, and Tiago B. Quental. "Continental Faunal Exchange and the Asymmetrical Radiation of Carnivores." *Proceedings of the Royal Society B: Biological Sciences* 282, no. 1817 (October 22, 2015): 20151952.

Pleszczynska, W. K. "Microgeographic Prediction of Polygyny in the Lark Bunting." *Science* 201, no. 4359 (September 1978): 935–37.

Pokorny, Monica, and Jane Mangold. *Montana's Noxious Weeds*. Bozeman: Montana State University Extension, 2012.

Pollock, M. M., G. M. Lewallen, K. Woodruff, C. E. Jordan, and J. M. Castro. *The Beaver Restoration Guidebook: Working with Beaver to Restore Streams, Wetlands, and Floodplains*. Version 2.01. Portland: U.S. Fish and Wildlife Service, 2018. https://www.fws.gov/media/beaver-restoration-guidebook.

Polziehn, Renee O., Curtis Strobeck, Jane Sheraton, and Robin Beech. "Bovine MtDNA Discovered in North American Bison Populations." *Conservation Biology* 9, no. 6 (December 1995): 1638–38.

Pool, Duane B., Arvind O. Panjabi, Alberto Macias-Duarte, and Deanna M. Solhjem. "Rapid Expansion of Croplands in Chihuahua, Mexico Threatens Declining North American Grassland Bird Species." *Biological Conservation* 170 (February 2014): 274–81.

Poor, Erin E., Andrew Jakes, Colby Loucks, and Mike Suitor. "Modeling Fence Location and Density at a Regional Scale for Use in Wildlife Management." *PLOS ONE* 9, no. 1 (January 8, 2014): e83912.

Popper, Deborah E., and Frank Popper. "The Buffalo Commons: Its Antecedents and Their Implications." *Online Journal of Rural Research & Policy* 1, no. 6 (January 1, 2006): 1–26.

———. "The Great Plains: From Dust to Dust." *Planning* 53, no. 12 (1987): 12–18.

Population Reference Bureau. "How Many People Have Ever Lived on Earth?" May 18, 2021. https://www.prb.org/articles/how-many-people-have-ever-lived-on-earth/.

Potter, Ben A., James F. Baichtal, Alwynne B. Beaudoin, Lars Fehren-Schmitz, C. Vance Haynes, Vance T. Holliday, Charles E. Holmes, et al. "Current Evidence Allows Multiple Models for the Peopling of the Americas." *Science Advances* 4, no. 8 (August 2018): eaat5473.

Poulin, Ray G., and L. Danielle Todd. "Sex and Nest Stage Differences in the Circadian Foraging Behaviors of Nesting Burrowing Owls." *Condor* 108, no. 4 (November 1, 2006): 856–64.

Proctor, Jonathan. "A GIS Model for Identifying Potential Black-Tailed Prairie Dog Habitat in the Northern Great Plains Shortgrass Prairie." Master's thesis, University of Montana, 1998.

Proffitt, Kelly M., Robert Garrott, Justin A. Gude, Mark Hebblewhite, Benjamin Jimenez, J. Terrill Paterson, and Jay Rotella. "Integrated Carnivore-Ungulate Management: A Case Study in West-Central Montana." *Wildlife Monographs* 206, no. 1 (November 2020): 1–28.

Protected Planet Report 2020. Last modified May 2021. https://livereport.protectedplanet .net.

Pulling, Albert Van S. *Fort Peck Game Range: Narrative Report: August–October, 1940*. Fort Peck MT: Fort Peck Game Range, 1940.

———. *Fort Peck Game Range: Narrative Report: May–August 1941*. Fort Peck MT: Fort Peck Game Range, 1941.

Raesly, E. J. "Status of River Otter Reintroduction Projects in the United States." *Wildlife Society Bulletin* 29 (2001): 856–62.

Ranglack, Dustin H., and Johan T. Du Toit. "Bison with Benefits: Towards Integrating Wildlife and Ranching Sectors on a Public Rangeland in the Western USA." *Oryx* 50, no. 3 (2016): 549–54.

Ratajczak, Zak, Scott L. Collins, John M. Blair, Sally E. Koerner, Allison M. Louthan, Melinda D. Smith, Jeffrey H. Taylor, and Jesse B. Nippert. "Reintroducing Bison Results in Long-Running and Resilient Increases in Grassland Diversity." *Proceedings of the National Academy of Sciences* 119, no. 36 (2022): e2210433119.

Rebollo, Salvador, Daniel G. Milchunas, Paul Staff, David J. Augustine, and Justin D. Derner. "Disproportionate Effects of Non-colonial Small Herbivores on Structure and Diversity of Grassland Dominated by Large Herbivores." *Oikos* 122, no. 12 (December 2013): 1757–67.

Redford, Kent H. "The Empty Forest." *BioScience* 42, no. 6 (June 1992): 412–22.

Reeves, Matthew C., Brice B. Hanberry, Hailey Wilmer, Nicole E. Kaplan, and William K. Lauenroth. "An Assessment of Production Trends on the Great Plains from 1984 to 2017." *Rangeland Ecology & Management* 78 (2021): 165–79.

Reid, Angela M., and Samuel D. Fuhlendorf. "Fire Management in the National Wildlife Refuge System: A Case Study of the Charles M. Russell National Wildlife Refuge, Montana." *Rangelands* (April 21, 2011): 17–23.

Renwick, W. H., S. V. Smith, J. D. Bartley, and R. W. Buddemeier. "The Role of Impoundments in the Sediment Budget of the Conterminous United States." *Geomorphology* 71, nos. 1–2 (October 2005): 99–111.

Retallack, Gregory J. "Cenozoic Paleoclimate on Land in North America." *Journal of Geology* 115, no. 3 (May 2007): 271–94.

Revive and Restore. "The Black-Footed Ferret Project." Accessed November 29, 2021. https://reviverestore.org/projects/black-footed-ferret/.

Richards, J. H., and M. M. Caldwell. "Hydraulic Lift: Substantial Nocturnal Water Transport between Soil Layers by *Artemisia tridentata* Roots." *Oecologia* 73, no. 4 (October 1987): 486–89.

Riley, Charles V. *Destructive Locusts: A Popular Consideration of a Few of the More Injurious Locusts (or "Grasshoppers") of the United States together with the Best Means of Destroying Them.* Division of Entomology Bulletin no. 25. Washington DC: U.S. Department of Agriculture, 1891.

———. *The Locust Plague in the United States.* Chicago: Rand McNally, 1877.

Riley, J. L., S. E. Green, and K. E. Brodribb. *A Conservation Blueprint for Canada's Prairies and Parklands.* Toronto: The Nature Conservancy of Canada, 2007.

Riley, Shawn. "Integration of Environmental, Biological, and Human Dimensions for Management of Mountain Lions (*Puma concolor*) in Montana." PhD diss., Cornell University, 1998.

Riley, Shawn, and Richard A. Malecki. "A Landscape Analysis of Cougar Distribution and Abundance in Montana, USA." *Environmental Management* 28, no. 3 (April 11, 2001): 317–23.

Ripple, William J., Aaron J. Wirsing, Christopher C. Wilmers, and Mike Letnic. "Widespread Mesopredator Effects after Wolf Extirpation." *Biological Conservation* 160 (April 2013): 70–79.

Roberge, Jean-Michel, and Per Angelstam. "Usefulness of the Umbrella Species Concept as a Conservation Tool." *Conservation Biology* 18, no. 1 (February 2004): 76–85.

Roberts, N. M., M. J. Lovallo, and S. M. Crimmins. "River Otter Status, Management, and Distribution in the United States: Evidence of Large-Scale Population Increase and Range Expansion." *Journal of Fish and Wildlife Management* 11, no. 1 (June 2020): 279–86.

Robinson, Hugh S., Toni Ruth, Justin A. Gude, David Choate, Rich DeSimone, Mark Hebblewhite, Kyran Kunkel, et al. "Linking Resource Selection and Mortality Modeling for Population Estimation of Mountain Lions in Montana." *Ecological Modelling* 312 (September 2015): 11–25.

Robinson, Michael J. *Predatory Bureaucracy: The Extermination of Wolves and the Transformation of the West.* Boulder: University Press of Colorado, 2005.

Rogowitz, Gordon L., and Michael L. Wolfe. "Intraspecific Variation in Life-History Traits of the White-Tailed Jackrabbit (*Lepus townsendii*)." *Journal of Mammalogy* 74, no. 4 (November 1991): 796–806.

Roosevelt, Theodore. *Hunting Trips on the Prairie and in the Mountains.* New York: Co-operative Publication Society, 1882.

Rosas, Claudia A., David M. Engle, James H. Shaw, and Michael W. Palmer. "Seed Dispersal by *Bison bison* in a Tallgrass Prairie." *Journal of Vegetation Science* 19, no. 6 (December 2008): 769–78.

Rosenberg, Kenneth V., Adriaan M. Dokter, Peter J. Blancher, John R. Sauer, Adam C. Smith, Paul A. Smith, Jessica C. Stanton, et al. "Decline of the North American Avifauna." *Science* 366, no. 6461 (October 4, 2019): 120–24.

Ross, Joseph V. H. "Managing the Public Rangelands: 50 Years since the Taylor Grazing Act." *Rangelands* 6, no. 4 (1984): 147–51.

Rowland, Mary M. *The Effects of Management Practices on Grassland Birds—Greater Sage-Grouse (Centrocercus urophasianus).* USGS Numbered Series. Professional paper. Reston VA: U.S. Geological Survey, 2019. http://pubs.er.usgs.gov/publication/pp1842B.

Ruth, Janet M. *Status Assessment and Conservation Plan for the Grasshopper Sparrow (Ammodramus savannarum).* Lakewood CO: U.S. Fish and Wildlife Service, 2015.

Sage, Jeremy, and Norma Nickerson. *Analyzing Economic and Social Opportunities and Challenges Related to Bison Conservation in Northeast Montana.* Missoula MT: Institute for Tourism & Recreation Research Publications, University of Montana, 2017.

Salis, Alexander T., Sarah C. E. Bray, Michael S. Y. Lee, Holly Heiniger, Ross Barnett, James A. Burns, Vladimir Doronichev, et al. "Lions and Brown Bears Colonized North America in Multiple Synchronous Waves of Dispersal across the Bering Land Bridge." *Molecular Ecology* (November 8, 2021): 16267.

Samson, Fred B., and Fritz L. Knopf, eds. *Prairie Conservation: Preserving North America's Most Endangered Ecosystem.* Washington DC: Island Press, 1996.

Samson, Fred B., Fritz L. Knopf, and Wayne Ostlie. "Great Plains Ecosystems: Past, Present, and Future." *Wildlife Society Bulletin* 32, no. 1 (2004): 6–15.

Samuels, Joshua X., L. Barry Albright, and Theodore J. Fremd. "The Last Fossil Primate in North America, New Material of the Enigmatic *Ekgmowechashala* from the Arikareean of Oregon." *American Journal of Physical Anthropology* 158, no. 1 (September 2015): 43–54.

Samuels, Joshua X., and Samantha S. B. Hopkins. "The Impacts of Cenozoic Climate and Habitat Changes on Small Mammal Diversity of North America." *Global and Planetary Change* 149 (February 2017): 36–52.

Sandler, Ronald L., Lisa Moses, and Samantha M. Wisely. "An Ethical Analysis of Cloning for Genetic Rescue: Case Study of the Black-Footed Ferret." *Biological Conservation* 257 (May 2021): 109118.

Santymire, R. M., E. V. Lonsdorf, C. M. Lynch, D. E. Wildt, P. E. Marinari, J. S. Kreeger, and J. G. Howard. "Inbreeding Causes Decreased Seminal Quality Affecting Pregnancy and Litter Size in the Endangered Black-Footed Ferret." *Animal Conservation* 22, no. 4 (August 2019): 331–40.

Saremi, Nedda F., Megan A. Supple, Ashley Byrne, James A. Cahill, Luiz Lehmann Coutinho, Love Dalén, Henrique V. Figueiró, et al. "Puma Genomes from North and South America Provide Insights into the Genomic Consequences of Inbreeding." *Nature Communications* 10, no. 1 (December 2019): 4769.

Sato, Jun J., Mieczyslaw Wolsan, Francisco J. Prevosti, Guillermo D'Elía, Colleen Begg, Keith Begg, Tetsuji Hosoda, Kevin L. Campbell, and Hitoshi Suzuki. "Evolutionary and Biogeographic History of Weasel-like Carnivorans (Musteloidea)." *Molecular Phylogenetics and Evolution* 63, no. 3 (June 2012): 745–57.

Sauer, John R., William A. Link, and James E. Hines. *The North American Breeding Bird Survey, Analysis Results 1966–2019.* U.S. Geological Survey, 2020.

Saunders, Aretas A. "A Preliminary List of the Birds of Gallatin County, Montana." *Auk* 28, no. 1 (January 1911): 26–49.

Sauquet, Hervé, Maria von Balthazar, Susana Magallón, James A. Doyle, Peter K. Endress, Emily J. Bailes, Erica Barroso de Morais, et al. "The Ancestral Flower of Angiosperms and Its Early Diversification." *Nature Communications* 8, no. 1 (December 2017): 16047.

Schechinger, Anne Weir, and Craig Cox. *"Retired" Sensitive Cropland: Here Today, Gone Tomorrow?* Washington DC: Environmental Working Group, June 2017.

Schrey, A. W., R. Boley, and E. J. Heist. "Hybridization between Pallid Sturgeon *Scaphirhynchus albus* and Shovelnose Sturgeon *Scaphirhynchus platorynchus*." *Journal of Fish Biology* 79, no. 7 (December 2011): 1828–50.

Schrey, A. W., and E. J. Heist. "Stock Structure of Pallid Sturgeon Analyzed with Microsatellite Loci." *Journal of Applied Ichthyology* 23, no. 4 (August 2007): 297–303.

Schullery, Paul, and Lee Whittlesey. *The Documentary Record of Wolves and Related Wildlife Species in the Yellowstone National Park Area Prior to 1882.* In *Wolves for Yellowstone? A Report to the United States Congress*, vol. 4, *Research and Analysis*, edited by John D. Varley and William G. Brewster, Yellowstone National Park WY: National Park Service, July 1992, 1-4-1-173.

Scott, J. Michael, Dale D. Goble, Aaron M. Haines, John A. Wiens, and Maile C. Neel. "Conservation-Reliant Species and the Future of Conservation." *Conservation Letters* 3, no. 2 (April 2010): 91–97.

Scott, M. L., G. T. Auble, M. D. Dixon, W. Carter Johnson, and L. A. Rabbe. "Long-Term Cottonwood Forest Dynamics along the Upper Missouri River, USA." *River Research and Applications* 29, no. 8 (October 2013): 1016–29.

Scott, Michael L., Susan K. Skagen, and Michael F. Merigliano. "Relating Geomorphic Change and Grazing to Avian Communities in Riparian Forests." *Conservation Biology* 17, no. 1 (February 2003): 284–96.

Seipel, Timothy F. "Plant Species Diversity in the Sagebrush Steppe of Montana." Master's thesis, Montana State University, October 2006.

Sells, Sarah N., Allison C. Keever, Michael S. Mitchell, Justin Gude, Kevin Podruzny, and Robert Inman. *Improving Estimation of Wolf Recruitment and Abundance, and Development of an Adaptive Harvest Management Program for Wolves in Montana.* Final report for Federal Aid in Wildlife Restoration Grant W-161-R-1. Helena: Montana Fish, Wildlife & Parks, December 2020.

Serheen, Christopher. "Grizzly Bear Recovery Plan." Missoula MT: U.S. Fish and Wildlife Service, September 10, 1993.

Severson, Keith, and Glenn Plumb. "Estimating Population Densities of Black-Tailed Prairie Dogs." *US National Park Service Research Station Annual Reports* 18 (January 1, 1994): 31–34.

Shaffer, Jill A., and Deborah A. Buhl. "Effects of Wind-Energy Facilities on Breeding Grassland Bird Distributions: Wind-Energy Effects on Grassland Birds." *Conservation Biology* 30, no. 1 (February 2016): 59–71.

Shaffer, Jill A., and John P. DeLong. *The Effects of Management Practices on Grass-land Birds—an Introduction to North American Grasslands and the Practices Used to Manage Grasslands and Grassland Birds.* USGS Numbered Series. Professional paper. Reston VA: U.S. Geological Survey, 2019. http://pubs.er.usgs .gov/publication/pp1842A.

Shaffer, Jill A., Lawrence D. Igl, Douglas H. Johnson, Marriah L. Sondreal, Christopher M. Goldade, Melvin P. Nenneman, Travis L. Wooten, and Betty R. Euliss. *The Effects of Management Practices on Grassland Birds—Mountain Plover (*Charadrius montanus*).* USGS Numbered Series. Professional paper. Reston VA: U.S. Geological Survey, 2019. http://pubs.er.usgs.gov/publication/pp1842E.

Shaffer, Jill A., Lawrence D. Igl, Douglas H. Johnson, Marriah L. Sondreal, Christopher M. Goldade, Amy L. Zimmerman, and Betty R. Euliss. *The Effects of Management Practices on Grassland Birds—Lark Bunting (*Calamospiza mela-nocorys*).* USGS Numbered Series. Professional paper. Reston VA: U.S. Geological Survey, 2020.

Shaffer, Mark L. "Minimum Population Size for Species Conservation." *BioScience* 31, no. 2 (February 1981): 131–34.

Shamon, Hila, Olivia G. Cosby, Chamois L. Andersen, Helen Augare, Jonny Bear-Cub Stiffarm, Claire E. Bresnan, Brent L. Brock, et al. "The Potential of Bison Restoration as an Ecological Approach to Future Tribal Food Sovereignty on the Northern Great Plains." *Frontiers in Ecology and Evolution* 10 (January 2022): 826282.

Shave, Justin R., Seth G. Cherry, Andrew E. Derocher, and Daniel Fortin. "Seasonal and Inter-annual Variation in Diet for Gray Wolves *Canis lupus* in Prince Albert National Park, Saskatchewan." *Wildlife Biology* 2020, no. 3 (August 19, 2020): 00695.

Shaw, James H. "How Many Bison Originally Populated Western Rangelands?" *Rangelands* 17, no. 5 (1995): 148–50.

Shen, Yanjun, Na Yang, Zhihao Liu, Qiliang Chen, and Yingwen Li. "Phylogenetic Perspective on the Relationships and Evolutionary History of the Acipenseriformes." *Genomics* 112, no. 5 (September 2020): 3511–17.

Sierra-Corona, Rodrigo, Ana Davidson, Ed L. Fredrickson, Hugo Luna-Soria, Humberto Suzan-Azpiri, Eduardo Ponce-Guevara, and Gerardo Ceballos. "Black-Tailed Prairie Dogs, Cattle, and the Conservation of North America's Arid Grasslands." *PLOS ONE* 10, no. 3 (2015): e0118602.

Sikes, Derek S. "Hidden Biodiversity: The Benefits of Large Rotting Carcasses to Beetles and Other Species." *Yellowstone Science* 6, no. 1 (Winter 1998): 10–14.

Silcox, Mary T., Jonathan I. Bloch, Doug M. Boyer, Stephen G. B. Chester, and Sergi López-Torres. "The Evolutionary Radiation of the Plesiadapiforms." *Evolutionary Anthropology* 26, no. 2 (March–April 2017): 74–94.

Sinclair, A. R. E., and Charles J. Krebs. "Complex Numerical Responses to Top–Down and Bottom–Up Processes in Vertebrate Populations." Edited by R. M. Sibly, J. Hone, and T. H. Clutton-Brock. *Philosophical Transactions of the Royal Society B: Biological Sciences* 357, no. 1425 (September 29, 2002): 1221–31.

Sliwinski, M. S., M. Burbach, L. A. Powell, and W. H. Schacht. "Factors Influencing Ranchers' Intentions to Manage for Vegetation Heterogeneity and Promote Cross-Boundary Management in the Northern Great Plains." *Ecology and Society* 23, no. 4 (December 2018): 45.

Sliwinski, M. S., and Nicola Koper. "Grassland Bird Responses to Three Edge Types in a Fragmented Mixed-Grass Prairie." *Avian Conservation and Ecology* 7, no. 2 (2012): article 6.

Smith, D. W., D. R. Stahler, K. A. Cassidy, E. Stahler, M. Metz, C. Meyer, J. Rabe, N. Tatton, J. SunderRaj, L. Carroll, M. Jackson, B. Cassidy, and E. Loggers. *Yellowstone National Park Wolf Project Annual Report 2019.* Yellowstone Center for Resources, YCR-2020-01. Yellowstone National Park WY: National Park Service, 2020.

Smith, Felisa A., John I. Hammond, Meghan A. Balk, Scott M. Elliot, S. Kathleen Lyons, Melissa I. Pardi, Catalina P. Tomé, Peter J. Wagner, and Marie L. Westover. "Exploring the Influence of Ancient and Historic Megaherbivore Extirpations on the Global Methane Budget." *Proceedings of the National Academy of Sciences* 113, no. 4 (2016): 874–79.

Smith, S. V., W. H. Renwick, J. D. Bartley, and R. W. Buddemeier. "Distribution and Significance of Small, Artificial Water Bodies across the United States Landscape." *Science of the Total Environment* 299, nos. 1–3 (November 2002): 21–36.

Soga, Masashi, and Kevin J. Gaston. "Shifting Baseline Syndrome: Causes, Consequences, and Implications." *Frontiers in Ecology and the Environment* 16, no. 4 (May 2018): 222–30.

Solounias, Nikos, Melinda Danowitz, Irvind Buttar, and Zachary Coopee. "Hypsodont Crowns as Additional Roots: A New Explanation for Hypsodonty." *Frontiers in Ecology and Evolution* 7 (May 3, 2019): 135.

Somershoe, Scott G. *A Full Annual-Cycle Conservation Strategy for Sprague's Pipit, Chestnut-Collared and McCown's Longspur, and Baird's Sparrow.* Washington DC: U.S. Department of the Interior, Fish and Wildlife Service, 2018.

Song, Hojun, Ricardo Mariño-Pérez, Derek A. Woller, and Maria Marta Cigliano. "Evolution, Diversification, and Biogeography of Grasshoppers (Orthoptera: Acrididae)." *Insect Systematics and Diversity* 2, no. 4 (July 1, 2018): 1–25.

Soulé, Michael E. "What Is Conservation Biology?" *BioScience* 35, no. 11 (December 1985): 727–34.

Soulé, Michael E., and Reed Noss. "Rewilding and Biodiversity: Complementary Goals for Continental Conservation." *Wild Earth* (Fall 1998): 18–28.

Soulé, Michael E., and Daniel Simberloff. "What Do Genetics and Ecology Tell Us about the Design of Nature Reserves?" *Biological Conservation* 35, no. 1 (1986): 19–40.

South Dakota Department of Game, Fish and Parks. *South Dakota River Otter Management Plan.* Division report. Pierre: South Dakota Department of Game, Fish and Park Wildlife, 2012.

Southern Plains Land Trust. "Our Preserves." Accessed January 18, 2022. https://southernplains.org/our-preserves/.

Sovada, Marsha A., Robert O. Woodward, and Lawrence D. Igl. "Historical Range, Current Distribution, and Conservation Status of the Swift Fox, *Vulpes velox*, in North America." *Canadian Field-Naturalist* 123, no. 4 (October 1, 2009): 346–67.

Staunton, Frederick T. *Fort Peck Game Range: Narrative Report: May–August 1960*. Fort Peck MT: Fort Peck Game Range, 1960.

———. *Fort Peck Game Range: Narrative Report: September–December 1960*. Lewistown MT: Fort Peck Game Range, 1961.

———. *Fort Peck Game Range: Narrative Report: May–August 1961*. Lewistown MT: Fort Peck Game Range, 1961.

Steffen, Martina L., and Tara L. Fulton. "On the Association of Giant Short-Faced Bear (*Arctodus simus*) and Brown Bear (*Ursus arctos*) in Late Pleistocene North America." *Geobios* 51, no. 1 (February 2018): 61–74.

Steffensen, Kirk D., Kimberly A. Chojnacki, Jeffrey A. Kalie, Meredith L. Bartron, Edward J. Heist, Kyle R. Winders, Nathan C. Loecker, Wyatt J. Doyle, and Timothy L. Welker. "Evidence of Limited Recruitment of Pallid Sturgeon in the Lower Missouri River." *Journal of Fish and Wildlife Management*, 10, no. 2 (December 2019): 336–45.

Stein, Walter W. "Taking Count: A Census of Dinosaur Fossils Recovered from the Hell Creek and Lance Formations (Maastrichtian)." *Journal of Paleontological Sciences* 8 (March 2019): 1–41.

Stewart, Robert. *Breeding Birds of North Dakota*. Fargo ND: Tri-College Center for Environmental Studies, 1975.

Strasser, Erin H., Maureen Correll, T. L. George, and Arvind O. Panjabi. *Identifying Limiting Factors for Wintering Grassland Birds in the Chihuahuan Desert*. Brighton CO: Bird Conservancy of the Rockies, 2018.

Stringer, Allison L. "Status of Northern Pearl Dace and Chrosomid Dace in Prairie Streams of Montana." Master's thesis, Montana State University, 2018.

Strömberg, Caroline A. E. "Evolution of Grasses and Grassland Ecosystems." *Annual Review of Earth and Planetary Sciences* 39, no. 1 (May 30, 2011): 517–44.

———. "Evolution of Hypsodonty in Equids: Testing a Hypothesis of Adaptation." *Paleobiology* 32, no. 2 (March 2006): 236–58.

Stroupe, Sam, David Forgacs, Andrew Harris, James N. Derr, and Brian W. Davis. "Genomic Evaluation of Hybridization in Historic and Modern North American Bison (*Bison bison*)." *Scientific Reports* 12 (2022): 6397.

Subalusky, Amanda L., Christopher L. Dutton, Emma J. Rosi, and David M. Post. "Annual Mass Drownings of the Serengeti Wildebeest Migration Influence Nutrient Cycling and Storage in the Mara River." *Proceedings of the National Academy of Sciences* 114, no. 29 (July 18, 2017): 7647–52.

Surovell, Todd A., Spencer R. Pelton, Richard Anderson-Sprecher, and Adam D. Myers. "Test of Martin's Overkill Hypothesis Using Radiocarbon Dates on Extinct Megafauna." *Proceedings of the National Academy of Sciences* 113, no. 4 (January 26, 2016): 886–91.

Sutton, Bruce D., David A. Carlson, Jeffrey A. Lockwood, and Richard A. Nuna-maker. "Cuticular Hydrocarbons of Glacially-Preserved *Melanoplus* (Ortho-ptera: Acrididae): Identification and Comparison with Hydrocarbons of *M. sanguinipes* and *M. spretus.*" *Journal of Orthoptera Research*, no. 5 (August 1996): 1–12.

Tack, Jason D., Andrew F. Jakes, Paul F. Jones, Joseph T. Smith, Rebecca E. Newton, Brian H. Martin, Mark Hebblewhite, and David E. Naugle. "Beyond Protected Areas: Private Lands and Public Policy Anchor Intact Pathways for Multi-species Wildlife Migration." *Biological Conservation* 234 (2019): 18–27.

Tack, Jason D., David E. Naugle, John C. Carlson, and Pat J. Fargey. "Greater Sage-Grouse *Centrocercus urophasianus* Migration Links the USA and Canada: A Bio-logical Basis for International Prairie Conservation." *Oryx* 46, no. 1 (2011): 64–68.

Tallamy, Douglas W., and W. Gregory Shriver. "Are Declines in Insects and Insectivorous Birds Related?" *Condor* (January 5, 2021): duaa059.

Tallian, Aimee, Douglas W. Smith, Daniel R. Stahler, Matthew C. Metz, Rick L. Wallen, Chris Geremia, Joel Ruprecht, C. Travis Wyman, and Daniel R. MacNulty. "Predator Foraging Response to a Resurgent Dangerous Prey." *Functional Ecol-ogy* 31, no. 7 (July 2017): 1418–29.

Teletchea, Fabrice. "Fish Domestication in Aquaculture: Reassessment and Emerging Questions." *Cybium: International Journal of Ichthyology* 43, no. 1 (2019): 7–15.

Teply, Mark. *Montana Rivers and Streams Assessment.* Lacey WA: Cramer Fish Sci-ences, October 2013.

Thompson, D. J., and J. A. Jenks. "Dispersal Movements of Subadult Cougars from the Black Hills: The Notions of Range Expansion and Recolonization." *Eco-sphere* 1, no. 4 (October 2010): article 8.

Thompson, Darrin A., Hans-Joachim Lehmler, Dana W. Kolpin, Michelle L. Hladik, John D. Vargo, Keith E. Schilling, Gregory H. LeFevre, et al. "A Critical Review on the Potential Impacts of Neonicotinoid Insecticide Use: Current Knowledge of Environmental Fate, Toxicity, and Implications for Human Health." *Environ-mental Science: Processes & Impacts* 22, no. 6 (2020): 1315–46.

Thompson, Jonathan. "The First Sagebrush Rebellion: What Sparked It and How It Ended." *High Country News*, January 14, 2016.

Thompson, Sarah J., Douglas H. Johnson, Neal D. Niemuth, and Christine A. Ribic. "Avoidance of Unconventional Oil Wells and Roads Exacerbates Habitat Loss for Grassland Birds in the North American Great Plains." *Biological Conserva-tion* 192 (December 2015): 82–90.

Time. "Top 10 Worst Cabinet Members." 2019. http://content.time.com/time/specials/packages/completelist/0,29569,1858691,00.html.

Titus, Keifer, and David S. Jachowski. "Persistent Negative Stakeholder Perspectives Limit Recovery of a Critically Endangered Carnivore." *Conservation Science and Practice* 3, no. 11 (2021): 3e526.

Toombs, Theodore P., and Martha G. Roberts. "Are Natural Resources Conserva-tion Service Range Management Investments Working at Cross-Purposes with

Wildlife Habitat Goals on Western United States Rangelands?" *Rangeland Ecology & Management* 62, no. 4 (July 2009): 351–55.

Tornabene, Brian J., Robert G. Bramblett, Alexander V. Zale, and Stephen A. Leathe. "Spatiotemporal Ecology of *Apalone spinifera* in a Large, Great Plains River Ecosystem." *Herpetological Conservation and Biology* 12, no. 1 (April 30, 2017): 252–71.

Tornabene, Brian J., Troy W. Smith, Anne E. Tews, Robert P. Beattie, William M. Gardner, and Lisa A. Eby. "Trends in River Discharge and Water Temperature Cue Spawning Movements of Blue Sucker, *Cycleptus elongatus*, in an Impounded Great Plains River." *Copeia* 108, no. 1 (March 18, 2020): 151–62.

Tóth, Anikó B., S. Kathleen Lyons, W. Andrew Barr, Anna K. Behrensmeyer, Jessica L. Blois, René Bobe, Matt Davis, et al. "Reorganization of Surviving Mammal Communities after the End-Pleistocene Megafaunal Extinction." *Science* 365, no. 6459 (September 20, 2019): 1305–8.

Towne, E. G. "Prairie Vegetation and Soil Nutrient Responses to Ungulate Carcasses." *Oecologia* 122, no. 2 (February 1, 2000): 232–39.

Trexler, H. A. "The Buffalo Range of the Northwest." *Mississippi Valley Historical Review* 7, no. 4 (1921): 348–62.

Trimble, Donald E. *The Geologic Story of the Great Plains.* Washington DC: U.S. Geological Survey, 1980.

Truett, Joe. C., Michael Phillips, Kyran Kunkel, and Richard Miller. "Managing Bison to Restore Biodiversity." *Great Plains Research* 11 (2001): 123–44.

Trust Lands Management Division. *Annual Report Fiscal Year 2020.* Helena: Montana Department of Natural Resources and Conservation, n.d. Accessed December 1, 2021. http://dnrc.mt.gov/divisions/trust/docs/annual-report/annual-report-fy20-final.pdf.

Twidwell, Dirac, William E. Rogers, Samuel D. Fuhlendorf, Carissa L. Wonkka, David M. Engle, John R. Weir, Urs P. Kreuter, and Charles A. Taylor. "The Rising Great Plains Fire Campaign: Citizens' Response to Woody Plant Encroachment." Supplement, *Frontiers in Ecology and the Environment* 11, no. s1 (August 2013): e64–e71.

University of California Museum of Paleontology. "Online Exhibits." Accessed January 21, 2022. https://ucmp.berkeley.edu/help/timeform.php.

Uno, Kevin T., Pratigya J. Polissar, Kevin E. Jackson, and Peter B. deMenocal. "Neogene Biomarker Record of Vegetation Change in Eastern Africa." *Proceedings of the National Academy of Sciences* 113, no. 23 (June 7, 2016): 6355–63.

U.S. Army Corps of Engineers. "Fort Peck Dam Test Releases Draft Environmental Impact Statement." Omaha: U.S. Army Corps of Engineers, Omaha District, March 2021. https://usace.contentdm.oclc.org/utils/getfile/collection/p16021coll7/id/17644.

———. *Missouri River Recovery Management Plan and Environmental Impact Statement.* Record of Decision. U.S. Army Corps of Engineers, November 2018.

U.S. Army Corps of Engineers and U.S. Department of the Interior. *Lower Yellowstone Intake Diversion Dam Fish Passage Project, Montana: Final Environmental*

Impact Statement. Final Environmental Impact Statement. Omaha: U.S. Army Corps of Engineers and U.S. Department of the Interior, October 2016.

U.S. Department of Agriculture. *Land Values 2021 Summary*. August 2021. https://www.nass.usda.gov/Publications/Todays_Reports/reports/land0821.pdf.

———. "1950 Census Publications." Accessed October 2021. Census of Agriculture Historical Archives. https://agcensus.library.cornell.edu/census_parts/1950-montana/.

———. "2017 Census of Agriculture." Accessed July 2021. https://www.nass.usda.gov/Publications/AgCensus/2017/index.php.

———. "USDA NASS Census of Agriculture, Ag Census Web Maps." Census of Agriculture. Accessed October 2021. www.nass.usda.gov/Publications/AgCensus/2017/Online_Resources/Ag_Census_Web_Maps/Overview.

U.S. Entomological Commission. *First Annual Report of the United States Entomological Commission*. Washington DC: U.S. Department of the Interior, 1878.

———. *Map Showing the Distribution, Permanent and Subpermanent Breeding Grounds of, and Region Periodically Visited by the Rocky Mountain Locust* (Caloptenus spretus). N.d. Entomology Today, accessed June 2022. https://entomologytoday.org/wp-content/uploads/2018/10/Rocky-Mountain-locust-historic-range-map.jpg.

———. *Second Report of the United States Entomological Commission*. Washington DC: U.S. Department of the Interior, 1880.

———. *Third Report of the United States Entomological Commission*. Washington DC: U.S. Department of Agriculture, 1883.

U.S. Environmental Protection Agency. "Proposed Interim Registration Review for Neonicotinoids." 2021. https://www.epa.gov/pollinator-protection/proposed-interim-registration-review-decision-neonicotinoids.

U.S. Fish and Wildlife Service. *Biological Opinion: Operation of the Missouri River Mainstem Reservoir, the Operation and Maintenance of the Bank Stabilization and Navigation Project, the Operation of Kansas River Reservoir System, and the Implementation of the Missouri River Recovery Management Plan*. Denver: U.S. Fish and Wildlife Service, April 13, 2018.

———. "Bowdoin National Wildlife Refuge, Montana." March 28, 2014. https://www.fws.gov/refuge/bowdoin.

———. *Final Comprehensive Conservation Plan and Environmental Impact Statement: Charles M. Russell National Wildlife Refuge, UL Bend National Wildlife Refuge*. Lakewood CO: U.S. Fish and Wildlife Service, Mountain-Prairie Region, 2012.

———. *Fish and Wildlife Service Determines the Mountain Plover Does Not Warrant Protection under the Endangered Species Act*. News release. Lakewood CO: U.S. Fish and Wildlife Service, May 11, 2011.

———. *Recovery Plan for the Black-Footed Ferret* (Mustela nigripes). Denver: U.S. Fish and Wildlife Service, 2013.

———. *Revised Recovery Plan for the Pallid Sturgeon* (Scaphirhynchus albus). Denver: U.S. Fish and Wildlife Service, 2014.

———. *Species Status Assessment Report for the Black-Footed Ferret (*Mustela nigripes*).* U.S. Fish and Wildlife Service, December 12, 2019.

———. *U.S. Fish and Wildlife Service Black-Footed Ferret Managed Care Operations Manual (*BFFMCOM*).* U.S. Fish and Wildlife Service, January 16, 2017.

U.S. Geological Survey. "McCown's Longspur *Calcarius mccownii.*" Patuxent Wildlife Research Center. Accessed February 2022. https://www.mbr-pwrc.usgs.gov/bbs/grass/a5390.htm.

———. "North American Breeding Bird Survey." Patuxent Wildlife Research Center. Accessed December 1, 2021. https://www.pwrc.usgs.gov/bbs/.

Veldhuis, Michiel P., Mark E. Ritchie, Joseph O. Ogutu, Thomas A. Morrison, Colin M. Beale, Anna B. Estes, William Mwakilema, et al. "Cross-Boundary Human Impacts Compromise the Serengeti-Mara Ecosystem." *Science* 363 (March 29, 2019): 1424–28.

Vosburgh, Tim. "Ferret Restoration on Fort Belknap Reservation." *Endangered Species Technical Bulletin* 25, no. 3 (June 2000): 18–19.

Wagner, Alexandra M. "Grasshoppered: America's Response to the 1874 Rocky Mountain Locust Invasion." *Nebraska History* 89 (2008): 154–67.

Wang, Xiaoming. "Systematics and Population Ecology of Late Pleistocene Bighorn Sheep (*Ovis canadensis*) of Natural Trap Cave, Wyoming." *Transactions of the Nebraska Academy of Sciences and Affiliated Societies* 16 (1988): 173–83.

Watson, James E. M., Nigel Dudley, Daniel B. Segan, and Marc Hockings. "The Performance and Potential of Protected Areas." *Nature* 515, no. 7525 (November 2014): 67–73.

Watson, James W., Ursula Banasch, Timothy Byer, Daniel N. Svingen, Robert McCready, Miguel Á. Cruz, David Hanni, Alberto Lafón, and Rick Gerhardt. "Migration Patterns, Timing, and Seasonal Destinations of Adult Ferruginous Hawks (*Buteo regalis*)." *Journal of Raptor Research* 52, no. 3 (September 2018): 267–81.

Weisberg, Peter J., N. Thompson Hobbs, James E. Ellis, and Michael B. Coughenour. "An Ecosystem Approach to Population Management of Ungulates." *Journal of Environmental Management* 65, no. 2 (June 2002): 181–97.

Welti, Ellen A. R., Karl A. Roeder, Kirsten M. de Beurs, Anthony Joern, and Michael Kaspari. "Nutrient Dilution and Climate Cycles Underlie Declines in a Dominant Insect Herbivore." *Proceedings of the National Academy of Sciences* 117, no. 13 (March 31, 2020): 7271–75.

Wenger, Seth J., Amanda L. Subalusky, and Mary C. Freeman. "The Missing Dead: The Lost Role of Animal Remains in Nutrient Cycling in North American Rivers." *Food Webs* 18 (March 2019): e00106.

Werdelin, Lars, Nobuyuki Yamaguchi, Warren E. Johnson, and Stephen J. O'Brien. "Phylogeny and Evolution of Cats (Felidae)." In *Biology and Conservation of Wild Felids,* edited by David W. MacDonald and Andrew J. Loveridge, 59–82. New York: Oxford University Press, 2010.

Western Association of Fish and Wildlife Agencies. *Greater Sage-Grouse Population Trends: An Analysis of Lek Count Databases 1965–2015.* Cheyenne: Western Association of Fish and Wildlife Agencies, August 2015.

Western Landowners Alliance. *Reducing Conflict with Grizzly Bears, Wolves and Elk.* Albuquerque: Western Landowners Alliance, October 12, 2018. https://westernlandowners.org/wp-content/uploads/2019/01/ReducingConflict_WLA-Guide_low-res-1.pdf.

Wheeler, Richard S. *The Buffalo Commons.* New York: Forge, 2000.

Whicker, April D., and James K. Detling. "Ecological Consequences of Prairie Dog Disturbances." *BioScience* 38, no. 11 (December 1988): 778–85.

White, P. J., Kerry A. Gunther, and Travis C. Wyman. "The Population—Attributes, Behavior, Genetics, Nutrition, and Status." In *Yellowstone Grizzly Bears: Ecology and Conservation of an Icon of Wildness,* edited by P. J. White, Kerry A. Gunther, Frank T. van Manen, and Daniel D. Bjornlie, 2–11. Yellowstone Forever, Yellowstone National Park and U.S. Geological Survey, Northern Rocky Mountain Science Center, 2017.

Whitlock, Cathy, Wyatt Cross, Bruce Maxwell, Nick Silverman, and Alisa A. Wade. *2017 Montana Climate Assessment.* Montana State University Scholar Works, 2017.

Wiedenfeld, Melissa G. "The Development of a New Deal Land Policy: Fergus County, Montana (1900–1945)." PhD diss., Louisiana State University, 1997.

Wildlife Society. *Lacey Act.* Policy brief. July 2017. https://wildlife.org/wp-content/uploads/2014/11/Policy-Brief_LaceyAct_FINAL.pdf.

Willms, Walter, Barry Adams, and Ross McKenzie. "Overview: Anthropogenic Changes in Canadian Grasslands." In *Arthropods of Canadian Grasslands,* vol. 2, *Inhabitants of a Changing Landscape,* edited by Kevin D. Floate, 1–22. Biological Survey of Canada, 2011.

Wilmers, Christopher C., Robert L. Crabtree, Douglas W. Smith, Kerry M. Murphy, and Wayne M. Getz. "Trophic Facilitation by Introduced Top Predators: Grey Wolf Subsidies to Scavengers in Yellowstone National Park." *Journal of Animal Ecology* 72, no. 6 (November 2003): 909–16.

Wilsey, Chad, Lotem Taylor, Brooke Bateman, Caitlin Jensen, Nicole Michel, Arvind Panjabi, and Gary Langham. "Climate Policy Action Needed to Reduce Vulnerability of Conservation-Reliant Grassland Birds in North America." *Conservation Science and Practice* 1, no. 4 (April 2019): e21.

Wilson, Edward O. *Half-Earth: Our Planet's Fight for Life.* New York: Liveright, 2016.

Wilson, Scott, Adam C. Smith, and Ilona Naujokaitis-Lewis. "Opposing Responses to Drought Shape Spatial Population Dynamics of Declining Grassland Birds." *Diversity and Distributions* 24, no. 11 (November 2018): 1687–98.

Wisely, Samantha M., Oliver A. Ryder, Rachel M. Santymire, John F. Engelhardt, and Ben J. Novak. "A Road Map for 21st Century Genetic Restoration: Gene Pool Enrichment of the Black-Footed Ferret." *Journal of Heredity* 106, no. 5 (September–October 2015): 581–92.

Wisely, Samantha M., Mark J. Statham, and Robert C. Fleischer. "Pleistocene Refugia and Holocene Expansion of a Grassland-Dependent Species, the Black-Footed Ferret (*Mustela nigripes*)." *Journal of Mammalogy* 89, no. 1 (February 19, 2008): 87–96.

Wishart, David J. *The Fur Trade of the American West, 1807–1840*. Lincoln: University of Nebraska Press, 1979.

Wockner, Gary, Randall Boone, Kathryn A. Schoenecker, and Linda Zeigenfuss. *Modeling Elk and Bison Carrying Capacity for Great Sand Dunes National Park, Baca National Wildlife Refuge, and The Nature Conservancy's Medano Ranch, Colorado*. USGS Numbered Series. Open-file report. Reston VA: U.S. Geological Survey, 2015.

Woodcock, B. A., J. M. Bullock, R. F. Shore, M. S. Heard, M. G. Pereira, J. Redhead, L. Ridding, et al. "Country-Specific Effects of Neonicotinoid Pesticides on Honey Bees and Wild Bees." *Science* 356, no. 6345 (June 30, 2017): 1393–95.

Wooten, H. H. *The Land Utilization Program, 1934 to 1964: Origin, Development and Present Status*. Agricultural Economic Report. Washington DC: U.S. Department of Agriculture, Economic Research Service, August 1965.

Worcester, Donald E., and Thomas F. Schilz. "The Spread of Firearms among the Indians on the Anglo-French Frontiers." *American Indian Quarterly* 8, no. 2 (1984): 103–15.

World Wildlife Fund. "Plowprint Report Map." Accessed January 18, 2022. https://www.worldwildlife.org/projects/plowprint-report.

———. *2016 Plowprint Report*. Accessed January 18, 2022. https://files.worldwildlife.org/wwfcmsprod/files/Publication/file/7xaffijdtj_plowprint_AnnualReport_2016_Final_REV09192016.pdf?_ga=2.238320000.1410015095.1667334139-703935230.1667334138.

———. *2021 Plowprint Report*. Accessed January 18, 2022. https://files.worldwildlife.org/wwfcmsprod/files/Publication/file/5yrd3g00ig_PlowprintReport_2021_Final_HiRes_b.pdf?_ga=2.227921247.374627115.1642607791-824389788.1641759857.

Wright, Christopher K., Ben Larson, Tyler J. Lark, and Holly K. Gibbs. "Recent Grassland Losses Are Concentrated around U.S. Ethanol Refineries." *Environmental Research Letters* 12, no. 4 (April 1, 2017): 044001.

Xerces Society. "Feds Plan Insecticide Sprays across 2.6 Million Acres of Montana Grasslands, Threatening Pollinators and Organic Farms." Accessed November 21, 2021. https://xerces.org/press/feds-plan-insecticide-sprays-across-26-million-acres-of-montana-grasslands-threatening.

Yackel Adams, Amy A., Susan K. Skagen, and Julie A. Savidge. "Modeling Post-Fledging Survival of Lark Buntings in Response to Ecological and Biological Factors." *Ecology* 87, no. 1 (January 2006): 178–88.

Yansa, Catherine H. "Lake Records of Northern Plains Paleoindian and Early Archaic Environments: The 'Park Oasis' Hypothesis." *Plains Anthropologist* 52, no. 201 (February 2007): 109–44.

———. "The Timing and Nature of Late Quaternary Vegetation Changes in the Northern Great Plains, USA and Canada: A Re-assessment of the Spruce Phase." *Quaternary Science Reviews* 25, nos. 3–4 (February 2006): 263–81.

INDEX

Page numbers followed by *f*, *m*, and *t* refer to figures, maps, and tables, respectively.

Ingram Content Group UK Ltd.
Milton Keynes UK
UKHW010019130623
423151UK00015B/264